INSTRUMENTAL
ENRICHMENT

INSTRUMENTAL ENRICHMENT
AN INTERVENTION PROGRAM FOR COGNITIVE MODIFIABILITY

by

Reuven Feuerstein
Director, Hadassah-Wizo-Canada Research Institute, Jerusalem
Director, Youth Aliyah–Hadassah-Wizo-Canada Child Guidance Clinic
Professor, Bar Ilan University, Ramat Gan, Israel
Adjunct Professor, George Peabody
College of Vanderbilt University, Nashville

in collaboration with

Ya'acov Rand
Co-director, Hadassah-Wizo-Canada Research Institute, Jerusalem
Dean, Faculty of Social Sciences, Bar Ilan University, Ramat Gan, Israel

Mildred B. Hoffman
Director, Teachers' Training and Field Operations,
Hadassah-Wizo-Canada Research Institute, Jerusalem
Adjunct Assistant Professor, George Peabody
College of Vanderbilt University, Nashville

and
Ronald Miller
Research Director, Hadassah-Wizo-Canada Research Institute, Jerusalem

Illustrations by **Eitan Vig**

University Park Press
Baltimore

UNIVERSITY PARK PRESS
International Publishers in Science, Medicine, and Education
300 North Charles Street
Baltimore, Maryland 21201

Composed by University Park Press, Typesetting Division.
Manufactured in the United States of America by the Maple Press Company.

Library of Congress Cataloging in Publication Data
Feuerstein, Reuven.
Instrumental enrichment.
Bibliography: p.
Includes index.
1. Mentally handicapped children—Education. 2. Mentally handicapped children—Treatment. 3. Cognition in children—Ability testing. I. Title.
LC4602.F48   371.9'28   79-16485
ISBN 0-8391-1509-1

The research reported in this book was prepared with the participation of:

Research design and implementation:	Yehiel Friedlander, Martin Hamburger, David B. Hoffman, Mendel Hoffman, Reimer Jensen, David Krasilowsky, Yael Levy-Minzker, A. Harry Passow, Evelyn Bloomfield Schachter, and Abraham J. Tannenbaum
Preparation of material:	Dalia Katz, Levia Kiram, Nilly ben-Shakher, Haim Shalom, and Eitan Vig
Field work:	Yitzhak Amiel, Nurit Bolotin, Don Davidi, Batya Eitan-Kimmelman, Sarah Eshel, Esther Gazit, Asher Haviv, Mattie Haviv, Judy Hirsch, Dalia Katz, Yehuda Klaus, Yehoshua Kolski, Yitzhak Meiri, Yehuda Nir, Eli Ofir, Esther Sharon, Pnina ben-Zakan, and Haim Zorfati

CONTENTS

FOREWORD

Feuerstein's *Instrumental Enrichment,* along with its companion volume, *The Dynamic Assessment of Retarded Performers,* represents an intellectual achievement of formidable proportions. Few single works in contemporary psychology equal it in originality and ingenuity, in scope, in theoretical importance, and in potential social significance.

The two books could have been given an embracing title like "The Making of Mind," or "Assessing and Teaching Intelligence." Mind? Intelligence? *Teaching* intelligence? Yes, for it is with such matters that the books deal. Although Feuerstein's work is based on extensive experience with Israeli adolescents who were retarded in intellectual performance for reasons associated with their diverse cultural origins, disrupted lives, and limited opportunities to learn, he in fact provides the foundation for a general theory of cognitive competence, coupled with a technology for assessing learning potential and for repairing functional deficits in the cognitive process. Feuerstein is concerned generally with the ability to learn and solve problems; with why this ability fails to develop in the absence, during early childhood, of systematic learning mediated by a caring adult; and how, much later than generally thought possible, identified cognitive deficits can be remedied by a formal instructional program. Thus the significance of his work extends substantially beyond its implications for programs for retarded performers—to, for example, general programs of child care and parent education.

Knowledge of Feuerstein's intellectual origins and of the staggering social and educational problems he was trying to solve will help the reader appreciate both his insights into psychological functions and the practical consequences of his work. While pursuing graduate study under André Rey at the University of Geneva (Feuerstein subsequently received his doctorate at the Sorbonne), he began to work with Youth Aliyah, the agency responsible for the ingathering and integration of Jewish children in Israel. Between 1950 and 1954 he and his colleagues examined large numbers of adolescents in transit camps in Morocco and southern France. The young people came from many cultures, some quite primitive, in Asia, Africa, and Europe. They had to be received, settled, classified, and schooled for citizenship in a new country with a unique and thoroughly modern technological culture. Tests of many kinds were given as a basis for planning their education after immigration. But all existing tests proved inadequate to the task because they reflected what the children had learned, or more accurately had failed to learn, not what they could learn; their achieve-

ment status, not their learning potential. Feuerstein notes: "Our clinical observations strongly suggested that a substantial reservoir of abilities was being left
untapped by the measuring instruments we employed." Inspired by "our two
great masters of the Genevan School, Professor Jean Piaget and Professor André
Rey," Feuerstein initiated work leading to "a radical shift from a static to a
dynamic approach in which the test situation was transformed into a learning experience for the child" (in the Learning Potential Assessment Device, or LPAD)
and ultimately to a formal instructional program (the Feuerstein Instrumental
Enrichment, or FIE, program) designed "to change the cognitive structure of
the retarded performer and to transform him into an autonomous, independent
thinker, capable of initiating and elaborating ideas." On the basis of 25 years of
clinical experience now buttressed by a growing body of research, Feuerstein insists that "except in the most severe instances of genetic and organic impairment, the human organism is open to modifiability at all ages and stages of development." Such a fundamental reconstruction of the nature of intelligence
could perhaps have occurred only in a country that could not afford to waste
people.

In developing the theoretical foundations for his work, Feuerstein had to
transcend three intellectual traditions in psychology: psychodynamic theory,
behaviorism, and the psychometric movement. The results have important implications for education and child development in general. Psychoanalysis ac-
corded emotional factors a primary role in determining individual conduct.
Behaviorism ruled out internal factors and concentrated attention on inputs and
outputs, on stimuli and response-related environmental contingencies, to account for behavior. Psychometrics was concerned with increasingly precise and
quantitative descriptions of static states, or of the end-products of development
and learning to enhance the predictability of the applied measures. These three
traditions gave insufficient attention to the most distinctly human of human attributes—the ability to think. One tradition said that man feels, another that
man acts, and the third that the end-states of both can be measured. Feuerstein
emphasizes that man also thinks. "Cognition [is] the focal point of successful
adaptation." Then, further: "The neglect of cognitive processes has conspired
to produce a widespread belief that intelligence is something that one either has
or does not have and that attempts to change the structure and course of intellectual development are futile, if not impossible." He then proceeds to demonstrate (as others have done with young children) the mutability of intellect in response to intended interventions even in late adolescence and early adult years.

Feuerstein's assessment of learning potential breaks with a half-century of
theory and technology in the measurement of intelligence. He is not interested
in *what* a child or adolescent has learned (which is what conventional intelligence tests measure, on the untenable assumption that all children have had an
equal opportunity to learn the materials covered by the test), but in *how* the
child learns and solves problems. He is interested not in the content of mind but

in the formal structure of thought. The LPAD examiner engages the child in a clinical, teaching, learning exercise (test-teach-test) to discover the way the child perceives the world, processes information acquired, and communicates the results. A conventional intelligence test is designed to disclose the child's average performance to permit a comparison with the average performance of children of the same age; the LPAD, in contrast, invites, calls forth, discovers the child's peak performance, or learning potential. Furthermore, the conventional intelligence test yields a score useful only in classification while learning potential assessment leads to a prescription for intervention through instrumental enrichment. The Feuerstein Instrumental Enrichment program consists of 15 instruments made up of paper-and-pencil exercises, providing materials for 1-hour lessons three to five times a week for 2–3 years. These are not set pieces but systematic guides to creative teaching. Each instrument focuses on a specific cognitive deficiency and provides experience in overcoming it. Instruments are selected to fit deficiencies identified in the prior learning potential assessment.

I first saw Instrumental Enrichment used in classrooms in Israel in 1975, accompanied by Feuerstein. In Jerusalem we visited a classroom for early adolescent girls whose appearance (miniskirts, lipstick, bubble gum) led me to anticipate the apathy or unruly behavior so often seen in inner-city schools. A superb teacher called the group to order, distributed Instrumental Enrichment materials, and then carried the group along in a highly creative transaction between teacher and children and among the children themselves, guided by the structure of one of the FIE tasks. At the outset what impressed me most was the high level of motivation of the students. Hands waved for recognition, and the performance of others was eagerly attended to. The FIE materials are evidently interesting. What impressed me later was that the children were both thinking and thinking about thinking; they were developing concepts they could apply in many other situations, and this they seemed to know.

We went next to a rural area to a day school for orphaned and disturbed children who boarded with families on a *moshav* or collective farm. There I watched and listened to Feuerstein talk with individual children. He knew a lot about each child from occasional visits to the *moshav* and from previous clinical work at the referral agency, the Hadassah-Wizo-Canada Child Guidance Clinic in Jerusalem, which he directs. The engagement between adult and child was intense, sometimes joyous; Feuerstein was providing a mediated learning experience for the child, sensitively adjusted to the edge of the child's growing capacity for formal thought. He asked a severely withdrawn child of perhaps 12 years of age to show me his marvelously intricate and imaginative drawing of a city. The three of us talked about it. The child was of borderline intelligence as conventionally measured, but his drawing and conversation indicated a potential far above his IQ. When we left, the child gave the drawing to me, and I still have it. Subsequently, Feuerstein arranged for the boy to take lessons with a distinguished Israeli artist. Instrumental Enrichment came alive for me that day.

Feuerstein was intellectually prepared to be a pioneer, and the task he faced demanded unconventional solutions. What has emerged from his work are:

A theory of the relationship between early mediated learning experience and later cognitive competence

An instrument for the assessment of learning potential that has the unique capability of specifying required remedial measures

A formal instructional program to repair identified deficits in cognitive functioning

An extensive training program to prepare examiners, teachers, supervisors, and consultants in learning potential assessment and instrumental enrichment

An already substantial but now burgeoning international research program to validate the procedures

An impressive demonstration of how a new theory and technology can be introduced to help solve a major problem of a developing society

This impressive performance is capped by the production of two beautifully written books to describe it all. The theoretical argument marches from point to point with disciplined precision. The ingenious procedures for learning potential assessment and cognitive enrichment are described meticulously and illustrated copiously, and their significance is exemplified in scores of clinical case studies. Feuerstein ends this book with an account of research results and a commentary on the future of LPAD and FIE, to use initials sure to become familiar to psychologists, educators, and the public. That future looks bright indeed.

Nicholas Hobbs, Ph.D.
Professor of Psychology
and of Preventive Medicine
Vanderbilt University

INTRODUCTION

In the realm of behavioral science and learning theory and in the search for improved methods of intellectual assessment and special education practices, *effective* challenges to long cherished beliefs have been comparatively rare. Many have tried, heroically, to significantly enhance the mental performance and scholastic achievement of low functioning children from disadvantaged families. Most efforts have taken the form of curriculum content manipulation or a range of early intervention strategies focused in varying degrees on the child or family. The success of these endeavors, measured in terms of enduring change, has been very limited, at best.

Instrumental Enrichment and its companion work, *The Dynamic Assessment of Retarded Performers,* depart radically from previous educational strategies. Unfettered by the tradition of special public education in the United States to adapt curriculum requirements to the manifestly deficient learning skills of certain categories of students, Feuerstein and his colleagues have conceptually reversed the process. The "watered down" versions of special class study assume a static cognitive structure in these children which precludes the mastery of higher learning skills. The concept of cognitive modifiability upon which this book fundamentally rests cogently argues the opposing point of view. According to this approach, it is the learner, rather than the material to be learned, that should and can be modified. The validity of this concept has already been dramatically demonstrated in thousands of Israeli school children and on a smaller scale in a number of major school systems in the United States.

The theory of mediated learning experience and its expression in the content-free system of mental exercises referred to as Instrumental Enrichment (FIE) is based on many components of Piagetian theory and the clinical insights of André Rey. Feuerstein has introduced a determinant of cognitive development that is not part of Piagetian theory and, more importantly, has converted a descriptive system to an instructional and operational one.

The author has achieved this very difficult goal through an unusual blend of talents: clinical acumen and insight of the highest order; a wealth of experience with troubled and handicapped children and youth from diverse cultures; a gift for conceptualization and integration of theory; ingenuity, resourcefulness, and open mindedness; and, above all, total commitment to the worth and dignity of all human beings and to their capacity for positive change. Applying these talents, Feuerstein has spectacularly bridged the gap from research to practice and provided educators with effective tools for improving the performance of children with a range of learning deficits. In the process, the practice of special education in this country may take on some exciting new dimensions.

To more fully appreciate the potential impact of this book on the field of special education, Feuerstein's work should be viewed in historical perspective. Several significant developments in the field occurred starting with the last decades of the 19th century. The basic structure of the public school system, including tax support, free tuition, and compulsory attendance, had been established. A second development was the emergence of the school's responsibility for social problems. Social reform at the turn of the century relied increasingly on the schools to train the young for civic, social, and economic roles. Health problems, citizenship education, and Americanization programs added further to society's perception of the schools as the primary defender of the social order and prophylactic against social ills.

With the growth of mass education systems, efficiency became a concern of educators, leading to managerial and organizational models and the adoption of industrial techniques. School boards were centralized, administrators appointed, and cost and pupil accounting methods introduced. The curriculum became the technology and the students the raw material to be processed.

The emphasis on efficiency raised immediate questions about the equality of educational opportunity. While education was ostensibly free and open to all, in practice the mass system did not treat all equally. Scores of surveys revealed that many students were dropping out of school without completing elementary coursework or were repeating grades several times. Such academic retardation was considered inefficient and undermined the presumed economic benefits of school education.

The response of educational reformers to this state of affairs was the promotion of vocational education. Vocationalism assumed that schools should prepare academically deficient students for the vocational roles they would ultimately play and that their coursework had to be directly relevant to their future economic and social status.

The fit between individual needs, abilities, and course of education, however, raised many questions about the decision-making process. Given the concentration of weak school achievers in the lower social classes, finding a democratic means of placement and ensuring equality of opportunity involved crucial issues of choice and classification.

The development of intelligence and educational tests, especially the Binet-Simon scales, seemed at the time to offer an objective solution to the classification dilemma. In applying these measures to public school children, Goddard concluded that "experience with these tests has continually reassured us as to their amazing accuracy; their usefulness as a means of understanding the mental development of children is beyond question."

Goddard's influence was directed primarily toward the socially deviant and mentally retarded, but it was Terman who applied psychological testing to soldiers in World War I and made mental testing a major influence in American education. The tests confirmed most of the stereotypes—still prevalent today—about the relationships between social class, race, nationality, and intelligence.

Furthermore, the assumption that intelligence was inherited led to the claim that IQ was a constant and caused or predicted school achievement. Since education was the presumed gateway to economic and social success, schools now had an instrument for scientifically classifying students for their future social roles.

The progress of special education since these early beginnings has been unremarkable. The arguments for segregating the retarded from regular classrooms closely resemble the logic underlying ability grouping more generally; segregation would free normal pupils from the restrictions imposed by the retarded and teachers would be relieved of the special problems and tensions created by the retarded student. Retarded children, under this system, would be protected from scorn and ridicule, would be shielded from the sense of inferiority generated by unequal competition on learning tasks, and would have the benefit of specially trained and sympathetic teachers and an appropriate curriculum.

The special education movement, designed to categorize students according to their mental abilities and train them for economically useful roles, never achieved full public acceptance. Most school systems provided for only a fraction of the children with learning problems, classes were located in the least desirable buildings, equipment and materials were scarce, few of the teachers were especially trained, and the curriculum was a watered down version of the regular course of instruction. The hostility in parents which these conditions evoked further impeded the movement and forced school systems to use such euphemisms as ungraded, opportunity, and adjustment classes.

The current movement toward mainstreaming—in the absence of solid empirical data regarding its presumed benefits—speaks strongly to the dissatisfactions with the special education system. These concerns have been heightened by the lack of community interest and support and the isolation and alienation of special educators from their colleagues. The tendency to make the special class the "dumping ground" for all types of problem children and the continuing confusion over terminology and etiology seriously hindered the development of consistent procedures and effective teaching technologies. Individualized tutoring was the exception, not the rule.

Against this background, Feuerstein's work stands forth as signal, innovative, and a potentially revolutionary contribution to the field of education. In *The Dynamic Assessment of Retarded Performers,* he attacks the theoretical and social significance of standard intelligence testing for school placement and other diagnostic purposes. Thus, he joins a growing legion of critics who impugn the value of IQ testing. Unfortunately, critics frequently overlook the fact that conventional tests measure samples of *current* behavior only. They have evolved by inference into a concept of general intelligence and have been used to predict future performance, a task for which they were never designed.

The disproportionate representation of the poor and minority groups at the lower end of the intellectual spectrum suggested to some that, since the tests were standardized on middle class, white children they did not measure the true abilities of other groups. The proliferation of "culture-free" and "culture fair" tests, however, did not change the pattern of IQ distribution across social class and other group variables.

In Feuerstein's conceptual framework, children from economically and psychologically impoverished homes perform poorly on intelligence tests and function generally at a low level because they have been denied appropriate mediated learning experience (MLE). This type of deprivation—the absence of adults in the child's life who can effectively focus attention and interpret to him the significance of objects, events, and ideas in his social surround—is the root of most failure. Inadequacies of mediated learning may occur in any family and derive from many sources, but they are obviously more common in homes characterized by economic deprivation, social and family pathology, and distortions in parent-child relationships.

Acting on the theory that retarded performance is, in large measure, attributable to a lack of MLE and that this environmental deficiency may mask the child's true learning capacity, Feuerstein has departed from the traditional mode of devising a better instrument. Instead of further refinements to measure what a child *has* learned (an equation clearly involving opportunity, or MLE), his *Learning Potential Assessment Device* (LPAD) has proved to be a successful approach in assessing what a child *can* learn—his learning capacity.

In a "test-train-test" paradigm, the examiner becomes a teacher-trainer and tries to promote the best possible learning and motivational conditions in the child. The tests begin with simple tasks and progress through more complex reasoning processes. This dynamic approach involves testing in the act of learning and assessing the process of learning, thus specifying differences in cognitive strategies and style. Such information is then used as a guide to what should be taught and how it should be taught.

Experience with the LPAD with large numbers of adolescents of varied intellectual abilities—as measured by standard tests—reveals hidden and unexplored potentials in a high percentage of these youngsters. Individuals referred to Feuerstein's clinic with reported IQs in the moderate and mild range of mental retardation have been evaluated far more favorably and have been able with the aid of Instrumental Enrichment to pursue satisfactory careers in the army and industrial community, thereby validating the LPAD diagnosis.

The LPAD is a novel and very significant addition to the growing armamentarium of diagnostic tools. For those individuals raised under relatively optimal conditions, that is, receiving a high quality of MLE, *abilities,* as measured by standard IQ tests, and *capacities,* as determined by the LPAD, may show similar outcomes. The latter, however, reveal more of the individual's cognitive processes, an extremely important dimension when learning difficulties are a consideration. For the disadvantaged, retarded, learning disabled, and emotionally disturbed, the LPAD may avoid mislabeling and inappropriate school placement and may provide guidance for educational treatment.

Instrumental Enrichment (FIE), the content of this volume, is a logical extension of the LPAD effort and is, in fact, the vehicle by which the validity of the diagnostic instrument was established. FIE is most simply described as a strategy for *learning to learn*. It uses abstract, content-free, organizational, spatial, temporal, and perceptual exercises that involve a wide range of mental operations and thought processes. The exercises do not substitute for, but supplement the traditional content materials of the regular classroom. In an experimental program, children subjected to FIE not only showed gains in IQ over their controls, but were also better in some academic subjects, even though they received less coursework because of the classroom time devoted to FIE.

The most important results of FIE are its apparent long term effects. If the program's claims of modifying the cognitive structures of adolescents for enhanced learning are valid, the ability to apply problem-solving skills to new learning situations should be demonstrated. And, indeed, this is so. Several years after the termination of the intervention program, the experimental group diverges significantly from controls in achievement levels. Preschool intervention—a primary content, curriculum-oriented approach—has been, for the most part, subject to "washout" effects. Perhaps in this approach, as contrasted with FIE, insufficient attention is directed toward cognitive modification and the provision of a strategy for learning.

The success of *Instrumental Enrichment* in the Israeli school system and some programs in Canada and the United States challenges cherished assumptions that intervention must begin in early infancy and be carried on well into the school years. Social policies based on this presumption would relegate millions of disadvantaged children and youth around the world to lives of underproductivity and unfulfillment. Adolescence is not too late.

The theories, concepts, and technology reported in this book and its companion work hold great promise for improving the learning skills of the mildly retarded, the culturally disadvantaged, the learning disabled, the emotionally disturbed, and other low performing children. It holds great promise, too, for the more precise identification and placement of children based upon what they can learn rather than have learned.

The practical and social significance of this book is clearly apparent, but the theoretical and conceptual contributions should not be overlooked. Cognitive psychologists, child developmentalists, educators, and psychometricians will find much provocative food for thought in this outstanding book.

Michael J. Begab, Ph.D.
Head, Mental Retardation Research Centers
Mental Retardation and Developmental Disabilities Branch
National Institute of Child Health and Human Development

PREFACE

The contents of this book revolve around a strategy for the cognitive redevelopment of retarded performing adolescents. However, the specific goal of introducing Instrumental Enrichment is transcended by the presentation of a theory of differential cognitive modifiability, of which Instrumental Enrichment is only one of the possible outgrowths.

The concept of mediated learning experience, which we describe as the proximal determinant of differential cognitive development, is based on the assumption that human development can be neither conceived of as a sole epiphenomenon of neurophysiological maturation nor considered as simply the product of the individual's chance encounter with and direct exposure to stimuli and his active interaction with them. In addition to these determinants, it is by the flow of information transmitted to the individual by a process of mediation through channels produced by mediation itself that higher mental functions are developed. It is the mediation process itself that constructs both its content and its structure. This may be understood by analogy to a river, whose stream not only determines the movement of its waters (content) but also carves the bed (structure) along which the waters flow.

Implied in the concept of mediated learning experience is an intergenerational relationship determined by the strong need for ensuring continuity beyond the biological existence of the individual. Cultural and spiritual continuity are materialized in a variety of ways and situations. The psychologist has seldom been concerned with the integration of cultural transmission within the processes of learning, leaving the definition of the modalities of cultural transmission and its teleological dimensions to the cultural anthropologist. Our theoretical framework, however, deals with the impact of mediated learning experience on the development of higher mental functions.

The development of higher mental processes cannot be fully understood without the powerful adjunct of mediated learning experience to those learning processes that take place through the direct interaction between the maturing organism and its environment. If this concept is accepted, one can readily see that Instrumental Enrichment is but a substitute for early mediated learning experience. It is a phase-specific method and technique for the alleviation of the ill effects resulting from the lack of mediated learning experience. The goal of Instrumental Enrichment is to modify the cognitive structure of the individual and thus to produce and set in motion his further development. The redevelopment goals of Instrumental Enrichment, described in this book, differ greatly from those usually set for individuals suffering from retarded performance, irrespective of the distal conditions underlying their difficulties.

Special education, the usual framework for the retarded performer, attempts to shape the modes of training and teaching so that they not only will respond to the needs of the retarded performer but also will correspond to what are considered more "realistic" goals, set for him on the basis of his current level of functioning. Because the cognitive structure of the retarded performer is accepted as an immutable entity, any changes that special education may attempt to elicit will be kept within the presumed limits of his capacity. The mind is regarded as a rigid container with ultimate limits to what it may contain. It is not considered a dynamic, flexible, and elastic system whose capacity and structure change as the organism interacts with new stimuli. To follow this metaphor, the difference in the goals set by Instrumental Enrichment, compared with those set by more traditional approaches to the phenomenon of retarded performance, lies in the fact that the theory underlying Instrumental Enrichment perceives of the mind and cognitive structure as a system accessible to meaningful change and to the broadening and enriching of the repertoire of functioning. More traditional enrichment methods, however, are content to provide the individual with only the amount and nature of cognitive repertoire that can be contained within the rigid confines of the container. It is therefore that Chapters 2 and 3 on the mediated learning experience should be considered a central part of this book since they provide the theoretical framework for the cognitive modifiability of a variety of retarded performers at different ages and levels of manifest functioning.

The term "retarded performer" is used by us to convey the idea that what is retarded is the individual's manifest cognitive behavior as reflected in his performance and not his *capacity*. The term "mental retardation" has come to imply an irreversible state in which the capacity of the individual for growth and development is regarded as fixed and immutable. The insufficient and inadequate cognitive functioning of the retarded performer is more pervasive than just simple academic failure, and is reflected in a variety of life situations that transcend his immediate needs. Retarded cognitive performance must be clearly distinguished from such transient conditions of cognitive inefficiency as those produced by temporary states of fatigue, diminished motivation, or any of the other internal or external factors that may obstruct the learning process. Although a pervasive state, retarded performance should not be considered permanent or irreversible. By changing the total cognitive structure rather than selected dimensions of behavior, we aim to achieve a permanent, enduring, and stable state of modifiability. Thus, by using the term "retarded performer" we attempt to describe the current manifest level of functioning of the individual rather than provide a label that supposedly refers to some stable characteristic of his cognitive capacity.

The deficiencies that impede learning processes and are responsible for reduced modifiability in response to direct exposure to stimuli are described in Chapter 4 as an outcome of the lack of mediated learning experience. The division of the mental act into the three phases of input, elaboration, and output permits the more precise localization of the areas of deficiency. We have used the deficient cognitive functions in conjunction with the cognitive map presented in Chapter 5 as a taxonomy for the construction of materials, didactics, and techniques that aim at changing both the cognitive structure and the manifest level of functioning of the retarded performer.

In Chapter 6 we present the objectives and nature of Instrumental Enrichment materials in anticipation of the reader's introduction to the instruments themselves. Sensitizing the retarded performer to direct exposure to stimuli and life experiences and changing his cognitive structure are accomplished through six subgoals. These form the foundation for the construction of the instruments and the means by which teachers of Instrumental Enrichment turn into powerful mediators to their students. It is from these subgoals that the teacher derives his didactics, and, by varying the emphasis placed on one or another of them, he adapts them to the specific needs of individuals and groups.

The reader is introduced to the instruments, their structure, their content, and the psychological functions with which they deal, in Chapter 7. The meaning of the interaction with the tasks and their mastery for cognitive structure, manifest level of functioning, motivation, and other more pervasive adaptational goals that depend on adequate cognitive functioning are outlined.

A deeper analysis of the instruments and of the way they converge to produce the desired effects is presented in Chapter 8. Although Chapters 6 through 8 may assist the teacher who uses Instrumental Enrichment in the classroom, the training of teachers will continue to be a prerequisite for the proper application of the program both in group situations and in individual, remediational tutoring. The scope and modality of teacher training and the support provided for the teacher in his first years of implementation of the program are described in Chapter 9.

Before the present wide-scale dissemination of the Feuerstein Instrumental Enrichment program, FIE was submitted to a controlled experiment. A full description of the target population, research design, criterion measures, and the quantitative and qualitative results of the research and its follow-up are presented in Chapter 10. Chapter 11 is devoted to a summary and a discussion of the implications and future of our work on Instrumental Enrichment.

Instrumental Enrichment, its theory and technique, relies heavily on a dynamic diagnostic method, the Learning Potential Assessment Device (LPAD) (Feuerstein, 1979). Similar to the Learning Potential Assessment Device, Instrumental Enrichment seeks to focus attention and understanding on the *processes* of cognitive functioning rather than on their *end products*. The work on the LPAD began more than 25 years ago and was inspired by our two great masters of the Genevan school, Professor Jean Piaget and Professor André Rey. Our efforts in dynamic assessment have proved successful in revealing the hidden potential of immigrant youngsters in Israel, whose manifest level of functioning on psychometric and school criteria indicated a gap in the level of cognitive functioning ranging between 3 and 6 years compared with their normally functioning peers. The LPAD has been a useful tool not only for diagnosis, but also for the generation of a wealth of clinically derived insights into the cognitive structure of the retarded performer, initially in our work with the cuturally different and later with other populations.

Following the improved diagnostic clarity and the specific prognoses indicating high modifiability of many of the low functioning adolescents assessed with the LPAD, we began to lay the basis for a focused attack on cognitive deficiencies (Feuerstein and Richelle, 1957). Within a few years this became crystallized as Instrumental Enrichment. This body of work could not have been conceived or developed without the active participation, encouragement, and support of numerous people and organizations.

ACKNOWLEDGMENTS

For the past 29 years, first in Europe and currently in Jerusalem, the author has served as Director of the Hadassah-Wizo-Canada Child Guidance Clinic of Youth Aliyah, a nongovernmental agency charged with the in-gathering of Jewish children and youth into Israel. Because of its strong commitment to the children in its care, Youth Aliyah confronted the author with goals whose attainment were only possible through innovative methods. In answer to this challenge, the Learning Potential Assessment Device (LPAD) and Instrumental Enrichment (FIE) were developed and found their first application within the framework of Youth Aliyah. We would like to express our gratitude to the former heads of Youth Aliyah, Moshe Kol, Joseph Klarman, and Yitzchak Artzi, and to its former directors-general, David Umansky, Hanoch Rinott, the late Yohanan Ginatt, and Shraga Adiel, and the current director-general Meir Gottesman, as well as to many other Youth Aliyah colleagues. By their words and deeds that expressed a dedication to the ideas and ideals of the founders of Youth Aliyah, Henrietta Szold and Recha Freier, they presented the author with the challenge leading to this work.

Over the years we have been fortunate in having the support, faith, and interest of the Hadassah-Wizo Organization of Canada and its presidents, Clara Balinsky, Neri Bloomfield, Blanche Wisenthal, Anne Eisenstadt, Nina Cohen, and the late Lotte Riven. The realization of many of our plans of earlier years were made possible by Freda and William Cohen, who, with the Besner brothers, established the *Bertha and Alter J. Besner Foundation for Child and Youth Development.* The active interest and generosity of Joyce and Myer Deitcher, Moise Deitcher, and Perla and Saul Josephson, together with that of the *Hadassah-Wizo Organization of Canada* resulted in the erection of the *Louis and Zelda Deitcher Center,* which has served as a site for the numerous activities of the *Hadassah-Wizo-Canada Research Institute.* We are grateful to them as we are to Anne Gross and the World Patron of Youth Aliyah, Baroness Alix de Rothschild, for their unflagging assistance throughout the years.

We would also like to express our warm thanks to Dr. David Krasilowsky, Shimon Tuchman, and Mendel Hoffman, able colleagues at the Hadassah-Wizo-Canada Research Institute, whose active participation and unfailing assistance have facilitated our work.

We would like to single out Dr. Michael Begab for special mention: In the course of our research, Dr. Begab insisted on rigorous scientific methodology, offered constructive criticism, and gained an intimate knowledge of our program and its meaning for the retarded performer. With the termination of the research described in this book, Dr. Begab became most helpful in conveying information about our approach to those in search of a way to improve cognitive functioning.

Many friends from abroad have been generous in sharing their time and professional counsel: Professors Cynthia and Martin Deutsch, Alfred Friedman, Martin Hamburger, Robert Harth, H. Carl Haywood, Nicholas Hobbs, Samuel Levine, A. Harry Passow, Milton Schwebel, and Abraham J. Tannenbaum.

The author's interaction with Professor Martin Hamburger at an early stage was important in the development of the theory of mediated learning experience. The cooperation of Professor A. Harry Passow, as well as his editorial advice, contributed immeasurably in the preliminary stages of this book. Professor Abraham J. Tannenbaum has contributed in a constant and direct way to the design and implementation of the experiment described in Chapter 10 in his role as Senior Research Consultant to the Hadassah-Wizo-Canada Research Institute.

For the past 10 years Professor H. Carl Haywood has conducted a most fruitful dialogue with the author both personally and in his many publications on the theory of mediated learning and its theoretical and applied aspects. In addition to his valuable consultation and advice, Professor Haywood has played a key role in the development and coordination of research on Instrumental Enrichment conducted in North America. Under the auspices of Professor Haywood, Professors Harvey Narrol, Harry Silverman, and Dr. Mary Waksman have established a center for research and dissemination at the Ontario Institute for Studies in Education in Toronto. Professors Martin B. Miller and Bluma Weiner of Yeshiva University, Dr. Ruth Smith and Jane Towery of the John F. Kennedy Center for Research on Education and Human Development, and Drs. L. and M. V. Hannel of Phoenix, Arizona, are currently contributing to the body of knowledge on the differential effects of Instrumental Enrichment by the studies they are conducting.

Francis Link deserves a special mention. After her initial exposure to Instrumental Enrichment, she recognized the need for the program and its potential for large scale implementation in the United States. This, coupled with her expert knowledge in the field of curriculum development and teacher training, has been of great assistance.

In Israel, Shlomo ben Eliahu and Yair Levine of the Ministry of Education, and M. Gottesman, current Director-General of Youth Aliyah, and Dina Harpaz, his project director, have extended assistance and encouragement in the ever expanding dissemination of the program.

We acknowledge the generous support of the National Institute for Child Health and Human Development, which made possible the research on the differential efficiency of Instrumental Enrichment by its grant R01 HD0 4634-01. We are grateful to the teachers and directors of the four settings involved in the study: Yehuda Klaus, Eli Ofir, Yitzhak Meiri, Esther

Sharon, Yehoshua Kolski, and Don Davidi; and to Dalia Katz, Sarah Eshel, Judy Hirsch, and Batya Eytan-Kimmelman of the Hadassah-Wizo-Canada Research Institute for their direct efforts in the implementation of the research program. The children in the four institutions, in particular, with their cooperation and enthusiasm made our work a joyful experience.

We should like to express our sincere gratitude to our publisher, University Park Press, and to our editor, Janet S. Hankin, for their valuable suggestions.

Last, but not least, we should like to express our appreciation to our long suffering families whose encouragement and belief in our work are surpassed only by their patience.

The Legend of Rabbi Akiba

Rabbi Akiba, the famous Biblical scholar, was forty years old when he first began to study. One day, standing at the mouth of a spring, he saw a stone with many grooves. He wondered how the stone came to be carved, and he was told: The water that daily flows over it wears away the stone. And Rabbi Akiba thought: If even a stone can be softened and shaped, how much more can I, soft flesh and blood. So he found a teacher and began his studies.

Many years later, Rabbi Judah the Prince likened Rabbi Akiba to an ample storehouse. Like a laborer, said Rabbi Judah, Rabbi Akiba would take his basket and walk through the fields. Whatever he found he put in his basket. And when he got home he sorted what he had gathered: the wheat he put with the wheat, the barley with the barley, the beans in one pile and the lentils in another. Thus did Rabbi Akiba act, and he arranged the whole Torah in rings.

To my beloved parents, blessed be their memory, who, by love and devotion, have mediated an ever-extending world.

1

INSTRUMENTAL ENRICHMENT AND THE CONCEPT OF COGNITIVE MODIFIABILITY

Instrumental Enrichment is presented in this book as a strategy for the redevelopment of cognitive structure in the retarded performer. It is designed as a direct and focused attack on those processes that, because of their absence, fragility, or inefficiency, are responsible for poor intellectual performance, irrespective of underlying etiology.

The aim of the Feuerstein Instrumental Enrichment (FIE) program is to change the overall cognitive structure of the retarded performer by transforming his passive and dependent cognitive style into that characteristic of an autonomous and independent thinker. It is our view that both the low level of scholastic achievement and the low level of general cognitive adaptation of the retarded performer, especially among socioculturally disadvantaged adolescents, are a product of a lack of, or inefficient use of, those functions that are the prerequisites to adequate thinking.

The Instrumental Enrichment program is addressed not to any specific skill or content area but to the *process* of learning itself. For this reason, the various components of the program have been deliberately called "instruments" and the entire program "Instrumental Enrichment." The contents around which each instrument is built serve only as a vehicle for the development, refinement, and crystallization of the functional prerequisites of thinking. Implicit in the conception of Instrumental Enrichment is the conviction that manifest low cognitive performance need not be regarded as a stable characteristic of an individual and that systematic intervention, directed at the correction of deficient functions, will render the condition reversible by producing a change in the cognitive structure of the individual.

ASSUMPTIONS UNDERLYING THE INSTRUMENTAL ENRICHMENT PROGRAM

Clearly, as an approach to the problem of retarded cognitive performance, Instrumental Enrichment represents an active-modification approach as opposed to one of passive acceptance (Feuerstein, 1970). Characteristic of the former approach is the goal of changing the individual by providing him with the means of successfully adapting to his environment. In contrast, the

1

passive-acceptant approach contents itself with changing the environmental conditions to suit the low level of performance of the retarded individual. Each of the above broad approaches is governed by a number of fundamental assumptions that find expression in the nature of the diagnostic tools used for assessing an individual's performance; in the procedure of classifying and labeling him; in the provision of treatment and training; and in the expectations for his future development leading to the establishment of educational, occupational, and general adaptational goals.

At the heart of the matter is the issue of whether the organism is viewed as an open or closed system, since the implications of this view are far-ranging. Advocates of the active-modification approach view the human organism as an open system that is receptive to change and modification. In this framework, modifiability is considered to be the basic condition of the human organism, and the individual's manifest level of performance at any given point in his development cannot be regarded as fixed or immutable, much less a reliable indicator of future performance. Tangible expression of this viewpoint is evident in the rejection of IQ scores as reflective of a stable or permanent level of functioning. Instead, and in accordance with the open system approach, intelligence is considered a dynamic self-regulating process that is responsive to external environmental intervention.

In contrast, when intelligence is conceptualized in quantitative terms, as a fixed product of ability that is constant across the entire life span of the individual, the natural outcome is a passive-acceptant approach. Attempts to modify an individual's course of development are thus regarded as futile and even as unfair because they demand the "impossible" from the child. The extent to which any gaps in the closed system are plugged is reflected in the common practice, leading to a tautological way of thinking, of confirming the observed low level of manifest performance by the use of tests especially designed to measure such performance. The child's low achievement at school is confirmed by his poor performance on an IQ test, and he is then classified, labeled, and treated accordingly.

The assumption that the human organism is open and amenable to change demands a very different method of assessment and evaluation, the purpose of which is to evaluate the individual's capacity to learn and, hence, to become modified. Thus, the purpose of assessment is to reveal the potential of the individual and identify the deficient processes that may be impeding development. Treatment may then be directed at the correction of deficiencies, as a result of which the individual will be able to alter the course of his development.

The aim of the Instrumental Enrichment program is to modify the individual rather than the environment. To appreciate this process-oriented approach, it is important to specify the nature of the changes that the program is intended to produce. We have selected the term "cognitive modifiability" to convey the idea of a process of autonomous and self-regulated change set into motion by this program. In the retarded performer, the first step in the process of reversing his low manifest level of performance is to effect a diversion from his current pattern of development. This necessitates an active interaction between the individual and sources of external and internal stimulation. Once activated, the dynamics of modifiability propel the individual along a course of development that could not be anticipated on the basis of his previous performance. In Chapter 2 consideration is given to the factors that contribute to the differential development of cognitive modifiability, but even before considering the issue in detail it must be emphasized that cognitive modifiability is a product of highly specific experiences and learning. In general terms, it is a means of adapting to the environment. The survival of any organism depends on its ability to adapt. For the human organism, successful adaptation involves the ability to respond not to a constant and stable environment but to situations and circumstances that are constantly changing.

In describing the adaptational mechanisms of the human organism, Freud (1924) distinguished between alloplastic and autoplastic responses to changes in the environment. Adaptation of an alloplastic nature is directed at modifying the external environment. It is the force behind man's need to conquer nature and harness its resources to meet humanity's needs. It is also reflected in various forms of aggressive behavior in which situations perceived as threatening may be neutralized by attacking the source of danger. On its own, successful alloplastic response is limited to those situations in which environmental change is possible. In many instances, however, it is the individual himself who must adapt to external reality. Such changes constitute an autoplastic means of adaptation and are reflected in a state of internal flexibility that enables the individual to cope with sudden and novel changes in the environment. Autoplastic adaptation depends heavily on the presence of adequate cognitive processes and autonomous exercise of control over those functions that render the cognitive system flexible and constantly modifiable. In terms of adaptation, it is the autoplastic changes that are crucial. The extent to which external changes may be brought about is contingent upon the organism's ability to initiate such changes.

It should now be evident that when we speak of cognitive modifiability we are concerned not with the acquisition of bits and pieces of knowledge or the mastery of specific academic or vocational skills but with, in the broadest sense, the ultimate destiny of the retarded performer. Adequate cognitive functioning has implications that reach far beyond the academic requirements of the school or formal educational system. Although a mastery of the "three Rs" is a necessary prerequisite for integration into modern technological society, success in such a social framework depends on the ability of the individual to use his own resources in drawing inferences, making decisions, and planning ahead to anticipate future contingencies. Because of the social and cultural discontinuity that marks today's society, the individual can no longer rely on an established order or traditional patterns of behavior. Greater social, political, economic, and religious freedoms place a heavy burden of responsibility on the individual. Decisions must be made concerning employment, use of leisure time, political and religious affiliations, morality — in short, individual destiny is today, more than ever before, in the hands of the individual himself. Without the necessary cognitive tools, the individual cannot carve a future that will enable realization of his potential for growth.

COGNITION AS THE DETERMINANT OF BEHAVIOR

Even today, in spite of the unparalleled commitment to education as a means of transforming society, it is still often necessary to justify an approach that regards cognition as the focal point of successful adaptation. A number of interrelated factors contributed to the previous neglect of the cognitive processes both as a field for scientific investigation and as a guide for educational principles and practice. Although at the turn of the century cognition was considered the main determinant of behavior by the Denk psychology of the Wurtzberg School, its preeminence was eclipsed by three major forces that have had, and continue to have, a powerful influence on psychology and education. These are the psychoanalytic, the behaviorist, and the psychometric schools of thought.

Psychoanalysis

The dynamic psychoanalytic approach, initiated by Freud, was an attempt to explore the unconscious affective determinants of behavior. Theorists of this school often maintained that behavior is a function largely of non-intellectual factors that may bypass or even neutralize cognitive processes. It was even argued that cognition is determined by unconscious emotional processes and that the latter should be regarded as the primary force rather than solely as an energizing or motivational factor in behavior. This one-sided emphasis on the primacy of emotional factors probably arose because the neurotic behavior that psychoanalysis intended to explain was almost exclusively manifest in a very selective group of individuals who had attained high levels of cognitive articulation. Thus, the conclusion was drawn that, because their cognitive abilities and skills in logical thinking had not prevented the occurrence of neurotic, irrational, infantile, and regressive behavior, cognitive factors should be assigned a secondary role in determining behavior. However, for the majority of children whose behavior is maladaptive, cognitive impairment cannot be relegated to a secondary role. The major determinant of their inability to adapt is a low level of cognitive functioning. Psychoanalysis tended to ignore this fact because very few children, and even fewer adults, functioning at low cognitive and intellectual levels, ever came to the attention or treatment of dynamically oriented theoreticians. In fact, the retarded child was considered immune to neurotic disturbances because of his low level of functioning and lack of personality differentiation.

In a study conducted with culturally different and socioculturally deprived adolescents immigrating to Israel from North Africa (Feuerstein, Richelle, and Jeannet, 1954), we were able to establish that the subjects' considerable maladaptive behavior was primarily a function of inadequate cognitive processes. Because of a lack of the requisite cognitive tools, these children, when confronted with a different and unfamiliar dominant culture, were unable to understand, learn, or become modified in order to adapt to their new environment. Their reactions were certainly determined by anxiety, but, as our tests revealed, their aggressive and impulsive behavior was not produced by neurotic or repressive tendencies. Rather, the anxiety was provoked by a state of cognitive disorientation. These adolescents were unable to understand the nature of their new environment, its social organization, and the roles played by their various caregiving personnel. They were unable to predict the outcome of their behaviors in novel situations, and this, combined with a failure to grasp abstract concepts, produced a state of tension in which the worst was always anticipated. Hence, the high levels of anxiety among this group of adolescents were primarily caused by their inability to adapt to the new environment and culture in which they found themselves. The problem was one of a lack of the necessary cognitive equipment to cope with reality. This, in turn, may have produced personality disorders, but they were the *result* and not the cause of the individual's inability to organize, integrate, and relate to his environment.

Whatever its merits, the psychoanalytic approach has exerted considerable influence on education, especially at the preschool and primary grade levels. For many years emphasis was placed on the emotional determinants of behavior, at the expense of the cultivation of cognitive processes, instead of taking a balanced approach that recognized that difficulties in either the cognitive or the emotional realm could produce concomitant problems in the other.

Behaviorism

Whereas psychoanalysis attempted to penetrate the depths of the "black box" of the mind, behaviorism emerged as a reaction against any form of introspection and "outlawed" the concept of mind. Only those behaviors directly observable were regarded as worthy of scientific endeavor. Thus, with a single stroke, behaviorism effectively removed from psychology the entire apparatus of man's capacity to think and reason. The notion that man's behavior could ultimately be explained by a psychology built on the principle of association, with observable stimuli and responses as its sole source of information, hampered our understanding of cognition. Until recently, little attempt was made within the behaviorist tradition to understand the underlying structure and function of thought. As a consequence, for many years experimental psychology was simply irrelevant for education. This also may have indirectly contributed to an uncritical acceptance of psychoanalytic theories by educationalists.

Modern behaviorist approaches, usually referred to as behavior modification, have been applied to educational problems and warrant merit for their expression of an optimistic attitude toward the possibility of change. But, because of the essential philosophy underlying the theory and practice of behavior modification, both the problems and the solutions concerning inadequate cognitive performance are conceptualized in terms of specific behavioral patterns. Intervention programs are directed at the end products of cognition and not at the processes that govern and determine the nature of the output. Thus, programmed learning, teaching machines, and verbal training are all efficient means of transmitting specific contents. But directing attention to the operation of the mental processes responsible for the mastery of any content area or skill is still assiduously avoided, and, although the "black box" is occasionally tampered with, the "lid" on cognition has not been lifted.

Psychometry

The third major force contributing to the limited attempts to influence the cognitive development of the child was the rise of the testing movement in psychology and education. Whereas psychoanalysis was directed at the treatment of neurosis, and behaviorism was concerned with methodological issues, the psychometric approach was associated from its inception with educational issues. The focus was the issue of prediction; yet, despite advances in statistical techniques, the underlying structure of IQ tests remains unchanged. The IQ test, constructed to yield a measure of the individual's manifest level of performance, is based on those very characteristics that are most likely to remain stable and constant over time. It is not necessary to document the extent to which IQ tests have permeated the entire educational and vocational system and become entrenched in it. Whatever reticence education may have had toward the adoption and application of psychological theories, its acceptance of the IQ test as the major assessment tool of educability, trainability, and general intelligence level has been almost total. The great paradox is that to this very day we still do not have any real understanding of what the IQ test measures; herein lies its great potential for abuse within education.

THE CONCEPT OF INTELLIGENCE

Because a score is obtained with the IQ test, the assumption is made that we are measuring an entity. The idea that this entity can be measured suggests that it is a fixed and immutable element. This attitude is further strengthened by the deliberate effort to eliminate from IQ tests those items that address the characteristics of an individual's functioning that are subject to change and to retain only those questions directed toward characteristics that are most resistant to change and demonstrate stability over time. Consequently, the IQ score reflects the *product* of a given quantum of ability. It does not tell us anything about the underlying *processes* responsible for an individual's performance or about the individual's capacity to improve it. In short, the IQ test may provide an indication of what has been learned in the past; but how the learning took place and whether an individual has the potential to improve his learning ability are not questions that can be answered by studying an IQ score. Yet questions such as these are of crucial importance in education, especially in relation to the retarded performer.

In recent years, there has been a shift away from the product-oriented approach toward a more process-oriented conception of intelligence. In discussing the concept of intelligence, McCall, Hogarty, and Hurlburt (1972) have commented:

> One may need to discard the reified notion of intelligence as an unchanging characteristic that governs nearly all of an individual's mental performance at every age. Despite the incredibly pervasive and restrictive character of its assumption, psychologists have apparently been willing to make it, explicitly or implicitly, throughout most of modern psychological history (p. 728).

Considering the above, it is not surprising that IQ testing has become deeply embedded in the entire rubric of education to the extent that cognitive processes have been largely ignored and certainly neglected.

The neglect of cognitive processes has conspired to produce a widespread belief that intelligence is something that one either has or does not have and that attempts to change the structure and course of intellectual development are futile, if not impossible. In the case of psychoanalysis, efforts at modifiability focused on personality changes. The assumption was that cognitive change was irrelevant to the emotional life and stability of the individual and, furthermore, was less attainable. Within the behaviorist framework, cognitive modifiability, directed toward internal structural changes, could not be contemplated because underlying mental processes were regarded either as scientific fictions or as inaccessible to control. But the case against cognitive modifiability was most strongly expressed by the psychometric approach, which placed considerable emphasis on the genetic determinants of intelligence, the level of which was fixed and not amenable to concerted efforts at modifiability.

This previous absence of a viable theory and approach to confronting the problems of cognition perhaps should be regarded as a further negative force in the conceptualization and understanding of intelligence. In recent years, however, cognition has increasingly received the attention of psychologists. The static, quantitative conception of intelligence has been challenged from many quarters. Probably the most cogent attack has emanated from the work of Piaget, whose writings have simultaneously provided a counterforce to psychoanalysis, behaviorism, and the psychometric approach to intelligence. Not only does Piaget's theory redress the overemphasis of psychoanalysis on the unconscious emotive aspects of thought and provide a scientific alternative to behaviorism, but it also has demonstrated that the essence of intelligence lies not in its measured product but in its active construction by the individual. Although Piaget's theory does not provide all of the answers for education, it has exposed the myth that intelligence is fixed at birth, and it has dramatically shifted attention away from the static and sterile concept of IQ toward a dynamic process-oriented approach to cognition.

THE ETIOLOGY OF RETARDED PERFORMERS

Many different reasons, ranging from genetic to environmental factors, have been suggested to explain low cognitive performance. A progression of pessimism regarding cognitive modifiability is associated with the proposed etiologies. On the one extreme is the approach of Jensen (1969, 1973), who holds that low cognitive performance is largely genetically determined, and therefore inaccessible to modification. Jensen has proposed a dichotomous model of intelligence in which humanity is divided on the basis of genetic endowment into two different categories: people whose capacities are limited to simple mental acts of an associative and reproductive nature, referred to as Level I type of intelligence, and people who are able to use complex transformational, operational, and abstract processes, referred to as Level II type of intelligence. In terms of this dichotomy, Jensen suggests that we should accept the limits imposed by heredity and accordingly set limited educational goals for individuals with Level I intelligence. This orientation is totally at variance with that embodied in our general approach and, in particular, with the Instrumental Enrichment program. The focal question is whether it is possible to derive an approximation of heritability from data that, at best, represent a manifest level of functioning determined from the static "inventories" of abilities reflected by IQ tests (see Feuerstein, 1979). We maintain that it is more appropriate to regard genetic factors as producing variations in the level of responsiveness of the individual to learning situations that may require corresponding variations in the quality and quantity of investment necessary for growth.

At the other end of the scale we encounter the notion of the "six-hour retarded child." In this case, the failure of the retarded performer is considered a function of demands imposed by an academically oriented and alien school system. This approach, which is characteristic of the "cultural difference" etiological position, implies that merely altering the environment will bring about the desired change or eliminate the apparent poor performance of the individual. It represents a gross oversimplification of the problem and fails to recognize that deficient cognitive functioning is neither culture bound nor limited to specific school skills. On the contrary, even if the "three Rs" of education have been mastered, a lack of the "fourth R" — reasoning — may lead to maladaptive behavior.

Between the two extremes of genetic and cultural determinants of retarded cognitive performance are numerous intermediate positions. A broad spectrum of organic causes are said to be implicated in the production of retarded performance. Whereas the genetic approach leaves no room for intervention, neurophysiological etiologies are sometimes open to modifiability, provided that intervention is initiated early enough. Similarly, the suggestion that poverty of stimulation during the early years of development may result in retarded performance also limits intervention to the earliest stages of development. What all of these approaches share in common, however, is the belief, either implicit or explicit, that retarded cognitive performance persisting beyond childhood is not a reversible condition.

THE CONCEPT OF COGNITIVE MODIFIABILITY

The defining characteristic of the approach represented by the Instrumental Enrichment program is the concept of "cognitive modifiability." The essential feature of this approach is that it is directed not merely at the remediation of specific behaviors and skills but at changes of a structural nature that alter the course and direction of cognitive development. To understand what is intended by the concept of cognitive modifiability, it is necessary to appreciate the difference between structural and other kinds of change that occur during the course of development. In the normal course of events, the developing organism undergoes a series of changes. On the one hand, changes of a maturational nature occur, such as the transition from crawling to walking. On the other hand, specific changes may occur as a result of exposure to a given set of circumstances, such as the learning of a particular arithmetic operation or a foreign language. *Structural changes,* however, refer not to isolated events but to the organism's manner of interacting with, that is, acting on and responding to, sources of information. Thus, a structural change, once set in motion, will determine the future course of an individual's development. When we use the term "cognitive modifiability," we refer to structural changes, or to changes in the state of the organism, brought about by a deliberate program of intervention that will facilitate the generation of continuous growth by rendering the organism receptive and sensitive to internal and external sources of stimulation.

In the section that follows, we provide an account of our approach to the problem of the etiology of retarded cognitive performance and the reasons for our insistence that, except in the most severe instances of genetic and organic impairment, the human organism is open to modifiability at all ages and stages of development. Evidence of the capacity for modifiability is beginning to mount, and the long held belief that adverse early experience produces permanent and irreversible damage is being seriously questioned. In fact, Clarke and Clarke (1976), in their presentation of little-known research and follow-up studies, incline toward the view that "the worse the early social history, the better the prognosis for change" (p. 72). The following case is presented as an illustration of how the products of adverse genetic, neurophysiological, and environmental conditions may be modified at a relatively late stage in an individual's development.

Eleven years ago, M was referred to us for life-long placement in custodial care. At the time of his referral, he was 15 years old and his IQ, according to the reports, was in the 35–45 range. His vocabulary consisted of 40–50 words and he manifested severe impairment of spatio-temporal orientation, imitation, retention, and social behavior. Echolalia and echopraxia were observed, but no psychotic-autistic signs were detected. Trainability had been considered very poor, and custodial care seemed unavoidable.

M was the second of three brothers. His father, a schizophrenic, alcoholic, and poorly adjusted Foreign Legion soldier, met and married M's mother in an Oriental country. The mother was retarded and illiterate, and died as a hospitalized, diagnosed psychotic. M suffered from brain damage caused by prematurity and low weight (2½ lbs.) at birth, and required prolonged incubator care. His infancy was marked by nutritional difficulties and by repeated and prolonged separations in nurseries and foster homes. His early adolescence was spent largely in socially and educationally restrictive environments.

Contrary to all expectation, our assessment of M, using the Learning Potential Assessment Device (see Feuerstein, 1979), yielded a surprising level of modifiability. Accordingly, he was placed in a foster home group care treatment program for the redevelopment of severely disturbed, low functioning adolescents (Feuerstein and Krasilowsky, 1967).

As a result of the intensive and concerted investment in M's development over the past 11 years, he has emerged as an independently functioning individual, oriented in space and time, with a full and rich command of spoken and written Hebrew, a sense of humor, social skills, and vocational ambitions. He is responsible for the maintenance of a large indoor swimming pool and has learned to speak French and some German. In spite of M's charged heredity, organic damage, maternal deprivation, and stimulus deprivation from his restricted early environments, all of which are considered responsible for retarded performance, he proved receptive to intervention, albeit of a sustained and systematic nature. The development of his capacity to use hierarchically higher levels of cognitive processes, such as representational, anticipatory, and inferential thinking, to a large extent determined his general behavioral adaptation. Thus, his entire destiny was changed from anticipated placement in life-long custodial care to the life of an autonomous, independent, adaptive young man, looking forward to building a future and starting a family.

The processes of redevelopment that so dramatically changed M's destiny are not nearly as rare as we have been led to believe and neither are they confined to isolated individuals. The research described in this book illustrates how the Instrumental Enrichment program may produce structural changes that transcend the acquisition of basic school skills in groups of adolescents. Thus, groups of children, many of them with organic and behavioral deficiencies necessitating placement in special classes, have been set on courses of redevelopment that have enabled them to expand their horizons and to not only be affected by life's experiences but to also actively contribute to the organization and planning of their own futures. The changes that these adolescents have undergone are reflected in the fact that the effects of the Instrumental Enrichment intervention tend to increase with time, after the completion of the program. Today, we find many of the individuals who participated in our research engaged in careers that were beyond any of the original expectations projected for the group. The factors responsible for such remarkable deviations from what is prematurely projected as the expected course of development are discussed in the next chapter, after the reader is introduced to the theory of mediated learning experience.

2
AN INTRODUCTION TO
THE THEORY OF MEDIATED
LEARNING EXPERIENCE

This chapter introduces the theory of mediated learning experience (MLE) as the underlying theoretical basis for the concept of modifiability described in the first chapter. It defines cultural deprivation and lays the foundation for the detailed description of MLE in Chapter 3 and, in fact, for what follows in the remainder of the book.

In terms of the theory of MLE, the deficiencies responsible for retarded cognitive performance are conceived of as belonging to the syndrome of what we refer to as *cultural deprivation*. Because of the pivotal role attributed to the concept of cultural deprivation as a conceptual link to our understanding of the phenomenon of retarded performance, it is important to realize that our definition of the term "cultural deprivation" is very different from that often encountered in the literature.

CULTURAL DEPRIVATION AND CULTURAL DIFFERENCE

Together with many cultural anthropologists, psychologists, and educators, we firmly reject the notion that certain cultures are themselves depriving or deficient and thereby create conditions of deprivation for the individuals and groups comprising them. The pernicious conclusions that may be drawn from judgments made by members of a dominant culture group about the deficiencies of minority cultures need no elaboration. Suffice it to mention in this particular context that value judgments of this nature can only hinder our understanding of the phenomenon of the retarded performer. Our use of the term "cultural deprivation" does not refer to the culture of the group to which an individual belongs. It is not the culture that is depriving, but it is the fact that the individual, or his group, is deprived of his own culture that is the disabling factor. In this context, "culture" is not defined as a static inventory of behaviors but, rather, as the *process* by which knowledge, values, and beliefs are transmitted from one generation to the next. In this sense, cultural deprivation is the result of a failure on the part of a group to transmit or mediate its culture to the new generation.

The notion that all socioeconomically or ethnically disadvantaged subgroups are necessarily culturally deprived is misleading and counterproductive. This is because the criteria relating to these kinds of disadvantage are extrinsic to the individual and the group, in that the criteria are based on sociological measures such as socioeconomic status, level of education (usually of parents), and social, cultural, and racial identity. That these factors do not necessarily stem from, or result in, cultural deprivation is attested to by the inescapable fact that many individuals from impoverished and disadvantaged backgrounds and racial and ethnic minority groups achieve remarkable levels of academic, social, and economic success within the dominant culture. In fact, many culturally different subgroups attain excellence in their levels of functioning despite their disadvantage in relation to the dominant culture. This apparent contradiction is resolved if the extrinsic criteria (e.g., environmental conditions) defining disadvantage are not confused with the intrinsic criteria (e.g., cognitive functioning) that govern individual performance.

The fact that many groups, culturally different relative to the dominant mainstream culture, are disadvantaged with respect to the more advantaged and affluent members of society, introduces a further source of confusion. It has been suggested that not only are disadvantaged groups culturally deprived but that the reason for both their disadvantage and their deprivation is the fact that they are also culturally different. Consequently, if cultural *difference* is equated with cultural *deprivation,* it has been argued that this accounts for the condition of disadvantage. A less vicious but equally circular version equates cultural difference with disadvantage and claims that this in turn explains the cultural deprivation.

In terms of our approach, cultural deprivation is defined as a condition not of the culture but of the individuals or groups, bearing no direct relation to the extrinsic and often antecedent conditions of disadvantage. Cultural difference is, in many respects, the very opposite of cultural deprivation because the defining characteristic of the culturally different individual is his identity with a given culture, whereas the culturally deprived individual is characterized by his lack of, or diminished, cultural identity. In short, we contend that there are no necessary causal links between cultural difference or conditions of disadvantage, such as poverty and discrimination, and cultural deprivation. These conditions may overlap, however, and cognitive dysfunction may accompany any of three conditions.

DEFINITION AND ETIOLOGY OF CULTURAL DEPRIVATION

So far the discussion of our conception of cultural deprivation has revolved around the central theme that retarded cognitive performance is a function of a condition in which the essential products of a culture are not transmitted or mediated to the individual. In order to advance our understanding beyond the descriptive level, two questions must be answered. First, what are the effects of cultural deprivation on the individual? Second, what is the etiology of the condition?

To answer the first question we start with an operational definition of what we call the *syndrome of cultural deprivation*. It is defined as a state of reduced cognitive modifiability of the individual, in response to direct exposure to sources of stimulation (Feuerstein and Rand, 1974; Feuerstein, 1978). At the core of this definition is the crucial fact that individuals exposed to similar environments and sources of stimulation respond to and are affected by them in very different ways. What distinguishes individuals at different levels of cognitive development is the extent to which they are able to become modified, i.e., to learn by direct exposure to stimuli.

To answer the second question concerning the etiology of cultural deprivation, cultural deprivation must be further defined as a condition of the organism that is produced by a lack of mediated learning experience. This lack of mediated learning experience (MLE) results in a reduced propensity of the individual to organize and elaborate stimuli to facilitate their future use by means of mental processes. Consequently, the theory of mediated learning experience is central not only to our understanding of the phenomenon of cultural deprivation and hence of retarded cognitive performance but also to our remediation efforts, which aim at reversing the deficiencies responsible for cognitive impairment.

CONCEPT OF MEDIATED LEARNING EXPERIENCE

We conceive of the development of cognitive structure in the organism as a product of two modalities of interaction between the organism and its environment: direct exposure to sources of stimuli and mediated learning.

The first and the most universal modality is the organism's direct exposure to sources of stimuli impinging on it from the very earliest stage of its development. This exposure produces changes in the organism that affect its behavioral repertoire and its cognitive orientation; these changes in turn affect its interaction with the environment, even when the environment itself remains constant and stable. Direct exposure to stimuli continues to affect the learning of the organism throughout its lifespan, to the extent that the stimuli present enough variation and novelty. This modality of learning as a function of direct exposure is consistent with the stimulus-response formulations of the learning theorists and also with Piaget's (1966) stimulus-organism-response formula. Although Piaget conceives of cognitive development as a function of an interaction between the organism and the environment, the environment is conceptualized as a domain of objects.

The second modality, which is by far less universal and is characteristic of the human race, is mediated learning experience. By mediated learning experience (MLE) we refer to the way in which stimuli emitted by the environment are transformed by a "mediating" agent, usually a parent, sibling, or other caregiver. This mediating agent, guided by his intentions, culture, and emotional investment, selects and organizes the world of stimuli for the child. The mediator selects stimuli that are most appropriate and then frames, filters, and schedules them; he determines the appearance or disappearance of certain stimuli and ignores others. Through this process of mediation, the cognitive structure of the child is affected. The child acquires behavior patterns and learning sets, which in turn become important ingredients of his capacity to become modified through direct exposure to stimuli. Since direct exposure to stimuli quantitatively constitutes the greatest source of the organism's experience, the existence of sets of strategies and repertoires that permit the organism to efficiently use this exposure has considerable bearing upon cognitive development.

The relationship between MLE and direct exposure to stimuli, the two modalities for the development of cognitive structure, can be set forth as follows: the more and the earlier an organism is subjected to MLE, the greater will be his capacity to efficiently use and be affected by direct exposure to sources of stimuli; the less MLE offered to the growing organism, both quantitatively and qualitatively, the lower will be his capacity to become affected and modified by direct exposure to stimuli.

MLE, therefore, can be considered as the ingredient that determines differential cognitive development (i.e., varying courses of cognitive development) in otherwise similarly endowed individuals, even when they live under similar conditions of stimulation. Thus formulated, the concept of MLE complements the formula suggested by Piaget, who conceives of the human factor as one object among others. The mediative value of human intervention is not regarded by Piaget as essential to the cognitive development of the child but, rather, as a direct source of stimulation that does not differ essentially from other sources located in the immediately experienced space and time of the individual. In our view, the cognitive development of the child is not solely the outcome of the process of maturation of the human organism itself and its autonomous independent interaction with the objectal world. Rather, it is the combined result of the direct exposure to the world and what we have termed the mediated experience by which cultures are transmitted. Whereas Piaget's (1966) approach is conceptualized in his stimulus-organism-response (S-O-R) formula, the theory of MLE may be expressed by the formula S-H-O-R, in which a human mediator (H) is interposed between the stimulus and the organism. In this manner, the child acquires appropriate behaviors, learning sets, and operational structures (i.e., approaches to mentally organizing, manipulating, and acting upon information gained from external and internal sources) by means of which his cognitive structure is constantly modified in response to direct stimulation. Thus the effects of mediated learning experience may be conceptualized as inducing in the organism a great variety of orientations and strategies that become crystallized in the form of sets and habits and constitute the prerequisites for proper cognitive functioning.

DISTAL AND PROXIMAL DETERMINANTS
OF DIFFERENTIAL COGNITIVE DEVELOPMENT

By recognizing the role played by mediated learning experience in the course of cognitive development, a new perspective is cast on the etiology of cultural deprivation, as manifested in retarded intellectual performance. In terms of the theory of mediated learning experience, it is possible and, in fact, necessary to distinguish between the *distal* and *proximal* determinants of differential cognitive development. Distal determinants include such variables as genetic factors, organicity, level of environmental stimulation, emotional balance of child or parents, and socioeconomic status. When these factors are deficient in some respect, for example, low socioeconomic status, poverty of stimulation, or emotional disturbance of child or parents, they can, but do not necessarily, lead to inadequate cognitive development. Thus, the distal etiological factors are defined as determinants that neither directly nor inevitably cause retardation. On the other hand, the proximal determinant is a lack of, or reduced exposure to, mediated learning experience, the outcome of which *is* retarded performance. Any of the distal conditions may trigger the proximal etiology, so that, although the indirect distal determinants contributing to the retardation may vary, the end result is, nevertheless, the same qualitative dimension, i.e., retarded performance. Conversely, if appropriate strategies of mediated learning experience are provided, such that the barriers obstructing mediation are overcome or bypassed, then it becomes possible to avert the expected course of retarded development and to restore a normal pattern of cognitive growth. The relationship between the distal and proximal determinants of differential cognitive development is illustrated in Figure 1.

Mediated learning experience forms the theoretical foundation for our belief in the reversibility of deficient cognitive processes under specified conditions of intervention. The program we have developed from the concept of mediated learning is the Feuerstein Instrumental Enrichment (FIE) program. It is a direct and focused attack on those cognitive functions diagnostically determined as being responsible, because of their weakness or nonexistence, for poor intellectual performance.

It is anticipated that attainment of the goal of inducing proper data-input strategies in the culturally deprived adolescent will foster in him a mental set that will make his future learning in its particular content-related aspects more meaningful and efficient. Set forth in these terms, it is clearly recognizable that the underlying assumption here is that an individual's defi-

18

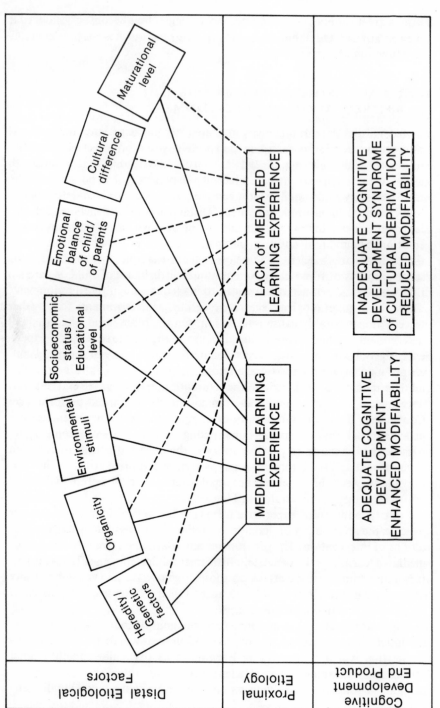

Figure 1. Distal and proximal etiologies of differential cognitive development. (Adapted from Feuerstein and Rand, 1974.)

ciencies are a result of a lack of mediated learning experience as previously outlined and are, therefore, reversible through strategies aimed at filling in the gap created by the lack of MLE.

RELATIONSHIP BETWEEN COGNITIVE PERFORMANCE AND MLE

Having discussed the various hypothesized determinants of differential cognitive development, a number of questions arise. In what way do these determinants produce the final outcome of cognitive performance, be it gifted or retarded? What are the mechanics by which genetic endowment, organic conditions, or environmental stimulation affect the capacity of the individual to use representational, abstract thinking? The fact that we find such great variability in the outcomes within various populations, despite the relative uniformity of the etiological factors, makes the relationships between the determinants highly questionable. However, in terms of the theory of mediated learning experience, the etiological categories just discussed are considered as distal and only indirectly related to the phenomenon of retarded cognitive performance. It is the proximal etiology of a lack of mediated learning experience that is the direct cause of the condition. Although a distal etiology is a necessary condition for the occurrence of retarded performance, it is not a sole determinant. It is the proximal etiology of a lack of mediated learning experience that is the prerequisite, and sufficient, condition for retarded performance. Hence, the concept of mediated learning experience provides both a theoretical rationale and the basis for a course of direct action, at the level of intervention, to alter cognitive development. By removing the focus from immutable distal etiologies for inadequate cognitive behavior to a proximal determinant of a lack of mediated learning experience, which is manifested in the syndrome of cultural deprivation, avenues for cognitive modifiability can be considered.

It is now possible to grasp the full implications of the definition of the culturally deprived individual as having a reduced capacity to modify his intellectual structures in response to sources of stimulation. There is no reason to assume that cultural deprivation, as a function of a lack of mediated learning experience, is an irreversible condition resistant to modification. On the contrary, it is the feature of modifiability which, more than any other, distinguishes the present approach from other more pessimistic and restrictive theoretical orientations.

What is at stake is not merely the transmission of specific skills or abilities but the development of the prerequisite cognitive schemata to enable an individual to derive maximum benefit from direct exposure to sources of stimulation. Our contention is that mediated learning experience is the foundation upon which cognitive structures are built and that, even as late as adolescence, major and significant cognitive modifications are possible. By interposing a program designed to facilitate the organization and transmission of information at increasingly more complex, more abstract, and more efficient levels of functioning, the retarded cognitive performance of the culturally deprived child may be modified and a normal pattern of development may be restored.

DEFINING CHARACTERISTICS OF MLE

In the present framework, MLE represents an interaction between the child and his environment. This interaction is strongly marked by a culturally determined need for each generation to shape the structure of the behavior of successive generations by transmitting to them the past, present, and future dimensions of their culture. The transmission of a culture, across the generations, is primarily a function of the nuclear family, but it is also effected, in varying degrees, by other institutions representing the society at large. Although the impact of cultural transmission in manifested through a variety of modalities, they all converge in the process of enriching the interactional patterns among the generations. MLE is, therefore, a group-supported behavior, which is generated by a primary need of human societies to preserve their cultural continuity.

The Intentional and Transcendent Nature of Mediated Interaction

The interactions that comprise MLE consist of a wide range of behaviors that are partly culturally determined and partly triggered by situational events and circumstances. However, not all interactions between the child and his physical or social environment are necessarily mediated learning experiences. An interaction that provides mediated learning must include an intention, on the part of the mediator, to transcend the immediate needs or concerns of the recipient of the mediation by venturing beyond the here and now, in space and time. Indeed, it is the intentional transcendent nature of the interaction that is the defining characteristic of a mediated interaction. The following example illustrates what is meant by the transcendent nature of mediated interaction.

Providing an infant with nourishment at a time when he is hungry is an act intended to fulfill an immediate need, especially when the feeding is conducted at no specific place or time especially designed for the purpose. The immediacy of the need and its fulfillment dictate where and when it should be satisfied. However, once the fulfillment of the need is intentionally delayed or anticipated for purposes not directly linked to the need itself but relating to temporal and spatial considerations, then the act of feeding becomes transformed into a mediated learning process and leads to the construction of spatial and temporal orientation. Thus, the mediated interaction attempts to expose the infant to dimensions of experience which, although not necessary for his immediate satisfaction, are important for the more complex and remote aspects of his development.

By the same token, the feeding interaction transcends the limited goal of gratifying an immediate need of the child. Because the infant is exposed simultaneously to the visual stimulus of the mother, he learns to distinguish certain constant and stable characteristics of her form from other highly changeable aspects. In this manner, the interaction transcends the elementary and immediate need of nourishment by producing in the infant patterns of attending and focusing such that he is able to relate changing events in his environment. Such activities on the part of the infant will have an important bearing on his pattern of functioning and the development of his cognitive structure.

On a higher level, when the mother, or other caregiver, uses verbal instructions in interacting with a child, and these interactions transcend the use of imperatives by including explanations and generalizations, the effects will be perceptible in the nature of the child's approach to reality. Rather than passively accepting verbal instructions and behaving as an extended limb of the instructor, the child learns to recognize the ideas implicit in the content of the expanded verbal instructions. For example, consider the difference between the following instructions:

"Please buy three bottles of milk."
"Please buy three bottles of milk so that we will have enough left over for tomorrow when the shops are closed."

The second elaborated instruction entails an understanding of its rationale and, hence, the individual is not just carrying out a command but is himself involved in the reasoning behind the command. If the instruction is also accompanied by the suggestion that extra quantities of milk should always be purchased before the weekend, when the shops are closed, a more expanded generalization is introduced. Understanding and executing the instruction now include an anticipation of a given set of conditions in a more or less remote future and a plan of behavior associated with a goal which guides the behavior of the individual. The effects of such instructions are not limited to their specific contents but rather produce an orientation that may not be conceivable without exposure to mediation of this nature. Viewed from this perspective, we may interpret Bernstein's (1964) concept of restricted linguistic codes as not necessarily producing cognitive deficiencies by themselves. Instead, they may reflect a lack of mediated learning experience, the manifestation of which may be more pervasive than that revealed in restricted verbal interactions.

In addition to the transcendent nature of the mediated interaction, MLE also requires a degree of intentionality on the part of the mediator. The intentional character of the mediated interaction is evident in certain well defined instances. For example, a bushman engaged in training a child to construct a spear or bow and arrow exhibits his intentions by requiring the child to follow his actions and by deliberately slowing down his own working rhythm when observed by the child. Thus, the child is able to register the transformations produced by the mediator's behavior in terms of the relationship between the sequence of acts and the specific outcome. Intentionality is not only a characteristic of the mediator but is also shared by the recipient of mediation as part of the interactive process. For both participants, the mediated interaction is a means for attaining a goal whose realization can only be anticipated in the future, in terms of the capacity of the individual to produce similarly to his mediator.

It is important to appreciate, however, that intentionality does not necessarily require a sharp or clear awareness on the part of both partners participating in the mediating process. The so-called primitive mother, whose mediating capacity may be extremely potent, may not be able to formulate the rationale or specific intention underlying her mediated interactions. Such interactions are simply an expression of culturally determined needs which are shared by all members of the society. Participation in the culture is the implicit reason for the occurrence of particular behaviors. Between the two extremes of explicit and implicit intentionality is a continuum of awareness. However, the degree of awareness does not necessarily affect the efficiency of the mediated learning experience. Provided that the element of intentionality and quality of transcending the here and now are present in the interaction, whether deliberately planned by the mediator or as an implicit expectation of the culture, the effect will be the same: a mediated learning experience that serves to nourish the child's developing intellect.

The Role of Content in Mediated Interactions

A further step in the understanding of the concept of MLE is that it is not necessarily contingent upon the content of a learning experience or the means by which a specific content is expressed. In order to avoid misunderstanding, it is important to clarify the role of content in the development of cognitive processes. No claim is made that content does not affect the functioning of the individual in a very specific manner, by producing a differential familiarity with objects, tasks, and events. However, the development of cognitive structure is not a direct function of exposure to specific kinds of contents. Whether a child is taught to build a canoe or to complete a puzzle, the underlying cognitive structure will not necessarily differ in a fundamental way. In learning to master a given situation, the child must learn to cope with a sequence of events situated in space and time, to dissociate the means from the goal, and to indulge in anticipatory representational thought. Such cognitive processes result in the establishment of structural elements, the import and meaning of which transcend the specific content and context within which they occur. It is when cognitive processes become detached from specific tasks that cognitive structures are established. These structures are of a more general nature than the learning of specific tasks and, hence, result in more adaptive behavior by the individual. Although, at later stages in the life of an individual, differences in content may appear to exert a greater influence on the development of differential, cognitive processes, this is not the case during early childhood when MLE has its greatest impact.

The most elementary basis for behavior is established in the earliest years when all experience is novel for the child. During this period, MLE occurs in relation to events, tasks, and interactions that have little to do with the immediate and specific content. For example, unlike older children, the young child focuses on very limited variations in the perceived elements of his world. Every mother has observed her baby focusing for hours on end on a tiny spot that he has discovered and to which he responds with vocalizations.

In this connection, the circular reactions described and elaborated upon by Piaget (1952) are of relevance. According to Piaget, at various stages of the sensorimotor period, the circular reactions evolving from repetitive interaction with objects and events, refined and changed through variations and innovations, are potent vehicles of the assimilation-accommodation process and are thereby directly responsible for the enlargement of schemata. However, the importance of circular reactions lies not in the particular content with which they are linked but in the production of stable and adaptive schemata. Certainly, some behaviors have a higher degree of priority because of their reliance on genetic determination. Thumb-sucking behavior, although dependent on the general nursing schema, is an outcome of a chance encounter with a strange object that is repeated until it becomes established as an independent behavior pattern. Thus, the primary, secondary, and tertiary circular reactions serve as an excellent illustration of the fact that it is the exercise of these reactions, irrespective of the objects involved, that provides the foundation for cognitive structure.

The Role of the Modality of Mediated Interactions

Apart from content, MLE is also not directly contingent upon the modality or language through which the mediation is expressed. Thus, gesture, mimicry, observation, and behavior in general may be as potent as instruments of mediation as speech. The present theoretical framework emphasizes the impact of MLE during the preverbal stage of early childhood. Consequently, at this stage verbal interactions, as such, are not as powerful as nonverbal and metalinguistic behaviors. Using the example of instruction in a preliterate society, it is clear that mediation may take a nonverbal form. The mediator illustrates his actions to an interested observer with only limited verbal, and even less semantic, interaction occurring. In our experience, the changes that occur as a result of nonverbal mediation transcend both the content and the means by which the content is transmitted. The end result is the development of a cognitive structure that determines the modifiability and, hence, the adaptability of the individual when confronted with other tasks of varying degrees of similarity and difference.

Of course, language in the sense of a verbal encoding system may be considered as the most economic and, consequently, the most efficient transmitter of learning. By virtue of its nature, verbal transmission is the preferred modality of mediation whenever higher mental processes are of concern. Nevertheless, Helen Keller certainly represents a remarkable illustration of the potency of MLE to break through apparently impenetrable barriers imposed by sensory limitations. The fact that learning could be mediated through the medium of the tactile sense alone is clear testimony that substitutions may be made for verbal mediation under specific conditions. A less dramatic example is evidenced by the work of Furth (1966), who has shown that the cognitive development of deaf children is not qualitatively different from that of their hearing peers and that their limited experience of language *per se* does not necessarily inhibit their development.

MLE as the Determinant of Cognitive Modifiability

If it is agreed that neither specific content nor the modality of expression is crucial to the mediating process, then it becomes possible to conceive of MLE as a universal phenomenon. Irrespective of culture, levels of technological development, differences in semantic encoding, and variations in levels of skills, a capacity to become modified and to adapt to new situations is common to all individuals exposed to some kind of MLE. This capacity to respond in an autoplastic way to encounters with a constantly changing environment is the common product of MLE. However, the onset of mediation and its extent and intensity may contribute to differences in the efficiency of MLE.

The universal characteristic of MLE, as the essential determinant of cognitive structures that enable individuals to make efficient use of their experience, casts new light on the differential capacity of culturally different groups to adapt to drastic changes in their life-style and environment. One of the apparent paradoxes that arises from the mass of data relating to the adaptation of culturally different groups to a new environment is that the degree of familiarity with the new environment and with its objects, language, and level of differentiation and technological sophistication is not necessarily related to successful adaptation. This is well illustrated in the comparison between the Yemenite and North African immigrants to Israel. Of the two groups, the Yemenites were considerably more remote from the dominant Occidental Israeli culture. It has been estimated that a time gap of some 400 years separated the Yemenite community from modern technological society. In contrast, the North Africans were judged as being much closer, in terms of familiarity, to Israeli culture because of their encounter with French culture in their countries of origin. Nevertheless, the initial adaptation of the Yemenite group in Israel was by far more rapid and efficient despite its confrontation with a totally new culture and life-style. The same is true of the American Chinese community, the members of which represent an extreme example of a culturally different subgroup with respect to the dominant culture of the society within which they live.

Stodolsky and Lesser (1967) have shown that groups with the highest levels of cultural identity also manifest the highest levels of cognitive functioning. The paradox in which cultural difference appears inversely related to cognitive adaptation is resolved if degree of familiarity with the new environment is replaced by the degree of modifiability of the individuals confronting new circumstances and life-styles. When group identity is nurtured by cultural transmission, MLE becomes the vehicle by which a culture ensures its continuity. In the case of both the Yemenite and American Chinese groups, the by-product of cultural identity is cognitive modifiability, as both depend on the phenomenon of MLE. Consequently, MLE for the individual, and cultural transmission for the group, comprise the major determinants of flexibility which enable the individual to transcend the here and now, to adapt to new modes of functioning, and to develop new patterns of behavior appropriate to new situations. In other words, MLE produces in the organism a propensity to learn how to learn, by equipping the organism with the tools necessary for this facility.

CATEGORIES OF MLE

Cultural Transmission

From the above discussion, it is clear that MLE includes not only mediated learning but also cultural transmission. This latter element includes information which would be unavailable to the individual if not communicated by the more initiated and experienced generation. Included in this category of MLE is a knowledge of events that belong to a time period outside the direct experience of the individual and information out of his immediate reach and, therefore, accessible only be means of mediation. The fact that an individual becomes party to information not directly available from his immediate sensorial and experiential field affects more than his reservoir of knowledge. Even more important is the fact that the acquisition of such knowledge produces a readiness to explore, or an orientation of curiosity toward, the more remote realms of knowledge. In this sense, mediated transmission enables an individual to conceive of the existence of a world by sheer knowing and without recourse to direct experience. Mediated transmission of the past and future is therefore enriching for the individual not only with respect to content but, more important, through its production of new needs and ways of relating to the world, which transcend those experiences directly available to the senses.

Mediated Learning

MLE also includes transactions between child and environment in which changes are produced in the nature of the stimulus impinging on the child's senses. This may occur as a result of the mediating processes either transforming the nature of the stimulus or producing changes within the recipient of the stimulation, such that the stimulus is perceived in a variety of ways.

Attributes of the stimuli, such as temporal, spatial, ordinal, and other such relationships, are mediated within this category of MLE. Mediation of this nature produces in the organism a need to relate events, objects, and experiences to one another, with the result that the experience of a specific object or event is transcended by means of the individual's own actions and operations. Hence, the world of relations is the primary product of the individual's activity, and, having become detached from the sensorial experience of the individual, these relations are governed by their own laws of organization and regulation. It is through MLE that operational systems are established which determine new modes of interaction with the sensorial world that are significantly different from those derived from direct, instant experiences of the world. Thus, the need to establish relationships among experienced elements, by means of comparative behavior, is the necessary outcome of MLE.

In order to appreciate the processes involved in MLE, consideration must be given to the nature of some interactions between the child and his human environment. Before examining in some detail the nature of various mediated interactions, it should be emphasized that there is nothing in our biological existence that necessitates abstract thinking with its reliance on elaborated symbols and higher mental processes. Such processes arise in response to cultural needs of an interpersonal and intergenerational nature. Therefore, MLE is directly responsible for all functioning that transcends the biological needs of the individual. One of the earliests forms of mediation that reflects the expression of cultural needs is the selection of stimuli offered to the child by the caregiving figure.

Selection of Stimuli   Selection of stimuli is usually oriented toward protecting the child, especially the newborn infant, from unpleasant experiences. These selection processes involve three phases: the first consists of linking simple perceptual elements to the sensory systems of the child; the second involves relational systems; and the third is concerned with social interactions. However, even at the most elementary level, the mediating mother, or caregiver, selects stimuli as a function of specific educational or child-rearing patterns, as determined by her socioeconomic and cultural needs. Three kinds of selection may occur: removing stimuli from the child ("Not for you"), relating certain stimuli to a time dimension ("Not now but later"), and relating stimuli to a spatial dimension ("Not here but there"). In this manner, the child learns to discriminate between things and non-things, their attributes, and the spatiotemporal elements associated with them.

In the development of higher mental processes and their efficient application, the selection of stimuli has two important functions. The first concerns the meaningfulness or saliency that is attributed to certain stimuli. From the mass of stimulation impinging on the child, certain stimuli are selected by the mother as being more relevant and meaningful than others at a given point, and, therefore, a background is provided against which categorization becomes possible at later stages of development. The second function is related to the development of focusing behavior in the child. Focusing entails an inhibitory, or limiting, process that enables the child to be selective and discriminatory in his perception of objects and events. This inhibitory process permits the child a greater investment in those elements that have acquired specific meaning. Thus, both the meaningfulness of the stimulus and the established patterns of attention ensure appropriate focusing behavior and, consequently, the capacity to efficiently register and collect relevant data.

One of the well observed phenomena in children who have not received MLE from a constant caregiver is the hyperprosexic or the diffused nature of their perception. These children scan their perceptual environment without attending differentially to the more relevant elements and, therefore, do not persist in developing the means necessary for attaining specific goals. Very often, these children are described as perseverative, that is, they repeat their perceptual and motor behaviors inappropriately and engage in sweeping perceptual activities without attending to the more meaningful elements of the environment. Thus the selection of stimuli has an enhancing effect on the infant's focusing behavior because the mediator serves to emphasize certain stimuli by attaching to them qualities not shared by other stimuli. In this manner, the mediator frames the reality experienced by the child, a process which occurs at the earliest point in the life of the child.

In reviewing the literature relating to infant capabilities, Korner (1973) points out that newborns are capable of many more responses than was previously assumed. With respect to the theory of MLE the following conclusion drawn by Korner is particularly relevant:

> The recent discoveries of the extent and the variety of the newborn's capabilities leave little doubt that the very young infant is able to avail himself of and respond to a great many more forms of stimulation than had been suspected (p. 312).

Today, it is a well documented fact that the vision of the newborn is far more developed than was previously thought (Korner, 1973). Given certain limitations, such as a lack of accommodatory functions, the newborn is capable of fixating on and pursuing objects, moving or stationary, and also shows preferences for certain configurations, such as the human face (Fantz, 1967). Together with other researchers, we believe that the mother is one of the richest sources of visual stimulation. Consequently, the more adequate the exposure of the mother's face to the child's perceptual system, the greater will be his focusing capacity and, hence, the more efficient his perceptual activities at later stages of development. This continuous exposure to the mother's face assumes importance because, being the most constant and familiar stimulus, it provides the child with an opportunity to experience the alterations or transformations that occur in his perception of objects and events which, nevertheless, retain some constant features. In the case of the mediating mother, such transformations gradually become related to other events and eventually culminate in the first implicit perceptions of causal relationships. Because transformations associated with the mother tend to follow specific behavior patterns, the chance that the relationships between these transformations will have a reinforcing significance is great. Thus, the selection of stimuli, in both its positive and negative aspects, will help in the differentiation within the perceptual system of the child, resulting in perceptual acuity and the active mobilization of the volitional processes of attention.

Unlike Hebb (1949), for whom perceptual stimulation is a condition for the development of cell assemblies, or Hunt (1961), for whom perceptual stimulation is a function of direct exposure, the theory of MLE does not regard a lack of perceptual stimulation as a meaningful determinant of differential cognitive development. Beyond a few rare and unusual cases, there are limited instances in which direct exposure to sources of stimulation varies in any meaningful way among populations that manifest considerable variations in the level of cognitive functioning. Clearly, an attempt to explain such variations among populations on the basis of direct exposure to stimuli does not appear tenable. By the same token, the hypothesis that the sheer physical proximity of mother and child is sufficient to provide for all of the child's emotional and cognitive needs cannot be considered specific enough to explain the development of the cognitive prerequisites for higher mental operations. Studies in early childhood have confirmed that culturally and socially deprived individuals who enjoy an intensive relationship and physical proximity with their caregiver develop normally up to the time they are required to use higher levels of operational thinking. At this point, they begin to manifest deficiencies in their use and exploitation of learning opportunities (see Feuerstein and Richelle, 1957; Jensen, 1977; Smilansky et al., 1976). The point is that, although direct exposure to stimuli and the emotional closeness of a loving mother may have an important bearing on the biologically determined development of the organism, they are not sufficient in themselves to ensure the development of those aspects of human behavior that transcend biologically determined needs. To achieve this, cultural transmission is a condition *sine qua non* for the passage from animal to human modes of relating to the world.

Scheduling of Stimuli   The selection of stimuli to be presented or filtered to the child is associated with the process of scheduling, which concerns the appearance of stimuli along both temporal and spatial dimensions. By assigning specific times for the appearance or disappearance of given stimuli, the significance of temporal factors will be accentuated. To the extent that such schedules represent rhythms, they mark the time and help establish implicitly the concepts of temporal distances, temporal orders, and sequences of before and after. They start out by being linked to an action, and, because actions are organized around specifically demarcated segments of time, segmentation becomes an implicit notion even on the preverbal level. "Not now but later," and "Not before but after," create the dimensions of a proximal action-based concept of time, which provides the skeleton upon which past and future orientation extends out from the immediate present. The more such scheduling occurs, the greater the awareness and the orientation toward time as a determining factor in the child's life. With the onset of verbal interaction, time transcends the individual's own action-oriented meaning and becomes progressively extended to other areas of functioning.

It is of interest to note the manner in which various cosmologic systems have made use of the temporal factor for establishing meanings and the significance of events. The solar system in the biblical description of the Creation not only provides light but enables the human being to divide time and use it for his temporal orientation. Furthermore, in the biblical tradition, great care is taken for the transmission and inculcation of an awareness of temporal factors by providing the factors with sacred, social, and political functions in addition to the rhythm associated with biological and natural functions. It is our contention that there is no more important factor affecting the human mind than the consciousness and awareness of time and the temporal dimensions in our lives. Henri Bergson (1919) ascribes to memory (which to a large extent is closely related to the factor of time) the most important characteristic of life as compared to other factors. Without a process of mediation, this awareness cannot become fully established.

Since the more remote past of human beings cannot be reconstructed except through cultural transmission, an initiated as well as intentioned adult is required to mediate the past. (By the initiated adult, we refer to the informed and knowledgeable member of society, while, by the intentioned adult, we refer to the person intending to transmit the culture, i.e., serve as mediator.) Lack of mediation of past events will leave the developing organism limited, to a large extent, to the very proximal temporal dimensions linked to his own life and actions. Thus, the absence of scheduling results in the individual lacking an awareness of the most important attributes of events: the time in which they occur and their coordinated order and sequence in relation to other events.

This lack of orientation toward time as a dimension of one's own experience may, of necessity, limit an orientation toward the future. One may use Henri Bergson's illustration (1919) describing the relationship between past and future as similar to the relationship between the taut bowstring and the distance of the arrow's trajectory. The more taut the string, the further the arrow is projected; the more remote the past to which an individual can refer, the further he can project himself into the future, planning and working constructively toward it. The frequent lack of temporal orientation in the culturally deprived child occurs because he has not had time mediated to him as a dimension that must be registered or associated with each experienced event. Lack of summative and comparative behavior will limit even further an awareness of experienced time, even more than it will restrict perception of other dimensions of the experienced world. An episodic grasp of reality will seldom evoke in these children a real need for organizing, sequencing, and understanding the relationships between events ordered along temporal dimensions (see Chapter 3).

Mediation of temporal factors occurs at an early stage of development by means of scheduling. Later, the process of scheduling becomes more efficient as more remote segments of time are dealt with by the transmission of the past experience of the learning organism itself. This is achieved by helping the child re-evoke and re-experience, in an internalized way, past events that become more and more remote and detached from his own actions, experience, and needs. A similar progression is followed for the representation of the future, which involves a process of extension and expansion, enabling the individual to project himself into time periods associated with the transformation of his own needs and interests.

The orientation of the culturally deprived child toward the immediate present, together with various other emotional, motivational, and aspirational limitations, is, in our opinion, explained by a cognitive factor. This is contrary to the view that the need for immediate gratification is attributable to some pathological deviation in the otherwise adequate cognitive functioning of the individual. When we speak of the need for immediate gratification on the part of the culturally deprived child, we think of it as determined by the cognitive limitations of the individual because of his restricted capacity to orient himself to temporal dimensions remote from his immediate actions and the gratification of his needs.

Anticipation   Closely linked to the mediation of temporal factors and scheduling is the mediation of positive or negative anticipation as a product of the outcome of the individual's own experience. The relationship between the child's own actions, or those of someone else, and the consequent result is stressed in producing for the child an orientation to temporally and spatially more distant effects. A variety of elements is produced when such anticipation is mediated to the child. One element, for example, is the production of a representation of an otherwise nonexistent object or effect, that has not as yet become observable. Any anticipation of an outcome is an internal construction of reality, which is dependent on a representation as well as an inferential thought process by the child. This involves enriching those parameters of the thought processes that are neither easily established nor readily produced by the child, without a request on the part of the mediating adult. Requests of this nature are not the product of a regular action-based, present-oriented interaction between the child and the adult or between the child and the objectal environment. In the process of anticipation, the mediating individual has to intend to transcend the immediate needs of gratification in favor of more remote goals. By producing such anticipation, the mediator attempts to affect the immediate action of the individual in favor of an as yet unexperienced future. In contrast to certain interaction modalities between the child and his human environment, in which the goal is merely the substitution of the fulfillment of an immediate act, an interaction that transcends the immediate fulfills the criterion of mediated learning experience. This is because it projects the child into a dimension that he could not master without mediation. Another factor involved in the mediation of anticipation is the establishment of a causal relationship between a given act and its anticipated outcome.

Imitation   One of the most powerful tools of mediated learning experience is the intentional provision of models that the child can imitate, including those that mirror his own actions. This is especially important in the early periods of the life of the newborn child when the limitations in his postural control and locomotor behavior confine his imitative behavior to models that are provided by a mediator. One can and often does care for and nurture the child without exposing him to models of imitative behavior. The establishment of eye contact is a prerequisite of imitative behavior, and yet mothers, and other caregivers, may hold the child in such a way that he does not come into eye contact with them. Mothers may nourish a child by bottle or by nursing from the breast without establishing any eye contact. There can be even less eye contact when an act does not involve physical closeness. The child may be kept on the lap of the mother without being looked at or able to look at the mother. On the other hand, parents may go to extraordinary lengths to establish eye contact. In one known instance, a father, because of the loss of his left arm, could not hold his baby in the usual manner. In order to maintain eye contact with the child, the father spent many hours looking at the child and teaching him to focus on his face. As a result, the child would twist his body in order to turn his face toward his father when cradled in the father's right arm. When eye contact was lost, the child would immediately start seeking to renew the contact.

Exposure of the child to models of imitation, at least during the period of limited locomotor behavior, will vary enormously from case to case and can be described as a potent proximal etiological factor for differentiated cognitive development. The more that mediated imitative behavior is enhanced, and the higher the capacity of the child to seek objects and explore their attributes, the greater will be his capacity to become affected and modified through direct exposure to sources of stimulation in later life.

According to Piaget (1962), imitative behavior at the very early period of life can be considered as the reconstruction of the perceived object through imitational activity. Working from this meaning, Piaget conceives of imitation as the prototype of accommodational activity of the organism. In imitating an object or an action, the organism assimilates the imitated model and by virtue of this reproduction of the act accommodates the existing schema to the assimilated object. However, Piaget describes the modalities and techniques of the behavior to be imitated as developing progressively through the sensorimotor period as a product of both motivation and the interaction of the organism with its objectal environment. Thus, Piaget sees the *existence of schemata* as a necessary condition for imitation. He does not consider imitation possible before the development of requisite schemata at a certain period in the life of the child.

Another criterion of imitation, which has to be considered as a relatively delayed phenomenon, concerns the volitional criteria of imitation. Imitative behavior, as suggested by Piaget, involves a volitional act on the part of the imitator that is already marked by the discrimination between goals and means, model and imitator. These criteria are not met by the child until the onset of representational behavior. The crying of a newborn child in response to the crying of other children surrounding him in the nursery is not regarded by Piaget as imitative behavior. He considers this response simply a confusion between external and internal sources of stimuli with the child responding to the models without knowing that the source is outside of him.

However, recent studies of perception and focusing behavior, such as those done by Fantz and his associates (1967), as well as the work on synchronicity of movement by Condon and Sander (1974), and earlier observations gathered by Zazzo (1962) in his work *Conduits de Conscience,* which are strongly supported by the recent work of Meltzoff and Moore (1977), provide strong evidence that imitation occurs much earlier than was previously considered possible. Zazzo, for example, provides evidence of the infant's imitative protrusion of the tongue at ages 7–14 days of life and even earlier.

Meltzoff and Moore (1977) have found that 12- to 21-day-old infants can imitate both facial and manual gestures, which implies that "[they] can equate their own seen behaviors with gestures they see others perform" (p. 75). In the Meltzoff and Moore studies, 2- to 3-week-old infants proved able to imitate the tongue protrusion, mouth opening, lip protrusion, and sequential finger movements that were demonstrated by an adult experimenter. These findings and similar ones cited by other researchers conflict with the Piagetian definition of imitation in which perceptual cognitive sophistication is required in order to match a gesture that is seen with a gesture that cannot be seen. Thus, the significance of mediating to the child, in his earliest days, models of imitative behavior is even greater, in light of these findings, than the Hebbian perceptual theory was able to anticipate.

Provision of Specific Stimuli   In addition to the selection of stimuli and scheduling, in terms of time, space, and order, mediated learning occurs as a result of the direct and intentional provision of specific stimuli which are considered necessary for the growth and general orientation of the child. Such stimuli are usually culturally determined, and the child's attention is constantly and repeatedly directed toward them. Not only is the child enriched in terms of content but the provision of specific kinds of stimuli also produces two kinds of behavior in the child. The first is the elaboration of the orienting reflex, which is manifested in a search for new elements in the environment. The second involves the development of a need to share and communicate to others new perceptions and experiences. This behavior is evident in children who have been exposed to the mediated provision of stimuli. They frequently indulge in pointing to new and interesting objects and attempt to share their experience with cries of "look, look, look," "see, see, see," and so on. Once established, the mediated provision of stimuli becomes a major means of communication in the family and is manifested in a variety of ways, including the verbal, emotional, and experiential levels. In this process, all of the siblings become amplifiers of mediation. However, in families where the child is provided with only the direct exposure of stimuli, irrespective of the range or extent of such stimuli, very little, if any, sharing occurs and, hence, the child does not learn to relate to the stimuli in culturally acceptable and desirable ways.

Repetition and Variation   Common to many forms of mediation is constant repetition. The amount of repetition, of necessity, will have to vary with the specific characteristics of the receiving organism. Thus, children with variation in their receptive threshold because of differences in sensorial acuity or because of central nervous system impairment may require considerable variations in the amount and the intensity of exposure for the mediational process to penetrate their system. The mediating adult who wishes to expose the child to certain events must ensure that the objects or events are actually perceived. This means that they must be brought to the attention of the child in his sensorial field to ensure that their appearance is actually registered as being of a repetitive rather than an episodic nature.

This concern for manner of perception has bearing on Piaget's views on circular reactions, which he considers to be automatically triggered in the following way. The child's first discovery and interaction with objects are largely of a fortuitous nature. When repeated, the interaction becomes more voluntary, and variations are produced by the changes of certain dimensions of the behavior. Finally, these variations bring about innovations. In order for circular reactions to become sources for the enlargement of schemata, through assimilation and accommodation, the repetition of the event and repeated exposure to the object must be ensured. Usually, it is the mediator who intervenes and provides the child with the opportunity of repeating a particular behavioral sequence. This is evident in many of Piaget's protocols in which the active nature of his own intervention is often eclipsed by his description of the child's activity.

A number of processes are involved in the repetition of a behavioral sequence. Repeated exposure to the same object or event permits a given schema to become first consolidated and then varied and expanded, and, in the process, various different attributes of the object also are assimilated. A meaning is assigned to the behavior, such that the underlying schema becomes detached from the specific behavioral sequence and acquires more general application. In addition, sets of intentions, common to all the behavioral variations, are transmitted or mediated to the child. Thus, the child is able to experience whether, under different conditions, certain behaviors are accepted or not, and is able to link specific behaviors to the dimensions of meaning, time, and space. Hence, mediated repetition serves either to reinforce existing schemata or to establish new schemata in instances where they did not previously exist.

Transmission of Past and Representation of Future   Of all the dimensions of mediated learning, perhaps the most clearly understood is that of the transmission of the past and the representation of the future. By definition, the past cannot be experienced by the child whose only access to past events is through transmission. Past events provide the child with sources of information that enrich and extend his own experience. Thus, not only is the child dependent on his parents to satisfy his biological needs but he is also dependent on an informed and intentioned adult to transmit a knowledge of the past. Transmission of the past and representation of the future serve to extend the life space of the individual to include experiences that are not directly available to him.

Of necessity, representational processes are involved if the child is to develop the ability to ascribe meaning to events not directly perceived or experienced. Probably one of the most important human characteristics is a readiness to be influenced by the past in arriving at decisions affecting the present and future. The transmission of the past starts with simple re-evocations and continues progressively to more remote temporal dimensions. Reference was made previously to Bergson's contention that knowledge of the past is related to the projection of the future. In this sense, transmission of the past may be regarded as a major determinant of anticipatory and planning behavior.

Comparative Behavior   One of the most fundamental processes to emerge as a result of mediated transmission is the development of comparative behavior. Although heavily dependent on verbal modes of interaction, the basis for comparative behavior is established long before the child develops elaborate encoding processes and the ability to educe relationships among objects. As a prerequisite to relational thinking, comparative behavior has its origin in the scanning behavior of the infant. In scanning the field, relationships of commonality and differences among objects are established, which provide the basis for comparative behavior. The precursors of comparative behavior involve the orientation of the organism toward increasingly more precise processes of perception, exploration, and attention. At later stages of development, discrimination is enhanced by labeling and relating objects and events to each other, rather than experiencing them as discrete and episodic events.

The need to link and relate objects and events is transmitted by the mediator to the child at very young ages. The behavioral results of comparative behavior in the young child may be witnessed by his reaction to new and unfamiliar events. Thus, a 2-year-old boy will exclaim that he sees a broken car when looking at a jeep without doors or windows. The disequilibrium experienced by the child is reflected in this reaction, which conveys that the child has grasped that something has changed or has been transformed in relation to a previously experienced object, rather than perceiving the object as a new and different experience. Similarly, the distress of the young child in response to a man who looks like his father, but is not, suggests that even though certain characteristics are perceived as similar their differences render them distinct.

Comparative behavior becomes more firmly established with the emergence of verbal interactions. Such interactions permit the use of the re-evocation of objects and events and facilitate the production of relationships between them, across temporal and spatial dimensions. The use of words as a means of comparison reflects the need of the organism to link and organize what is perceived and experienced. This propensity may well be regarded as the psychological basis, or cognitive correlate, of the cell assemblies described by Hebb. In these terms, the individual goes beyond his experience by introducing dimensions that do not themselves derive from, or originate in, his immediate perceptual experience. It is significant that one of the most common characteristics of culturally deprived retarded performers is their limited need to compare objects and events beyond very specific and immediate needs.

Summary

It should now be evident that the two basic categories of MLE, transmission of information and mediated interaction, affect the human organism's capacity to use direct exposure to stimuli from a very early point in the individual's development. As stated previously, the earlier that MLE begins, the greater the individual's efficiency in becoming modified through direct exposure to stimuli and, consequently, the greater his capacity for further learning and development. In contrast, a lack of MLE drastically limits the meaning and significance of experienced events because these experiences are grasped in an episodic manner without being related to other events experienced by the individual. Thus, the effects of a lack of MLE may be conceptualized as depriving the individual of the prerequisites of higher mental processes, despite a potentially normal capacity inherent in him. It is in the realm of the need system or attitudinal orientation of the individual that the effects of a lack of MLE are manifest. Although a neurophysiological or neurochemical involvement cannot be dismissed as a corollary of a lack of MLE, the ill effects do not have the permanent, stable, and irreversible characteristics usually ascribed to the neurophysiological organization of the organism (see Feuerstein, 1978).

3
DETERMINANTS OF A
LACK OF MEDIATED
LEARNING EXPERIENCE

The cause of a lack of MLE may be rooted in two broad sources: the nature of the individual's environment and the condition of the individual at a given point in his development. Of course, both of these potential areas of cause for a lack of MLE may become interrelated such that the individual's condition affects his environment or vice versa. In addition, a lack of MLE may be a group-determined phenomenon or an isolated event that occurs within a particular nuclear or extended family. A lack of MLE, however, most frequently occurs as a group-determined phenomenon, as the result of a lack of cultural transmission in certain socioeconomic, cultural, and ethnic subgroups. This is reflected in the limited investment, made on the part of the adult generation to communicate the values, attitudes, and past history of the group to the new generation, at either formal institutionalized levels or through informal means.

ENVIRONMENTAL DETERMINANTS

Cultural Transmission

No one would deny that in all human societies a great deal is transmitted from one generation to the next. However, among culturally deprived groups what is transmitted tends to be limited to those aspects to which the child is directly exposed by means of his sensory, perceptual, and motor behavior. This exposure, by its very nature, is characterized by its directness and immediacy and, as such, is not a transmission in the sense of being mediated, filtered, or interpreted to the growing and learning organism. In those cases where interactions are limited to behaviors that are oriented to the present and represent a horizontal dimension of experience, there is little concern for the transgenerational vertical dimension that spans both past and future.

A breakdown in cultural transmission, which results in a lack of MLE within the nuclear family, may be caused by a variety of historical conditions. Certain groups may experience a transition from one established way of life to another and may react to their past (and also to their future) as a burden that must be discarded as soon as possible. In some cases, the attempt to obliterate the past may be a deliberate and conscious act accompanied by an elaborate rationale. This process is highlighted in the clash of a minority culture and a dominant culture when the minority perceives specific advantages as accompanying the adoption of the dominant culture. In order to adopt and become part of the dominant culture, the past must be relinquished, often to the extent of rejecting one's previous cultural identification and severing one's ties with it. Through this process, transmission of the past is obstructed, the effect of which will depend on the length of the transitional period and the extent of integration into the new and dominant culture. In many cases, integration is by no means complete or successful, with consequent accompanying effects of alienation from both cultures that vary in severity. The obstruction of cultural transmission can become a harsh and even cruel condition for parents to bear as they feel compelled to reject their past to gain acceptance. To free themselves and the younger generation from what they consider an impediment to integration, parents attempt to erase the past and to conceal whatever traces of their culture exist. The extent to which parents may go, and the sad consequences for their children, are well illustrated in the following case.

J is the son of parents who had to wipe out the evidence of a traumatic past, despite the fact that a daughter who was a part of this past was still living. This need to obliterate the past went so far as to include the destruction of works of art and photographs that were connected with this past. The rather glorious history of one part of the family was totally negated. The resulting limitation of communication to the "here and now" among the members of the family resulted in very poor familial interaction. Associated with this verbal restrictiveness were many taboos that prevented certain knowledge from becoming known to the nucleus of the family as well as to others.

J was referred to the author because of a total incapacity to function in school, acting out predelinquent behavior, and a variety of signs indicative of poor control of reality. Using conventional assessment methods, the author found a low level of functioning with an IQ close to 54, which was confirmed by a consulting psychometrician. Following this diagnosis, the parents were directed toward a lower level of aspiration for their son, who seemed to be genuinely and endogenously retarded. However, various attempts at integration in work and placement with a foster family failed totally. J was again referred for evaluation. This time, the author applied the Learning Potential Assessment Device method and to his surprise a high level of modifiability was revealed. Following these findings, he decided on a remediational program that had to be carried out almost totally on an individual level. Again, the results pointed clearly to J's capacity to function once the deficient functions responsible for his failure were corrected.

A number of years later, J became interested in intellectual activities, and, after completing his army service, he devoted himself to religious studies for three years during which he performed on a very adequate level. In long discussions with the parents, the dynamics of the interaction in the family pointed clearly to the obstruction of mediational processes for J, as a consequence of the family's perceived need to hide and wipe out the past. Had cultural transmission not been obstructed, J's cognitive development may not have needed the author's intervention.

Clashes between cultures are frequently observed as a result of immigration. This is especially the case when people from culturally different and disadvantaged minority groups are confronted with the requirements of a dominant culture that is largely unfamiliar to them. Certain elements of the dominant culture are different from, and may even be opposite to aspects of, the culture of the disadvantaged groups. This incompatibility between the cultures will have an important bearing on the capacity of the group members to adapt both as a group and as individuals. For example, if storytelling is a well established tradition within the disadvantaged group, compatible with their more relaxed way of life, adaptation to a technological society may deprive the group of the time to indulge in this activity. Similarly, other traditional means of cultural transmission may come to be considered inappropriate, and the community may decide to eliminate them because of their incompatibility with the new culture whose acceptance of the minority is reflected by factors of economic and social status. In this event, the past takes on negative connotations, leading to an increase in the centrifugal forces of the group that acts to disrupt its cultural and social unity.

An example of the above process is provided by the initial reaction of some of the Oriental Jewish immigrants to Israel. Many of them were reluctant to acknowledge their origins, preferring to call themselves Southern Frenchmen, and sought to escape from their past. The author vividly remembers the violent reaction of an adolescent group of these immigrants to his request that they sing a few songs from the "old country" with which he was familiar. Despite the fact that he had worked with the group in North Africa and in a transit camp in France, and had conveyed to the members his regard for their cultural values, religious practices, folklore, and customs, the adolescents were shocked and dismayed to be reminded of their past. "Why do you remind us that we were primitive, ignorant, and uncultured?" they asked.

This attitude toward such an important and vital aspect of one's past cannot but result in a rejection of oneself and will affect, in the first instance, the nature of the relationship between mother and child. By rejecting one's own worth as a person, the mother limits her relationship with her child to the fulfillment of his biological needs. Inclination to provide the child with anything beyond his immediate requirements is diminished, if not eliminated. Many such parents openly declare that they are ignorant, illiterate, and unskilled people and have nothing to give their children and, indeed, express concern that their offspring will grow up like them. In this manner, an entire community may relinquish its responsibilities in shaping the future generation. Clearly, such an attitude will have a considerable impact on the self-image, identification, socialization, and moral and cognitive development of the child.

Often, groups that have attempted to become fully assimilated into the dominant culture but have been rejected, end up reaffirming their identity in an exaggerated manner. Stereotyped characteristics attributed to them by the mainstream culture are adopted in an extreme form and are manifested in an antisocial manner, accompanied by acts of rebellion and acting out behavior that represent a hypertrophy in what was formerly a somewhat atrophied ego.

The passage of cultural transmission may also be obstructed as a result of changes occurring in the structure of society and, hence, in the characteristic modes of transmission at a given time. For example, in Morocco, migration from the rural Mellah (small Jewish ghetto) into the large urban slums resulted in a discontinuation of the traditional intensive modes of cultural transmission. Two mechanisms were responsible for the breakdown in transmission. First, the extended patriarchal family structure, typical of the rural communities, was disrupted by the migration to the cities.

Previously, life in the Mellah was organized around a patriarchal nucleus with many collaterals in the extended family. The presence of both horizontal and vertical components in the enlarged family produced a rich variety of stimulation. The past was constantly and vigorously represented by the elderly members of the family, who were no longer as actively involved in the daily routines as were the parents of young children. The father, usually a peddler, was only available to his children on the weekends, and even then considerable time was spent with them in the synagogue. By virtue of their leisure and continual presence, it was the grandparents who fulfilled the role of transmitting to the child his culture, both past events and future expectations. In light of the absence of mass media, such as newspapers, radio, and books, the role of the grandparents assumed particular importance.

With the move to the city slums, with its crowded conditions of life, migration of the entire extended family was not possible, and life becamed organized around the restricted nuclear family. Within this new family framework, with its absence of vertical and lateral components, the amount of MLE was considerably reduced. Responsibility for the transfer of cultural transmission shifted from the family circle to institutions like the Heder and Kutab (Jewish and Moslem religious schools), without these institutions being equipped to meet even the most rudimentary scholastic skills required by the child, let alone the transmission of his substantial cultural heritage. In many cases, the outcome for the child was a void; he was deprived of a meaningful cultural identity to which he could relate.

The second mechanism responsible for breakdown in cultural transmission, which usually operates in conjunction with the disruption of family structure, concerns the passage from a preliterate to a literate mode of cultural transmission. Again, the Moroccan example serves as a good illustration since both Moslem and Jewish communities relied heavily on nonliterate modes of communication. Very little use was made of books, newspapers, pamphlets, and the like, for communication purposes. Even when prayer books existed, prayers were learned by rote at an early age, with the entire community chanting the prayers aloud rather than reading them. The limited reliance on the written word elevated the spoken word to a high level of importance, and the elderly members of the community became particularly skilled in conveying important information to the younger generations. In this milieu, the storyteller was an established institution who could captivate his audience for hours on end, manipulating the drama to ensure remuneration before the last act. In addition to such specialized cultural transmitters, the entire·adult community participated in the process of transcending immediate needs and concerns by verbally mediating their world view to the younger generation.

However, the sudden passage from this informal mode of transmission to a literate mode, which accompanied the migration to the city, served to impoverish the process of cultural transmission. This, combined with the limited reading habits of the migrants and the scarcity of written materials, served to reduce the effectiveness of cultural transmission in terms of content and, of greater importance, reduced the capacity of the individual to benefit from direct exposure to sources of stimulation for becoming modified.

A typical consequence of a lack of experiences that transcend the here and now is the reluctance of the individual to engage in any form of representational thinking. This is particularly apparent with respect to if-then propositions. The sharp and sudden transformation from preliterate to literate modes of communication may leave an entire generation devoid of vital information about themselves which, in turn, prevents them from transmitting such information to their progeny. Thus, a hiatus is produced in the cultural continuity of a community, which cannot be reversed except by a deliberate restitutive process. Recently, the Moroccan community in Israel made a successful attempt to actively promote an awareness and pride in their culture, encouraging the transmission of their cultural heritage to the younger members of their community.. This positive innovation has already proven beneficial to the development of children whose parents now feel not only the need but also the right to transmit to their children their past, their social values, and their life-style. As long as parents resisted the transmission of their culture, many of the deficient functions of their children could be attributed to their lack of MLE, produced by the disruption of cultural transmission. It is our contention that the many instances of cognitive dysfunctioning and low academic achievement that occur in certain populations arise during, and as a result of, the transition from the condition of culturally different to culturally deprived. This process is marked by a loss of one's own culture and a reduced capacity to become modified by direct encounters with the new culture.

Poverty

Poverty has often been invoked as a determinant of cultural deprivation and cognitive dysfunction. Many reasons are advanced in support of the role of poverty in producing differential cognitive development. Poverty is said to be associated with reduced opportunities for stimulation by producing an environment that is characterized by a limited variation in the sources of stimulation. In addition, the conditions of poverty limit the resources of parents for providing the emotional, nutritional, and physical conditions of life to support the growth and development of the child. However, it has been well documented that poverty alone does not inevitably or unavoidably produce cultural deprivation. The point has been cogently stated by Begab (1977):

> The relationship of poverty to sociocultural retardation is associative, not causal. While an overwhelming majority of the retarded are poor, only a small fraction of the poor are retarded. This fraction is concentrated in families where the mothers are of low intelligence and education. The root causes of retardation in these families still need to be specified, but the evidence points more to the quality of life than to level of income (p. A-3).

From our perspective, poverty may be associated with a lack of MLE and, hence, may result in cognitive dysfunction. Because of the hardships imposed on families in satisfying primary needs, the mother may not be able to focus on anything beyond the most urgent and immediate needs of her child, thereby reducing the opportunities for MLE. Nevertheless, in many cultures that are rooted in poverty, compensatory mechanisms are provided by the culture that ensure intensive mediation.

This is well illustrated in Jewish sociocultural history. Many Jewish communities were subject to conditions of abject poverty, political oppression, and social discrimination, but MLE persisted at the informal and formal levels of Jewish communal life. Within these communities parents would pay exorbitant prices for lessons to their children, often exposing themselves and their families to deprivations including hunger. The ideal of the "Talmid Haham" (wise scholar), who was granted the highest status in the community, inspired parents to transmit to their children a love and knowledge of their culture and to set high standards of cognitive excellence. In such families, communication is marked by a high level of intergenerational transmission and communication. In the course of learning, the flow of information is multidirectional, with the younger generation providing a source of enrichment for the older generation, a process perceived as acceptable and even desirable. In view of this situation, which is also true in many other cultures, the claim that poverty alone is a direct determinant of cultural deprivation cannot be accepted.

It has been suggested that, in large families, typically associated with poverty, IQ decreases with an increase in the number of children. Of course, if no framework exists for the provision of MLE to the child, the presence of many children will reduce even further the capacity of the mother to serve as a mediator to each child. However, if despite poverty or precarious economic conditions mediated interactions are the prevailing modes of communication, the presence of many siblings will only serve to enhance and amplify the mediational processes. Younger siblings will be able to benefit from multiple sources of mediation through their interactions with older members of the family. The precocity of language development and other cognitive processes in children whose older siblings share with the mother in the task of raising them is well known. The "pointing finger," while a source of dismay to well mannered parents, serves as a means for young children to share with each other their perceptions and experiences.

There is no doubt that the physical conditions imposed by poverty may set priorities for the organism that are not productive for MLE. The frequently observed phenomenon of a lack of curiosity of primates deprived of food is a good illustration of the priority needs of the organism. Maslow's hierarchy of needs is an expression of the idea that only when the basic biological needs of the organism are satisfied are other more remote and complex goals sought. It has been demonstrated that hungry monkeys will not explore a box that does not contain food beyond establishing the absence of the food incentive. Once satiated, however, the same monkeys will vigorously explore the previously ignored stimulus. By the same token, a poverty-stricken group may, unless otherwise oriented by powerful cultural determinants, abandon more remote goals in favor of satisfying immediate needs.

Despite the many ill effects produced by the conditions of poverty, the causal factors leading to cultural deprivation should not be confounded. Poverty may trigger a state of cultural deprivation by reducing the exposure of the child to MLE, but this is not a necessary or inevitable outcome. The fact that MLE may be lacking under conditions of economic affluence mitigates against the conception of a culture of poverty as necessarily producing cognitive deficiency. Whatever the reasons for the absence of cultural transmission, the end result is the same, i.e., retarded performance, even though on the surface various groups may seem quite different, as in respect to socioeconomic level.

Ideology

Cultural deprivation as a result of a lack of MLE may occur even in cognitively and academically high achieving groups. In such cases, the mechanisms producing the syndrome of cultural deprivation are often of an ideological nature and are characterized by a high degree of intentionality and even ostentation. This may be illustrated by the hippie movement, whose followers were dubbed by William Soskin (personal communication, 1964) the "flower children of a beat generation." In this case, a detachment from the past is a direct product of an ideology that advocates the circumscribing of human concern to the immediate present. The past is not available, either to oneself or the next generation, to the extent that a conscious attempt is made to neither impose oneself nor one's past on the new generation. Fortunately, this ideology, because of its fundamentally untenable position, has never fully materialized; but, in the attempt, some hopelessly abandoned, neglected, and deprived children have emerged.

In the course of his psychotherapeutic practice, the author has encountered the problems manifested by the children of parents who, having freed themselves from their own oppressive communities, have attempted to raise their children in a cultural void. The intention of such parents is to provide their children with the opportunity for free and autonomous growth and development. In many cases, the result is a manifestation of cultural deprivation affecting the personality, behavior, and cognition of these children. Whatever the nature of their specific problems and reasons for referral, common to these children is a feeling of missing links and an inability to relate their experiences in a continuous and integrative manner. The episodic grasp of their reality, that is, their perception of objects and events in isolation, is reflected in their inability to relate specific events to a broader system of meaning and purpose. An imposed detachment from one's past carries with it a very limited concern for the future. Being unable or unwilling to view oneself as a continuation of the past, which transcends biological existence, results in a lack of concern for one's own future beyond the level of immediate biological needs. Happily, many of those adopting this philosophy, when confronted with the reality of a growing child, abandon their beliefs and attempt to reconcile their own past with their anticipated future and to transmit this cultural dimension to their children.

Parent-Child Relationship

A lack of MLE as a result of environmental factors need not necessarily be confined to group phenomena, such as the absence of cultural transmission, or even to a lack of mediation within a particular family. In some instances, it occurs as a highly specific phenomenon between a parent and a particular child. Such occurrences are equally frequent in families of varying socioeconomic status, culture, and ethnic background. In such cases, any of the children suffering from the effects of cultural deprivation are regarded as genuine cases of mental retardation or, even more usual, are labeled with the ubiquitous term *minimum brain damage* after all other diagnostic entities have been exhausted. This is illustrated in the following case.

> F was born into a family which was in the midst of a strong pull toward upward social mobility. His undesired conception and birth interfered with the parents' aspirations. An unsuccessful abortion attempt provided the mother with an explanation for F's subsequent difficulties at school, which she attributed to organic causes produced by her abortion attempt. In reconstructing the relationship between the mother and child during infancy and later, it became evident that the child had been subjected to a lack of MLE. The parents were reluctant to admit that the nurses, servants, and many toys provided the child were, in fact, substitutes for a constant and intense caregiving figure. The mother could not accept that her lack of attention and interest, beyond providing the biological and material needs of the child, was responsible for his condition, which was assessed at the level of educable mentally retarded. Despite the many sources of direct exposure to stimuli offered to the child, in terms of toys and equipment, no one took the care to interpose himself between these stimuli and the child. The syndrome of cultural deprivation was manifest in F by his strong need for immediate gratification and his limited capacity for modifiability by exposure to new situations and events. The inadequacy of the diagnosis of organicity was demonstrated by the ease with which F's condition was later reversed with a

limited investment of effort. However, for a long time the parents continued to believe that F's condition was of an organic nature caused by the unsuccessful abortion attempt. Their belief was reinforced by others who accepted the explanation of endogenous determination, since the quantity of stimulation offered the child, through material objects, seemed more than adequate. What was difficult for all to accept was that F had been subject to continuous deprivation by the absence in his environment of a mediator to provide meaning and to frame, schedule, and organize the rich sources of stimuli at his disposal.

Cases such as the one described above occur with unusual frequency among adopted children. An analysis of the relationship between the mother and an adopted child has enabled us to better understand the role of emotional factors in producing cultural deprivation and its consequent detrimental effects on cognitive development. The many instances in which adopted children pose developmental and achievement problems are all too often attributed directly to the emotional condition of both the mother and child. In many cases, however, these emotional and affective factors serve only as a trigger to a lack of MLE; it is this absence of mediated learning that causes deficient cognitive functioning. Certainly, emotional attachment between the mother and child is a necessary condition for optimal development. But it is a mistake to believe that this attachment alone is sufficient to ensure adequate cognitive development. The following cases are illustrative.

K was referred to us at 6½ years by both the school and his mother in order to assess whether he should repeat nursery school or be referred to the first grade in a school for the educable mentally retarded. Conventional psychometric measures yielded an IQ score in the 70s with limited higher potential. K's manifest level of functioning was even lower as a result of a host of behavior problems, including infantilism, impaired attention span, hyperkinesis, and a general lack of cooperation. The mother, who appeared strikingly old considering the age of the child, was very concerned about K's condition. Her concern, however, was coupled with a peculiar detachment and a strong insistence that his condition was organically determined. She described a full-term pregnancy and a delivery free of complications and expressed a strong desire to have the child.

On examining the child, we were struck by his cooperation with the examiner and willingness to work for more than 1½ hours on a variety of tasks, which he quickly learned to master (e.g., organization of dots, building blocks). The mother reacted to our findings with disappointment, hinting that she could not accept that the child was normal or would ever be normal. Despite our commitment to prepare K for school, she resisted our recommendation that K be placed in a nomal first-grade. In order to better understand the mother and help her change her attitude toward her child, we began to include her in our work with K. During a session in which K succeeded in a task that was difficult even for older children, his mother reacted angrily and sent K out of the room. She then asked in an agitated tone if it was important for us to know that K was an adopted child — indeed an uncomplicated pregnancy and delivery for her. It was then that the discrepancy in age and complexion, and the continuous rejection of the child, became clear.

For a long time we had observed the mother as she left the clinic. She never held K's hand or talked or interacted with him except to issue instructions on how to walk, not to run, or not to go in the street, but never reaching out to him or having him in close physical proximity. During one of K's preparatory lessons, in which he wrote in mirror letters, his mother could not refrain from remarking that all children like K (referring to the ethnic group to which K belonged) write upside down and reverse their letters. When it was pointed out that the opposite was true and that such children usually show high levels of functioning, the mother sought reassurance that K would succeed and achieve higher levels of performance. Since adopting K, the mother's anxieties had induced her to prepare for the worst, and her inability to accept the child prevented her from investing those cognitive elements that would have enhanced his development. After having prepared K, and especially after having involved the father, who showed a much greater capacity to accept K, a dramatic change occurred in the parents. This positive change has continued with K's growing capacity to cope with school and the social environment.

M, the daughter of a highly intellectual couple, was referred to us at the age of 13 years. It had been suggested that M be placed in a vocational school for low achievers and borderline children. The mother was ambivalent about the placement of M in this school, and it was her ambivalence which led to M being referred to us. On the one hand, the mother was partly responsible for the suggested placement because of her description of M's deficiencies to the psychologists. On the other hand, the mother tried to fight against the placement recommendation. The mother's ambivalence toward her daughter produced a very low level of tolerance and frustration in M when she experienced failure, accompanied by a state of dependence, clinging behavior, and a strong resistance to forming new attachments.

At the first testing session, the mother was asked to observe M's performance from behind a one-way mirror. After voicing her doubts regarding M's abilities, she immediately reversed her attitude in response to M's successful performance by claiming that the task was too simple. Even after failing herself to successfully complete the task, she could not be convinced of M's ability. Nevertheless, she did follow our instructions and advice, with the result that M was placed in a normal school. Throughout this period, the mother was convinced that M's condition was irreversible due to an organic cause. She constantly sent us newspaper cuttings on organic children and tried to convince us that, despite M's tremendous strides and successful mastery of a variety of tasks, the underlying problem was organic in nature.

Having been alerted by the previous case, we embarked on a fact-finding mission in order to understand the irrational resistance of M's mother to accept her as normal despite the evidence provided by our dynamic assessment and M's successful mastery of tasks. It transpired that M was an adopted child. After cautiously revealing our information to the mother, a new basis was established in our relationship with the mother. She agreed to allow us to discuss the adoption with her daughter, something we believed that M already knew. M has since completed high school and has passed her matriculation examinations. In the case of M, the mother convinced herself over many years not to place any pressures on M nor to build any expectations. Instead, the major emphasis was on rest, isolation, moderate stimulation, and very limited verbal interaction. This resulted in a great reduction in her involvement and active interaction with the child. In this way, the mother sought to protect herself against any slip of the tongue that would reveal the past history of the child.

In conjunction with the factors identified in the cases reported above, consideration should also be given to the relationship between the emotional interaction of mother and child and the child's cognitive development. In explaining the occurrence of cognitive deficiencies, the most pervasive approach tends to confuse a *necessary* condition with a *sufficient* condition. It is undoubtedly true that, for MLE to occur, affection and emotional involvement of parents and siblings are important. It is by virtue of these affective ties that interest in and commitment to the development and future of the child are fostered. However, under certain circumstances, a lack of MLE may occur despite a strong emotional bond between mother and child. This is well illustrated in the following case study.

> At 14½ years, D was totally insensitive to the wealth of information he encountered in many trips with his parents. His only reaction to the many unfamiliar environments with which he was confronted was to run away in an attempt to restore a familiar environment. This response, however, was more emotional than rational, as evident by the fact that no attempt was made to master the new situation at a cognitive level. Indifference to exposure to stimulation extended to all of D's behavior and included such pleasurable events as visits to zoo, cinema, and so on. Curiously, the only exception was the world of television commercials, an interest which D shared with his mother. D's mother was attached to him in an almost symbiotic manner. Not only did she fail to mediate the world to him, but she almost deliberately obstructed the mediation process by preventing and withholding from her son sources of stimulation. The mother did this in order to maintain the *status quo* in an attempt to adapt to what she had always considered to be an unchangeable condition of her son. In this case, affection and emotional ties led to patterns of interaction that were totally devoid of providing the child with active patterns of coping with the present or adapting to the future. Thus, when asked to stop answering D's repetitive questions with stereotyped answers, the mother replied that it was necessary to comfort him with the kind of answer he liked to hear. This gentle and sensitive attitude of the mother failed, however, to take into account the kinds of problems generated by a constant passive and resigned approach to the condition of her child. For a long time any attempt to involve D in a broader area of interest proved unsuccessful. However, with the introduction of a planned substitute for MLE, an entire system of interests, needs, and skills was revealed. D's behavior became modified to the extent that he became able to learn and master things that he had been unable to achieve during his previous 12 years of life.

In many other cases, in which a lack of mediation is bound up with appropriate affective ties, the mother may not even be aware that she is withholding mediated experiences from the child. Thus, in cases where poverty sets priorities, such that attention is focused entirely upon meeting essential needs, affective ties may be operative but only in terms of the behaviors and actions necessary to fulfill those immediate needs. Similarly, as reported in the cases discussed previously, a specific mediational content and orientation may be withheld because of a feeling of inadequacy, on the part of the parents, to plan and direct the future of their children. Our own observations of the interaction between the child and his caregiving environment in North Africa yield ample evidence of this phenomenon. Not only did an intensive emotional relationship exist between mother and child, but a great deal of time was devoted to the child during the infancy period. Although mothers typically spend many hours of the day with their children, many of these children subsequently manifested symptoms of cultural deprivation because of a lack of MLE. It seemed clear to us that the prevailing mother-infant relationship was of a dual-union nature, rather than a mediating interaction, with mother and child existing within a close physical and psychic proximity. This closed relationship did not provide the distance necessary for the differentiation of partners in a relationship that included other sources of stimulation that required shaping, filtering, interpretation, and mediation.

Research findings (Feuerstein and Richelle, 1957; Mathieu, 1947; Smilansky, Shephatia, and Frankel, 1976) have confirmed the normal pre-, para-, and postnatal developmental patterns of children in the North African Jewish Community, and they compare favorably with those of Moslem and European children. Mathieu (1947) interpreted the subsequent failure of these children to achieve normal levels of cognitive development as attributable to environmental factors associated with inadequate education. Smilansky et al. (1976), in a study of the early development of Israeli children of Oriental origin, have described a developmental precocity of these children when compared with other more advantaged groups. They attribute this finding to the greater emotional involvement of the Oriental mother and the role of the extended family. Again, at later stages of development, these children fall behind other groups to a significant extent. The question that arises is to what should this loss of initial advantage be attributed? Jensen (1969), of course, may regard these findings as evidence for hereditability. In his recent research (1977), however, he maintains that there is a progressive loss of an IQ point per year in children from certain environments, and indicates a willingness on his part to accept a more important role of the environment in determining the level of cognitive functioning of these children.

In terms of the theory of MLE, research findings, such as those mentioned above, require a different interpretation. Satisfying the infant's biological needs and providing him with direct exposure to stimuli will produce a normal pattern of early development. However, once the activity required from the organism transcends the limits imposed by biologically determined adaptive mechanisms, adequate development is only possible through MLE. It is at the subsequent stages of early development that a lack of MLE becomes apparent, especially when the child is not able to effectively learn from direct exposure to sources of stimulation. When the affective ties between parents and child are not accompanied by MLE, they are not sufficient alone to ensure the adequate development of the child. Furthermore, when such affective ties are absent, the energizing principle of MLE is removed, and, under these conditions, MLE is bound to be absent from the parent-child relationship.

Pathological Conditions of Parents

Another reason for the failure of MLE to occur is the existence of pathological conditions affecting both or one of the parents, especially the mother. Under these circumstances, a parent may not have the capacity to provide MLE to his or her children, in general, or to a single child, in particular. In the course of our diagnostic and therapeutic work, we have encountered many cases in which an individual child, or an entire family of children, has become culturally deprived as the result of the incapacity of the parents to serve as mediators and the absence of parent surrogates, such as relatives, foster parents, or older siblings, to fulfill the role of mediator at early stages of the child's development. When pathological disorders are one factor among many other conditions, such as impoverished home environment and physical impairments of the parents, it is very difficult to identify the specific pathology responsible for the lack of MLE. Consequently, parental pathology is most striking when, rather than being part of a broader constellation of factors, it is the sole determinant of the withdrawal of MLE, particularly in cases in which only one specific child is affected. This is the situation when the parental pathological condition develops at the time of the arrival of the child and particularly if the pathology is determined by the birth of the child.

In many instances in which one child from a normally functioning family performs at a lower level than that expected of him, on the basis of the performance of the other children in the family, the conclusion is drawn prematurely of an endogenous determinant. All too often the search for endogenous factors is determined to be successful, even if support comes only from scant and equivocal evidence. In such cases, the confirmation of an endogenous basis for the child's deficiencies serves to obscure the critical role of the relationship between the particular child and one or more or his caregivers. Usually, the task of uncovering the dynamics of the troubled relationship is difficult because of the defensive reactions of parents, produced by their own feelings of guilt. When provided with the proper support, these parents may acknowledge their aversive reaction to their child at an early stage of his development. Such feelings, on the part of parents, will have resulted in a restricted relationship in which interactions have been limited to what is strictly necessary and an inclination to leave real caregiving activities to others has been evidenced. In other cases, where some traumatic event has affected the mother-child relationship, a more explicit attitude may be encountered, but even this greater awareness on the part of the mother does not necessarily alter the nature of the relationship.

In addition to pathological states inherent in the parents, mention should also be made of reactions that are triggered in otherwise normal parents by a transient condition in the child. Such a condition may establish an attitude that is not readily abandoned by either partner in the parent-child relationship. For example, transient neurophysiological or health conditions of the child may determine a lowered responsiveness on the part of the child to the mother's attempts at mediation. Such reactions may produce feelings of futility in the mother. If these feelings of not being needed by the child are compounded with a limited need on the part of the mother to provide care, as in the case of certain adopted children and children for whom commencement of the mother-child relationship was delayed by illness, then the result will be a relationship in which MLE interactions are kept to a minimum.

In an extensive discussion with the mother of a disturbed, low functioning child, an attempt was made to reconstruct the nature of the early interaction patterns between her and her child. This was done in order to understand the different child-rearing approaches used by this mother with her three adopted children. Each of the children was brought up in a very different way, and the relationships between them and their mother were also distinctly different. Of course, it may be argued, with good reason, that each child was constitutionally different. However, the attitudes of the parents toward their three adopted children were inconsistent and had become crystalized into patterns of behavior that were perpetuated beyond the initial condition that may have triggered them. Thus, the mother confided that P, immediately on his adoption, manifested a "happy" and "contented" disposition. He never required attention and had to be awakened for meals, even missing them because of the mother's reluctance to disturb him. Only when her other two children were discussed did the mother realize, to her dismay, that she could hardly recall anything of P's past up to the age of about 6 years. At this point, his placidity and passivity, initially interpreted by the mother as a happy, contented disposition, became a source of concern, especially when he failed to meet the demands expected of him. Only much later did the mother realize that she had never felt any need to penetrate P's personality. She felt that he never needed her and also admitted that, despite her desire to have a child, she never looked upon P's presence as fulfilling this need in her. Thus, a disturbance on the part of the parents may act in a selective manner such that certain kinds of interaction may produce in a child a high degree of resistance to modification, in turn resulting in a state of impenetrability to the parents' attempts at mediation.

By way of summary, the range of environmental determinants of a lack of MLE extends from historical, cultural, and socioeconomic factors to emotional, affective, and physiological conditions that influence the child-rearing practices of parents. In all of these instances, a lack of MLE, its moment of onset, its severity, and its length of duration will affect the growing organism's capacity to become modified by direct exposure to stimuli.

ENDOGENOUS CONDITIONS OF THE CHILD

The second broad category of determinants of a lack of MLE is anchored in the nature of the organism itself. Various conditions render the organism transiently or permanently, partially or totally, impenetrable to attempts at mediation by external agents. A host of conditions may produce a lack of MLE as a result of sensory impairments in which the ability to register stimuli is limited to certain sensory modalities and specific kinds of stimulation. In other cases, absence of receptivity to MLE may be the result of central processes or emotional and affective dynamics involved in the child's personality. To the extent that the child's impenetrability to MLE may be bypassed, either by varying the intensity or the modalities of the mediating process, or even by changing the mediator, many of the ill effects caused by distal determinants may be avoided. In this way an appropriate pattern of cognitive development may become possible, as is illustrated in the following case study.

> G is the child of a marriage between first cousins. Both of G's parents have similar signs of motor dyspraxia and a lack of coordination which visibly affects their appearance. Of their three children, G showed genuine signs of retarded development and deficient cognitive functioning. All of G's motor and other developmental landmarks, including speech and ideational processes, were delayed. The family, which was a highly motivated and efficiently functioning cohesive group, recognized the developmental risk entailed in G's condition. A determined and systematic attempt was made to mediate to G despite his low level of receptivity. Stimuli normally requiring few presentations for mastery were repeatedly and intensively provided, and life in general was organized to provoke G's interest and attention. A special feature of G's case was the inclusion of a non-family member in the mediating process with whom G established a meaningful and close relationship. This proved to be very beneficial to G because it moved the emphasis from the mother, who was burdened by emotional conflicts and anxiety, to a more neutral figure. Despite G's very limited motor control, he received a normal education and, surprisingly, achieved remarkable proficiency on the piano. However, school proved tedious for G, and pressures were exerted from many quarters to lower his expectations and to provide him with an environment that would more closely match his capacity. The parents were strongly advised by the author to continue with a normal educational curriculum for their child. G persevered and managed to master tasks of growing complexity. After completing high school, he enrolled in a course for laboratory technicians but was unable to continue because of his general slow disposition and motor deficiencies. To prevent a sense of failure, G was given a position in the family business and received training in accounting and bookkeeping and was paid a nominal salary. Today, G is responsible for the accounts department of a large chain of supermarkets in which he prepares the balance sheet for the company, a position he has held for the past 12 years. Without the continued mediating efforts of his parents, G's growth into adulthood might have taken a very different course.

Autism

One of the most extreme manifestations of reduced receptivity to MLE occurs in cases of autism. The autistic child may have an excellent capacity to register events, including outstanding attentive functions, immediate memory, photographic visual recall, calculation skills, and many other discrete cognitive abilities. However, these abilities are manifested in a fragmented way and are, therefore, meaningless activities, devoid of any purpose or goal. Attempts at mediation by various agents are usually totally rejected by the child with the result that his experiences occur in isolation, are characterized by a lack of organization, and remain in a state of fragmentation. This is an extreme manifestation of our description of the episodic grasp of reality, which characterizes culturally deprived children, although in a far more moderate fashion. However, even in such severe cases, on those occasions in which a mediator (usually not the parents) has been able to penetrate the child's resistance, meaningful changes have occurred (see Alpert and Crown, 1953; Hanegbi, Krasilowsky, and Feuerstein, 1970). A case study follows:

> A few years ago, a mother of an autistic child was advised by us to actively communicate her feelings to her child. This included crying when she felt sad, expressing joy when she felt happy, and giving free expression to her feelings of anger. In addition, the mother was instructed to involve the child in purposeful activities: setting goals and linking these to the child's needs, summing up activities, and relating the activities to each other. In short, an entire program of mediation was suggested. At the time, this advice was given because the child displayed a degree of sensitivity that apparently had not existed previously. Despite the mother's opinion that her child would not respond, she asked a relative to assist her, and, by observing the behavior of the relative, she increasingly managed to adopt the role we had suggested to her. After a period of 2 years, very significant changes occurred in the child's behavior and in the nature of his interactions with his environment.

Constitutional Factors

Variations in the receptivity of the individual, because of constitutional factors that produce different thresholds to stimulation, may also affect the process of MLE. This is the case for many placid and apathetic children for whom a high degree of intensity, frequency, and amplitude of stimulation is necessary in order to reach their threshold. Many children categorized as organically impaired and functioning at the slow hypoesthesic end of the sensitivity continuum are impoverished by virtue of their limited readiness to search for and reach out for stimulation. Often, these children are regarded as "good kids" because their demands are minimal; as a consequence, however, they elicit considerably less from their environment than the child who needs less mediation and attention from his parents. In this situation, as in many others, the normal child receives the "cream," while the more subdued child gets only the "leftovers."

At the other end of the spectrum, the hyperactive child, who is constantly on the move, is exposed to a multitude of stimuli. This exposure, however, is of a brief, discontinuous, and disorganized nature, with little sustained attention and systematic, purposeful exploratory behavior. The hyperactive child is only marginally affected by attempts at mediation because of the fleeting quality of his perception and experience. Thus, filtering, selecting, and scheduling stimuli, and establishing relationships between events, meet with great resistance because of the child's propensity to act out and move around and his limited readiness to delay reactions in favor of anticipated future ends. The first-stimuli-to-come, first-to-respond behavior of the hyperactive child prevents the establishment of relationships. Impairments in conceptual thinking may occur, not because of the alleged organic basis of the hyperactivity, but because the child's episodic interactions prevent the formation of learning sets through MLE. In terms of this hypothesis, it is not the elaborational capacities of the child but his readiness to acquire adequate modalities of data gathering and output that are affected by a lack of MLE.

In the case of both the hyper- and the hypokinetic child, a barrier is created by the condition of the child, which renders him impervious to mediation. In some cases, the child's condition may be of a transient nature, but, once a nonmediating pattern becomes established between the child and his caregivers, it may tend to become perpetuated beyond the condition that initially gave rise to it. Thus, the child may never learn to accept mediation and the parents may not learn to provide it. One often hears parents remark how attentive and grateful their child is when taught by others but how impatient in response to their own efforts. We have recorded on videotape the resistance of a child to eye contact with his mother, preferring instead to catch the attention of his caregiver. In this case, the child developed an early resistance to interactions with his mother, presumably because of a lack of familiarity with and gratification derived from such interactions. If the mutually caused and perpetuated barriers to MLE are removed by means of suitable intervention, it is possible to prevent the ill effects associated with a prolonged and continuous lack of MLE.

Many children afflicted by genetic disorders are, by virtue of their condition, faced with barriers to MLE. Their level of deficient functioning is a result of these barriers, which in many cases affect the peripheral phases of input and output rather than permanently affecting their elaborational capacities. The child suffering from Down's syndrome provides a good illustration. The various deficiencies associated with this condition occur with different degrees of severity and negatively affect the child's capacity to search for, and respond to, stimulation. The state of hypotonicity common to these children renders them dependent for stimulation upon a caregiver for long periods of time. It is generally accepted that children suffering from Down's syndrome have a low IQ ceiling. This assessment is based on statistics yielded by those children who are available to scientific research. These children are not a representative sample but tend to reflect the more severe cases who are institutionalized and subject to restrictive social and intellectual interactions. The view that the Down's syndrome child may reach, at best, an IQ of about 70, accompanied by a constant decrease in his level of competence, both normatively and absolutely, is open to question with respect to the following two related issues. To what extent is the above assertion rooted in empirical evidence? What are the current conditions that surround these children and that may contribute to their level of performance?

As previously mentioned, many of the physical, sensory, and neurophysiological deficiencies of these children may be instrumental in creating barriers both for adequate input of stimuli and for the capacity to use the MLE offered them. Certainly, the hypotonicity of the children produces a considerable delay in their ability to seek out stimulation, which, together with their general slowness in behavior and development, produces a restricted environmental input. Even the available stimulation may be only partially registered if it does not reach the amplitude, intensity, and frequency necessary to penetrate the barriers present in these children. Thus, it is reasonable to assume that much of the extero- and proprioceptive stimulation that is actually absorbed by the system is of a diluted quality and is insufficient to produce modification. Unless otherwise instructed, parents of Down's syndrome children tend to provide these children with less stimulation than that which their normal children receive, and, in so doing, they inadvertently produce even greater deprivation. It is common to hear parents maintain that their child needs sleep and rest; that he is a "good," undemanding child; that he plays alone. Eventually, parents begin to describe the stereotyped behavior associated with the condition, behaviors that the children learn to use as a source of proprioceptive stimulation to replace the inadequate and insufficient exteroceptive stimulation.

The same is true with regard to verbal stimulation, and the dictum that "the rich get richer while the poor get poorer" is certainly applicable. The mother will initiate stimulation in accordance with the responsiveness of the child and his capacity to initiate and actively use the stimulation she provides. However, to the extent that the child remains unresponsive, the mother will more or less consciously refrain from providing the necessary stimulation. This situation is further exacerbated by the influence of both uninformed public opinion and "expert" guidance and advice offered by pediatricians and other professionals. Regrettably, it has become standard practice to inform the parents of Down's syndrome children, in an almost callous fashion at the crucial start of the mother-child relationship, of the irreversibility of the condition. Often, the mother is told soon after the birth of her child that there is no chance of proper development, and that, if possible, the child should be placed in a home from the start. Resistance on the part of parents to this advice is met with charges of their being unrealistic and warnings that disillusionment will certainly follow their attempts to provide the child with a normal environment. Parents are also cautioned that they may incur heavy financial burdens and threaten the equilibrium of the home and their other children. Even if the mother does succeed in keeping her child at home, public opinion and stereotyped attitudes mitigate against a thorough understanding of the child, necessary to permit an individualized approach conducive to his specific condition. The value derived from regarding each child as an individual is illustrated by a rebellious mother who insisted on rearing at home her child, who showed remarkably few stigmata and limited hypotonicity. The pediatrician, who insisted that the child would eventually require placement outside the home, dismissed the author's contrary advice as over-optimistic. Yet, the mother's active MLE approach to her child has resulted in a remarkable relatively early development of the child, despite the professional forecasts to the contrary. Similar results have occurred with other children for whom the prognosis was initially far less positive.

B, a Down's syndrome boy with trisomy 21, had a severe condition with a number of stigmata such as scrotal tongue, hoarse voice, webbed neck, and moderate to severe hypotonia. B's case is a good illustration of how intensive stimulation, constantly provided by the environment and supported by specific mediators, has produced a level of functioning that approaches the normal for his age except in those areas, such as speech, where the emergence of specific functions was delayed. At 8½ years, B is reading and writing on a first- to second-grade level, although his understanding is more developed, especially with respect to social activities. As a small child, B managed to conceptualize family relations such that he could classify each of his many uncles, aunts, and cousins from various parts of his family. The intensive MLE regimen that B was provided not only affected the richness of his knowledge but, of greater importance, established modalities of operational thinking and an orientation not only toward objects but to the nature of the relationships between them.

Before B was properly able to orient himself in time by keeping account of the days of the week, he learned to make use of cues to anticipate the days to come. This was particularly evident with regard to the Sabbath, with its many obvious cues, and was followed by the identification of other days on the basis of recurrent events specific to the particular day. The point is that B developed the ability to generalize from one instance to other situations. Similarly, he learned to anticipate the kind of meal he would receive on the basis of the cutlery and tablecloth laid on the table. (In traditional Jewish homes different utensils are used for meat and milk dishes.) Eventually, B was able to help set the table, and if more places were required than usual he would ask about the additional person.

B learned to anticipate the reactions of adults and children by means of both verbal and nonverbal cues, with the result that he developed a highly manipulative personality. An offer to attend the theater together with a group of children with whom he enjoyed interacting was met with a blunt refusal by B. His attempts to dissuade his peers from accepting the offer were not successful. Because he did not want to be left alone, he began to explore the possibilities of joining the group and to establish conditions for his participation which, at the same time, served to allay his fears. For example, he asked if it would be dark in the theater, if it would take a long time, if he could be held on a lap if he could not see. In the end, B participated in the visit and thoroughly enjoyed the performance. How many parents of Down's syndrome children would even consider taking their children, particularly at such an early age, to a performance at the theater?

Although confidence and security are important ingredients in the child's development, alone and under inappropriate conditions, they may produce overprotection and a passive acceptance of the child's condition. In this event, the experiences offered the child become limited and restrictive. In B's case,

MLE was provided by an extended family unit in which siblings and cousins learned how to enrich the life of this child by constantly providing him with new modalities of functioning. The input was both intensive and frequent, and was amplified by the many participants in the mediating process. Nevertheless, the mother had to overcome a crucial and painful problem. She had to be prepared to expose herself and her child to the reactions and comments of others. In order not to confine the child, the mother had to encourage friends and visitors to come to her home and to explain that she was not embarrassed by her child. This was necessary to reverse the good intention of people not to visit the home for fear of embarrassing the mother. In many cases, B's mother initiated visits to others in order to "break the ice." In general, B's mother, rather than limiting her son's exposure, invested far more effort than with her other children, thereby providing B with what he needed. The normal occurrence of stimuli was reinforced by presenting them in a more systematic and enriched manner to ensure that they were registered and absorbed.

Against the background of the above, rather unusual case, it is important to present the more typical account of a Down's syndrome child. A was born with Down's syndrome. Paranatal anoxia and other complications contributed to a precarious developmental prognosis for the child. A's young parents, persuaded by the advice of their pediatrician and their own lay knowledge, arranged for the child to be institutionalized so as not to disrupt the life of the other siblings in the family.

Although A's parents visited her periodically, they did not hope to have any impact on her since A was considered incapable of responding to significant people and events in her environment. The parents' main concern was that A was well cared for and that her basic needs were met. Beyond the routine physical care, few opportunities existed for the child to establish a relationship with a constant figure.

The author's first contact with A was when she was 4 years old. The child was placid and immobile in her crib. In addition to her impaired motoricity, the child was hampered in her motility and standing by a very soft crib mattress. With her weight, the mattress sank in the center and pushed up around her so that there was limited exposure to stimuli. Even those activities that occurred within the vicinity of her crib were not visible to A.

A initially cried when lifted and held but soon showed contentment. It took only a short time to elicit adequate responses to a variety of stimuli to which she had been considered impervious. She was able to discriminate between objects and quickly learned object permanence, as described by Piaget and established by Uzgiris and Hunt (1975) as a developmental landmark.

As a result of this demonstration, A's daily regimen was enriched. Subsequent development confirmed that A could have reached even higher levels had the proper treatment been initiated earlier. The question of how much was lost during her first 4 years remains unanswered; nevertheless, her level of functioning today is considerably beyond what was expected.

Our conviction, that even after an early age it is not too late to produce meaningful changes in the course of development of Down's syndrome children, bears repetition.

The question arises, to what extent do genetic or organic conditions produced by chromosomal or metabolic deviations affect the cognitive behavior of the individual directly, unavoidably, and irreversibly? Or, rather, to what extent do these conditions affect the capacity of the organism to make proper use of MLE and thereby impair his capacity to become modified by direct exposure?

One of the conditions for which a direct relationship between a metabolic disorder and behavior was thought to exist was that of phenylketonuria (PKU). PKU is a disorder of amino acid metabolism, which usually leads to mental retardation, unless a strict low phenylalanine diet is begun within the first few months of life. Among the behavioral problems associated with PKU are irritability, hyperactivity, athetoid movements, uncontrollable temper, and seizures. Nevertheless, cases have been known and documented (Howell and Stevenson, 1971) in which the behavioral signs ascribed to PKU failed to materialize in untreated mothers who had this condition and even transmitted it to their children. (Treatment for this disorder only started some 10 to 12 years ago. Unfortunately, the documented accounts do not describe the development or educational antecedents of these PKU mothers. Hence, it is difficult to understand how, despite their condition, they managed to function normally.)

The same is true of many other disorders that have been considered to relate directly to cognitive dysfunction, as has been pointed out by Sameroff and Chandler (1975). It is true that genetic and organic conditions may produce barriers that affect the threshold of stimulation, the capacity to attend to stimuli, and the child's general vitality and curiosity. Consequently, the probability of being affected by stimuli in the environment is reduced. However, the crucial question is to what extent and by what means can these barriers be bypassed or penetrated and thereby overcome?

Emotional Disturbance

Emotional disturbances of children provide another set of conditions that may result in the creation of barriers between the child and his environment. Traumatic experiences, rejection, and even constitutional dispositions of the organism may hinder the transmission of MLE. A good example of how a combination of these factors may occur is provided in the following case study.

> S was referred to us at the age of 15 years after all attempts at rehabilitation had failed. His case was regarded as hopeless, and the social welfare agency, supported by psychiatric evaluations, had decided on custodial care within a psychiatric ward for disturbed and retarded children. S was considered both deeply disturbed and irreversibly defective, cognitively and motorically. The parents of S were in favor of this decision, and, were it not for the intervention of an uncle, the institutionalization would have been implemented. On examination, it became apparent that S manifested a constant instability in his motor behavior. He responded to our attempts to inhibit and control this behavior by explaining that he suffered from a condition of persistent skin irritation necessitating scratching and moving his body. Interviews with the parents revealed that S had always suffered from this condition. His skin was covered with small protuberances that made him react in a hyperesthesic way to tactile stimuli, especially those produced by particular fabrics. From his earliest childhood, S had cried in-

cessantly and slept badly. Only at a much later stage did the parents become aware of S's affliction and even then they could do little to alleviate his suffering. He was unable to wear certain kinds of clothes and could not touch buttons made of specific materials. As a result, he was dependent on adults to unbutton his pants and was enuretic and encopretic until an advanced age. S's mother could not tolerate his perpetual crying and rejected him, avoiding his presence as much as possible beyond providing for his basic biological needs. The outcome was a very retarded level of performance, accompanied by the syndrome of low modifiability. Even more serious was the severe state of disturbance which rendered S impervious to mediation by the mother or anyone else.

Having pointed out the multiple adverse circumstances of S's development, we suggested a phase-specific program of MLE as a means to rehabilitation for this unfortunate young man. Today, 14 years later, S is a well adjusted, self-sufficient, and independent adult. He completed the 11th grade at school and his military service, is now responsible for the horticultural department of a large zone of his township, and maintains an interest in cultural activities. The methods employed in S's case were mainly oriented to corrective object relationships (see Alpert, 1957), individual tutoring based on the principles of Instrumental Enrichment, and a re-elaboration of the parent-child relationship. The major obstacle was to remove S's barrier to MLE, which was established as a result of his disturbed relationship with his parents and then generalized to all other relationships. This resistance, which resulted in overt psychotic behavior, had to be overcome and a pattern of confidence, trust, receptivity, readiness to imitate others, and motivation to modify his own behavior had to be instilled.

The spearhead of S's treatment was to break through his emotional barrier without which meaningful penetration into the system could not be achieved. This alone, however, would not have been sufficient. Cognitive modification was necessary and was achieved by the direct intervention of MLE in a number of ways. Temporal and spatial dimensions, comparative behavior, discrimination, and many other functions necessary for reflective thinking and psychological differentiation had to be mediated to S. Relative to the massive deprivation to which S was subjected, the amount of investment required to reverse S's "hopeless" condition was rather moderate.

That many of the deficiencies produced by a lack of MLE are reversible, provided that the proper steps are taken, should again be clear from this case study.

Conditions of emotional disturbance which produce barriers to MLE may be established at various stages in the child's development. Thus, differences in development arise and may be understood in terms of the syndrome of cultural deprivation, with the severity being contingent on the amount and nature of the deficiency of MLE. Whether produced by environmental or endogenous factors, and although differential treatment may be required, the essential and fundamental need remains the same: to overcome the deficiencies produced by a lack of MLE. The precise nature of these deficiencies is defined and discussed in the next chapter.

EVIDENCE FOR THE THEORY OF MLE

The final issue to which attention must be devoted concerns the source of evidence for the theory of mediated learning experience (MLE), which has evolved over many years of observation and the study of a variety of groups of children and young adults characterized by cultural differences and cultural deprivation. The capacity of these children to become modified has produced evidence of the plasticity of the human organism, which has made modifiability possible and has led to the concept of MLE as the proximal determinant of cognitive performance. At the core of the theory of MLE is the implication that low cognitive performance is a reversible condition. For more than 20 years, evidence of a clinical and empirical nature has accumulated with respect to three converging sources of evidence for modifiability. The first concerns the question of uncovering, assessing, and measuring the potential for modification on the part of individuals or groups; the second source relates to the evidence for long term and permanent modifiability; and the third involves the dimensions of cognitive function to which efforts at modifiability must be directed.

Much of the evidence in support of the notion of modifiability derives from the results of the author's work with Youth Aliyah, a unique institution dedicated to the task of the ingathering and integration of Jewish children into Israel. Initially, during the pre-war period of the 1930's, Youth Aliyah was involved in rescuing children threatened by the Nazi regimes in Germany and Austria. During and after the war, the rescue operation spread throughout Western and Eastern Europe in an effort to reach orphaned children who had survived the Holocaust. With the establishment of the State of Israel, Youth Aliyah was confronted with the task of rescuing children and adolescents from Islamic countries where they were subject not only to political oppression but also to conditions of severe economic impoverishment and status deprivation. It should be emphasized that the Youth Aliyah population from North Africa represented a biased selection of the various Jewish communities since, in addition to their Zionist ideals, the first to immigrate were those living in the most impoverished conditions.

The Youth Aliyah population, which provided the major source of inspiration for the theory of MLE, consisted of large numbers of Jewish adolescents from North Africa. These adolescents were examined by us from 1950 to 1954 in Morocco and in the south of France where they were organized in transit camps before immigrating to Israel. A large variety of tests were administered to these adolescents, both individually and in groups, with the dual purpose of assessing their educability and understanding the nature of their severe instructional, educational, and behavior problems. The assessment of these adolescents revealed that they were functioning 3 to 6 years behind their age norms, with many of them yielding IQs between 50 and 70 and even lower. Even though great caution was exercised in the interpretation of these results, which were obtained even on so-called "culture-free" tests, developmental tests, and Piagetian tasks, the high correlation between the scores obtained on these static tests and other objective, cognitive, intellectual, and achievement criteria could not be negated. Israel at this time was in a precarious economic and security situation, and many educators questioned the wisdom of her policy of opening the door to a flood of non-selective immigration. The severe problems facing the state could only be exacerbated by the task of absorbing a population totally unprepared to confront an occidental and technologically oriented society. One could anticipate that the sudden confrontation would create immense problems even under the best of circumstances.

The problems experienced by these adolescents were manifold. Cognitive difficulties immediately arose as a result of cultural differences reflected in language barriers and a general lack of familiarity with the new culture and environment. But, above all, the adolescents manifested many signs of cultural deprivation in a wide variety of situations that related even to their own cultural background. In their countries of origin, an awareness of their past traditions and customs had faded in the migration from the village to the city slums. Their language was an unstructured mixture of French, Arabic, and Judeo-Arabic, which produced an inadequate level of receptive language and an even lower level of expressive language.

A great number of these adolescents were either fully or functionally illiterate in all three of the languages they used. Writing ability was even lower than that of reading. Only 20% to 25% of them were able to perform three of the four basic arithmetical operations by the age of 12 to 15 years. Their general knowledge was very limited and demonstrated a narrow range of curiosity, interest, and exploration. Processes involving conceptualization, abstraction, symbolization, and representation were poorly developed not only because of language difficulties, but also because of extensive perceptual difficulties, an impaired need for precision, and unrestrained impulsivity. The syndrome of cultural deprivation was manifest by their very limited capacity to become modified through direct exposure to the new culture and a tendency to perpetuate a stereotypic and maladaptive mode of functioning.

In the attempt to modify the condition of these adolescents, many educators came to question the efficiency of the regular didactic methods. The extent to which the usual cognitive, social, and vocational goals should be offered to these adolescents was also in doubt since many psychologists and educators were inclined to the view that the deficiencies manifested by these children were basically immutable. Psychologists confronted with the difficulties experienced by these adolescents in structuring spatial dimensions, such as those required by the Bender-Gestalt test, even tended to believe that a large number of these children suffered from organic conditions. Consequently, it was suggested that academic activities involving representational, symbolic, and abstract behavior were inaccessible to these children. Even the more optimistic and cautious among the professionals involved with these adolescents had strong reservations regarding the likelihood of modifiability, given the relatively advanced age and socioeducational background of the adolescents.

It was in response to an urgent need to study the modifiability of these adolescents that the Learning Potential Assessment Device (LPAD) (Feuerstein, 1968, 1972, 1977, 1979) was developed. The manifest level of functioning of these adolescents on both academic achievement and general behaviors, as measured by conventional psychometric tests, was such that attempts at redevelopment were doomed to failure from the outset since they were governed by negative expectations. The problem was to distinguish between poor manifest levels of functioning and a potential capacity for modifiability that could be observed, measured, and interpreted. Initially, an attempt was made to solve the problem by means of a wide range of testing devices, such as culture-free and culture-fair tests, developmental tests, practical problem-solving tasks, and Piagetian tests of cognitive operations (Feuerstein and Richelle, 1957; Feuerstein, Richelle, and Jeannet, 1953). The results did not differ in any meaningful way from those obtained on the conventional tests, and we were led to the inescapable conclusion that the failure of all the tests to reveal the real potential of these children, beyond their low level of manifest functioning, was caused by the static nature of the tests themselves; that is, the measures obtained served only to establish the repertoire of existing behaviors. Our clinical observations strongly suggested that a substantial reservoir of abilities was being left untapped by the measuring instruments we employed.

A fundamental revision in the concept of assessment was required in order to meet our goal of establishing a dynamic measure of their ability. Rather than limiting the search to the stable characteristics of the organism, which meets the traditional requirement of predictability by isolating the least modifiable aspects of behavior, the very opposite procedure was adopted. Our goal became the development of an assessment technique oriented toward eliciting those very characteristics of the organism that are amenable to change and that may be provoked, measured, and interpreted in the test situation. Moreover, the elicited changes and identified potential for further change would, we hoped, provide the basis for planned long term intervention. Thus, as the name implies, the Learning Potential Assessment Device involved a radical shift from a static to a dynamic approach in which the test situation was transformed into a learning experience for the child. Attention was focused on the process of learning rather than on its product and, accordingly, on the qualitative rather than the quantitative dimensions of the individual's thought. By means of the LPAD, it was possible to identify a number of deficient functions responsible for poor cognitive performance. Over the years, we have attempted to elaborate and refine our understanding of the nature of the more typical deficient functions.

The above account of the LPAD is not intended to provide a comprehensive description of the system of assessment and evaluation (see Feuerstein, 1979). However, it is important to appreciate that the Instrumental

Enrichment program is a reflection of the underlying philosophy and principles of the LPAD. Although the deficient functions, which are the target for Instrumental Enrichment, and the cognitive map, which provides the theoretical scaffold for the program, are discussed in the chapters that follow, both are derived from observations and insights gained from our work with the LPAD. For the past 25 years, the LPAD has been used in the assessment of culturally deprived and culturally different children and adolescents. It has provided overwhelming evidence of the capacity for modifiability of a wide variety of individuals of different ages and levels of functioning, suffering from various distal etiological conditions, and with contrasting redevelopmental goals. Empirical studies in which the LPAD has been used with EMR children at the individual and group level have confirmed the hypothesis of modifiability. By means of the LPAD, it is possible, within a period of between 5 to 25 hours of training and testing, to observe individuals who were incapable of grasping simple relations become able to produce inferential and even syllogistic reasoning. Similarly, children with manifest perceptual and discrimination difficulties are able, in a relatively short span of time, to solve problems that demand a high level of proficiency in these abilities. In this manner, the potential of many of the North African adolescents was revealed. This served to raise the expectations of those involved in their education and integration into Israeli society.

The high level of modifiability demonstrated by the Moroccan adolescents as a result of their migration to Israel and the intervention programs offered by Youth Aliyah has totally invalidated the pessimistic hypotheses concerning the etiology of their low level of functioning. It has shown that given proper conditions they may accede, even at so late a stage in their development, to normal and even high levels of functioning.

FOLLOW-UP STUDIES

The evidence for meaningful cognitive modifiability must be sought in studies of the changes that occur in individuals over long periods of time. Whereas the LPAD serves as the source of evidence of the potential for modifiability by providing an intensive but brief intervention during which examinees are provoked and prodded, long term and permanent changes can only be assessed by means of follow-up studies. In particular, confirmation of modifiability should derive from studies that use as criteria of adaptation those very factors that were responsible initially for the child being considered at high risk. In terms of our previously stated definition, modifiability involves the capacity of an individual to benefit from, and make use of, opportunities provided by life's experience and his ability to adapt to situations more remote and more complex than those to which he was initially exposed. Thus, the concept of modifiability implies the introduction of divergent patterns of change initiated by some kind of intervention. Once set in motion, the changes become more and more effective as the individual's encounters with stimuli become more meaningful and provide a source for growth and learning. Our evidence for the occurrence of such changes, and the overall potential for modifiability of the retarded performer, derives from three sources: clinical case studies; long range follow-up studies, extending over a period of some 20 years, of high risk adolescents varying in degree of severity of their deficiencies; and empirical studies in which various types of intervention were manipulated. Two case studies are presented and the findings from follow-up studies are discussed below. The major empirical study in which the effects of Instrumental Enrichment were assessed is presented in a subsequent chapter. Although we do not intend to review the literature, the reader is referred to Clarke and Clarke's (1976) excellent book, which represents an eloquent and powerful statement of the modifiability of individuals subject to the most extreme conditions of privation.

Clinical Case Studies

The clinical assessment of modifiability was made possible through the direct involvement of the author with hundreds of children and adolescents referred for treatment. Although most of the cases involved multiple symptoms, including cultural and emotional deprivation, the most prevalent symptom was severe cognitive dysfunctioning. This was manifested in a very reduced capacity to learn and make use of the regular redevelopment programs provided before entering the therapeutic environment of Youth Aliyah. The students' illiteracy was not simply attributable to a lack of opportunity to learn reading any more than to their failure to learn elementary adaptive social behavior. Rather, it was caused by a host of deficient functions that were expressed in their daily activities and emerged during assessment on the LPAD. Many of these youths have since undergone a process of redevelopment that would have been readily predicted on the basis of their initial performance. Of particular interest is the fact that the process of redevelopment continued in an autonomous and independent manner long after the admittedly potent and intensive intervention program. The following cases serve as illustrations:

> H was referred to us at the age of 14 years after many unsuccessful attempts to help him. His history was complicated by severe separation traumata, caused by his young mother abandoning him and the death of his aged father shortly thereafter. H, who was the only child of this marriage, was actively rejected by his half-brothers from his father's previous three marriages. Not only was he the son of an unwanted stepmother but he was considered by all, including the various caregiving agencies with whom he came in contact, to be mentally defective. For many years H was neglected and his conditions of life were barely sufficient for his physical survival. He existed on handouts from benevolent people who provided him with food and temporary shelter, and most of his time was spent in a slaughter house where his father had once been influential.

At the age of 14 years, H was functioning on a level of moderate to severe mental retardation; he had a poor mastery of language and was in a constant state of excitation that was manifest in uncontrolled, unpredictable, aggressive, and destructive behavior. Attempts to assess H's potential for modifiability were tedious and difficult, but fragments of his behavior, elicited after elaborate efforts, provided sufficient evidence of his ability to learn. It was decided to provide H with intensive therapy and remediation rather than place him in the custodial care that, on the basis of his performance and behavior problems, had been recommended. At this time, H developed a highly contagious ringworm condition, which prevented his placement in our own specialized therapeutic environment. Instead, H was admitted to the dermatology department of a hospital in which children between 1 and 5 years were being treated for the same condition.

After considerable adaptational difficulties, H learned to live with the younger children, and this induced regression (indulgence in a state of socially acceptable and encouraged regression to an earlier stage of social behavior and development), forced on him by circumstances, served to facilitate intervention and remediation. Within the relatively short space of 6 months, H changed in a dramatic way. He not only learned to speak in a more intelligible manner but also learned to read, write, and to do elementary computations. His previous avoidance of meaningful and prolonged contact with people was replaced by an ability to form significant relationships with his caregivers.

After acquiring the basic school skills, he was placed in a Youth Aliyah Kibbutz setting. After graduating from Youth Aliyah, H joined the pioneer wing of the Israeli army and became the leader of a new settlement. Today, H is a noncommissioned officer in the regular army and lectures on the educational problems of the disadvantaged to soldiers training to be teachers of disadvantaged youth.

The personality development of H was no less remarkable than his cognitive development. This is reflected in his warm and understanding attitude toward his mother who had abandoned him at a young age in his country of origin. After many years, his mother arrived in Israel with two children, and H provided her with love and filial devotion, even building a house for her and her children literally with his own hands.

The first signs of H's modifiability occurred in the realm of perceptual-motor behavior. Initially he could hardly draw a square and was totally unable to draw a diamond. After overcoming initial problems of inattention and uncooperativeness, H mastered these skills and expressed his delight by painting over a number of walls. In other areas, H began to show signs of mastery, and, as each function was acquired, it provided a point of departure for repeated self-initiated activities, much the same as the circular reactions observed in infancy. This readiness of H to continue his activities after the learning of a new element facilitated the process of modifiability. It was largely on the basis of these aspects of H's behavior that we were able to plan an appropriate intervention program and provide the necessary conditions for the materialization of his true ability.

At the age of 3 years, J was placed in the care of a maternal uncle after her mother died and her father abandoned the family. At the age of 12, J was referred to us as illiterate and functioning at a low level, as reflected on static, psychometric measures. Her drawings were infantile and reflected a gap of about 6 years in her cognitive development. She did not have a proper grasp of the concept of number and possessed very limited verbal skills. All in all, her developmental prognosis was poor. In contrast, her performance on the LPAD was promising. Not only did she cooperate, but her level of motivation proved to be high and she was able to use a variety of modalities in the training and subsequent assessment of its effects. Her results on the LPAD indicated a high degree of modifiability. She was provided with an appropriate intervention program and placed in an environment selected to foster motivation. After completing high school, J continued her studies at the university and successfully completed her course of study. Rather than seeking remunerative employment commensurate with her university degree, J decided to continue her studies in a field in which she could provide services to disadvantaged high risk children. Today, J has achieved academic distinction and occupies a teaching position at a university.

Many of the children who have received special intervention, having been aware of the changes that occurred in themselves, have subsequently felt obliged to help others overcome similar difficulties. Many of the graduates of special intervention programs have become teachers and school principals and have adopted a far more optimistic attitude toward the possibility of cognitive modifiability.

Long Term Follow-Up Studies

Follow-up studies on individuals provide a rich source of information; however, this information is not readily quantifiable. Although group studies conducive to statistical analysis and comparison include a reduced amount of information, they do permit a great degree of generalization.

In an extensive study, which is in the process of analysis, a group of 38 adolescents was selected on the basis of the presence of one or more of the following parameters: low scholastic achievement, low psychometric scores (IQs below 70), behavior and/or emotional problems, and difficult family background. The preliminary results obtained indicate a high level of subsequent adaptability of these high risk individuals. Differences in the degree of their adaptation are related to the nature and quantity of the intervention they received in the setting of a Kibbutz or Youth Aliyah village rather than to the severity of their initial condition.

In another study of cognitive modifiability at the group level (Feuerstein et al., 1976), a number of Youth Aliyah groups were assessed on the basis of their performance on tests administered by the army. Of particular interest was the "treatment group," which consisted of children who entered the program practically illiterate, with severe retardation symptoms, and serious social adjustment problems. These children could not be integrated with normal children and were provided with a special treatment technique (see Feuerstein and Krasilowsky, 1967) within the framework of a Youth Aliyah village. After a period of 2 to 3 years of intensive mediation, these children were fully integrated into a normally functioning peer group at about the age of 16 years. The results obtained by the "treatment group" on tests administered by the army reflected an astonishing level of functioning when compared with other groups whose initial prognosis was far more optimistic. On the army intelligence test they scored above the national norm and obtained the highest scores compared with other Youth Aliyah groups. On the army language test, the treatment group functioned at the average level. The results on a measure that combines the scores obtained on tests of intelligence, language development, and educational achievement indicate that the treatment group performed significantly better than all but one of the other groups. Thus, it is clear that the treatment group, which entered the program as a high risk population, emerged on an equal, if not better, footing than their initially more advantaged peers.

In addition to the case studies and follow-up studies mentioned above, the effects of the Instrumental Enrichment program have been the subject of an extensive empirical study. This study is presented in some detail in a subsequent chapter, but some of the major findings are mentioned below. After receiving the Instrumental Enrichment program for 2 years, the children proved superior to comparison groups on tests of general cognitive functions, specific cognitive functions, some scholastic skills, and behavioral measures. Despite the fact that the program was administered at the expense of attendance in a regular school curriculum, this did not prove detrimental and in no case was the performance of the groups who received Instrumental Enrichment worse than that of the comparison groups. In general, the results indicated the emergence of a more salient, analytic cognitive style, a more pronounced facility for differentiation, and a more efficient overall intellectual functioning by the recipients of the program.

Finally, it should be mentioned that the development of the Learning Potential Assessment Device made it possible to isolate the nature of the deficient functions responsible for low cognitive performance. The deficient functions will be discussed in Chapter 4, but it should be appreciated that the LPAD is more than an assessment device. It also operates as a diagnostic tool by means of which specific deficiencies may be pinpointed. This, in turn, permits a directed and planned intervention strategy, based on the specific needs of the individual. On the basis of the information regarding the nature and locus of deficient cognitive functions, the Instrumental Enrichment program was devised. The program is fully described in the chapters that follow. The empirical studies that are discussed in Chapter 10 have confirmed that Instrumental Enrichment, which is based on and represents an application of the theory of MLE, does indeed serve to produce cognitive modifiability and, thereby, to reverse the process of low cognitive performance. It is, however, important to recognize that the theory of MLE did not emerge as a result of controlled experiments in the psychological laboratory. Its source lies in our work with thousands of children, adolescents, and adults. In developing the theory we have relied on clinical, observational, and empirical data. Research of a strictly experimental nature is more limited at this stage, although hypotheses deriving from the theory of MLE have been tested (Feuerstein and Rand, 1974).

SUMMARY OF MLE-RELATED ISSUES

What Is the Nature of Retarded Cognitive Performance?

Identifying the nature of retarded cognitive performance is the most crucial question because it requires answers not only of a descriptive but also of a conceptual nature that will facilitate our understanding of the etiology of the condition and its manifestation. At the heart of our conception of retarded cognitive performance is the phenomenon of cultural deprivation. This term is defined operationally as a state of reduced cognitive modifiability of the individual in response to direct exposure to sources of stimulation. The syndrome of cultural deprivation includes a number of deficient cognitive functions that impede the process of modification. These deficient functions, which are responsible for the low level of performance, are discussed in detail in the next chapter. However, it is with respect to the etiology of cultural deprivation that the present approach may be sharply distinguished from all others. Cultural deprivation is not directly determined by distal factors such as poverty, low socioeconomic conditions, emotional disturbances of either the child or parents, or even by organic disorders. Common to all manifestations of cultural deprivation is a lack of MLE, and it is to this proximal factor that retarded performance is related. Inadequate MLE may arise in a variety of ways. Parents may not provide MLE as a result of poverty, alienation, indifference, or emotional disorders. Children may not be receptive to MLE as a result of organic impairments or emotional disorders. Whatever the reason, when MLE is impeded and the barriers produced by the organism are not bypassed, the result is cultural deprivation. Although a number of conditions, ranging from environmental to organic factors, may trigger the circumstances that limit the provision of MLE, the end result is the syndrome of cultural deprivation, that is, lack of modifiability in response to direct exposure to stimuli, as manifested in a wide range of deficient cognitive functions.

What Is the Prognosis for Redevelopment?

The prognosis for redevelopment serves as a barometer of the level of optimism, explicit or implicit in the theory, with regard to the remediation of retardation. The theory of MLE provides for a maximum commitment to the conviction that retarded cognitive performance is a reversible condition. This is not merely a matter of faith or blind optimism. The case studies reported in this chapter represent a minute sample of the children who have defied conventional and traditional theories by overcoming their difficulties and have emerged as normal, well adjusted adults. It is on the basis of cases such as these that the present theory was built. Rather than attempting to bend existing theories to meet the facts, an explanation consistent with the evidence had to be provided. By distinguishing clearly between distal and proximal etiologies and recognizing that the mechanisms responsible for retarded performance are not immutable organic impairments, depressed environmental circumstances, or emotional disabilities, it becomes possible to conceive of the phenomenon as a highly modifiable condition. However debilitating the prolonged effects of a lack of MLE may be, there can be no good reason for believing that its effects need remain permanent or that MLE cannot be instituted at any stage of development with positive and constructive results.

Is Redevelopment Dependent on
Intervention at Specific Ages, Stages, or Critical Periods?

In answering the question of the effectiveness of redevelopment in relation to time of initiation of intervention, it is necessary to distinguish between two issues. It is one matter to argue that early intervention may facilitate redevelopment. This, however, should not be confused with the issue of whether redevelopment is dependent on early intervention. The point has already been made that the greater the quantity and quality of MLE, the higher the capacity of the organism to become modified by direct exposure to stimuli. Purely in terms of age, the longer a child is deprived of MLE, the greater will be the effort required for successful redevelopment. Although early intervention may serve to facilitate redevelopment, late intervention does not preclude the possibility of redevelopment. It is when the notion of stages and, even more so, critical periods, is introduced that the question becomes more complex.

The stage concept is usually employed in developmental theories in a structural sense. Stages occur in a particular sequence, with the earlier stages preparing the ground for those that follow. From this line of reasoning, it may be argued that if stages are age related then earlier stages become critical since a failure to develop the cognitive requisites, which define the stage at a given period of development, results in an irreversible deficit. This approach is particularly evident when development is viewed as closely linked to maturational processes. A weaker version of the stage concept is that failure to master the requirements of a particular stage results in inadequate preparation for the subsequent stages, with the damage being progressively compounded. In this case, intervention may have to be structured to account for more fundamental deficiencies, but there is no necessary restriction on the age at which the intervention may be introduced. In terms of MLE, the human organism is viewed as an open system within which modifiability is not limited to specific ages or stages of development. Many of the deficient cognitive functions resulting from a lack of MLE are not stage specific but cut across all stages of development. For example, deficient functions at the input and output levels, such as impulsive exploratory behavior and acting out, may be operative at any stage of development. Furthermore, and perhaps most important, because the focus is removed from distal factors of an organic or physiological nature to the proximal cause of a lack of MLE, there is no sound theoretical reason for assuming that redevelopment need be dependent on specific ages or stages.

The distinction between critical period and optimal periods is essential (see Moltz, 1972). The construct of "critical period" implies that the structure and organization of behavior will be affected by events if and only when they take place in a specific and delimited period in the organism's development. The term, borrowed from embryology, implies the occurrence of certain stimulus conditions within a specific temporal period for the development of a schema. Imprinting in the duckling is the classic example of the development of a response system in a critical period. It should be apparent that the theory of modifiability, with its emphasis on reversibility, does not assume that the provision of MLE is limited temporally to a specific stage or age, nor to a particular set of stimuli, for the development of schemata.

What Is the Nature of Intervention?

Theoretically, the answer to the question of what is intervention is straightforward. Intervention is directed at the elimination of deficient functions resulting from a lack of MLE. This is achieved by providing the individual with mediated learning experiences structured according to his phase-specific needs and his particular condition.

At a more practical level, the Instrumental Enrichment program, for example, reflects an application of the principles of MLE. Although specifically developed for use with adolescents, the underlying principles of the program are applicable to all age groups. The program, and for that matter the entire theory, lends itself not only to remedial intervention but also to use as a preventive measure in cases where there may be reason to anticipate future problems. In terms of Instrumental Enrichment, the intervention is directed squarely at the individual rather than at factors external to his condition. The view that improving environmental conditions, be they poverty or discrimination, will necessarily eliminate the problem of cultural deprivation appears to be an oversimplification according to the theoretical framework of MLE, despite the compelling moral force of this argument. In the same way that preventing the occurrence of organic disorders reduces the probability of a lack of MLE occurring, eliminating impoverished environmental conditions *may* reduce the occurrence of cultural deprivation. But it must be recognized that cultural deprivation is a function not of environmental conditions, *per se,* but of a lack of MLE, which can and does occur in the best of material, social, and emotional circumstances. The danger inherent in the extreme environmental approach is that it removes the responsibility for intervention from those responsible for the transmission and mediation of the culture, such as parents, communities, educators, and psychologists, and places it in the hands of politicians and economists. Indeed, the utopian dream has always been that a society based on freedom, justice, and equality would provide the conditions for the elimination of differential cognitive development. But, until such time as this dream may be realized, educators must accept the responsibility of providing meaningful and effective intervention in those situations where the demand is pressing and the need urgent. Poverty and inequality of opportunity are only partial reasons for a lack of MLE, and the need for a clear appreciation of the role of MLE as a proximal determinant of differential cognitive development is therefore crucial.

What Are the Goals Set for Retarded Performers?

The goal of any intervention based on MLE is always to restore a normal pattern of development. The purpose of MLE, as reflected in the Instrumental Enrichment program, is never to train the individual merely to master a set of specific skills that will enable him to function in a limited way. Instead, the goal is to change the cognitive structure of the retarded performer and to transform him into an autonomous, independent thinker, capable of initiating and elaborating ideas. This necessitates a rejection of the passive-acceptance approach and all that it implies in terms of training and placement. Instead of directing training at routine mechanical skills, the retarded performer can make use of, and therefore must be provided with, the cognitive prerequisites that will enable him to derive maximal benefit from exposure to the widest possible variety of stimuli. In the final analysis, the aim is to develop in the organism a state of modifiability. The answers provided by the theory of MLE to this and all the previous questions may be crystallized in our firm conviction that the organism is an open system and that redevelopment must produce changes of an alloplastic as well as of an autoplastic nature. The development of autoplasticity is limited only by the extent of the effort that society is prepared to invest in order to ensure that all children develop to their maximum potential. In short, the goal set for retarded performers according to the theory of MLE is adaptation to a normal environment as opposed to adapting the environment to meet the specific needs of the retarded performer.

4
DEFICIENT COGNITIVE FUNCTIONS

The deficient functions, which are explained and discussed in this chapter, are conceived of as being a product of a lack of, or insufficiency of, mediated learning experience and are responsible for, and reflected in, retarded cognitive performance. The deficient functions relate to and help identify the *prerequisites* of thinking. In this sense, they refer to deficiencies in those functions that underlie internalized, representational, and operational thought and should not be confused with the operations or contents of thought. It is crucial to understand what is intended by the concept of deficient functions for two related reasons. First, the deficient functions provide a means for understanding and diagnosing the reasons for an individual's low manifest level of performance. Second, the Instrumental Enrichment program is intended to correct and redevelop those functions that, because of their deficient nature, are responsible for retarded performance. All too often, a child's failure to perform a given operation, whether in the classroom or test situation, is attributed either to a lack of knowledge of the principles involved in the operation or, even worse, to a low intelligence that precludes his understanding of the principles. What is overlooked is that the deficiency may reside not in the operational level or in the specific content of the child's thought processes but in the underlying functions upon which successful performance of cognitive operations depends. For example, underlying the operation of classification are a number of functions such as systematic and precise data gathering, the ability to deal with two or more sources of information simultaneously, and the necessity to compare the objects or events to be classified. Failure to correctly classify objects or events may either be caused by an inability to apply the logical operations governing classification or may result from deficiencies in the underlying functions that are presupposed in the operation. Clearly, a failure to locate the source of a child's errors will seriously affect the efficacy of any corrective action on the part of teachers or psychologists.

Before turning to a discussion of the deficient functions, careful consideration should be given to the following points:

1. Our sources of information concerning the deficient functions stem from a great variety of situations in the life space of culturally deprived children, gathered by means of a dynamic clinical assessment using the Learning Potential Assessment Device (LPAD). (LPAD is summarized in Chapter 2;

for more detail, see Feuerstein, 1979.) The LPAD has facilitated a deeper inquiry into the cognitive processes, particularly through the manipulation of the test situation which produces insights into the relationship between the cognitive functions of an examinee and certain behavioral outcomes. Furthermore, certain types of investment, oriented toward modification of the cognitive behavior of the child, have made possible the evaluation of hypotheses concerning the role of the deficient functions; the degree to which the different functions are accessible to change; and the differential nature of the investment required, in order to produce desired modification in specific deficient functions.

2.   We make absolutely no claim that the list of deficient functions is either definitive or exhaustive. On the contrary, we recognize that our description of the deficient functions may require additions and refinements. Despite a certain amount of overlap, the elements are conceptualized for purposes of analysis, understanding of the underlying processes, and for didactic purposes.

3.   These deficiencies do not necessarily appear *in toto* as a complete repertoire of the cognitive characteristics of each culturally deprived individual. Certain deficiencies may appear in an individual while others are absent. Accordingly, the retarded performer will need more or less investment in one function rather than another, and he may be more or less resistant to change in the specific function. The presence of a deficient cognitive function and its particular saliency will determine the nature of the intervention, the amount of resistance encountered, and the extent of the investment required to overcome it. It is for this reason that one has to seek a more individual profile in order to single out the specific instructional needs of the individual and to generate prescriptive teaching approaches with the help of the instruments.

4.   The deficient functions are not necessarily considered as elements that are totally missing from the cognitive repertoire of the individual and, therefore, need to be implanted in him. Rather, they are conceived of as elements that are weak and vulnerable. Under certain conditions, especially when a strong need emerges in the individual, adequate functioning may appear. However, such elicitation of functions that are usually deficient is rare and infrequent because of the lack of a requisite "need system" so that the effort involved in their mobilization makes their use uneconomical. A state of impairment or deficiency is to be understood in the sense that these functions do not appear spontaneously, regularly, and predictably in the cognitive behavior of the individual.

5.   Our attempt to distinguish the deficient functions on the basis of the three phases of the mental act (input, elaboration, and output) has to be understood as an artificial allocation since the three phases are dimensions that cannot be regarded in isolation from each other. A subdivision is important, however, because it provides us with the possibility of producing the desired changes in the cognitive functioning of the retarded performer by

focusing our intervention on the appropriate phases while taking into account the current responsiveness of the organism. (The three phases of the mental act are discussed in detail in Chapter 5.)

The deficient functions are presented in the following four categories:

a. Impairments in cognition at the input phase
b. Impairments in cognition at the elaborational phase
c. Impairments in cognition at the output phase
d. Affective-motivational factors

a. *Impaired cognitive functions affecting the input phase* include all those impairments concerning the quantity and quality of data gathered by the individual as he begins to solve, or even to appreciate, the nature of a given problem. Some possible impairments include:

Blurred and sweeping perception
Unplanned, impulsive, and unsystematic exploratory behavior
Lack of, or impaired, receptive verbal tools and concepts which affect discrimination
Lack of, or impaired, spatial orientation, including the lack of stable systems of reference which impair the organization of space
Lack of, or impaired, temporal orientation
Lack of, or impaired, conservation of constancies (i.e., in size, shape, quantity, orientation) across variations in certain dimensions of the perceived object
Lack of, or deficient need for, precision and accuracy in data gathering
Lack of, or impaired, capacity for considering two sources of information at once, reflected in dealing with data in a piecemeal fashion rather than as a unit of organized facts

b. *Impaired cognitive functions affecting the elaborational phase* include those factors that impede the individual in making efficient use of the data available to him. In addition to impairments in data gathering, which may or may not have occurred at the input phase, there are deficiencies which obstruct the proper elaboration of those cues that do exist. These include:

Inadequacy in experiencing the existence of an actual problem and subsequently defining it
Inability to select relevant, as opposed to irrelevant, cues in defining a problem
Lack of spontaneous comparative behavior or limitation of its appearance to a restricted field of needs
Narrowness of the mental field
Lack of, or impaired, need for summative behavior
Difficulties in projecting virtual relationships

Lack of orientation toward the need for logical evidence as an interactional modality with one's objectal and social environment

Lack of, or limited, interiorization of one's behavior

Lack of, or restricted, inferential-hypothetical thinking

Lack of, or impaired, strategies for hypothesis testing

Lack of, or impaired, planning behavior

Non-elaboration of certain cognitive categories because the necessary labels either are not part of the individual's verbal inventory on the receptive level or are not mobilized at the expressive level

Episodic grasp of reality

Note that we have not included in the above list the content of elaborative mental processes and operations, such as analogical thinking, syllogisms, transitive thinking, logical multiplication, and so on. These may be deficient as well, but this deficiency derives, in many cases, from inadequate learning experiences that focus on such specific content. In this list we have limited ourselves to the necessary *prerequisites* for the acquisition or application of such operations.

c. *Impaired cognitive functions affecting the output phase* include those factors that lead to an inadequate communication of the outcome of elaborative processes. Some possible impairments include:

Egocentric communicational modalities

Blocking

Trial-and-error responses

Lack of, or impaired, verbal tools for communicating adequately elaborated responses

Deficiency of visual transport

Lack of, or impaired, need for precision and accuracy in communicating one's response

Impulsive acting-out behavior, affecting the nature of the communication process

d. *Affective-motivational factors affecting the cognitive processes* can combine negatively in such a way as to influence the attitudes of the disadvantaged. These attitudes may affect the general involvement with cognitive tasks, as demanded by academic studies, tests, and real life situations.

Although reference to cognitive deficiency in terms of a division of the mental act into three phases, input, elaboration, and output, is intended to bring some order into the array of impaired cognitive functions, the interactions occurring between and among the phases is of vital significance in understanding the extent and pervasiveness of cognitive impairment. Input, elaboration, and output affect one another to various degrees and are not in a linear relationship with each other. The graphic model in Figure 1 illustrates, but does not do justice to, the intricate relationships among these

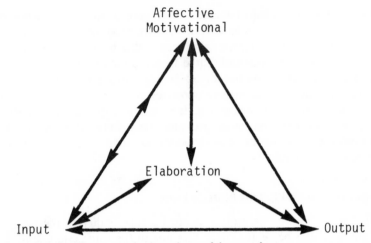

Figure 1.   Relationships among the three phases of the mental act.

three phases and the affective-motivational factor. One must be aware of and consider the great overlap and intricacy among the various phases in producing the mental act, as opposed to the rather simplistic conception presented by certain behavioristic approaches.

As previously stated, distinguishing between and among the phases and components of human cognitive behavior benefits both the diagnosis of deficiency and the prescriptive approach to teaching. A great deal of the data on retarded performers, which serves as the basis for contentions of their levels of functioning and the labels attached to them, is contaminated by the very limited distinction made between deficiencies occurring at the three phases of the mental act. This lack of precision precludes consideration of the behavior of the individual from the viewpoint of a hierarchy of cognitive processes. In contrast, by locating and defining the source of a failing response, it is possible to ascribe a relative weight to it according to the specific phase(s) under consideration. Thus, input and output have to be regarded as peripheral determinants of the cognitive processes, in contrast to the elaboration phase, which certainly has a more central position and should be considered as more essential for proper cognitive functioning. Deficiencies of input and output do not impair the child's functioning to the same extent as do deficiencies in his elaborational system.

In the final analysis, it is elaboration that determines our cognitive behavior. Impaired input and output may exist, but if the child is able to elaborate he can bypass the barriers obstructing the regular channels of input or output such that his level of functioning may go beyond what could have been expected on the basis of specific peripheral deficiencies. An excellent model of such bypassing of regular channels of input and output can be found in the achievement of Helen Keller, who, in spite of blindness and deafness, was able to function cognitively with a high level of efficiency.

The nature of the elaborational process in disadvantaged, low functioning adolescents is very often obscured by the presence of behavioral deficiencies at the input and output levels. Failure to take into account these peripheral deficiencies contaminates our assessment processes and results in our frequent inability to realize that elaborational capacities are intact and appropriate and that failing responses are, in many instances, caused by the use of incorrect data or the incorrect expression of adequate elaborational functions.

BLURRED AND SWEEPING PERCEPTION

Blurred and sweeping perception is attributable neither to the peripheral limitations of the perceptual processes nor to the way certain stimuli are sensed, but rather to the manner in which things are perceived. The perception of stimuli is marked by a blurredness of the various dimensions that characterize or define them. What characterizes the blurredness is a poverty of details or their lack of clarity, a poor quality of sharpness, an imprecise definition of borders, and an incompleteness of the data necessary for proper distinction and description. The fact that an object or stimulus is perceived in a blurred way totally affects, as well as is affected by, the processes of elaboration and output. Because we are not dealing with peripheral, sensory limitations, we are in the realm of a deficiency whose effect upon the elaborational process determines both the nature of the input and the subsequent output.

How can one explain this type of perception? The nature of the child's investment in the perceptual process, as defined by the amount of time and the degree of his persistence in focusing on an object or event, will determine the accuracy and pervasiveness of the perceptual process. So, too, speed and rhythm may be important factors in the clarity of the perception. The perceptual process may be a very rapid one in which a great deal of information is gathered during a short exposure, or it may be a slower process requiring much more investment for the same amount of information, or even less. Slow perceptual processes, combined with limited focusing, may result in reduced or inappropriate input, reflected in blurred perception. Finally, the nature of the perceived stimulus, according to such parameters as simplicity/complexity and familiarity/novelty, has important bearing on the types of perceptual investment and the amount of focusing. Thus, the adaptation of the individual will be a function of his capacity to discriminate stimuli along these parameters and vary his investment accordingly. Because such an adaptation is directly linked to the elaborative process, it very often fails in the culturally deprived, retarded performing child, whose perception may well be described as sweeping over the characteristics of the stimuli in a highly indiscriminate way.

However, sweeping perception and blurredness do not characterize all of the perceptual behavior of the culturally deprived child; there are certain instances in which his perception is sharp. Even when devoid of the verbal tools necessary to describe and formulate the perception, his perceptual processes can be complete and highly discriminating. However, these instances are usually linked to supercharged needs. When the perceptual processes are elicited by very specific and highly intensive needs that require corresponding variations in the amount and nature of investment, one is confronted by a "perfect" perception produced by the retarded performing child. Such perceptual activity, however, is rather limited in terms of the nature of the stimuli and the types of eliciting needs. It may occur rarely and for a limited universe of objects and events, corresponding to the limited need system of the culturally deprived individual.

In these children perceptual inadequacy arises because purpose, focusing, and investment are not the result of an intrinsic need system of the organism. An intrinsic need for appropriate perceptual functioning would elicit these behaviors at any time, so that appropriate functioning would not be strictly contingent upon a chance event in the life of the organism, but would rather characterize a generalized and pervasive mode of functioning.

Ample opportunity to exercise and continue perception beyond the satisfaction of primary needs is offered through the impetus of mediated learning experience. Whenever MLE has not been provided, however, perception is limited to basic needs, and its adaptive role in encounters with situations unfamiliar or not directly relevant to these needs is considerably restricted. Yet the fact that the organism is able to adapt to specific situations under certain conditions is testimony to the underlying intactness of the system. Thus, deficiencies in this function are due to a lack of appropriate habits, attitudes, and specific techniques which are acquired and established during early periods of the interaction of the organism with stimuli.

IMPULSIVITY

The retarded performer often demonstrates impulsive, unplanned, and unsystematic exploratory behavior. When presented with a number of cues that must be scanned, the individual's approach is so disorganized that he is unable to select those cues whose specific attributes make them relevant for a proper solution. For example, in the task of placing letters on a formboard, culturally deprived children often attempt trial-and-error placement, without a coordinated visual or tactile exploration of the two objects to be matched. When asked to estimate the size of an object using only tactile cues, the culturally deprived child invariably "palms" instead of keeping one finger in place as a point of reference for identifying the object. Consequently, his recognition and estimation of objects are highly inaccurate because of his inability to use proper investigational strategies as a result of fragmented and unsystematic exploratory behavior.

We should emphasize that impulsive, exploratory behavior is not the result of an incapacity to attend, although these two phenomena frequently appear together. Instead, it is the product of inadequate training in exploratory skills. This is reflected in a poor definition of the problem to be solved, a lack of goal orientation, and unsystematic exploration. Ultimately, the definition of a problem is itself a function of appropriate exploratory behavioral skills.

We must distinguish between three types of impulsivity. The first type may be determined by the basic biological rhythm characteristic of the biophysical constitution of the individual. On this dimension, there are certain basic individual differences that seem to appear only when one measures rapidity on very elementary tests, such as tapping.

A second type of impulsivity involves control over motor behavior as a function of a process of inhibitions. Such inhibitory processes have their origin in the need to keep the response, especially that which involves a motoric act, oriented toward a more complex goal that requires both a more enriched input and a more complex elaboration. In tasks requiring both rapidity and precision, there is an inherent conflict between the corresponding processes of acceleration and inhibition. Thus, the rapidity-precision complex illustrates how the two antagonistic trends, activation and inhibition, are coordinated and converge into the obtained response. The need to balance these two antagonistic trends is very often deficient in the culturally deprived child, and the child's behavior alternates between acceleration and inhibition in an uncoordinated way.

A third type of impulsivity represents, in a more or less pure form, a cognitive dimension of the behavior of the individual. In this type of impulsivity, lack of control is not necessarily caused by the accelerated rhythm of the individual or by his lack of control over his motor behavior. It is attributable, rather, to a lack of awareness on the part of the child that certain dimensions, other than those that he has already considered, will have to be used to reach the final solution. Here, the major determinant of impulsivity is conceptual or epistemic with the acceleration of the response directly linked to the limited awareness of the need for additional data to produce the proper answer.

An illustration may be taken from an LPAD session with a Russian boy. Described as suffering from organic damage, he was referred to the clinic because of his apathy, stuttering, and slowness, both motoric and verbal. On tasks in the Raven Progressive Matrices in which the child has to select the correct answer from six choices, he usually was slow in responding and never answered before being asked to do so. This enabled us to exclude the constitutional type of impulsivity as the source of his many errors. However, when presented with the task, the boy explored for a while, then raised his eyes, looked around and ceased to focus on the task. When asked for a response, he usually gave one that was based on the use of only one source of information and was therefore incorrect. It was clear that what determined the premature cessation of his exploratory behavior was not a lack of attending, nor a lack of control, nor the instability of the perceptual process, often observed in impulsive children. Rather, his response reflected his lack of awareness that in order to solve the problem properly there were dimensions to be considered in addition to those that he had already taken into account.

In contrast to the cognitive impulsivity, the phenomenon of biorhythmical impulsivity is not necessarily more prevalent in culturally deprived children than in those who function normally. When groups of culturally deprived, low functioning Moroccan children were compared with a sample of children from Geneva on a simple motor test, such as tapping, no differences were found between the two groups. In certain instances, our clinical observations demonstrated that the deprived child behaved in a rather slow way, with greater latency periods, which reflected, perhaps, conditions of reduced energy due to undernourishment, caution, suspicion, and the like. However, differences in disfavor of the culturally deprived group were found whenever the task was based on the rapidity-precision complex which required coordination between acceleration and control. In these instances, we witnessed either blockage, affecting the rhythm in which the response was elicited, or an indulgence in an imprecise, inaccurate type of activity.

The phenomenon of conceptual or epistemic impulsivity, however, is observable in the culturally deprived child in tasks in which a rich input is required, with a variety of data to be derived from different sources, in order to solve the problem at hand. What typifies the conceptual or epistemic impulsivity is a probabilistic-accidentalist approach to the cue offered. This produces a limitation in which an arbitrary selection of data is used for the solution of a task. Of course, a combination of the three types of impulsivity may result in an aggravation of the failing behavior, depending on the requirements of the solution, its complexity, and the degree of familiarity that the individual has with the particular tasks. A good example of conceptual impulsivity at the input phase is the phenomenon of the "hand-to-mouth" response, in which the child responds to the first and most salient stimulus before he has had an opportunity to gather all the data available to him. In a test involving the reproduction of a complex figure (Rey, 1959; see Figure 2), the behavior of the impulsive child is typified by his responding in a probabilistic way to each stimulus as it appears in his visual field. This does not allow him to integrate all of the information necessary in order to produce the correct answer. Many incomplete or failing answers to the questions of teacher or examiner are the result of incompletely perceived instructions. Often an examiner is interrupted by the "I know! I know!" reaction of the

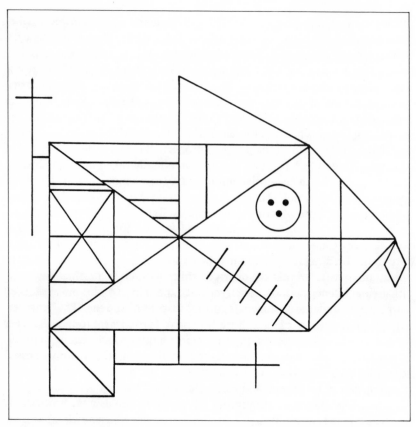

Figure 2.   Rey's Complex Figure Test. (From: Rey, A. 1959. *Teste de copie d'une figure complexe*. (Manual). Reprinted with permission from the Centre de Psychologie Applique, Paris.)

examinee before the intent of the instructions has been properly transmitted to the child.

Impulsivity may also be manifest at the output phase. One common phenomenon is the absurd, and often totally unexpected, erroneous answers offered by children in the areas of basic arithmetic computational operations. The child answers in a totally unexpected way, which is frustrating to the questioner and to the respondent, because it is clear to both of them that the respondent really possesses the correct answer in his repertoire. Usually, this is related to the fragility of the operational system which results in its unpredictability. However, the teacher often interprets this behavior as a lack of knowledge and takes the failure as the true measure of the child's level, rather than considering those instances in which he does show mastery. What really occurs is often the outcome of impulsivity at the output level, attributable to the fact that the child, as well as the examiner, expects an automatic mechanical response. Consequently, the operational process is displaced by an impulsive answer. In many cases, impulsivity on the output level is followed by the spontaneous correction on the part of the examinee because of his own feeling of the inadequacy of his response. However, the pressure and anxiety generated in the child by his initial inadequate answer may result in a second answer that is no better than the first. Thus, the appropriateness of the data gathered at the input phase and the adequate elaborational processes involved in the solution of a problem become inadaptive and inappropriate only because of the child's impulsive behavior in responding.

We are often confronted with a child providing failing responses in one specific modality of output, such as oral communication, whereas his responses to the same tasks in another modality, such as gestural or written communication, are correct. The observed difference regarding failure or success on certain tasks among children is often a direct function of the preferential modality characteristic of the individual. Thus, many children will be able to provide verbally correct answers but will fail when the response involves visual or motor behavior. If this dimension is not taken into consideration, one may easily tend to confuse the inappropriateness of the output with an elaborational incapacity.

As described above, impulsive behavior may be observed in the three phases of the mental act: input, elaboration, and output. The isolation of impulsivity as one of the determinants of the cognitive performance of the individual is of great importance because its study may assist us in defining the nature of failure and in better understanding the cognitive structure of the individual, an understanding that can lead to more effective intervention strategies. In this respect, Instrumental Enrichment focuses its attack on the phenomenon of impulsivity within the three phases of the mental act by including in its tasks an *explicit* and *implicit* need to gather all existing information, by necessitating the inclusion of all the data provided in order to solve the problem at hand, and by introducing reflective thinking in an attempt to change the conceptual tempo of the child by imposing a temporal distance between the input and the output. Planning ahead and feedback also serve to restrain impulsivity. The tasks included in the instruments demand enumeration, comparison, and summation of objects and events, and also aid in combating rhythmical, motoric, and conceptual impulsivity.

LACK OF VERBAL SKILLS

It is clear that a lack of appropriate verbal labels will affect the input phase. This deficiency may result in the limitation of the operational use of perceived elements to specific conditions rather than the generalization of those dimensions to other tasks when possible. The fact that a child cannot formulate the outcome of a comparison by using relational terms may result in his inability to apply the relationship deduced from comparing two objects or events, even if intuitively he is able to perceive their commonality or difference. Haywood and Switzky (1974) provide evidence that deficiencies in verbal skills among culturally deprived children are characterized not by an inability to form verbal abstractions but by a reduction in the intake of information. They found that enriching the supply of information produced normal performance levels on verbal abstracting tasks.

A lack of verbal skills may also severely affect a child's ability to elaborate certain cognitive operations. The absence of a specific verbal code to designate certain attributes of an object will not only affect efficiency at the input phase; on the elaborational level, lack of operational terms, such as "opposite," "relation," and "identity," may keep the child bound to specific tasks that he can handle on a concrete level and may impair his ability to generalize the same operation to tasks differing in content and complexity. Without entering into a discussion of the role played by language in the generation of thought processes, which is an area of dispute (see, for example, Bruner, Olver, and Greenfield, 1966; Piaget, 1968; Vygotsky, 1962), no one denies the facilitative role that verbal labeling plays in processes of generalization. In this particular case, the verbal labels represent important tools for designating the mental operation itself. In teaching an analogy task to the child, the most important aspect is to make him deduce the relationship that will then permit him to use it for the construction of a similar pair. However, in teaching this relationship, the capacity of the child to generalize his behavior will depend on his ability to understand the concept and the operational meaning of the term "relationship" and some of its specific contents. Inappropriate or imprecise verbal tools may still allow the child to operate, but the existence of the appropriate labels will turn this operation into a more universal key in solving similar problems.

In discussing the lack of verbal skills, a sharp distinction must be made between the culturally deprived and the culturally different. Both may lack the appropriate concepts or labels for functioning in a situation, but for very different reasons. For the culturally different, this deficiency may reflect a cultural difference in verbal and cognitive styles. In this case, the basic concept may exist but there may be a difficulty in selecting the correct corresponding linguistic term. The culturally deprived child, on the other hand, may have the label but not the corresponding concept. Alternatively, he may lack the verbal label because he does not discriminate between two otherwise distinctly perceived objects.

Mediated learning experience is not solely and necessarily dependent on the verbal capacity of the mediators, but also depends on their readiness and ability to transmit the appropriate verbal tools to the child. The lack of a proper term to designate an object, sequence, relationship, or concept will not, of necessity, limit mediational processes between the child and the adult. Whenever such verbal tools are missing, they may be substituted for by intonation, mimicry, gestures, and metalinguistic types of communication. However, if the absence of transmission is combined with a lack of verbal tools, the outcome will be a severe lack of the prerequisites of operational thinking. Of course, the existence of verbal codes permits the use of more complex relationships and facilitates both the understanding and communication of more abstract components. Confronted with more abstract and formal logical operations, the lack of verbal tools makes the mastery of such tasks very difficult, and, in many cases, uneconomical to the point of being prohibitive.

In short, many operational activities and their prerequisites can be conceived of as being independent of a verbal, semantic system of labels. Labels are necessary, however, when more complex and abstract relationships are required and ensure their more efficient use and application.

LACK OF, OR IMPAIRED, SPATIAL AND TEMPORAL ORIENTATION

Temporal and spatial dimensions are among the cognitive functions whose development is strongly dependent upon mediated learning experiences because they are based mainly upon relational thinking. They represent a level of functioning that transcends the "here" and "now," and the isolated unique existence of an object or of an event. They describe, rather, the way objects or events relate to others in terms of order and sequence, distance and proximity, and the like. Direct exposure to stimuli without an adequate orientation toward time and space reduces cognitive functioning to the level of simple identification and recognition of objects without permitting the establishment of relationships between them.

Temporal and spatial orientation more than certain other cognitive dimensions depend on MLE to become established into the cognitive repertoire of the individual. What would we know about a past that is not directly experienced by us if it had not been transmitted to us? The mediational processes reflected in the transmission of the past create representational thinking as a modality to relate to and act upon the "represented" as one would to the "experienced." Continuous exposure to the past also has important bearing upon the capacity to plan ahead and to relate to the future, operate on it, and produce transformations in it by hypothetical "iffy" thinking. This may result in a habitual disposition to register time and to order space, to organize and coordinate them according to specific needs, and to use them as the necessary condition for the precise definitions of objects and events.

Clinical observations of culturally deprived individuals have demonstrated again and again an impairment in their level of functioning in tasks requiring spatial orientation. This deficiency is clearly observable in a positional learning test in which children have to learn the position of five particular squares on a 5 × 5 grid. The gradualness of the learning curve or their failure to learn at all is easily traced to an incapacity to orient themselves by the help of directions like "left-upper," "right-upper," "left-lower," and so on. The fact that these children have to rely on the perceptual pattern of the cues, which itself is difficult to establish because of their episodic grasp of reality, makes learning very slow and unstable and, in some cases, even impossible (Feuerstein, Krasilowsky, and Rand, 1978).

The culturally deprived individual frequently is dependent on his own body movements for spatial orientation. For example, when giving directions, culturally deprived individuals will often use gestures that are limited to their own movements rather than using terms like "right" or "left." They may even propose accompanying an individual who has asked for directions to the site in question because it is easier to do so than to conceptualize spatial relations. Our experience indicates that merely inhibiting the gestures and movements of the culturally deprived child often results in the emergence of more conceptualized, interiorized handling of spatial orientation.

Impairments in representing, projecting, conceptualizing, structuring, and organizing space have implications both for psychological testing and for actual learning. Culture-free and culture-fair tests, which are designed largely for the culturally deprived populations, normally have many items that require spatial discrimination. The impairments of culturally deprived youth in this area, however, often preclude their succeeding in the very nonverbal performance tests specially designed not to penalize them for their generalized or specific deficiency.

Temporal orientation seems to be deficient more often than other factors in culturally deprived populations. Because time is an abstract element and requires representational relational thinking, it is a concept far more difficult to master than certain types of spatial relationships, especially those of functional space. Of the two, the concept of time, even more than that of space, is especially dependent on mediated learning experiences for its acquisition. Thus differences in the registering and orientation of time may be found between the culturally deprived and the culturally different. The culturally deprived child's attitude is characterized by the lack of a need for ordering, summating, comparing, and sequencing, all of which must be produced initially by a volitional act on the part of the individual. In contrast, the attitude toward time that may characterize certain culturally different individuals is reflected in a more casual and inefficient attitude and use of time. A readiness to "kill" time or to "waste" time does not necessarily imply a lack of temporal orientation as such an attitude may be accompanied by a great deal of awareness, even to the point of registering and summing up the time wasted.

A lack of temporal orientation is not necessarily linked to the lack of, or inaccuracy in the use of, proper verbal tools. In certain cases, there may be a generalized episodic grasp of reality and a lack of summative behavior that make the child neglect the grouping of objects and events because he has not yet established quantifiable or ordering relationships among them. However, the most prevalent factor in this deficient cognitive function is the lack of orientation toward time in attributing meaning to one's experience of objects and events and the relationships among them. Thus, "before" and "after," as well as the "now" and "then," are very vaguely defined, if mentioned at all, as attributes.

This lack of temporal orientation and the inaccurate use of temporal concepts affect the individual's capacity to use the data registered by him in an accurate and well defined way. Both spatial and temporal concepts are needed in order to define our perceptions. The uniqueness of a percept, in contradistinction to its general or universal character, is provided by inserting the object or the event into the matrix of time and space.

When relationships between objects and events are the content of our mental operation, a clear understanding of the concepts of time and space is essential. Causal relationships and concepts of transformation cannot be conceived of without recourse to spatial and temporal dimensions. Of the two, the temporal is less accessible and, consequently, much more deficient in the culturally deprived child. Whereas the spatial orientation may be dealt with by the culturally deprived in a more concrete operational manner, the temporal dimension is inaccessible to the concrete and therefore produces greater difficulties. The difficulty in grasping temporal dimensions is related to the fact that they are handled almost exclusively by an internal feedback and representational registration. Therefore, they depend not only on the generalized attitude of summative grouping behavior but also on the need and the capacity of the retarded performer to represent to himself, and to act on, data derived and summed representationally.

An orientation toward time and space, produced by MLE, crystallizes and becomes an automatic response, which is then regarded as an attribute of human perception rather than as a product of special effort and a volitional act. It is this automatic character of our time-space orientation which is then conceived of as an *a priori* condition of our thinking. However, temporal and spatial functions are heavily impaired in the retarded performer and the result is an imprecise grasp and organization of objects and events and relationships between them.

LACK OF, OR IMPAIRED, CONSERVATION OF CONSTANCIES

Perceptual stability is, to a large extent, dependent on the capacity of the individual to conserve the constancy of objects across variations in some of their attributes and dimensions. Such constancy is produced either by perceiving the variation in given attributes as irrelevant to the identity of the object or by conceiving of the variation as being produced by a transformation of the given attributes of the particular object that does not affect the identity of the object because it can be easily reversed to the original state through another transformation.

Reversibility is the mental process underlying the conservation of constancies under conditions of transformation. Lack of, or impaired, conservation of constancy often is associated with an episodic grasp of reality in which objects and events are not related to each other. Because an episodic grasp does not result in the establishment of a relationship between the perceived objects and experienced events, it does not make possible the understanding of the identity between them by eliminating, as irrelevant, transformations of the attributes. For example, a square placed on its angle is often considered a triangle by a child because the variation in the square's spatial orientation has made the child use the irrelevant attribute of its standing on its angle in his identification of the object. The shift in orientation has made the child neglect the more important dimension of a square, its four angles rather than three. The lack of conservation of constancy is manifested in a limited disposition to conceive categories of objects above and beyond differences between them because of the lack of readiness on the part of the retarded performer to accept a common factor as constant and to abstract this common factor from other dimensions on which the objects may differ. Thus, the phenomenon of the conservation of constancy can explain the difficulties experienced by the child on a conceptual level in producing proper superordinate concepts.

LACK OF, OR IMPAIRED NEED FOR, PRECISION AND ACCURACY

The function of a lack of, or impaired need for, precision and accuracy was mentioned in the previous discussion of impulsivity. However, the level of recognized need for precision is also affected by cultural differences and/or individual differences in the focus of interest.

The distinction between the lack of precision of the culturally different and of the culturally deprived can be seen in the ease with which the need for precision emerges in the culturally different individual once he is confronted with tasks that elicit such a need. In contrast, the culturally deprived child evinces a resistance to the establishment of such a need despite the requirements of a specific task. The response patterns established in the culturally different child as a result of MLE, with respect to culture-specific contents, will be readily applied to new contents with which the individual is confronted. This is because of the modifiability produced in an individual as a result of MLE. However, where the lack of precision is the result of a lack of MLE, as in the culturally deprived individual, the child will be more resistant to changes imposed by the nature of a task requiring precision.

Two categories of imprecision may be distinguished: missing data and distorted data. In the first category, the individual does not take the care to gather all the data he is offered and hence cannot use the information when he has to produce an answer or is required to report on a perceived object or event. Imprecision is thus manifest by partial gathering or partial transmission of data on the input and output levels, respectively. In the second category, imprecision may be the result of a distortion of certain dimensions. In this case, data are not missing but there may be approximations rather than precise attributions or the use of qualitative rather than quantitative dimensions.

The dynamics of the orientation toward precision is based on a generalized need, the application and use of which are affected by more specific needs. The general need is established by a variety of strategies very early in the interactional processes between the child and his human environment. This interaction, reflected in a dialogue in which each partner is provided with feedback on the efficiency of his communication, is certainly one of the most potent factors in establishing the general need for precision. The more a dialogue bears upon topics distant from the immediate perceptual field, the greater is the reliance upon precision in the communication of the specific subject of the dialogue. Feedback on communication gaps produced by imprecision will produce in the individual a need to gather all the data and express them in such a way that his partner is able to understand and react accordingly.

This interaction starts at a very early age, with the gathering of data as a product of instruction or as an answer to an explicit request. It is then followed by corrective responses, and, throughout the process of habit formation, precision becomes less dependent on explicit instruction and is manifested as an internalized intrinsic need to be exhaustive and precise in gathering all the necessary data. This need may also result in incidental learning, in which certain sets of data not of immediate relevance are registered, stored, and readily mobilized, despite the absence of specific instructions to do so.

Precision may be impaired or lacking not only because it is not experienced as a need, as such, but also as a secondary result of deficiencies in other cognitive functions. There are some types of imprecision that may arise as a function of deficiencies of the elaborational processes. For example, certain dimensions and relationships become salient and relevant only when they gain a specific meaning through comparison. Therefore, if one does not compare, then the accuracy and the precision of the description of the dimensions included in the perception of the object will be far less than if, in perceiving, one sets out with the intention to compare. Lack of precision at the output level may differ from that on the input level. In addition to cognitive factors, differences may also be attributable to the nature of the relationship between the individual and his partner in the communicational interactions, which may be reflected in egocentric modalities of output.

LACK OF, OR IMPAIRED USE OF, TWO OR MORE SOURCES OF INFORMATION

The function of lack of, or impaired use of, two or more sources of information is included as a deficiency at the input level, despite the fact that it is actually the outcome of an elaborative process. The use of two sources of information is a prerequisite of thinking because it is the basis of all relational thought processes. Two elements must be used as sources of data in comparative behavior and whenever a problem is confronted. In fact, no problem can be experienced as such unless an incompatibility of data stemming from two or more sources is identified and confronted.

The capacity to conceive of the congruity and incongruity among multiple sources of information is the *a priori* condition for the need to reinstate, by means of a specific operation, the equilibrium (i.e., to solve the problem). From this point of view, the use of two sources of information is, in itself, an elaborational process. If the individual constantly tends to relate to each source of information separately, either successively or alternately, but does not coordinate the two, the elaborative process will be impaired because the relationship between the two sources will not be available for further experiences.

If the individual is not oriented to gathering all the data from various sources, but rather satisfies himself with only one source, then the input is inadequate and his functioning will be limited to the simple identification or recognition of perceived elements. The lack of disposition to use two sources of information at the input level is a phenomenon observed in many situations and accounts for much of the unsuccessful performance of children on psychometric tests and in particular academic and everyday life situations. For example, in tasks relying on visual perception, this phenomenon is clearly evident when the child is offered a variety of possibilities and takes into account only one source from a series of alternatives. That he has used or looked at only one source becomes clear when analyzing the nature of his error. Often the response is appropriate if one takes into account that it corresponds to the single source of information that was considered.

Results obtained with Moroccan and Israeli children on the Raven Progressive Matrices (Raven, 1947, 1960) have been analyzed in terms of the children's errors. This analysis produced evidence that the majority of errors were attributable to the use of only one source of information. In tasks requiring the completion of missing parts by selecting from six alternatives (see Figure 3) the French-speaking Moroccan children almost invariably chose the part that was identical to the given lower-left section of the square, instead of selecting the appropriate complementary part. Unlike their French-reading peers, Hebrew-reading culturally deprived examinees chose the part corresponding to the given upper-right section. They did so because, accustomed to starting the perceptual exploration from right to left, as in reading Hebrew, they encountered the right part of the page first. In both cases, the use of only one source of information prevented the children from establishing the necessary relationship between the parts.

The limited need of the retarded performing child to use a variety of sources of information makes for difficulty in his grasping the point of view

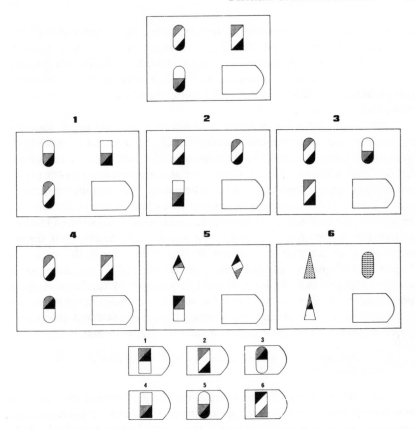

Figure 3.   LPAD Variations I.

of someone else and coordinating it with his own. The use of two sources of information is a prerequisite to what Piaget calls "decentration." Piaget maintains that egocentric behavior occurs because the individual is unable to see the "other" and represent himself in the situation of the perceived "other." Before disengaging oneself, one must be able to seek two or more sources of information. This lack of orientation toward, or search for, two sources of information produces limited input and heavily determines deficient elaborational processes.

INADEQUACY IN EXPERIENCING THE EXISTENCE OF, AND IN SUBSEQUENTLY DEFINING, AN ACTUAL PROBLEM

The function of inadequately recognizing and defining a problem involves the inability of the individual to grasp the disequilibrium existing in a given situation. If the disequilibrium does not produce an awareness in the individual of the change that occurs in his internal state, the existence of the problem will not be experienced. The origins of reflective thinking, as noted by Dewey (1933), lie in perplexity, confusion, or doubt. Reflection does not arise spontaneously in an individual but must be evoked by the disequilibrium inherent in a situation in which incompatibility exists between two or more sources of information.

Why is the culturally deprived individual not sensitive to, or disturbed by, the existence of a problem situation readily experienced by others? We hold that a number of poorly developed cognitive functions are responsible for this unawareness. First, the experience of a problem requires the gathering of data for the subsequent establishment of relationships between the various cues. This is followed by an appreciation of incompatibilities, discrepancies, incongruities, and missing cues via the establishment of relationships between various sources of information that may be present in the perceptual field or in stored information. By way of illustration, the reaction of Moses to the burning bush (Exodus 3.2) may be cited. Stored information made him expect that the bush would be consumed by the flame while his perceptual experience conveyed that the anticipated result did not occur. The incompatibility between the stored and current information produced a problem, which was experienced as a state of disequilibrium.

> ...and Moses said "I will turn aside now, and see this great sight, why the bush is not burnt" (Exodus 3.3).

This state of disequilibrium acted as the energetic determinant of a reaction whose aim was to restore the equilibrium between the perceived facts and those anticipated on the basis of previous experience. In the Biblical situation, the solution was offered by the miraculous nature of the incompatible and unexpected condition. In other cases, additional information, such as the condition of the wood or the illusory nature of the phenomenon perceived as fire, might have solved the problem.

Unless the necessary initial step of data gathering is undertaken with a modicum of attention and skill, the understanding of a problem will be nonexistent or partial, at best. Dewey (1933), in his classic book *How We Think,* commented on the importance of the initial steps of data gathering and the establishing of relationships for reflective thinking. The way in which the subject matter is supplied and assimilated is, therefore, of fundamental importance. If the subject matter is provided in too scanty or diffuse a fashion, or if it comes in disordered array or in isolated scraps, the effect is detrimental to cognitive processes. However, if the data gathered are adequate, whether through personal observation or through transmission of information by others, half of the battle is won, because this is the prerequisite for elaborating relationships and experiencing them as a problem to be solved.

The lack of a variety of culturally and experientially developed needs also contributes to a nonawareness of problems. Consider culturally deprived youths' lack of need for logical evidence. Cognitive systems, which do not demand that events necessarily follow from a given set of circumstances, will not appreciate discrepancies existing in the field. On the other hand, a complete lack of interest in the field, which is a frequent reaction of these youths to academic studies, will not lead to an arousal of curiosity that would signal an encounter with a problem situation.

On a more practical level, in the classroom when the retarded performer is presented with a problem situation and is instructed in its solution, both the phrasing of the problem and the instructions may not be understood purely on a verbal level. As has been stated, not attending to appropriate cues is the basis for the lack of awareness of the existence of problems, but the fact that a problem is not recognized, as such, acts circularly to perpetuate the chain of not organizing the field toward the solution of problems.

INABILITY TO SELECT RELEVANT AS OPPOSED TO IRRELEVANT CUES IN DEFINING A PROBLEM

The relevancy and irrelevancy of cues are a direct function of the specific goals established by cognitive process on the elaborational level. Relevance is always related to a specific goal. Therefore, in describing an individual as unable to discriminate between the relevance and irrelevance of certain cues, it is necessary to first define the specific goals that will determine his awareness, his amount of focusing, and the degree of relevance of each cue. In other words, relevance and irrelevance of cues are a direct function of the purposefulness and degree of goal orientation of the mental activity of the individual. The more purposeful and goal oriented are one's cognitive processes, the greater is the differentiation of the perceptual field with regard to the relevance of specific cues to meet these particular goals.

It is clear that we are dealing here with the need system of the organism, which renders him receptive to recognition of a problem and creates a search in the field for relevant data that may help reinstate the equilibrium by solving the problem. In this search, cues will be assessed with respect to their relevance or irrelevance according to their capacity to reduce the state of incompatibility of the processed data. For example, when a child is presented with six choices of equal size that differ in color and shape, and is asked to complete a missing part, size is irrelevant because it does not discriminate between the various alternatives. Thus, by defining the goal the common features of the alternative choices are judged as irrelevant to the problem at hand.

In certain other cases, the discrimination between the relevant and the irrelevant is produced by an analytic process that permits the elimination of certain cues and the assignment of preference to others. Hypothesis testing, which aims at the isolation of the determining factors of a given situation, is the case of discrimination between relevant and irrelevant cues. In distin-

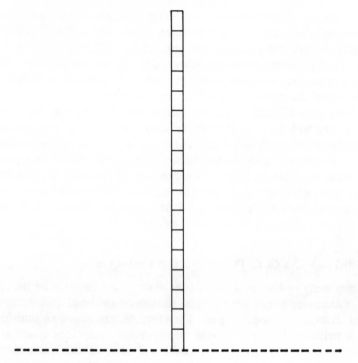

Figure 4.   Horizontal-vertical illusion.

guishing between factors that determine the horizontal-vertical illusion
(Figure 4), in which there is an illusory difference of size between the two
lines, the search for determinants may result in the ascription of causality to
irrelevant factors such as differences in the color of the lines, until their irrelevance is proved in an analytic experimental way. Lack of discrimination
between the relevant and irrelevant units of information is also linked to an
inappropriate or inexplicit definition of the problem, which produces a lack
of purposefulness in the perceptual processes of the individual. This leaves
the cues unorganized with little or no difference in the degree of relevance as-
cribable to each of them.

LACK OF, OR IMPAIRED, SPONTANEOUS COMPARATIVE BEHAVIOR

Spontaneous comparative behavior may be viewed as the primary condition for the establishment of relationships because it entails the organization
and integration of discrete units of information into coordinated thought.
As such, it is considered by the author to be one of the most fundamental
building blocks of higher cognitive processes. A deficiency of spontaneous
comparative behavior limits cognition to the most elementary processes by
excluding the involvement of higher mental processes. By means of the prod-

ucts of spontaneous comparative behavior, an individual is able to transcend his immediate perceptual experience and is able to draw logical inferences which lead to abstract, propositional, and hypothetical thinking. Thus, it is on the basis of comparative behavior that the child's construction of reality relies, as aspects of the outer world are organized into meaningful systems in terms of the relationships that he imposes on them.

We do not contend that the culturally deprived child is unable to compare or even that he does not do so in all situations. On the contrary, the fact that the child is usually successful in comparing when specifically requested to do so is sufficient evidence of his ability to compare. The deficiency in this case lies in the failure of the child to compare spontaneously. We have witnessed many children who perform poorly on psychometric and academic tasks because the necessity for comparison, in order to solve a problem, was not explicitly stressed. When the necessity to compare is indicated to the child by verbal or even nonverbal means, he is often able to proceed successfully with the task. Because the need to compare is usually taken for granted, very little experimental work describing and measuring spontaneous comparative behavior has been undertaken.

In short, comparative behavior is a prerequisite of relational thinking which leads to conceptual processes. It determines, as well as is determined by, the nature of the input and output processes. Factors such as systematic organization, need for precision, summation of attributes, and ordering of relationships may be outcomes of adequate comparative behavior.

NARROWNESS OF THE MENTAL FIELD

The culturally deprived child often demonstrates a narrow mental field which limits drastically the number of units of information that can be processed and manipulated simultaneously. This limitation results in an incapacity to use varied bits of information for the internal combination and coordination necessary for the production of conceptualized operational thinking. In many cases, this is manifest by an alternation and succession rather than a coordinated integration, so that objects and events are not considered in relation to each other but as independent entities.

On the level of memory, there is a loss of fragments of previously acquired information once the individual changes the focus of his attention to other information derived from the same source. This is illustrated figuratively by the "short blanket" phenomenon in which one uncovers one's legs by covering one's head and vice versa. On the Plateaux test, for example, in which the child has to learn the position of one fixed knob out of nine on each of four plates, or even in a test of memory for fifteen words, many of these children are unable to retain those elements that they are able to recall at first, once they succeed in remembering others. This phenomenon can be ascribed to a variety of factors, but in the retarded performer it seems to be linked to the passive attitude of the child toward his own self as the medium through which cognitive processes operate but over which he exercises no volitional control. Remembering is conceived of as a "happening" that involves limited control of the individual rather than as an active process of reconstruction of the experienced reality. It occurs *to* him and not *by* him. Thus, children asked in clinical assessment about the control over their memory describe it as either "there" or not.

The retarded performer does not manifest a belief in his own capacity to recall a memory, which is not evoked immediately and spontaneously, at will. This may be regarded as a particular case of the more generalized phenomenon of extrinsic locus of control, characteristic of these children, which makes them dependent on what will happen to them rather than on what they can make happen to themselves and to others. They do not consider themselves generators of information beyond what emerges within them as a consequence of a specific directed effort. Therefore, if a child remembers certain dimensions quickly and spontaneously by virtue of their greater immediacy or saliency or through increased vigilance, he will be inclined to renounce other information of greater relevance and importance because it is not as easily accessible to him.

An acceptance of oneself as a vehicle through which information passes in a passive and random manner rather than as a source and generator of information, combined with an inability to combine and coordinate units of information, produces a narrow and restricted mental field.

LACK OF, OR IMPAIRED NEED FOR, SUMMATIVE BEHAVIOR

A lack of summative behavior is a characteristic of the culturally deprived individual that leaves the stimuli registered by him isolated and unique. A common tendency, observable in even young children, is that a sort of running computational system is used, which manifests itself in adding objects and events and summing their appearance and frequencies without a very specific goal-oriented need to do so. The so-called child arithmomania, which manifests itself by the child's propensity to count sticks, telephone poles, cracks in the pavement, fence pickets, and the like, is but one manifestation of this need to have things summed up in inclusive terms. This purposeless and gratuitous type of behavior, often executed aloud as a soliloquy, with time and exercise becomes an internalized activity, permitting children to group, compare, subtract, and even multiply events, thus updating them as they occur. When asked, children may well be able to offer a summative account of these events without having to add them at that particular moment. Summative behavior represents a basic need to produce relationships in the world, and it reflects the active contribution of the organism in his interaction with the external and internal processing of stimuli.

The child who manifests a deficiency in summative behavior is often unable to give a spontaneous accounts of events with which he is confronted daily and with which he is thoroughly familiar. When asked, "How many children are there in your family?", "How many rooms are in your house?", or "How many children are in your classroom?", he will be taken by surprise at not having done what seems to be most natural. The child will start to enumerate names and events. His difficulties are not technical, because he is able to count when requested to do so. Instead, they reflect a lack of orientation to sum up reality as a part of a need to organize one's interaction with stimuli. Such a need is the product of mediated learning experience and is not generated directly by exposure to reality.

Summative behavior not only is confined to quantitative dimensions, but also includes a qualitative aspect. In both its quantitative and qualitative form, summative behavior represents a necessary prerequisite for logical operations. However, the need to summate objects and events should not be confused with the operation itself, which may involve any of a number of different logical operations.

DEFICIENCIES IN PROJECTING VIRTUAL RELATIONSHIPS

Deficiencies in projecting virtual relationships are concerned with those relationships that have been established and grasped but have not yet been applied in the handling of a new situation. The relationships exist "virtually" in the individual but remain to be projected into a specific constellation of objects and events. Thus, this deficiency involves the need to restructure a given constellation and then to shift from one type of relationship to another as required by new tasks confronting the individual.

LACK OF, OR IMPAIRED NEED FOR PURSUING, LOGICAL EVIDENCE

The definition of problems and the search for their solutions is strongly contingent upon the presence of a feeling of cognitive dissonance (Festinger, 1957) and disequilibrium (Dewey, 1933; Piaget, 1952), generated by the incompatibility or incompleteness of data in a given situation. A feeling of compatibility is derived through the grasp of the relationships either between objects present, or between a given object or event and previously stored information. However, even if the problem is experienced and incompatibilities are felt and registered, a search for solution may still be lacking if no need to change the situation in order to restore the disrupted equilibrium is felt. When we are confronted with an attitude that induces an acceptance of things as they are, the need for logical consistency is not deemed essential in the same way that other needs are experienced. "So what?" is often heard in response to situations that, in the regular child, would give rise to a storm of questions and search for answers.

The lack of need for logical evidence does not necessarily reflect a low level of intelligence, even though it certainly impairs cognitive functioning. Rather, it should be understood as an attitude of the individual toward the quality of interaction between himself and his external and internal environment.

In analyzing many of the responses given by children to some of the Piagetian type of tasks, it has been found that the failing behavior of the children can be explained by the fact that they are not disturbed in the least by the illogical relationship between the reality of the situations and the instructions accompanying the task or by the even more frequently occurring illogic of their own responses. Our conclusion is that a lack of need for logical evidence does not necessarily reflect a deficiency to operate logically, because the child's responses sometimes do demonstrate logical understanding. Rather, the inconsistency frequently observed in the child's responses may be ascribed to a faulty need system in which logical evidence is not prominent and pertinent, a condition which, in fact, may be noted even among some normal initiated adults.

Lack of need for logical evidence is commonly observed in the communication patterns of the culturally deprived child. Frequently an inferential question of *"Why?"* will be responded to with a sequence of "Because" *"Because why?"* "Because of because." This is but one example of the typically given inappropriate answers to simple informative questions, and simply attributing this inadequacy of the answers to emotional states is not supportable. Instead, logical evidence is not experienced as a compelling force or dimension with which the individual should be concerned.

A lack of need for logical evidence affects not only the output phase, in which the individual supports a statement and his judgments in a way that will be acceptable to his partner, by using rules commonly accepted by both, but strongly affects the input levels as well. If, in proposing a statement, one is not compelled to bring to bear evidence that will be acceptable to one's discussant, then the data supporting the proposition will accordingly be imprecise and incomplete. Lack of need for logical evidence is, therefore, a major determinant in the failure of the culturally deprived child and has important implications not only for academic activities but for behavior in a wide diversity of areas.

This particular function is often confounded with certain defense mechanisms characterizing neurotic, regressive behavioral patterns. As pointed out by Odier (1956), there are important common features between the regressive thinking of the neurotic and patterns of behavior typical of early stages in the development of cognitive functions in children. Our claim is that we are not dealing here with regressive types of behavior reflecting inadequate defense mechanisms, nor with fixation on lower stages of development, but with functions that are deficient as a result of the lack of mediated learning experience.

LACK OF, OR IMPAIRED, INTERIORIZATION

One of the frequently observed and well recognized phenomena in the retarded performer is a strong reliance upon concrete perceptual cues accompanied by a lack of readiness to use representational mechanisms by actively manipulating stored information. This has as its corollary the frequently cited pervasiveness of task-bound concrete behavior, with inappropriate generalization and a low level of abstraction. The distance between the mental act and the objects on which it operates is usually very narrow, with a limited use of mediating symbols, signs, and concepts. The child frequently tends to refer back to the initial object or event on which he was operating. In many cases, this concrete approach is the expression of the child's disbelief in his capacity to invoke or "hallucinate" the reality which he seeks and which is not accessible to his sensorial system; to represent to himself the object without having it in front of him; and to retrieve, by way of representation, something that is not in his immediate sensorial field. When asked to free associate, many of these children will limit themselves to the evocation of words for the objects perceived in their immediate environment and will have relatively greater difficulties in evoking things that are not present. The same is true for reports of events in which only very limited aspects are mentioned, usually those that have had a material and observable impact. When asked an inferential question based on data gathered and analyzed, the child will answer, "But, how can I say what it will be if I haven't seen it yet?" In requiring the child to represent to himself the outcome of a transformation, his initial response will be, "How can I know if it has not yet been done?"

This tendency is often supplemented by an educational approach that emphasizes sensorial stimuli and concrete motor behavior as the preferred, if not the sole, way to teach these children. Thus, the lack of interiorized representational behavior not only is the product of a lack of mediated learning experience, at both early and later stages of development, but is reinforced as well by prolonged and exclusive exposure to and reliance upon concrete sensorial data. The lack of interiorized representation has an important bearing on both academic and nonacademic behavior. Planning cannot be conceived of without interiorized representation as a plan in the attempt to bridge between the present and a nonexistent future. It aims at a goal which, by definition, is not yet concretized. Planning is exclusively dependent on the representation of interiorized goals. The incapacity of the individual to represent to himself the future or the outcome of a transformation may severely limit his behavior because it will reduce his judgment and, even more, confine his needs to the "here" and "now."

The well known and frequently cited incapacity of these children to delay gratification, often characterized as a personality and motivational trait, is interpreted differently in our framework. We see the unwillingness to delay gratification and the "here and now" orientation as attributable mainly to the limited capacity of the retarded performing individual to represent to himself a nonexistent future. This does not of course negate the importance of many non-intellective factors active in the life of the deprived child, such as a lack of security or a lack of prospects for a better future, which contribute to a predisposition for opting for the immediate. The choices of the culturally deprived are strongly delimited by the few existing alternatives that are usually taken from the "here and now." It is easier for the child who lacks the capacity for interiorization to represent to himself the pleasure of using all of his money on goodies than to anticipate the pleasures and benefits involved in delaying his gratification. By the same token, the capacity to delay gratification for the benefit of a more remote goal is strongly limited by the lack of capacity of the individual to represent such goals to himself or to compare the represented goals with his current status or with the expected outcome of his yielding to immediate gratification. Interiorized representational thinking is a highly complex product involving a great variety of cognitive components that combine with motivational and emotional determinants of behavior. Therefore, the readiness to plan ahead will vary in different individuals according to cognitive, emotional, and attitudinal dimensions.

The author remembers his own experiences of being shocked at the long-term planning behavior of his colleagues in the Kibbutz. Their 5-year plan seemed to him futile and totally unrealistic against the background of his previous day-to-day experience in a concentration camp where one could not conceive of a future beyond the hour. The same is true in many other situations in which planning is not economical. Failure to plan ahead thus does not always reflect an incapacity for or lack of interiorization. It can be attributable to the environment or internal motivational attitudinal conditions of the organism. However, in the case of the culturally deprived, the cognitive components, such as lack of interiorized representational behavior, should not be underestimated and may even be more prominent than the motivational affective factors.

LACK OF, OR IMPAIRED, PLANNING BEHAVIOR

Deficient planning behavior is mentioned above in the description of interiorization with respect to the construction and representation of more remote goals. However, planning not only consists of setting of goals that are located both temporally and spatially at a given distance from the "here" and "now" but also involves the dissociation of the aims set forth from the means necessary to achieve them. This dissociation requires a further differentiation of the means in terms of the steps that are necessary to achieve the final goal. The steps must be planned according to a certain degree of detail, must be ordered in terms of their temporal sequence, and must be judged for suitability in terms of investment, feasibility, economy, and other criteria that may be critical for the individual. Thus, the planning of one's vocational future may require unpleasant detours involving a maximum of investment in, and commitment to, activities that are not necessarily consonant with one's immediate needs. The readiness to plan and accept such an investment is closely related to the capacity to enumerate and sum the required activities and compare them with the anticipated outcome. Such planning behavior is usually learned and exercised on short term goals and is then applied to long range objectives as a response to the enlarged system of needs and the possibility of anticipating satisfaction and fulfillment.

The incapacity to anticipate the outcome of behavior may be caused by deficiencies inherent in the individual, such as a lack of representation, a lack of intrinsic locus of control, and so on. It may also be attributable to the objective situation which makes prediction a very difficult, if not impossible, task. In the case of the culturally deprived, these two determinants may converge and combine in reducing planning behavior to a minimum. Individuals who have been raised in conditions of poverty and constant danger may fail to plan and anticipate because their life conditions have never allowed them to actively determine their own future. Such individuals have been taught by circumstances that there is no alternative to a hand-to-mouth existence because they cannot foresee, much less determine, what the next moment will bring. This may be, and in certain cases may become, the reason for a reduced need to plan one's behavior. Because the individual is never put into a position of having to predict, he does not acquire the necessary skill and orientation toward planning behavior. This, in turn, may affect other functions at the input and output levels and thereby render attempts at future planning uneconomical.

EGOCENTRIC COMMUNICATIONAL MODALITIES

Egocentric communicational modalities refers to an impairment of communication output as a consequence of the way in which an individual regards his partner with whom he is involved in a transaction. Egocentric communication is a function of a lack of differentiation, which does not allow the individual to see his partner as different from himself. This differentiation is a necessary condition for making communication explicit by producing all the evidence necessary for the listener's comprehension of the information conveyed to him. In many cases, the child limits his communication in terms of detail, precision, and argumentation because of the attitude "How can he think differently than I do?" or "How is it possible that he doesn't know what I know?" This type of undifferentiated approach to another is even more accentuated when the interaction is between a child and a teacher or examiner. The child is not willing to accept the idea of being examined and limits his responses to the necessary minimum because it is clear to him that his responses are well known to his partner and, therefore, futile to communicate.

The egocentric communication modality is apparent when there is a necessity to provide evidence for claims and arguments. Here, the lack of need for logical evidence may further aggravate this impaired communication modality.

BLOCKING

A frequently observed phenomenon in culturally deprived children is the polarity between acting-out, agitated, unplanned, impulsive behavior, and quasi-total blockage of responses. This blocking often follows a prolonged trial-and-error activity that results in failure. Blocking may range from a lack of initiation of new responses to an open avoidance of encounter with stimuli that may place the individual in a position to react. Blocking, in this context, must be considered as a response to cognitive failure, affecting the readiness of the organism to enter again into an endeavor that may lead to failure.

This behavior requires an understanding beyond the motivational aspect to which it is usually attributed. It seems to resemble somewhat the reaction found in Pavlovian conditioning experiments during which blocking reactions were observed in response to ambiguous stimuli.

TRIAL-AND-ERROR RESPONSES

Trial-and-error behavior is often suggested as an efficient means to teach the child rules and principles through discovery, as opposed to ready-made responses or imitative reproductive types of learning. This is certainly true for the learner who, by virtue of his mastery of the prerequisites of cognitive processes such as precise perception, comparing, summation, reflective thinking, and an orientation to search for causal relationships, can relate the obtained effects of his behavior to the specific antecedent behaviors that have produced them. However, the fact that the culturally deprived child is deficient in these very functions disables him from making proper use of the experiences offered to him by trial and error. The sequence in which events occur, their order in space, and their quantitative or qualitative dimensions, even if observed, are not related to the outcome, its quality, its property, its nature, and its location. To a certain extent, then, exposure to, or encouragement of, trial-and-error learning may actually reinforce a kind of probabilistic, random behavior, diverting the attention of the individual and distracting him from the relationships to be discovered. This is consonant with our definition of the culturally deprived as an individual seldom sufficiently modified by direct exposure to sources of stimuli, irrespective of whether they are only perceived or whether they are acted upon. Trial-and-error behavior is, from this point of view, a typical situation in which direct exposure is the prevalent mode of interaction between the child and the environment.

The environment *per se* is not structured to elicit appropriate and adaptive responses that enable the child to focus on the relationship of one specific behavior directed toward achievement of a desired outcome, as compared with other less adaptive behaviors. Thus, trial and error in a child who cannot, on his own, systematize his search for a goal, or who does not always conserve the goal he has set for himself, will of necessity be of limited value in establishing the relationship between his response and its outcome.

In many instances in which trial-and-error behavior has been used as a training procedure, rather limited results have been obtained, and, in certain cases, a slowdown of training may be observed. The same is true when the nature of the materials and the structure of the task, which the child is asked to act upon, involve him in trial-and-error behavior. Such conditions reduce significantly the capacity of the child to deduce the rules and their application to new situations. Knowing the propensity of the culturally deprived child to acting out, trial-and-error behavior should be discouraged until the corrected cognitive functions will permit him to benefit from this activity.

DEFICIENCY OF VISUAL TRANSPORT

Deficiency of visual transport is defined as the incapacity of the retarded performer to complete a given figure by visually transporting a missing part from a given distance or by choosing the complementary missing part from a number of alternatives. That the difficulty is engendered by the visual transport of data from a given distance to the place where they belong is evidenced by the fact that the same child often succeeds in the task when his response involves a visual-motor gesture, such as drawing the completed figure in the air with his finger, or even when his response entails a graphic presentation of the completed figure. It seems that, in transporting the missing part visually, something is lost on the way, and, therefore, an inappropriately oriented figure is chosen (often after the task has been successfully completed through motor or even verbal modalities). It is known that difficulty in visual transport is observed in normally developing individuals when complexity is increased by factors surrounding perceptual elements that make a discrimination between them difficult. Thus, in a task in which the response must be made on a control panel, identical to that on which the stimulus was presented, the individual is likely to produce more errors than when reacting to the stimulus on the original panel.

In the culturally deprived child, two factors often seem to be involved in the experienced difficulty in visual transport. One is an instability of the perception itself, attributable to the vulnerable nature of the systems of reference supporting the perceived elements. The second relates to the narrowness of the mental field as the child becomes diverted by his encounter with irrelevant data, once his eyes stray from the source of the data to other sources of information. Consequently, he fails to conserve the image which he has formed and which was the original object of his search.

EPISODIC GRASP OF REALITY

A common thread running through virtually all of the above-described deficient functions is the phenomenon that we refer to as an episodic grasp of reality. Occupying a central position in our conception of deficient functions, it represents both a cognitive modality of interaction with reality and an energetic principle that determines the nature of the interaction. Episodic grasp of reality is, therefore, a bridge between the cognitive and affective-attitudinal determinants of behavior.

In essence, grasping the world episodically means that each object or event is experienced in isolation without any attempt to relate or link it to previous or anticipated experiences in space and time. An episodic grasp of reality reflects a passive attitude toward one's experiences because no attempt is made by the individual to actively contribute to his experience by organizing, ordering, summating, or comparing events and thereby placing them within a broader and more meaningful context. In this respect, the affective energetic principle is important because the organizational activity of the organism is, at least in its early stages, a product of a volitional, intentional, and purposeful effort on the part of the individual. This is in contrast to the more elementary cognitive processes, such as identification, recognition, association, and even reproduction, which do not necessarily rely for their adequate functioning on a purposeful and intentional orientation of the organism. Thus, an episodic grasp of reality is related to deficiencies in extrinsic and intrinsic need systems of the individual that render the active organization of information unnecessary and uneconomical.

As an umbrella concept, episodic grasp of reality must be understood as being determined by and, at the same time, determining many of the deficient functions previously discussed. Grasping an event episodically reduces it to vague and undefined dimensions with little relation of its most relevant characteristics to other events that have preceded and that may follow. A lack of comparative behavior, which epitomizes an episodic grasp of reality, limits our experiences to unique and unconnected events closely tied to the concrete here and now. Similarly, a lack of grouping or summative behavior confines our experiences of the world to more concrete sensorimotor modalities. In contrast, when organizing and linking activities occur, the individual is forced to detach himself from direct sensorial experiences and to accede to levels of abstraction and conceptualization. It is only when reality needs to be represented, in order to categorize and establish relationships between objects and events, that the need for encoding information arises.

The passivity of the individual, reflected in an episodic grasp of reality, influences his self-image as a recipient rather than a generator of information. Generating information is, of necessity, contingent upon the need of the individual to bring together facts, to compare, re-evoke, order, re-order, group, and re-group objects and events that are remote in space and time. An episodic grasp of reality is also responsible for the limited readiness of the individual to respond to incompatibilities in the field that provide the basis for the recognition of the existence of a problem. This passive approach is often characteristic of the culturally deprived child, and, when asked to establish relationships between objects, his reaction will be one of surprise or resistance.

The propensity to contribute to one's interaction with the environment and experience of the world goes beyond that required by our biological needs. The development of the need to create order, to make sense of, and to provide meaning for our experiences is inconceivable without mediated learning experience. Very often, the behavior attributed to the retarded performer is an expression of his episodic grasp of reality, which is manifested in his failure to act on and go beyond the mere registration of incoming stimuli and information. In terms of our approach, any attempt to modify a child must involve a fundamental reorientation of his encounter with reality. What is required is a change from a passive episodic grasp of reality to an active mode of interacting with the environment by operating on and transforming experiences and, thereby, detaching oneself from the constraints and limits imposed by the sheer sensorial perception of the world.

5
THE COGNITIVE MAP

Instrumental Enrichment is based on a theoretical framework that takes into account the structure of intelligence of the retarded performer; the motivational aspects of his functioning, influenced not only by his cognitive structure but also by environmental and cultural dimensions that determine his needs system; and the necessity for his redevelopment as determined by the conditions of life in the modern technological society to which he must adapt. The construction of Instrumental Enrichment materials, as well as the didactics of their application, is based on a cognitive map that aids in the categorization and definition of the components of mental acts. The cognitive map is the basis for the analysis of the cognitive behavior of the retarded performer and for a better understanding of the more general goals of the FIE program, above and beyond the nature of the instruments with which one attempts to attain them. The specific parameters of the map, or model, serve in analyzing the various components of the program, much like a taxonomy to establish the sequence of processes included in the educational goal.

PARAMETERS OF THE COGNITIVE MAP

The model involves seven parameters by which a mental act can be analyzed, categorized, and ordered. A brief description of the parameters, together with some illustrations of their application, follows.

1. Content

Each mental act can be described according to the subject matter with which it deals and can be analyzed in terms of the universe of content on which it is operating. Subject matter can be derived from geography, history, mathematics, physics, philosophy, or a combination of such broad fields, in which the tools from one discipline can be applied to another. Thus, mathematics may be used to understand geological data, and psychological rules may explain historical events, while leaving the focus, however, on the specific universe of knowledge with which one is primarily concerned.

Content is one of the areas of cognitive functioning in which people differ greatly, with differences determined directly by experiential background, educational history, and the culturally determined saliency of certain universes of content. In comparing relative competency in specific areas of knowledge, consideration must first be given to the cultural characteristics of the individuals compared, and only then may a specific weight be ascribed to degrees of excellence or incompetency. Certain content may be so strange and different to an individual that it requires a very specific and intense investment for him to reach mastery. Therefore, when attempting to teach a specific cognitive operation, the role of content is important. If instruction is attempted with content that, itself, is so difficult that it absorbs all of the attention of the individual, the learner may be left with little or no capacity to focus on the specific operation that is the target of the teaching. In other cases, it might be unwise to use elements that are too familiar because they may not induce the state of vigilance necessary to arouse the attention and interest of the individual and to mobilize his capacities to function.

In constructing teaching materials, these considerations should influence the selection of content. Familiarity with the material may deter interest and motivation, even though the familiar content may be purposefully selected for the elaboration of mental operations. In diagnostic work, the capacity to assess and weigh the role of familiarity with the particular content in the success or failure of the child is of the utmost importance (see Feuerstein, 1972; Feuerstein et al., 1978).

Instrumental Enrichment attempts to avoid the teaching of specific content, and the rationale for the content-free nature of the program is presented in the next chapter. Reasons based on the resistances of the student, teacher, and curriculum are offered in support of the content-free aspect of the program.

2. Operations

An operation may be understood as an internalized, organized, coordinated set of actions in terms of which we elaborate upon information derived from external and internal sources. In the analysis of a mental act, it is necessary to define the precise nature of an implied operation. The operations may range from the simple recognition and identification of objects to more complex activities such as classification, seriation, logical multiplication, and the like. Furthermore, operations may be applied to existing information or may themselves require the generation of new data that are not immediately present in the existing informational repertoire of the individual, as in the case of syllogistic, analogical, or inferential reasoning. In defining the nature of an operation, it is important to identify the prerequisites necessary for its generation and application.

In designing exercises or curricula that involve certain operations, the definition of the operation must be followed in order to outline all the components of intervening elements necessary for its acquisition and/or application. The child, to make an analogy, must deduce the relationship existing between two sets of data. However, in order to be able to deduce that relationship, he will have to compare the components of the analogy. The attainment of the operation will be a goal that requires the planning of a series of steps that take into consideration both the structure of the operation and the individual's equipment for its acquisition.

3. Modality

A mental act may be expressed in a variety of languages. Its modality may be figurative, pictorial, numerical, symbolic, verbal, or a combination of these or others. There are a great many codes, ranging from mimicry and metalinguistic modes of communication to conventional signs that are totally detached from the content they signify. It is necessary to identify within which of these modalities the mental act occurs. Modalities of communication involve differentiation of various sensorial or motor systems, enabling rather complex mental processes to take place despite the limitations of certain modalities (e.g., sign language and gestures). The efficiency of specific modalities of communication may differ among various ethnic, socioeconomic, and cultural groups or among individuals, according to their level of functioning and special deficiencies. By way of illustration, the case of one child is briefly described below.

> On examining a child with an IQ of 40, who had been diagnosed as moderately retarded (a diagnosis challenged by the author with the help of the Learning Potential Assessment Device, Feuerstein, 1972, Feuerstein et al. 1978), it was discovered that many of his difficulties were linked to a severe impairment of eye-hand coordination and visual-motor behavior. Thus, for example, he showed a total inability to draw a cross of two bisecting lines. When asked to produce a cross he usually superimposed the two lines or drew them as parallels. After hundreds of trials in which he repeatedly failed to reproduce the cross, it was decided to abandon all graphic work with him. However, one final attempt was made. This time the examinee was neither given a model to copy nor was a cross drawn in front of him but, instead, he was given the verbal instructions: "Draw one line and another line to cross it." The examinee suddenly proved able to perform the act successfully and consistently, showing his definite preference for the receptive verbal modality of presentation of the problem, despite his limited and impaired expressive verbal behavior. This insight changed drastically the instructional strategies used with the child and their efficiency in modifying his cognitive behavior.

The modality in which tasks are presented deserves careful consideration by the examiner and teacher in the construction and use of both diagnostic and instructional materials. Answers should be provided to the following questions: What will most readily be accessible to the examinee or the student? What is most necessary for the examiner to assess or to teach? What is the role played by the specific modality in producing a given successful or failing response? These are only a few of the questions to which an analysis of the modalities of presentation may offer an answer. A quasi-total failure in the response to an analogy presented in a numerical form will not necessarily reflect the child's ability to handle analogies as such because he may prove able to use such operations when the modality of presentation is figural or verbal. Can one decide, on the basis of his failure on the numerical modality, that the analogical operation *sui generis* is inaccessible to the child? On the other hand, using the same example, the difficulty involved in using a particular modality, numbers in this case, may have to be understood in order to be challenged. However, as long as the operation is erroneously considered responsible for the failure, rather than the modality in which it was presented, no meaningful target may be established for producing the desired change and improvement.

4. Phase

A fourth parameter deals with the phase in which the specific mental act takes place. The mental act can be broadly divided into three phases: *input, elaboration,* and *output.* These phases are interconnected and the role of each phase can only be considered in relation to the others.

However, bearing in mind the interplay between the phases, it is beneficial for didactic and descriptive purposes to isolate each phase in attempting to explain the relationship between a response and the stimulus which elicited it.

For obvious reasons, the isolation of the phase and the assignment of a differential weight will be neither necessary nor possible whenever the response is successful. However, the opposite holds in the case of failure. The individual may have failed because of inappropriate data gathering, which has resulted in incomplete or imprecise information. Furthermore, the inappropriate data may have been properly elaborated and, on that basis, an adequate response produced and communicated, yet the solution will be considered a failure because of the deficient input. The same may occur with the deficiencies in the output phase. Again, one may have gathered the data and elaborated them with mental operations appropriate to the specific task. But the result of a proper input and elaboration may nevertheless be communicated in a way more or less discordant and inconsistent with both the data and their elaboration. Failure may also occur during the elaboration phase as a result of the nonexistence or improper application of certain operations in the cognitive repertoire of the individual.

In the culturally deprived retarded performer and many other dysfunctioning children, deficiencies on the levels of input and output are frequently observed with a relatively less deficient capacity for elaboration. In many cases, elaboration, or the capacity of the child to operate mentally, can be modified with relatively little investment. On the other hand, deficiencies of input and output, which are responsible for the low level of efficiency, are much more resistant to change. It is our experience that input and output deficiencies require Sisyphean action to be changed in the desired direction.

Phase is an important parameter in the analysis of a child's mental act in that it helps to locate the source of an inadequate response. This enables consideration to be given to the nature of the investment needed to elicit higher levels of efficiency in the individual.

5.   Level of Complexity

Level of complexity may be understood as the quantity and quality of units of information necessary to produce a given mental act. The number may involve separate objects or groups, but the emphasis is on the units and/or operations. Although difficult to define, we consider a "unit" to involve those dimensions that are of immediate necessity for a specific mental act to take place. Complexity, then, requires a differentiated count that considers simultaneously the number of information units and the quality of the units in terms of their degree of novelty or familiarity. The more familiar the units, the less complex the act, even if units are multiple; conversely, the less familiar, the more complex will be the mental act. The parameter of complexity, based on number and novelty of units, is of importance in both assessment and preparation of instructional materials, and has broad implications for didactics.

6.   Level of Abstraction

By means of the parameter of abstraction level, we define the distance between the given mental act and the object or event on which it operates. The parameters described above can be conceived of as operating directly on objects or events. Thus, the content may involve objects that can be sensorially perceived or handled completely by motor manipulation. Different modalities may be used and operations involving adding, subtracting, and grouping real objects or their substitutes may be applied. However, the previously discussed parameters do not take into account the extent to which the elements upon which operations are performed are removed from the originally perceived objects or events.

Thus, a mental act may involve operations on the objects themselves, such as sorting them according to some classification system. At a more abstract level, operations may be performed on representations of objects, such as applying a classification to a set of hypothetical objects. Even more abstract is the application of operations to purely hypothetical propositions without reference to real or imagined objects or events. Thus, a hierarchy of levels of abstraction can be established, using as a criterion the distance between the mental operation and the universe of objects or events to which it is applied.

7.   Level of Efficiency

The mental act can also be described and analyzed according to the degree and level of efficiency with which it is produced. As a criterion for efficiency one may use the rapidity-precision complex and/or the amount of effort objectively and subjectively exerted by the individual in his production of the particular act. The concept of efficiency can be conceived of as a dimension that is different, both qualitatively and quantitatively, from the other six parameters even though it may be determined or affected by one or more of the parameters or a combination of them. For example, a low level of complexity, as a result of familiarity with a given content or with particular cognitive operations, may render efficient the mental act operating on these particular areas.

Lack of efficiency, as defined by slowness, reduced production, or by imprecise, inefficient handling of a problem, may be totally irrelevant to the capacity of the individual to grasp and elaborate a particular problem. Our inability to isolate efficiency from capacity is an important source of error in assessment, not only of the individual's true capacity but even of his repertoire of information and skills. Such an error, stemming from the confusion between efficiency and capacity, results in faulty labeling and the formulation of a prognosis based on an erroneous assumption of low capacity that has been derived solely from an observed low level of efficiency. This, in turn, determines the low level of educational, vocational, and other life goals established for the individual.

Efficient handling of a task is always contingent upon a variety of task-intrinsic and/or task-extrinsic factors affecting the individual. Anxiety or a lack of motivation may disrupt one's efficiency in a particular task. However, the degree of crystallization of the mental act and its automatization may determine the nature and the magnitude of the impact of these variables on the individual's efficiency. The more recently acquired the pattern of behavior, the greater its vulnerability and the less resistant will it be to the impact of interfering factors. The more established and crystallized the pattern, the less will emotional factors disrupt its proper functioning.

The same is true of motivation. In describing the nature and quantity of motivation of groups of children demonstrating different levels of achievement, one tends to explain the lower levels of functioning by the concept of "motivation," which is regarded as being different and correspondingly lower in low performing children. However, as the individual's efficiency is determined, at least in part, by his familiarity with the objects, events, and operations involved, so the degree of motivation required to mobilize the energy needed to produce a mental act is much higher for the culturally deprived than for the more advantaged student. The differential investment, determined by the different levels of efficiency characteristic of these groups, will itself determine the amount of motivation required to produce the necessary investment. Thus, even if motivation is kept equal, the outcome of a mental act may differ since lower levels of efficiency require greater amounts of effort.

One of the most important dimensions in the development of efficiency in cognitive operations is the progressive automatization of certain behaviors, a process which results in a reduction in the amount and level of effort needed to produce a given mental act. The process of automatization, through familiarization with certain components of the task, brings about a capability of expending most of one's energy in those areas that still require investment for the mastery of the task in a more rapid and precise way. The less automatic the operation, the greater is the vigilance required to master all of its components and the less efficient the handling of the task. By the same token, inefficiency may be produced in a familiar task if an attempt is made to discover in the task unimplied relationships, because effort is diverted into areas other than those for which the task was initially intended. One may observe a slowdown in the functioning of highly intelligent individuals when they are presented with tasks too easy for them because they invest much more than they need by searching for more complex elements than actually exist in the task.

If our concept of efficiency is accepted, the meager results often obtained with disadvantaged individuals following recent intervention may require a very different interpretation (Jensen, 1969). What seems to be an *inefficiency* of a program designed to modify the level of functioning of an individual or the resistance of the learner to attempts at modification may very well be only a measure of the low efficiency demonstrated by the subjects of intervention in the implementation of their newly acquired skills or operations. This inefficiency may obscure the real changes produced by the intervention that may have affected the elaborational capacities of the individual but not, as yet, their efficient use. Whenever newly acquired operations and strategies are assessed, one must consider the high level of investment required in the initial stage of their use. Correspondingly, a weight must be ascribed to an individual's low efficiency, which is attributable to the recency of acquisition and the lack of automatization of the cognitive tools used for the solution of a given problem. Such an interpretation would direct the analysis of the data toward areas of functioning that may produce evidence of the role played by the level of efficiency. Consequently, a more accurate meaning may be ascribed to the induced change in areas of cognitive functioning that are not affected, or are less affected, by the recency of the newness of the situation.

The concept of crystallized intelligence may be equated here with the concept of automatized behavior. In common to both is a relatively low level of investment and vigilance for the production of a given mental act, as compared with the operations described as the fluid type of intelligence in which the use of previously acquired elements is more limited. The concept of inefficiency produced by the newness of a situation is supported by Konrad and Melzack (1975) in their work entitled "Novelty Enhancement Effects Associated with Early Sensory-Social Isolation," in which they reinterpret the results obtained by Hebb on the inefficiency in problem-solving behavior of organisms that were sensory-deprived through isolation. Konrad and Melzack contend that there is a direct relationship between the degree of novelty represented by the environment, which produced in the deprived organism a greater need for exploration, and a higher level of investment in certain parts of the stimuli. These parts of the environment are familiar to the nondeprived organism and therefore easily mastered by it. However, the greater amount of investment and higher level of effort required by the deprived organism are then translated into the relative inefficiency of the organism in its coping with new situations. Konrad and Melzack produced evidence for the progressive increase in efficiency with the corresponding decrease in novelty until a state of total recovery is reached by the deprived organism exposed to stimuli. This interpretation is significant in that it places the main emphasis on functional determinants of the behavior of the organism rather than on organic substrata of the deficiency that are usually considered irreversible.

In analyzing a mental act, the reason for inefficiency may be located and associated with any of the previously mentioned parameters: the content; the level of complexity, which is defined by the number of units of information as corrected for the degree of novelty; the level of abstraction, which requires the organization of data; the establishment of relationships; the organization and categorization of the relationships themselves; and the level of familiarity of the operation, or the differential amount of investment needed to decode a specific modality of presentation of the problem.

ANALYZING A MENTAL ACT WITH THE COGNITIVE MAP

The use of the cognitive map in an analysis of inferential thought processes may be illustrated by the following example of a transitive ordered set:

$$\text{given } A > B, \ B > C, \ C > D,$$
$$\text{then } A > D, \ B > D$$

The information that $A > D$ and $B > D$ is not offered in a direct way through observation or statement but is available indirectly from other observations. It must be derived, logically and inferentially, from the previously given information. This enables us to analyze the various parameters involved in this process. The first step involves a symbolic representation of the given entities, A, B, C, and D. In terms of content, they may be countries, plants, animals, or political groups. In terms of operations, $A > B > C > D$ represents a transitive thought process, permitting the derivation of new information from previously gathered data. The modality in which this mental act is presented is strictly symbolic since no verbal, numerical, or figurative modes are used. $A > B$, $B > C$, and $C > D$ represent the input phase of the mental act. Here, what is required from the individual is that he become aware of and store the relationships of "larger than" as identities that exist between these terms.

The elaboration phase starts when new information is sought from the previously given relationships. The relationships of "larger than" established between A and B, B and C, and C and D have the identity of the relation "larger than" in common. This permits the enunciation of the newly generated relationships between A and D, and B and D. The whole statement $A > B$, $B > C$, $C > D$, $A > D$, $B > D$ involves three units of information that are given on the input phase and two that are derived on the elaborational phase. It can therefore be considered as a complex task, relative to other tasks, such as one that includes only $A > B$ and $B > C$ so that $A > C$. In addition to increasing the number of units, the level of complexity may also be increased by introducing novel relationships. However, in other cases, increasing the number of units of information may facilitate the operation, as demonstrated by Haywood, Filler, Shifman, and Chatelnat (1975).

The sixth parameter, the level of abstraction, is defined by the distance between the mental act and the content on which it operates. The present example has a relatively high level of abstraction because it involves the generation of new information derived from the relationships obtaining between the objects or events rather than from the objects themselves.

The seventh parameter, the level of efficiency, will be reflected in the manner, rhythm, pace, precision, and degree of ease with which this mental act is produced.

SUMMARY

The cognitive map represents a model in terms of which mental acts may be analyzed according to seven parameters: content, operations, modality, phase, level of complexity, level of abstraction, and level of efficiency. In our theoretical framework, the map, in conjunction with the inventory of deficient functions, explains cognitive behavior by analyzing its components, and locating and interpreting any weaknesses that may occur. Through a process-oriented approach, the cognitive map and the repertoire of deficient functions enable a dynamic assessment of a child's functioning. The cognitive map also assists the examiner and teacher in the selection of instruments and the techniques for their application according to the specific needs of a child. It is helpful, as well, in setting goals for intervention and in the construction of the means and didactics of attaining these goals. The manner in which the cognitive map is used in the analysis of the instruments and preparation of lessons is illustrated in Chapter 7.

6
GOALS AND STRUCTURE OF INSTRUMENTAL ENRICHMENT

The major goal of the Feuerstein Instrumental Enrichment (FIE) program and the six subgoals through which it is attained are briefly presented in this chapter. After a discussion of the structure of the material and an introduction to the instruments themselves, the initiated reader will be better prepared to explore with the author the way in which the subgoals of Instrumental Enrichment and the cognitive map served as the guidelines for the construction of the material.

The following description of the characteristics of Instrumental Enrichment is therefore presented for the reader who is interested in developing an organizing orientation to the material discussed in depth in later chapters. The goals of FIE are discussed in greater detail in Chapter 8.

GOALS OF INSTRUMENTAL ENRICHMENT

Major Goal

The major goal of Instrumental Enrichment is to increase the capacity of the human organism to become modified through direct exposure to stimuli and experiences provided by the encounters with life events and with formal and informal learning opportunities.

Specific Subgoals

In order to attain the major goal of Instrumental Enrichment during adolescence, the following six subgoals serve as guidelines for the construction of the Instrumental Enrichment program and its application.

I. The foremost subgoal is, of necessity, the *correction* of the deficient functions that characterize the cognitive structure of the culturally deprived individual. Although the severity of the impairment of individual functions and the degree of resistance to intervention attempts may differ among the culturally deprived in accordance with the distal etiological determinants that have contributed to the condition, the impaired functions are greatly interdependent. Their appearances at the input, elaboration, and output phases of the mental act call for a generalized attack on these deficient functions as a means to changing the structure of the cognitive behavior, and the attitude and the motivation of the culturally deprived.

II. The second subgoal, the acquisition of basic concepts, labels, vocabulary, operations, and relationships necessary for FIE, represents the content dimension of the instruments, which themselves are purposely content-free. Many, although not all, culturally deprived children are devoid of the basic concepts and grasp of relationships necessary for mastery of cognitive tasks such as those presented to them in FIE. Such concepts have to be taught actively and systematically in order to make the instrument accessible to the child. FIE does not attempt to teach these operational terms as goals, *per se,* but rather as prerequisites for the representational, relational, and operational thinking required by the program.

III.   The third subgoal is the production of intrinsic motivation through habit formation. This subgoal is a unique characteristic of Feuerstein's Instrumental Enrichment in contrast to many programs that purport similar overall goals. One of the problems confronting those who attempt to modify the cognitive structure of the deprived child and adolescent is that many of the changes induced in the child depend for their reinforcement on the active mobilization of needs that the environment of the child is very unlikely to produce. Thus, whatever is learned in an enrichment program may be totally useless once the child has stepped out of the school, because outside of the school environment nothing will encourage, much less require, the use of these skills. Categorization or use of a spatial system of reference may be totally useless in the social environment of the child. Syllogistic thinking, implicit or explicit, may not be of operational value in an environment in which immediate, direct, and concrete evidence serves as the only way to convince one's partner.

Whatever is acquired in a program that aims at the creation of higher levels of mental operations may, therefore, be totally dwarfed and abandoned because its use is dependent on a need that seldom appears in the social environment of the child. In order to ensure that whatever is taught will become part of an active repertoire, spontaneously used by the individual, one has to ensure that the need for its use will be an intrinsic one rather than a response to an extrinsic need system. Such an intrinsic need can be produced in this population only by habit formation. Habit can be defined as an internal need system, the activation of which has become detached from and independent of the extrinsic need that initially produced it.

IV.   The fourth subgoal is the production of reflective, insightful processes in the student as a result of his confrontation with both his failing and succeeding behaviors in the FIE tasks. This particular goal both is bound to the tasks of FIE and, of more importance, transcends them. It is also a goal that can be reached only by the direct intervention of the teacher, and its achievement is often augmented by group processes in the classroom. The culturally deprived adolescent is very often described as an individual who is addicted to acting-out behavior. He is said to be involved in a variety of peripheral motor manipulations with little tendency to reflect on his behavior by asking Wh-questions (e.g., "What?", "Why?"). The tendency toward introspection, in which the individual takes himself as an object of observation and study, is rarely observed in the deprived adolescent. Rather, he constantly searches for external stimuli with very little investment in relating them to certain conditions they produce in himself. This is very similar to the minimal effort made by the adolescent to bring order into the stimuli impinging upon him from the outside. Reflective thinking is also closely linked to the capability of the individual to delay or even to inhibit responses in order to allow a more organized, articulated, and differentiated response, which can result only from taking into account more related factors.

V.   The fifth subgoal is the creation of task-intrinsic motivation. Task intrinsic motivation has two aspects: the enjoyment of a task for its own sake and the social meaning of success in a task that is difficult even for initiated adults (see Chapter 8). Paradoxically, despite the appealing nature of the instruments, FIE is neither defined nor designed as a play activity. Instead, the learner must consider it as a purposeful and meaningful investment in a program of cognitive development, by means of which his learning process will become facilitated and accelerated. In order to achieve this attitude, the instruments had to be constructed with a power to attract the learner, a quality that would make the individual view the tasks not only as a means for reaching an objective, which is external to the activity itself, but as a source of an autotelic pleasure. One of the well known phenomena of the cognitively deficient adolescent is his limited readiness to become involved in activities that do not provide him with material- or status-oriented immediate gratification. Performing for performance' sake is very seldom observed. Gratuitous activities that are not given proper material or social sanctions are seldom initiated and, even less frequently, continued. It is therefore of greatest importance, and a very vital component of any strategy of redevelopment, to enrich the repertoire of behaviors of the cognitively deficient adolescent with activities that are neither limited to nor leading directly to immediate extrinsic goals.

VI.   The sixth subgoal of FIE is probably one of the most vital aspects of the program, because it concerns the energetic principle underlying autonomous cognitive behavior. This subgoal deals with the attitude of the retarded performing individual toward himself as an organism able to generate information and his readiness to function as such, as a result of this self-perception. Self-perception is a very important component of human behavior because it represents the sum total of the expectations an individual has of himself. These expectations elicit certain types of behavior from the individual, according to the attributes he exhibits. The culturally deprived, retarded performing individual perceives himself as a recipient of information and accordingly, at best, as its reproducer, rather than as one who can become a generator of new knowledge and information.

The operational reflection of this attitude will easily be perceived in the limited readiness of the individual to engage in any cognitive operation for which no direct external model for reproduction has been offered to him.

His attitude toward his competencies and the nature of his cognitive functioning limits his readiness to operate on the information available to him from external sources in order to generate information not immediately accessible. The passivity of the culturally deprived retarded performer toward incoming stimuli and toward himself is also responsible for a host of other attitudinal, motivational, and emotional determinants of his behavior. Thus, the aim of the sixth subgoal is to arouse the learner from his role of passive recipient and reproducer of information and turn him into an active generator of new information.

CHARACTERISTICS OF INSTRUMENTAL ENRICHMENT MATERIAL

Structural Nature of Material

The Instrumental Enrichment material is structured as units, or instruments, each of which emphasizes a particular cognitive function. Despite the specificity of subject for each instrument, its tasks address themselves to a multiplicity of deficiencies. Furthermore, attainment of all six subgoals of the program is an objective common to all of the instruments.

This structural nature assists the teacher in his choice of the instruments to be taught and their sequence of presentation. Knowledge of the focus of each instrument enables a selection and matching of specific material to the needs and deficits of particular children in remedial work or prescriptive teaching. At the same time, since the construction of all of the instruments was in accordance with the same principles and objectives, their successful utilization is ensured with groups that are heterogeneous with respect to etiologies of retarded performance and the deficient functions of their members.

By isolating the source of retarded performance in terms of deficient cognitive functions, the Learning Potential Assessment Device, administered individually or in group settings, is of tremendous benefit in the selection of the particular instruments to be used. However, when testing is not possible, the structure of the instruments still enables their effective utilization in mixed classroom settings. Even in the rare case of an individual student within the group who evinces mastery of the tasks of a specific topic before intervention, participation in the study of that instrument has been determined to be of value to him. Not only is there a boost to his self-image as a result of his successful utilization of the cognitive functions emphasized in the instrument, but he acquires insight into his cognitive behavior, both its strengths and weaknesses. He also profits from the intervention of the instrument in other functions in which he may still be deficient.

Instrumental Nature of Material

An "instrument" is defined as "that by which or by means of which something is effected" (Stein, 1966). It is this view of the material, as a means for attaining adequate cognitive structure, not as an end in and of itself, that governed the construction of the material. This instrumental nature is also of prime importance in the didactics of presentation, the plan of the lesson, mode of student-teacher interaction, and evaluation of achievement. The shift from material as an objective to material as a tool has as its corollary a shift from product orientation to process orientation, with a corresponding emphasis on "how" rather than on "what." A student's errors are not merely recorded as evidence of his failures or as indicative of a need for further review of information, but their source is explored in terms of the parameters of the cognitive map to produce insight in the learning process.

Such analysis may reveal that the student's response was actually correct on the basis of his perception of the input. The statements "I turned on the radio" and "The doorbell rang" are presented, among others, in an exercise in which the student is asked to indicate whether the relationship between the two events is one of cause and effect or coincidental. One student indicated that a causal relationship existed between the two events. When the teacher insisted that this answer was incorrect, the boy exclaimed, "But, teacher, you don't know our neighbor. Every time I turn on the radio, she's at the door, telling me to turn it off!" By the same token, a correct response may be the result of chance, a guess, or perseveration without any attempt by the student to cope with the question he is answering.

The instrumentality of the material is demonstrated by its content-free nature. The rationale behind this characteristic is considered below.

Content-Free Nature of Material

Instrumental Enrichment does not attempt to teach either specific items of information or formal, operational, abstract thinking by means of a well defined, structured set of data. As much as possible, Instrumental Enrichment actually avoids the use of content. It is true that one cannot totally eliminate content when dealing with prerequisites of operational thinking or with the cognitive operations themselves. However, the content of an instrument is only a vehicle and is considered as secondary to the major goal, which is the acquisition of prerequisites of thinking. Simple, familiar material has been selected and presented in order to hold the attention of the child, while his orientation and his efforts are on the deficient function to be corrected, rather than on the content itself. The teacher is then able to keep the child aware and conscious of the goal of the tasks without the dissipation and diffusion of his efforts on aspects of content.

This content-free approach has raised many questions among learning theorists, especially among those who deal with the didactics of enrichment programs for the cognitively deficient. Their question is to what extent should noncurricular materials, rather than the content situations of the academic curriculum, be used as a source of development of cognitive operations and the prerequisites of thinking. Moreover, they raise doubts as to the efficiency of pure formalized exercises that are detached from content and unrooted in a specific reality in affecting the real-life behavior or approach of the child. In other words, to what extent can one hope that cognitive behavior taught with content-free material will then be applied to real life situations or to content-oriented learning when the student is confronted by them?

SOURCES OF RESISTANCE TO USE OF CONTENT

The content-free structure of our instruments was determined in response to four major resistances that, in our consideration, impede the use of curricular contentual learning for enhancing and modifying cognitive behaviors. The first resistance is that of the learner, the culturally deprived retarded performer. The second resistance is that of the material and of the content. The third is the resistance of the teacher, and the fourth resistance is that generated by previous experience of failure.

Resistance of the Learner

The culturally deprived adolescent, in many ways similar to the younger child, is an "action addict." Any units of concrete information attract him and keep him in a state of vigilance as long as there is action involving him in a state of tension toward the anticipated end. Once the tension is released, however, the child displays little readiness to stop his constant search for further stimulation in favor of organizing, articulating, elaborating, and reflecting on the recently gathered information. He offers great resistance to any attempts by the teacher to make him enter into a discussion of the material or into an analysis of its various components and the relationship existing between them.

The prolonged dwelling on the formal dimensions of the content and on the prerequisites of thinking makes the learner feel that time is being stolen from activities that are more appealing in favor of those that are of little immediate interest and/or of no use to him. This is especially true for the child who lives in an environment in which he is neither required nor encouraged to reflect upon his or others' behavior and the relationship of such behaviors to specific outcomes. The retarded performer is not accustomed to investing time and effort in reflecting on events rather than merely directly experiencing them by either acting or perceiving. Therefore, attempts to make him use content-rich subject matter for enhancing his cognitive functions by deriving from the material strategies instrumental to more efficient curricular learning (and such attempts have frequently been made) prove to be of little efficacy.

Another source of student resistance is the great propensity observed in the cognitively deficient to relate sets of stimuli to a specific concrete task. This task boundedness, determined largely by limited representational and hypothetical thinking, makes generalization based on exposure to specific content difficult, if not impossible. The "one-time" events presented to him in the content curriculum learning system neither permit nor facilitate the formation of more generalizable rules.

A final difficulty in the attempt to use content learning is the observed difficulty of the retarded performer in selecting and using relevant elements from a given set of data. Therefore, the exposure of the learner to situations that, by their very structure, focus his attention on the formal, operational prerequisites of thinking is of great advantage wherever these prerequisites have not been established in the individual by mediated learning experience.

Resistance of the Material

The second source of resistance lies in the structure of the materials of a content-oriented program. The goals set forth by FIE require a concerted attack upon a variety of deficiencies, with corrected cognitive functions established as habits by repetitive yet varied exposure. Any attempt to use curricular programs to achieve these objectives will either result in the production of hybrid-like content, with neither proper sequence nor flow of information, or will detract from the goals of producing the prerequisites of thinking. It helps very little, therefore, to impose the constructional rules of FIE on a curriculum of subject matter materials which has its own structure and needs. We find it preferable to present FIE as a stream of learning, complementary to the curricular program, with bridges between the two to mutually reinforce each other.

Resistance of the Teacher

One of the reasons for teacher-centered resistance emerges from the teacher's role as a representative of a system that demands a certain degree of efficiency and an identifiable end product as a result of the process of teaching. Any prolonged, repetitious elaboration of information is often perceived by educational systems as an impediment to the amount of new information, i.e., material, that can be taught. The teacher is confronted with the need to adhere to a materialistic approach toward the information he is supposed to transmit to his pupils, i.e., how much material can be covered in a particular period of time. This is even more pronounced when the teacher is faced with the pressure of supervisors as well as that imposed by the children themselves. "How much did we learn today? Only half a page. We haven't finished the first chapter yet." Such remarks by children and their parents represent an otherwise justified demand for a quantitative criterion of achievement.

A more important source of difficulty in using curricular learning for our specific goals is to be found in the incapacity of certain teachers to seize the opportunity presented by the curriculum for teaching and training the child in the appropriate cognitive behaviors. This inability should not be considered as reflective of the level of intelligence of the teacher or even the extent of his competency in more traditional teaching roles. It is attributable, rather, to the little orientation a teacher has to the prerequisites of cognitive processes. He takes their existence in the normal child for granted, and he is therefore more oriented to molar cognitive processes, such as those that are required by the transmission of information and establishment of basic school skills.

It is clear that one cannot expect the teacher to become efficient enough to be able to produce by himself, on an *ad hoc* basis, the necessary tools for teaching the prerequisites of thinking. More than two decades ago, the author (Feuerstein and Richelle, 1957), more naive than he is today, produced a set of paradigms for teaching cognitive processes by means of a language-based program. He hoped that the initiated and intelligent teacher would be able to produce more elaborate exercises for work with the deprived child by using the proposed paradigms. These paradigms proved inspirational, and many teachers adopted them for use in the regular teaching process. However, the teachers' capability of turning the paradigms into a systematic and sustained sequence of exercises was limited, and therefore the exercises were of no real meaning for the masses of children in need of a steady and continuous systematic intervention program.

After this experience, the author felt a need to offer ready-made instruments to the teacher. The construction of each instrument proved to require a sound theoretical basis in cognitive processes and in didactics with which the regular, and even the talented, teacher is not always equipped. Certain mental operations often go unrecognized by the classroom teachers as explicit and well defined entities, despite the teachers' implicit use of them in common everyday situations or even in teaching procedures. The automatic nature of these cognitive processes within the teacher is such that his failure to isolate the operations as entities that can be taught represents not a lack of capacity on the part of the teacher but rather a lack of orientation. Achieving the proper orientation requires special training and constant use and application.

The lack of orientation to the processes of operational thinking, much less the analysis of specific difficulties encountered by the deprived child, makes the teacher too task bound and consequently unprepared to fully derive from the materials a specific list of functions to be taught to the child. By involving the teacher himself in the training of operational thinking and by orienting him, through his active confrontation with the structure of the instruments, to the thinking process, we may enhance his capacity not only to apply FIE but also to make increasing use of the formal components of thinking in his work as a curriculum teacher.

Finally, the teacher of retarded performers tends to underestimate the capacity of these children to accede to higher levels of functioning. Consequently, he avoids involving them in unfamiliar cognitive processes, particularly those that he believes are completely inaccessible to them. This affects in a very deleterious way the retarded performer's amount and quality of exposure to levels of functioning not within his immediate repertoire. Very little, if any, opportunity is offered to him to become acquainted with, or even aware of, the existence of such operations. His condition is likely to perpetuate and reinforce the *status quo* of low level performance and functioning. However, once the teacher uses an instrument that requires a higher level of functioning and is prepared both theoretically and didactically for teaching it in a classroom situation, he may not only be successful in teaching, but, it is hoped, he may also become more convinced of the possibility of these children becoming modified, both in the structure of their intelligence and their level of achievement.

Previous Failure as a Source of Resistance

Many of our children have failed to achieve in regular school situations and in specific academic areas. Much of the curriculum content is unfair to the retarded performer because of his lack of familiarity with the material because of cultural differences or because of his lack of capacity to acquire information in a meaningful way because of cultural deprivation. The lack of content in the instruments fulfills the double role of making thought processes available to the child, despite all cultural differences, and of helping him to overcome the avoidance reaction to academic material commonly exhibited by children who have experienced failure throughout their school activities. Naturally, the lack of specific content in Instrumental Enrichment is not absolute and is relative to the meaning and weight ascribed to the content, the limited amount of investment it requires, and the previous experience needed by the child in order to achieve mastery.

SUMMARY

The major goal and the six subgoals of Instrumental Enrichment have been briefly reviewed in this chapter. The rationale for the content-free nature of the instruments has been analyzed from the viewpoint of the four identified resistances to the use of curricular material: that of the teacher, the student, and the material, and that stemming from previous experiences of failure. This brief presentation of the objectives, structure, and nature of the Instrumental Enrichment material should serve as a guide to the reader as he is introduced to the instruments, themselves, in Chapter 7. An analysis of these goals and the way in which they relate to the specific instruments is presented within the discussions of the instruments in Chapter 7 and then in more detail in Chapter 8.

7
INSTRUMENTAL ENRICHMENT: DESCRIPTION OF INSTRUMENTS

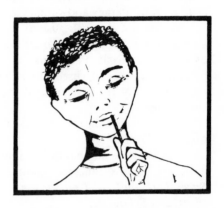

The Feuerstein Instrumental Enrichment program consists of more than 500 pages of paper-and-pencil exercises, divided into 15 instruments. Each instrument focuses on a specific cognitive deficiency but addresses itself to the acquisition of many other prerequisites of learning as well. Fourteen of these instruments are regularly used in any classroom implementation of the program and provide sufficient material for a 1-hour lesson, 3 to 5 days weekly for, depending on the program, a period of 2 or 3 years. For prescriptive remedial purposes, the psychologist, counselor, and/or educator select those instruments whose emphases match the specific needs of the pupil under treatment.

In this chapter, only those instruments that comprise the regular course of study at this point in the development of the FIE program are presented. This introduction to the instruments is not intended as a handbook or a manual for teaching. Instead, it limits itself to a discussion of each instrument in terms of its objectives, its structure, and the means by which it attempts to reach its specific goals. Some exercises and typical anecdotes from the field reports received by the author and his colleagues have been included to illustrate points made elsewhere in this text. When the anecdote has been translated into English, an effort has been made to preserve the style and tone of the speaker with all the slang and agrammatisms of the original. In the rare cases when it was impossible to translate the statement literally, the spirit was preserved, although the level of language was not. A few of the instruments have been analyzed in terms of the cognitive map and objectives of the program to demonstrate how the teacher is asked to approach the instrument. Where anticipated errors have been shown, they are typical and have been copied from the work of FIE students.

The Instrumental Enrichment exercises can be divided into two broad categories: 1) those that are accessible to even the more or less totally or functionally illiterate individual, and 2) those that require a relatively proficient level of literacy and verbal comprehension.

We do not delay the use of Instrumental Enrichment materials with adolescents or young adults until they overcome their difficulties in the use of written materials. Even those parts that require certain levels of competency in reading can be used with illiterate adolescents because of the limited requirements of the material and the careful selection of words to be read and written.

The nonverbal instruments are *Organization of Dots, Analytic Perception,* and *Illustrations.*

The instruments that have a limited vocabulary and may therefore require teacher assistance in reading the directions include *Orientation in Space I, II, and III, Comparisons, Family Relations, Numerical Progressions,* and *Syllogisms.*

The instruments requiring independent reading and comprehension skills are *Categorization, Instructions, Temporal Relations, Transitive Relations,* and *Representational Stencil Design.*

Several other instruments, not included in the 2-year curriculum, but in various stages of development include *Absurdities, Analogies, Convergent and Divergent Thinking, Illusions, Language and Symbolic Comprehension, Maps,* and *Auditory and Haptic Discrimination.*

All of the instruments have been constructed along the Learning Potential Assessment Device (LPAD) model (see Feuerstein, 1979). Except for *Illustrations* and *Temporal Relations,* exercises in each instrument are graded in difficulty and complexity, with later learning based on mastery of the earlier tasks. The order in which the instruments are taught depends on both the needs of the class and the characteristics of the instrument, although for some of the instruments there is a definite teaching sequence. Thus, *Orientation in Space I* must precede *Orientation in Space III; Comparisons* is the prerequisite for *Categorizations, Transitive Relations,* and *Syllogisms;* and *Representational Stencil Design* follows work in *Organization of Dots, Analytic Perception, Orientation in Space, Temporal Relations, Comparisons,* and *Categorization.* Obviously, nonverbal instruments precede those that require a high level of competency in reading and writing when one is working with illiterate students.

Two different instruments are taught in alternate lessons to prevent the frustration that would commonly accompany the use of only one instrument in which either its modality or the deficient function it emphasizes would be unduly problematic for a student with specific deficiencies. If a student in a

Figure 1. Each instrument has a cover page that bears the FIE identifying picture of a learner, the slogan of the program, and the symbol for the specific instrument it accompanies. The cover page is used to introduce the instrument and to arouse the interest and motivation, and in turn the need, of the students to cope with its exercises. The students must feel that the subject is not only interesting but relevant and important for them. The teacher orients the introductory discussion to include consideration of the symbol on the cover so that the student will start to gain insight into the meaning of the instrument for the attainment of the program's goals. (The cover page shown here is for *Organization of Dots.*)

class finds the material in a particular instrument relatively easy, he will still benefit from its instruction because of the reinforcement it provides. His success in the subject boosts his self-image and fosters his motivation. In prescriptive, individual work with a student, if the time at the teacher's disposal is limited, he will be able to concentrate on material that will correct the diagnosed deficiencies of the child in treatment.

Each instrument has a cover page (Figure 1) and is implicitly divided into units. Pages of exercises at the end of each unit can be used by the teacher to evaluate the student's mastery of the tasks. Each instrument also contains pages of mistakes in which the student learns to identify the source of errors. Usually when a culturally deprived child is confronted with an error in his own work, he tends to tear up the whole page or erase the entire problem rather than just the part in which the error occurs. Because the pages of errors are objective, they are nonthreatening to the child. Thus, the errors in either the instructions or the expression become a source of insight and further learning for the student.

The FIE program is taught along with the regular class curriculum by the classroom teacher, who has been especially trained in the material and the didactics of its presentation.

ORGANIZATION OF DOTS

The instrument, *Organization of Dots,* is based on a task produced by the late Professor André Rey of Geneva (Rey and Dupont, 1953). It was originally used as a selective device for persons who were to be oriented toward technical vocations and professions requiring specific spatial skills.

Molar and Molecular Aspects of *Organization of Dots*

The molar aspect of the task is to identify and outline, within an amorphous cloud of dots, a series of overlapping geometric figures, such as squares, triangles, diamonds, and stars (see Figure 2). The molecular components of the task are numerous and reflect a wealth of elements that can directly challenge the difficulties experienced by the retarded performer. The exercises therefore address themselves to the correction of a variety of deficient cognitive functions.

Projection of Virtual Relationships

The first component of the instrument involves organizing the dots and introducing into them a structure according to a given standard. To find the square and triangle, relationships have to be projected among otherwise discrete and separate existences, i.e., the individual dots.

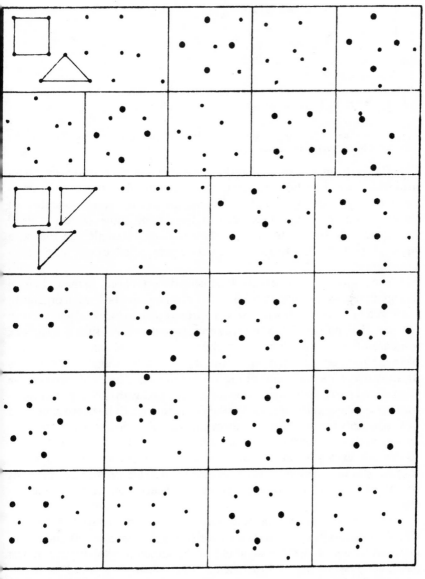

Figure 2.   Page 1 from *Organization of Dots*. Completion of the task requires the projection of virtual relationships; discrimination of form and size; constancy of form and size across changes in orientation; use of relevant information; restraint of impulsivity; precision; planning; systematic search; and comparison to the model. The thickened dots aid in the projection of the square, but also serve as a distractor by preventing the perception of the similar arrangement of dots in pairs of frames in the bottom row on the page.

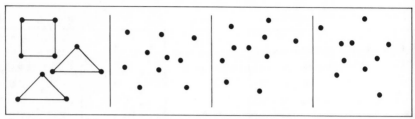

Organization of Dots (exercises 1, 2, and 3, page 2)

A square and two triangles, identical in size and form to those of the model, must be projected into each frame.

The performance of the culturally deprived children who were examined with these tasks did not substantiate the Gestaltist concept of the emergence of a structure as a result of isomorphic nature of our perception of the good form. Nothing was compelling, nor did the frames of dots "force" the retarded performer to perceive three dots as a triangle and four as a square, especially when to do so required a desegregation of various overlapping figures.

The projection of a virtual relationship does not occur in these children as a spontaneous response to the pressure of stimuli on the human organism, sensitized by a mental structure which is isomorphic to the good gestalt. Presented with opportunities to close the open part of a figure, such as a circle or a square, many culturally deprived children do not feel compelled to complete the good gestalt. That this is true, as well, with a fragmented gestalt is illustrated in work with some of the Raven Matrices. The child perceives the fragmented parts of the figures in an episodic way, with each part having its own autonomous existence, so that the parts from which he has to choose do not necessarily seem to him to be those that complete the gestalt. Work done by Rey and others on the filling in and closure of the gestalt has brought forth ample evidence that these are outcomes of learned behavior and, therefore, are not necessarily present following the development or emergence of structures through maturational processes (Feuerstein, Jeannet, and Richelle, 1953).

The projection of virtual relationships requires on the part of the individual an orientation or readiness to search for interconnections and meanings that do not necessarily stand out of the stimuli as vital attributes. The particular task, then, of Instrumental Enrichment is to produce in the learner a need to link episodically perceived events into a system by projecting into them relationships that are not necessarily obvious, and therefore not compelling. The projection of virtual relationships is a fundamental component of cognitive processes and leads toward higher mental operations.

Conservation of Constancy

After the projection of relationships, a second function of the instrument concerns the capacity to seek the constancy of perceived objects above and beyond variations in certain of their particular characteristics. In this case, the individual is required to identify the object's characteristics despite changes in its topological and orientational relationships. The difficulty inherent in this task is clearly observed when children, having already learned to identify the square when its base is parallel to the horizontal lines of the page, must identify the figure once it is oriented differently. Not only does the learner's established set make the task difficult for him to grasp, but the idea that the object can remain the same, continuing its constant existence above and beyond certain changes in its characteristics, must also be understood.

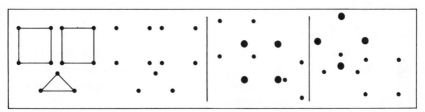

Organization of Dots (exercises 1, 2, and 3, page 3)

Constancy of the form of the square is conserved despite changes in its orientation.

Visual Transport

A third function is the visual transport of relationships, which requires a proper scanning process, focusing on the model figure and transporting its image visually to the field where it must be overlapped, compared, and judged as to the degree of its appropriateness to the given model. This requires a great deal of stability of the perceptual process and a variety of corrective devices to overcome the difficulties involved. Thus, many culturally deprived children do not conserve the model they have scrutinized and lose it en route to the place where they must find the figure again. In many cases, the perception of the figure is distorted by movements of the body; between the point of the gathering of the stimuli and the area into which they must be projected, something is either lost or altered. This has to do, to a large extent, with the vulnerability and fragility of the perceptual processes of these children.

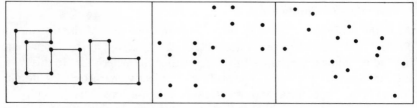

Organization of Dots (exercises 1 and 2, page 11)

Asymmetry of the figures makes their interiorization and visual transport difficult.

Precision and Accuracy

A fourth function is concerned with the need for the individual to accurately identify dimensions such as size, distance, and parallelism of lines. Accuracy as a need is seldom found in the attitudinal repertoire of the culturally deprived child.

Summative Behavior

A fifth function, the need for summative behavior, is very limited in the culturally deprived child. To solve a given problem properly, before taking any action, the individual must define the structure by summing the number of dots required to form the standard figure.

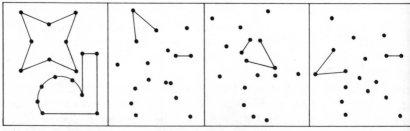

Organization of Dots (exercises 1, 2, and 3, page 9)

In the absence of angles, the number of dots in the curved line are of assistance in the drawing of the figure.

Three dots in a triangle do not differ from three dots in a square; the difference arises in that a triangle does not include the fourth dot necessary for the square. A child who begins with three dots in his search for the square may very well stop looking if he does not find the fourth dot immediately; or he may ignore the existence of the fourth dot entirely and close the three into a triangle because he has not appropriately summed up all of the existing stimuli in the perceived universe.

Planning and Restraint of Impulsivity

The sixth function, planning, and its correlate, the inhibition of impulsive acting-out behavior, are important requirements in fulfilling the exercises of *Organization of Dots*. Any unplanned move runs the risk of failure. Even if such a move succeeds in meeting the demands for one of the figures, subsequent work will reveal that the remaining dots are inappropriate for the other figures that must be projected. The responsiveness of the task itself provides the individual with an immediate feedback of the results of his unplanned behavior. Planning must encompass the entire activity, with all of its components.

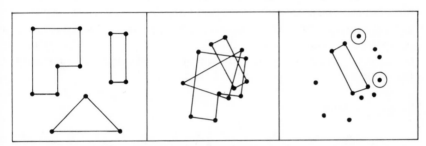

Organization of Dots (exercises 18, page 7)

    Impulsive use of improper dots for the rectangle ultimately results in inappropriate dots remaining for the other two figures.

Discrimination

A seventh function can be described as the capacity to withstand and resist the seduction of an element that seems, at first, to respond closely to the established criteria. Two dots in close proximity, or two different sets of dots with the same characteristics of distance, angles, and so forth, need additional criteria to aid in their differentiation and use.

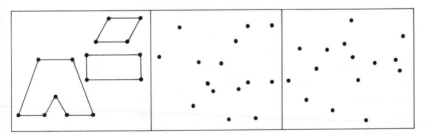

Organization of Dots (exercises 1 and 2, page 12)

    If the distance between the two dots in the short sides of the rectangle is used as the sole criterion for search, an error is likely since that same distance is characteristic of many other pairs of dots in the model figure.

The temptation to use an inappropriate dot is here closely linked with impulsivity and the probabilistic use of stimuli. The capacity to resist such a temptation requires the development of a great need for accuracy and becomes progressively more essential as the complexities of the tasks presented to the learner increase.

Segregation of Proximate Elements

An eighth function is the need to segregate interwoven, overlapping elements that are very close to each other yet belong to different sets or groups of figures. This function has application in social as well as occupational areas. To be able to disentangle various components from a given complex social situation, one must be able to identify the patterns that characterize the different groups and relate the individuals to the specific pattern. This is not achieved without an orientation to searching for such relationships, where they are not immediately apparent, with the help of relevant cues, and then searching for supportive data to confirm the inferences.

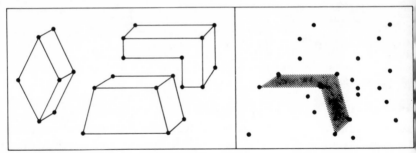

Organization of Dots (exercise 6, page 20)

The complexity of the three-dimensional figures and the proximity between the dots create the need for segregation and differentiation.

Structure of *Organization of Dots*

The 26 pages of *Organization of Dots,* each with between 14 and 18 exercises, provide the learner with ample opportunities for the activation of the various functions, for an understanding of the parts they play in the specific exercises, and for an awareness of their roles in the more molar behavior of the individual.

The instrument has been constructed so as to present each individual with a relatively high degree of difficulty, despite individual differences attributable to specific cognitive structures. Within the same exercises and level of complexity, through differentiation of the various spaces, the learner must discover geometric figures that become more intermingled and require progressively higher levels of discrimination, precision, and segregation. Even for the individual who has an easy grasp of such tasks, a great deal of mental power has to be invested in scanning, focusing, transporting, planning, and anticipating.

Errors as a Source of Critical Thinking

The instrument provides pages of exercises with intentional errors to provoke in the learner a conscious critical approach, associated with a verbal description of the source of errors in a given task. This experience permits the learner to anticipate the types of errors which may result if certain basic dimensions, such as size, angles, and orientation, are not considered.

The objective nature of the tasks makes the study of errors nonthreatening to the culturally deprived student. After sufficient practice in identifying the source of mistakes in these pages of errors, the student displays a readiness and an ability to apply the same critical approach to his own work.

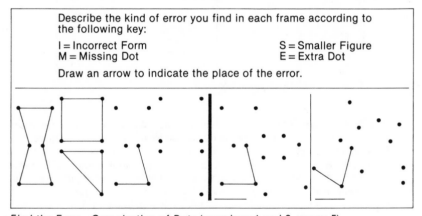

Find the Error—Organization of Dots (exercises 1 and 2, pages 5)

The student learns strategies for the critical examination of his own work through the identification of errors and their source.

The following anecdote, taken from a classroom discussion in a social studies class, illustrates how students can gain insight into using errors as a source of further learning.

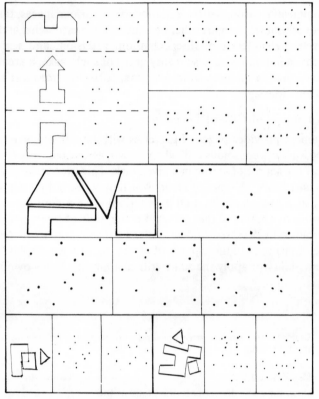

Figure 3.   Children's productions.

"In *Organization of Dots,* we are given a model. We have trouble in finding the figure and we do it wrong. What do we do? Do we tear up the page? Do we throw it away? Do we yell? Do we sit down and cry? No. . . . We see if it can be fixed. And, if it can be fixed, how can we fix it? Now let's look at our real-life situation. Is this the kind of government we want? Is this the kind of public we want? What happened? Something isn't right. Shall we cry? Shall we throw it all away? Or do we see where we made our mistakes? Is it possible to fix it? Just like in *Organization of Dots,* we saw whether the figure we drew was too big or too small, or crooked; here, too, we have to see. Slowly, in a systematic manner, we can find what isn't right. And we can correct it. And after we correct it we must keep the model of the kind of government we want firmly in mind, so that we don't make similar mistakes in the future."

Children's Productions

The activities in *Organization of Dots* are not limited to the discovery of relationships and their rediscovery in a variety of situations. The possibility of building such relationships and, on this basis, constructing a new universe of elements is offered as well (see Figure 3).

The opportunity to produce sets of instruments based on the discovered relationships is offered to the students as another way of enhancing their capacity to deal with the principles not only receptively but also actively and expressively. In many of our groups, adolescent learners have spontaneously produced pages with tasks involving the basic goals of our instruments. Their original productions demonstrate that they have been able to use many of the criteria employed in constructing the FIE instruments.

Additional evidence of the students' ability to internalize the goals of *Organization of Dots,* as well as those of other instruments, is their work as teachers' aides. In many classes, students who have completed their work assist the teacher with their peers who have been absent. These tutors have learned that to help a classmate does not mean to complete the task for him, and they are effective in the proper teaching of the material.

Classroom Implementation of *Organization of Dots*

Organization of Dots is the first instrument presented to students at the start of the FIE program. The reasons for the selection of this instrument are numerous. Because its tasks are very remote from those encountered in academic subjects, they are not accompanied by the negative affect associated with previous experiences of failure. Inasmuch as neither knowledge nor school-associated skills are required for engaging in the tasks, even illiterates are able to participate, without the onus that usually accompanies their schoolroom activities.

It is interesting to note that even children suffering from visual and motor deficits are able to work on *Organization of Dots.* For those with visual difficulties, a complete and precise verbal description of the form will aid in the interiorization of the standard and in the search for the figure. Inasmuch as the actual drawing of the line to connect the dots is neither the prime objective nor *raison d'être* of the task, it is sufficient to ask the student with motor difficulties to indicate where the line should be drawn; the line can be drawn for him. The advantages to be gained through this instrument warrant its use even under these difficult conditions.

The exercises are very different from those of the usual classroom curriculum for retarded performers in which primary grade material is introduced to adolescents without making the changes that age and life experience would seem to make necessary. The tasks are highly motivating and difficult. The fact that the teacher, although exposed to these tasks previously, must himself rediscover relationships well known to him if he is to correct and guide the child, creates the "equilateral triangle" of the teacher-material-student relationship (see page 282). Since the task requires an effort on the part of the teacher, as well as the learner, successful completion not only reinforces the student but also contributes to his readiness to accept and ascribe meaning to his mastery.

In providing evidence of the capacity of the students to master difficult tasks, to concentrate for long periods of time, and to work with task-intrinsic motivation, *Organization of Dots* is effective in changing the teacher's attitude toward retarded performers in general and toward those students who do not usually participate or are unable to perform adequately in subject-matter and vocational areas, in particular. The status of the retarded performer can also be raised with his normal peers by distributing some of the more difficult pages to those who feel themselves superior. It soon becomes evident that successful mastery requires a great deal of effort even from them.

In the hands of an experienced teacher, the instrument permits diagnosis of the student's deficient cognitive functions. It is possible, through *Organization of Dots,* to emphasize systematic work and restraint of impulsivity and to introduce all of the goals of the FIE program.

Analysis of *Organization of Dots* in Terms of the Cognitive Map

Content: Dots to be organized into geometric figures.

Modality: Figural.

Phase: Elaboration and output with the projection of virtual relationships; all three phases (input, elaboration, and output) with the utilization of almost all of the functions.

Operations: Organization of the field with articulation and segregation; differentiation and discrimination; categorization; anticipation and representation; inference; induction and generalization.

Level of abstraction: Low in actual solution of the problem; very high when principles and rules are generalized and applied.

Level of complexity: Low when model consists of familiar geometric figures and a relatively small number of dots; very high with the introduction of unfamiliar, asymmetrical figures, an increased number of dots very close together, and the necessity for fine discrimination and choice between dots that proximate those sought.

Level of efficiency: Shows effect of practice; decrease in number of errors and increase in speed of solution, with restraint of impulsivity and use of adequate strategies for search; reduced investment necessary for solving problems of increased complexity and difficulty, in terms of both time and subjective expression of affect.

Anticipated Difficulties

The teacher can anticipate the problems that will arise as the students are confronted with the demands of the tasks. An appreciation of the errors that are apt to occur guides the teacher in the presentation of the material. This can be illustrated by the types of errors that may occur, for example, on page 2 of *Organization of Dots:*

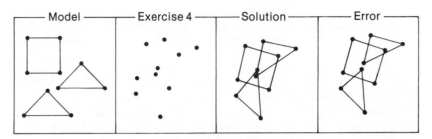

The difficulty stems from the necessity to discriminate between two dots that are very close together in order to assign the appropriate dot to the triangle to which it belongs. Errors may be caused by a lack of precision; impaired strategies for hypothesis testing; impulsivity with a probabilistic use of the first stimulus encountered; lack of comparison to the model after completion; and/or a deficiency in visual transport or interiorization of the model.

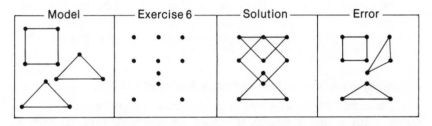

The difficulty stems from a tendency to use a gestalt or an inability to resist the temptation of using the first four dots that fit a pattern of a square. Errors may also be caused by the use of only one source of information, that of the figure, with no attention to size; impulsivity; a lack of interiorization of the model; a lack of comparison to the model; and a lack of self-criticism.

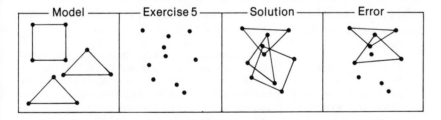

The difficulty stems from the necessity of defining a strategy for search. Errors may result from sweeping perception of the triangle; a lack of planning; impulsive behavior; inappropriate, uncritical use of a strategy; no exploration of alternatives; a lack of consideration of the sequence necessary for completion of the task; and a lack of comparison to the model.

In discussing errors of the type described above, and their sources, students' comments have included the following:

"The person used trial and error. Like somebody who has to go someplace and tries different routes instead of asking somebody or looking at a map. He wastes time and effort."

"The person forgot the correct figure. It's like somebody who can't remember exactly what he's looking for. He happens to find all kinds of things, some that he's been looking for before, in his search."

"The guy wasn't exact. He was satisfied with something that was about right. That might be okay for some things but wait until the first time he has to walk a long way in shoes that are too small for him."

When asked by the teacher, "Where else is precision important to us?" students had the following responses:

"In doing math, especially in a test."

"When plans are drawn to build something. Then I have to follow them exactly or else things won't fit together right."

"If a woman isn't exact in the amount of spices she puts in the food, it ain't fit to eat."

"If I have to catch a bus that only runs twice a day. I'd better get there right on time because the bus don't wait for nobody."

Organization of Dots **in Terms of the Subgoals of FIE**

The attainment of the subgoals of the program can perhaps best be illustrated by presenting fragments of lessons, anecdotes, and reports from the field that indicate the spontaneous use by students of the functions, strategies, and principles acquired in *Organization of Dots*.

I.   Correction of Deficient Cognitive Functions   Aside from the previously discussed (pages 128–134) eight cognitive functions that may be identified in the presentation of this instrument, an attempt is made to involve all other functions that may have been identified. Within a very short time, the spontaneous behavior of students shows evidence of improvement in more than one function. The following case is illustrative.

> Less than 3 months after the start of FIE, to celebrate the holidays, each class in the school was asked to decorate its homeroom for a contest in which the best decorated classroom receives a prize. Therefore, the students were asked to work without any assistance from a teacher. A member of the school staff, in charge of the contest, reported that only the FIE students sketched plans, measured windows and walls, and categorized and summarized the materials needed. They assigned tasks to members and made a schedule of the order in which things should be done. The other classes proceeded impulsively without advance planning. There were quarrels, acrimony, and blame casting.

This report, echoed year after year in many schools in which FIE is taught, is evidence of students' spontaneous use of techniques of organization, planning, summation, categorization, and analysis, both of materials and the sequence of operations. Precision, the use of time and space dimensions, restraint of impulsivity, and reduction of egocentric behavior are also indicated. There is an improvement both in problem-solving techniques and in social interactions. The replacement of competition by cooperation is illustrated by another passage from the same report:

> A student had placed a chair on a table in order to decorate. The chair teetered. A classmate called, "Wait! If you leave the chair that way, you'll fall. Let me fix it right and then I'll hold it for you."

In addition to hypothetical thinking and the ability to anticipate and represent the results of a cause-and-effect relationship, this interaction demonstrates an increased readiness to give and receive assistance from a peer.

II.   Acquisition of Basic Concepts, Vocabulary, Labels, Operations, and Relationships   The student learns to label not only the figures but also the operations and strategies he uses to construct them. Verbal mediators assist him in the interiorization of figures too complex to transport visually. Both vocabulary and strategies are transferred to other subject-matter areas.

> Overheard in a classroom: "Boy, he and I sure don't communicate."

> In a discussion of current events: "The lack of precision and common meaning in the United Nations Resolution 242 is what is responsible for all the disagreement." "Sadat has his own strategy."

> In geometry, the students immediately applied what they had learned about the square and the triangle. Math teachers reported that with the FIE students there was not the anticipated problem of differentiation between the square and the rectangle. "In computing the perimeter of a rectangle and a square, they know before any explanation that one must multiply the length of one side by 4 because there are four equal sides in a square, and that they must take twice the sum of the length and the width for a rectangle."

III.   Production of Intrinsic Motivation Through Habit Formation   The repetition of essentially the same task throughout the instrument creates a crystallization of the process of problem solution in *Organization of Dots*.

> "What do we do when we are given a page? We define the problem and see what we have been given. We look at the model carefully; we label it; if it is complex, we break it into manageable parts; we count the number of dots we need for each figure; we decide which figure we will look for and define its attributes so that they are points of reference; we plan our work; we select a starting point; we search systematically, using the strategy we have set for ourselves; in our search, we look for the attributes of the figure that are invariable and constant. We look for cues. We resist the temptation of an irrelevant dot; we use hypotheses and logic; we compare to the model if we think we have found the figure. If we make an error we examine it to discover the source of our mistake so that we do not make it again."

Teachers of other subject matter report hearing the FIE children start their work with: "Now what do we do when we are given a problem? We first have to find out what the problem is and then what is given...." There is also spontaneous application of other automatized schemata. In a geometry class, FIE students were critical of the lines the teacher had drawn on the board to illustrate parallels, contending that, if the lines were extended far enough, they would ultimately intersect. They demonstrated an ability to project virtual relationships, a need for precision, hypothetical thinking, and a need for evidence.

In a physical education class test for kicking distance, pushing, shoving, quarreling, and cursing ensued as most of the boys tried to kick the one ball at the same time. An FIE student took charge and told the boys to get organized into a line in order to save time and ensure each boy his turn to kick, undisturbed. The student's behavior indicated a spontaneous definition of the problem, a framework for its solution, organization, and a strategy for efficiency.

IV. Production of Reflective, Insightful Processes   Insight into the meaning of the activity is developed beyond the task of connecting the dots to form geometric figures according to a model. It is a realization of how the principles and strategies learned are generally applicable. For example:

> In response to the teacher's question of why the page should not be turned in the search for the figures, a student exclaimed, "What do you mean? If they give me a car engine to fix, I can't turn it around or turn it over just to suit me. I have to make the best of it and get along with it like I get it." Another student added, "But I will use my recollection of what the engine looks like when it's okay, and then I can see from that what is not right." And a third student said, "Until I can keep the model in my head I can use a plan of a motor to work with."

A physical education coach, in a request for information on the FIE program, commented on the development of insightful processes:

> In my physical education class there are three groups of boys, only one of which could be called "culturally deprived." The assignment for the day was volleyball and on the court on which the culturally deprived boys were playing the normal kids the game was slow in starting. I wandered over to see what was keeping them and heard a brisk discussion of the organization and strategy of the volleyball team. Who would stand next to the net and who would play in the last row, the strong players or the weak players? Was it better that all the best players start the game or would it be better to put them in after the opposing team started to tire? What would be the basis for deciding? Should the substitutions be arranged beforehand to prevent misunderstanding and allow the substitutes to be alert to the need for their entry into the game, etc.
>
> This discussion was surprising enough but the real shocker was that it was the culturally deprived kids who were doing the analyzing, thinking, and planning. I looked into it and found they were all FIE students. I thought you would like to know.

V. Creation of Task-Intrinsic Motivation   Motivation is enhanced by tasks that are genuinely challenging and difficult. Although students are initially intrigued by the pages of *Organization of Dots,* they approach the lessons rather warily, still loath to participate in conversations or to volunteer information. Within the first 3 weeks, after successful completion of several pages of increasing complexity, they approach the teacher with requests for more pages. "If I could do that last page, I can do anything!"

A principal reported that a young substitute teacher returned to his office in tears after her class had locked her out of the classroom. Some of the students met her in the hall prior to the lesson and asked her if she knew *Organization of Dots*. When it became obvious to them that she did not know what they were talking about, they refused to admit her. "Go tell the principal to send a substitute who knows Instrumental Enrichment."

VI. Change in the Attitude of the Retarded Performer from Perception of Himself as a Passive Recipient and Reproducer of Information to Perception of Himself as an Active Generator of New Information The student is an active partner in the exploration of strategies and the bridging from the principles learned in the exercises to other areas of his experience. As a consequence of work in *Organization of Dots,* the student's self-image is changed.

A teacher reports that one of her students had no effective strategy for self-criticism and/or any recognition of the existence of errors in his work. Once he learned to compare to a given model, he brought a perfect page to the teacher, saying, "You know, I used to think I was really stupid. Now I know that isn't true at all."

A shift in the locus of control and a readiness to assume responsibility are evident. From three different reports:

When students return to school after an absence, they themselves ask for the pages they have missed.

They bring their own pencils and erasers to class.

They have started to keep their folders organized according to subjects and page numbers.

A communication received by the author from a teacher in a vocational school for dropouts and rejects from other schools is particularly salient testimony to the cognitive enrichment that can be achieved through FIE. The teacher had announced to the class that in the next meeting he would summarize what they had learned in *Organization of Dots*. At the beginning of the next session, a girl approached his desk and offered him a very neatly written piece of paper entitled "Summary of the Subject: *Organization of Dots.* What We Learned from the Subject." Listed were 16 items:

1. To take advantage of cues.
2. To organize according to a certain principle.
3. To define problems and recognize rules and characteristics.
4. To find the relationship between given data.
5. To take advantage of an error as a source of learning.
6. To start with and finish a problem you start with.
7. To use given lines for assistance.
8. To recognize figures, symmetrical and asymmetrical.
9. Self-criticism.
10. To plan a starting point.
11. To overcome difficulties.

12. To pay attention to several factors at the same time.
13. To find a strategy and its importance.
14. Order and its importance.
15. To pay attention to size and form.
16. The danger in using the dots that stand out in the pages.

Although some items on the list are repetitive, there is little doubt that the student saw *Organization of Dots* as a source of learning. As another child aptly put it, "It only goes to show you that you don't have to suffer to learn."

ORIENTATION IN SPACE I, II, AND III

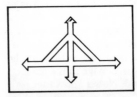 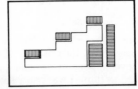 

Deficiencies in Spatial Orientation

Orientation in Space is composed of three instruments that aim at producing a direct attack on one of the most commonly observed deficiencies in the retarded performer: his limited use of articulated, differentiated, and representational spatial dimensions. This deficiency is most obvious when the orientation in space has to be detached from the learner's own action and must take on a point of reference outside of his own body.

Difficulties are twofold. The first has to do with the limited amount of representational, internalized behavior available to the individual, the corollary of which is his propensity to act motorically rather than to abbreviate the process in short-circuited form through representation. Thus, when an individual is required to indicate a point in space, his readiness and capacity to use representation may well be limited to those situations in which the possibility of using a motor modality is precluded. Such situations, however, occur infrequently in the life of the culturally deprived child, and his needs to orient himself in remote space are often limited. When he is called upon to act, he can easily master problems with motoric, gestural types of response. Therefore, representation and internalized behavior are not responsive to a real need for him. Such a need is only rarely aroused by a mediator who forces the child to use representation rather than motor behavior.

> "John, will you please tell Bob how to get to the nurse's office. . . . No, it's nice of you to offer but you don't have to take him. Just tell him."

A second difficulty has to do with the generalized lack of need to relate objects and events to the specific temporal and spatial dimensions that represent relational and sequential causal factors. According to various developmentalists (Piaget, 1956), the mastery of representational space is the result of a developmental process. Difficulties in temporal and spatial orientation, with certain more complex tasks, may occur in normal individuals even as late as 10 to 12 years of age.

Changing the Level of Representational Space

The necessity of producing a change in the level of representational space is twofold. First, there is the importance of such an orientation in the proper perception of objects and a great number of experiences. Second, the articulation of representational space can be used as an efficient carrier for the development of relational abstract thinking and the correction of a host of deficient cognitive functions. Relating two elements to each other, and coordinating one's view to that of another, with the basic comparative behavior involved in each of these processes, are only two of the many functions that can be activated in the acquisition of representational space.

Many classroom discipline problems stem from the inability to coordinate one's view with that of another:

"Teacher, it wasn't my fault. I open the window 'cause I'm hot. He close it 'cause he's cold. I tell him to put on a sweater and then I open it again. He punches me in the stomach and I hit him in the mouth."

The perception and understanding of transformations as deriving from certain operations can also be acquired through representational space perception.

Description of *Orientation in Space* Instruments

The first of the three instruments deals with spatial orientation relative to one's own body in which the frame of reference is one's own movements; the second adds dimensions of topological space with *on, above, below, up, down,* and *between;* and the third deals with an external stable system of reference, that of the cardinal points of the compass, which then combines with the first two systems of reference.

These three instruments are directed primarily toward the creation of specific strategies for the differentiation of the spatial frame of reference from other criteria and toward the introduction and demonstration of the relativity of certain systems as contrasted with the stability of others.

Plasticity of Orientation

At the beginning of *Orientation in Space I,* a turning pinwheel is the symbol of a system that relates to one's movement. It illustrates the concepts of *front/back* and *left/right* as being relative and dependent upon the relationship between two or more objects. "What" is located "where" is a function of movement. Following a certain movement, what was previously "right" will become "left" or "in front" will become "in back." This concept is fairly difficult for some retarded performers who will insist, "When I turn, my right hand will be my left hand." This response is not due to an inability to express verbally the product of a correct elaboration, but stems from the lack of perception and understanding of the nature of the transformation.

Orientation in Space I (page 1)

The movement illustrates the relative nature of the relationship between two objects. However, the internal relationship of the four directions, one to the other, is stable.

The need to produce flexibility and plasticity in the individual's orientation goes beyond the specific area of space and is, to a large extent, similar to the need to decentrate the individual so that his views are no longer egocentric. The individual is then able to consider hypothetically and representationally another's point of view, which may differ from his own.

The teacher started a discussion by asking, "Why is it important to know what others think? Why isn't it enough just to know how I think about something?"

Student: "My sister found a purse with 100 dollars in it. She took it to the police station and they found the owner."

Teacher: "Was that smart? Just think of the number of things she could have bought if she had kept the money!"

Student: "Yes, but she could only think of how terrible the person who lost the money felt."

Once a comparison between the two perceived points of view has been made, they can be judged more objectively. Relative positions can then be decided on the basis of data derived from two or more sources of information, with proper weight attributed to each. Rendering the perception of space flexible is to be seen not necessarily as a content-oriented need, although it fulfills an important one, but rather as the need to create a capacity and readiness within the individual to act on the world in a representational, internalized way, since this is the basis for abstract mental operations.

Distance as a Factor in Interactions

One may use the concept of distance in describing the interaction between the organism and the world. The sensorimotor interaction represents the smallest interactional distance, while the representational and abstract modalities represent the widest and the most distant ones, which permit both a range of activities in time and space and a high degree of reversibility and flexibility (i.e., equilibration).

Moving around in history and contemplating the future demand the use of representational and abstract thinking for hypothesizing and predicting possible outcomes of certain events. This kind of interaction between an individual and the world has a meaning that is more remote and of broader range than that entailed in the concrete and sensorial dimensions of the experienced world. Thus, representational, internalized activities may enhance the repertoire of the individual and his capacity to act on more remote space.

Description of *Orientation in Space I*

Orientation in Space I, 16 pages in length, deals mainly with the concepts of right/left and front/back. In a sequence of tasks these relationships become more and more devoid of figural support and consequently more and more remote from the body's own movements. Even when figural elements are used to represent changes produced by movement, it is always the representation of a relationship toward which one strives and that is required from the learner. The need to render the required flexibility into a stable and easily elicited function is ensured by the repeated exposure to the same task. The generalizability of this representational approach is attained by varying the nature of the tasks while keeping the principles and concepts that are involved constant.

> In a history class: "It's just like in politics. If you take the Liberal party as your starting point, you turn right to get to the Conservative party and turn left to get to the Socialist party."
>
> "We learned the story of Saul and Samuel in the Bible lesson. I think I can understand why Saul felt that he had to give booty to his soldiers, but I can also understand why Samuel was so angry. You can't just say who was right and who was wrong."
>
> "Also Samuel was angry because Saul didn't wait for him. It's like the time I waited and waited for my boyfriend, and he didn't come, so I left without him.

Boy, was he mad! But how long is a person supposed to wait for somebody else?"

In discussing the importance of orientation: "The sign + cannot be turned on its side without changing its meaning. It would become an × and then we'd have to multiply instead of adding."

The tasks of the first part of the instrument deal with the relationship between objects and a human figure. The four objects, a house, a tree, flowers, and a bench, are fixed in a stable position on the field, whereas the human figure changes in its orientation. He is depicted so that one sees him from the front, from the back, from the left, and from the right. The relationship between each of the objects and the human is relative and contingent upon the latter's changing position. The shifts in the position of the human are encoded with numbers and then become referents for the establishment of new relationships.

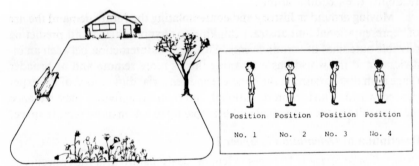

Orientation in Space I

The position of the figure and the objects in the field must be coordinated in tasks on pages 6, 7, 8, and 9 in order to arrive at the relationship between them.

The student is asked to represent the relationships between the object and the human from a variety of points of reference: Once he is asked to describe the relationship between the position and the object in terms of direction; once he is asked to describe which of the positions is appropriate so that the relationship between it and an object will yield a given direction; once he is asked which of the objects is required in order to qualify for a given direction in relation to the human. In a page that summarizes the unit and can be used to evaluate mastery, a mixture of tasks similar to those on preceding pages is provided (see Figure 4, *left*).

A student commented, "This is like a question in math. Once they ask you $2 + 3 = ?$; once $3 + ? = 5$ and once $? + 2 = 5$. But if you have any two of the numbers in the problem you don't have any trouble in finding what the third will be."

The teacher asked for a discussion of the problem in which relationships are sought, but no information is given and all the spaces are blank: "I can start with anything I want. I hate questions like these. It's like when I am supposed to write a composition about any subject I want. I never know what to write about."

"No, it's not. It just *seems* like you can do anything you want. But once you choose one thing, you're already limited, and then when you choose the second thing to go with it, you're stuck. There is only one possible answer. It's just like teacher saying, 'When you finish your work, you may do what you like.' What I'd like to do is go home, but I can't do that. I can do anything I want as long as I stay in class, don't talk, don't make noise, and don't bother nobody who's still working."

The second half of the instrument introduces arrows and dots, with the dot in place of the object and the arrowhead symbolically representing the face of the human. The symbols force a detachment from one's own body movement, which has served as the basis for the initial discrimination and division of the world into the dimensions of left/right or front/back. The axis of the body, permitting the distinction, serves as the basis, but it no longer serves as the sole criterion. The level of abstraction becomes higher as the tasks move from a depiction of concrete objects. Tasks are again varied and culminate in a page that blends exercises similar to those on preceding pages (see Figure 4, *right*). In the report below, a teacher takes up a discussion of symbols, facilitated by the later exercises of *Orientation in Space I:*

Teacher: "The arrow serves as a symbol for a boy standing in a certain position. What other symbols do you recognize from other subjects?"

"In algebra, $a + b = b + a$. The letter a serves as a symbol for any number. We can put any number in the place of a and b. + means add, and = means same as."

"In music, there is a symbol that tells you the key and the notes are symbols of sounds."

"Temperatures are symbols. For instance, 0 stands for a certain amount of cold."

"This is not in a subject, but there is a symbol for the telephone company in the shape of a bell. Many organizations and governmental branches also have symbols."

(In the above example, the teacher could perhaps have differentiated between symbols and signs.)

For some retarded performers, this work on representation of space is, in many cases, the first time the student experiences a detachment of his self from the concrete, motoric modality of operation in the world. An approach that requires representation is seldom, if ever, requested from the retarded performer in other intervention programs. The use of this operation is significant as an initial attempt to provide the child with such an experience. From this, he may accede to more complex and higher levels of representation and operation.

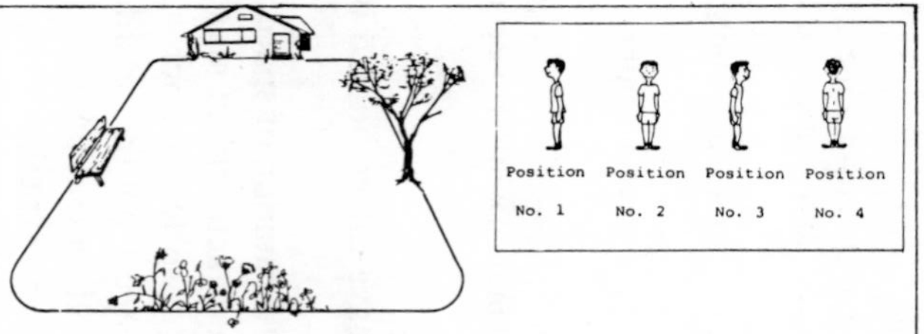

IV. Fill in what is missing:

Position	Object	Direction in Relation to the Boy
1	The tree	
4		right
2		back
	The house	front
3	The bench	
2	The house	
	The tree	left
4		back
	The bench	
		left
3		back
4	The tree	
		right

OSI 9

Orientation in Space I (page 9)

Fill in the missing so that each square contains an arrow, a dot, and a word which describes the relationship of the dot to the arrow.

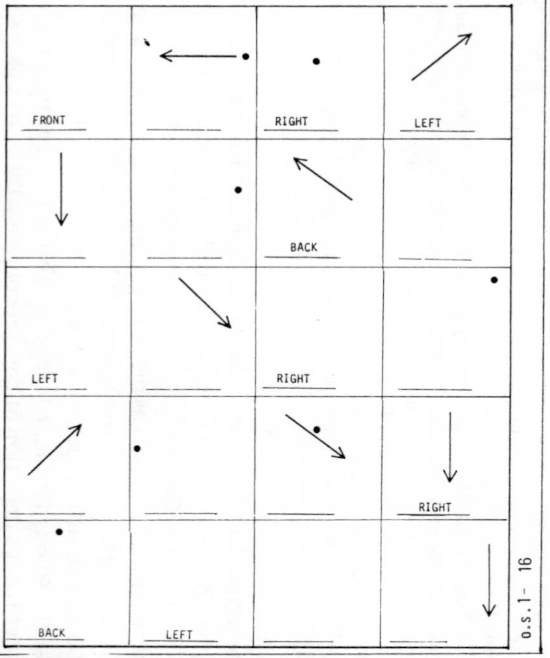

Orientation in Space I (page 16)

Figure 4. (Legend on opposite page.)

Description of *Orientation in Space II*

Orientation in Space II numbers only seven pages. To the elements of *Orientation in Space I*, it adds the parameters of *up, down, between, above, below, beneath,* and *beside* to describe the orientation of an object in space.

In the picture on the ___*right*___ the hat is ___*on*___ the chair.
In the picture on the _____ the cat is _____ the chair.

In the picture on the _____ the bottle is _____ the table.
In the picture on the _____ the cat is _____ the table.

Orientation in Space II (exercise 1, page 2)

The task requires the use of recently acquired concepts to describe the relative location of the object.

In addition to reinforcing the system of reference acquired in the first instrument, the exercises also elicit the need to view the same object or event from differing points of entry. For example, if a book is on the table, the table is under the book. The retarded performer is required to be an active participant in the construction of material by composing sentences that describe the same event from the viewpoint of the two or more referents in the interaction.

Orientation in Space II is included in FIE at the discretion of the teacher to meet specific needs and deficiencies of a student or a class.

Description of *Orientation in Space III*

Orientation in Space III, 29 pages in length, introduces an independent external frame of reference. In the exercises in the first unit, the four cardinal directions of the compass are presented as a stable system for describing the

---

Figure 4. *Orientation in Space I.* To enhance the ability to use concepts and stable systems of reference for orientation in space — concrete, abstract, and interpersonal. Distinction is made between relationships that are relative and can be described from a multiplicity of angles and those that are stable and can be fixed by coordinates. Precise and accurate communication of information lessens egocentricity. *Left:* This page summarizes preceding exercises and illustrates varied repetition of a principle to facilitate habit formation. Solution requires: definition of the problem; visual transport or internalization; simultaneous use of several sources of information; systematic work; and hypothetical and inferential thought as a basis for logical conclusions. The student learns of delimitation of alternatives and how to summarize his data, using a table. *Right:* Solution involves: redefinition of the problem with each frame; the use of symbols, encoding and decoding; the conservation of the constancy of the relationship across variations in the orientation of the arrow; projection of virtual relationships; hypothetical thought; and precision in gathering and communicating information.

position of an object in space. The orientation of an object can be perceived directly or inferred from the knowledge of the internal relationship between north, south, east, and west and their positions relative to one another.

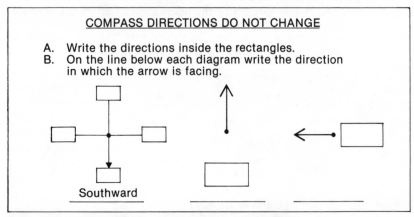

Orientation in Space III (exercises 1, 13, and 14, page 3)

The exercises require the coordination of information and inference in order to fill in the direction to which the arrow is pointing and the direction of the rectangle in relation to the arrowhead.

In the second unit, the stable system of reference of north, south, east, and west is coordinated with the relative system introduced in *Orientation in Space I*. The two systems are integrated in a way that permits their simultaneous use for the shifts in orientation that occur with movement. The relationship between the sides of the boy and the fixed compass directions are taught thoroughly, with a variety of possibilities for grasping the differentiated nature of the two systems and their points of congruence.

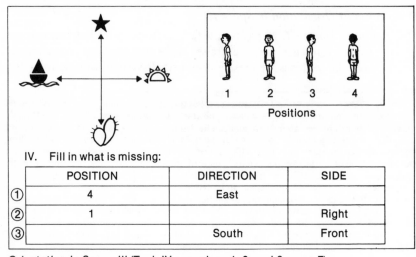

IV. Fill in what is missing:

	POSITION	DIRECTION	SIDE
①	4	East	
②	1		Right
③		South	Front

Orientation in Space III (Task IV, exercises 1, 2, and 3, page 7)

The human figure, in four positions, and the field with its compass points were coordinated in the preceding three pages, in each of which the referents and the given information differed.

In the task at the bottom of page 152, exercise 1 represents tasks in I in which the direction and position are given, and exercise 2 exemplifies II in which position and side are given, while exercise 3 gives an example of tasks in III in which the side and directions are given. IV involves a definition of the problem and may be used to indicate mastery.

In the third unit, the tasks are geared toward the establishment and reinforcement of internalized relationships in space, a grasp of these relationships, and an understanding of the operational nature of manipulating them. Represented movement, involving the number of turns or revolutions necessary to reach one direction from another, is taught as a function of the fixed interrelationship between compass points. Divergent thinking is encouraged in tasks eliciting alternative possibilities of reaching an objective.

F.   Use "north," "east," or "west" to fill in what is missing:
You are looking at the North Star.

In order to face _____ turn once to the right.

In order to face _____ turn twice to the left.

In order to face _____ turn once to the left.

Orientation in Space III (exercise F, page 8)

The need to use two or more sources of information to solve problems is specifically dealt with in the fourth unit through exercises in which two coordinates are the basis for trajectories. The system of reference is expanded to include the secondary compass points and is applied in exercises of increasing complexity. The student learns that representation of movements can be eliminated, altered, or undone by doing the reverse, directly or indirectly.

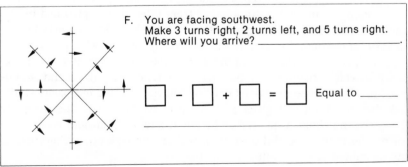

Orientation in Space III (exercise F, page 18)

In the last unit, both stable and relativistic frames of reference are applied in a series of exercises in which the student is given a starting point and a goal and asked to describe an itinerary. These exercises have as their major orientation and objective the constant use of internalized, representational movements, including numerical elements, as the determinants of the outcome. There are ample opportunities for crystallization of habits and attitudes for the proper grasp of the internal and external worlds.

B. In order to view the New Year's Day parade, people from different places gathered in Boston. Write the directions in which these people drove in order to arrive at Boston.

1. from Hartford _____   4. from New Bedford _____
2. from Manchester _____   5. from Albany _____
3. from Waterbury _____   6. from Montreal _____

Orientation in Space III (exercise B, page 24)

A map is provided in the instrument so that solution is not contingent upon prior knowledge. The changing description of the relationship between Boston, whose position is fixed, and the other cities is a function of the location of the city of origin with reference to Boston.

Meaning of the Instruments

The meaning of these instruments beyond their general goal is clear: their content, as such, is a condition of efficient problem-solving activity in a variety of day-to-day and more specialized tasks that involve both the receiving of instructions concerning sources of information and the carrying out of those instructions. Lack of orientation toward the dimensions of space, associated with limited or even nonexistent representation in their use, will, of necessity, bring about failure at both the input and output levels of the mental act. Even in such controlled situations as the classroom, the teacher's instruction, "Look at the figure in the upper left of page 2," will not orient the individual to the required place, and his focusing will be diffuse. If there is not discovery through extrapolation from other details provided by the teacher and accidentally grasped by the student, the individual may fail totally; or, at the output phase, he will incorrectly indicate what he may have correctly perceived. This is even more true when subject matter, like geography, in which orientation in space is crucial, is involved. In vocational subjects, in which coded directions must be understood, the incapacity or the lack of orientation to register and interpret symbols and codes properly leaves the individual with trial-and-error behavior. Trial and error, even when it leads to successful operation, will remain task bound, inefficient, and of limited adaptive value.

Need for Flexibility

The need for flexibility is especially clear in occupations requiring behaviors of a rather sophisticated level, which demand a high degree of representation, a strong automatization of the spatial concepts, and the cognitive flexibility to overcome the sets that have been established through experience. Many adults have to readjust to situations that are presented to them in a way that is unfamiliar or, in some instances, incompatible with their previous experience. This can be exemplified by trying to remove a screw from the underside of a stove.

The mirroring phenomenon shows that for many initiated adults constant alertness and vigilance are required to overcome orientational difficulties inherent in unfamiliar or set-opposed situations. A most common example is attempting to fix a stray lock of hair while looking in the mirror. In driving, calisthenic drill, gymnastics, and other tasks requiring coordination and reversal of stimuli in order to function properly, representational, flexible, spatial orientation is of highest importance.

Analysis of *Orientation in Space* in Terms of the Cognitive Map

Content: Systems of reference that permit the localization of objects in space and in relation to one another.

Modality: Mainly figural and graphic, with limited verbal elements; symbolic coding system; maps.

Orientation in Space I has only eight words, which are repeated throughout; it can therefore be used with illiterates.

Orientation in Space II and *III* have limited vocabularies but require a certain level of mastery of the reading process. Not withstanding a low level of lexical function, students can master key words with the help of the teacher.

Phase: *Input:*   The provision of basic concepts relating the individual to his surrounding space.

Elaboration: The acquisition or induction of basic functions, such as comparative behavior and planning behavior, internalized as prerequisites for proper mental functioning and enhanced by this particular activity; the constant confrontation with two or more sources of information as the condition *sine qua non* for the proper solution of a presented problem.

Output: The detachment of the individual from a system of reference limited to his own body, thereby leading to a process of decentration, which results in a higher level of flexibility, an openness toward different views, and a reduction of egocentricity.

Operations: Enhancement of a greater reliance on the representational modalities of action by use of a variety of situations, beginning with figural elements and ending with symbolic coding systems in which the identification process or the capacity of the individual to be helped by the movement of his own body is progressively reduced; the coordination and integration of two or more systems of reference through the confrontation between one that is stable and relative and another that is unstable but constant; production of relationships through coordination and deduction in a variety of modalities in which to operate with these concepts.

Level of abstraction: Relatively low in exercises having figural elements; moderately high with symbolic encoding; high with representation devoid of figural support.

Level of complexity: Low to moderate.

Level of efficiency: Moderately high with use of figures; slight, barely discernible body movements of students give evidence of motor behavior as aid; with decentration and use of symbols and codes, level of efficiency drops until practice shows results.

Anticipated Difficulties

The retarded performer's propensity to act motorically may be complicated if, in his indication of right and left, he centers his attention on his hand as an external instrument that can transcend the median axis of his body or its interior and intrinsic order. In such a case, if the individual is asked to point to the left part of an object, he may designate the part in accordance with the hand with which he points. Left, then, is where he places his left hand. He passes through the border of the axis of his body and manifests instability in the use of the only frame of reference that permits the division of the world into left and right.

Verbal labels may present a problem both in the input and output phases. If the child uses the word "relation" or "relative," it is usually to indicate a member of his family. "Side" and "direction" may become confused when the same word (e.g., "right" or "left") is used to indicate both.

An inability to answer logically is exemplified by the tautological response in the example below:

5. Why was it impossible to know the correct direction before you placed the boy in the center of the picture? *because it is impossible to know until you put the boy in the center of the picture.*

Orientation in Space I (exercise 5, page 5)

In the example on the next page there can be several sources of difficulty. The child must define the problem, which shifts from line to line (a). He must use several sources of information. He must identify the boy he seeks from a given code (b); transport him visually into the center of the field (c); identify the relationship between him and a given object (d); and then produce the answer in terms of object, relationship, or position using the code in the appropriate space (e). With a narrow mental field, an inability to define the problem, difficulty in eliminating the noise of extraneous and irrelevant stimuli, or an inability to coordinate several sources of information, he is unable to succeed in the task.

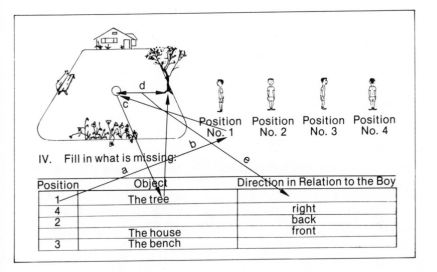

Rigidity of response can be demonstrated by the following example. A child may go to great lengths in order to squeeze an arrow between the dot and the side of the frame, despite unlimited possibilities of fulfilling the request in other ways. The lack of flexibility and plasticity is readily apparent. Another type of error in the same exercise is indicative of the apparent use of self as the referent.

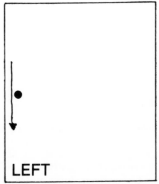

Orientation in Space I (exercise 10, page 15)

In the exercise on page 157, the task is to draw an arrow so that the dot appears on its left. The inability to see alternatives, impulsivity, insufficient reflection, and a lack of flexibility may account for the product.

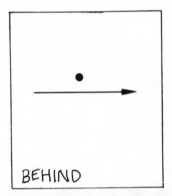

Typical error—*Orientation in Space I* (exercise 10, page 13)

The task is to describe the position of the dot in relation to the arrow. This error stems from an incorrect definition of the problem and decoding the written instruction into an action, so that the arrow is described in its relation to the dot.

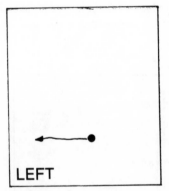

Typical error—*Orientation in Space I* (exercise 18, page 16)

The task is to draw an arrow and a dot so that the dot occupies the given position in relation to the arrow. This type of error indicates the use of self as the referent and the inability to divorce spatial representation from one's own body.

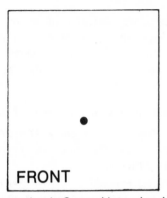

Orientation in Space I (exercise 4, page 15)

In one class the children excitedly revealed that they could draw arrows all around the dot and still comply with the instructions to draw an arrow so that the dot would appear in front of it. "We could draw 360 of them to correspond with the number of degrees in a circle," said one student. Another added, "And if we had a bigger circle, we would have more degrees and more arrows." The teacher agreed.

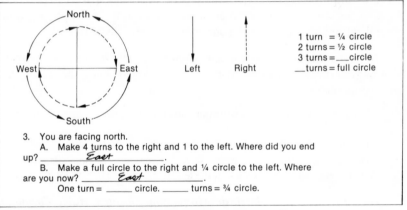

Typical error—*Orientation in Space III* (exercise 3, page 10)

The error above may arise from the inability to derive the appropriate information from the key: that one must stand in the center of the circle. Both hypothetical thought and representation are necessary. An error may also be caused by the lack of understanding of the principle of the nullification of a movement by its reversal. An additional difficulty stems from the necessity of translating from code to code, from turn to circle, and finding equivalents.

Inappropriate Use of Stable System of Spatial Reference

Teachers, too, may sometimes use inappropriate systems of spatial reference. For example, a teacher asked the students to write their names on the northeast corner of the paper, by which she meant its upper-right corner. This, obviously, is an inappropriate use of the cardinal points as a system of reference. This error is often made by children who are taught that north is at the top of their heads so that they automatically label the top of anything as its north.

The *Orientation in Space* Instruments in Terms of the Subgoals of FIE

I. Correction of Deficient Cognitive Functions   In the following anecdote there is evidence of the effect of *Orientation in Space* on the correction of deficient cognitive functioning:

> In discussing an accident in which a girl had been hit by a car in front of the school but had run away from the scene as soon as she was able to stand: "How could she have crossed the street without looking to her left and to her right?" "She shouldn't have run away." "She should have realized how concerned the driver of the car would be." "She should have stayed and found out how it happened and who was to blame." "She didn't think. She just got scared and ran. It's always a good idea after an accident to be checked by a doctor to be sure that everything is all right and to get the name of the driver in case there is trouble afterwards."

This discussion evidences use of the concepts of spatial orientation; criticism of impulsivity; empathy; analysis of cause and effect; hypothetical thinking; search for cause of an error so as to prevent its happening again; generalization; and need for the acceptance of responsibility.

II. Acquisition of Vocabulary, Concepts, and Operations   Within 2 months after the students start to learn *Orientation in Space,* they use its concepts spontaneously:

> "Teacher, do you want us to write our names in the upper left hand corner of the first page?"

> "Teacher, what is the third word in the fourth column from the right?"

> "The caption of the picture in the newspaper was wrong today. They said 'on Golda's left,' and it was really on the left of the picture but on Golda's right."

III. Production of Intrinsic Motivation Through Habit Formation The crystallization of acquired modalities of functioning by the formation of habits can be well illustrated by *Orientation in Space I.* There is ample opportunity to actively use a specific behavior in situations and tasks that do not repeat themselves. Each of the 16 pages presents the same principle in a different situation, modality of presentation, and/or mode of response. The required flexibility and generalization are produced by variations of the task in which the rule is applied (Figure 5).

What has been learned is then spontaneously applied in other subjects:

> In geography, relationships and the relative positions are used in locating places: "Germany is north of France."

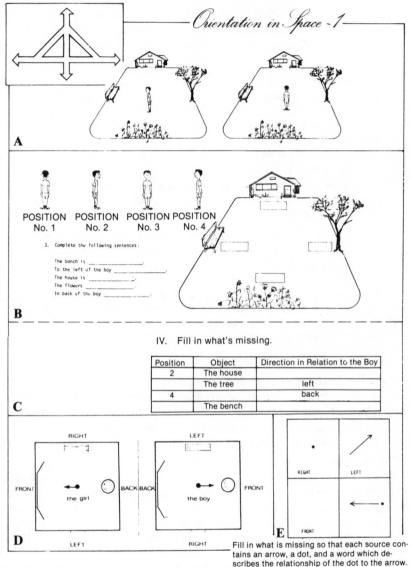

Figure 5. *Orientation in Space I. A:* Pages 1, 2, and 3. *B:* Pages 4 and 5. Tasks vary while situation is the same. *C:* Pages 6, 7, and 8. Format constant while referents and given data change. *D:* Pages 10 and 11. *E:* Pages 12, 13, 14, 15, and 16.

Teacher: "What about the Isle of Rhodes off of Turkey?"
Student: "The sea is to the south of Turkey, but the water is all around the island. That's what makes it an island."

In learning about longitudes, latitudes, the poles, and the hemispheres students invariably and spontaneously refer to lessons in FIE.

IV.   Production of Reflective, Insightful Processes   The immediate and correct use of appropriate referents and strategies in other subject-matter areas by the retarded performer gives evidence of the insight he gains.

> Carryover from the FIE exercises on wind and wind directions occurs in agriculture classes with the discussion of the necessity for considering wind direction and rain before planting.

> In nature lessons students speak of the necessity of meteorological services and wind direction for sailors, fishermen, paratroopers, and housekeepers who must hang out the laundry.

> A history teacher was surprised to hear his students talk of the influence of wind direction on maritime nations.

> A literature teacher writes of the increased empathy of her students: "Feuerstein's Instrumental Enrichment shows its influence on the affective, aesthetic and moral judgments of the child and has made a deep impression."

The student becomes aware of his ability to communicate more adequately and precisely. He gains understanding and self-confidence in his interpersonal relationships.

> A teacher corrected a student's listing of the four cardinal directions on the blackboard. The student politely said, "Excuse me, teacher. I listed them clockwise, while you listed them according to pairs. Both of us are right, but you can correct mine only if you explain why yours is preferable."

With decreased egocentricity and increased empathy, the retarded performer is able to understand how the same action can be viewed differently by two different participants, or even by the same participant at different times. Peace negotiations, such as the Arab-Israeli relations and the necessity for direct discussions, are often brought as examples.

V.   Creation of Task-Intrinsic Motivation   The exercises are highly motivating, not only for retarded performers, but for more initiated individuals and young adults as well. In Israeli Defense Forces, noncommissioned officers who introduce basic concepts of topology report increased efficiency on the part of soldiers who have been exposed to these instruments. The same is true of marksmanship, in which students demand that corrections for aim be given in more precise and stable terms than "a little higher" or "a little lower."

VI.   Change in the Attitude of the Retarded Performer from Perception of Himself as a Passive Recipient and Reproducer of Information to Perception of Himself as Active Generator of New Information   Starting from the beginning of *Orientation in Space I,* and continuing throughout all three instruments, the student is offered countless opportunities to generate new information by coordinating the data offered to him. When the two or more sets of data converge or are transformed by him, he produces new information that is available to him for the adequate solution of problems or adaptation.

A principal reported the results of a Bible test given to a class of FIE students and two other regular classes. The test was based on the first 12 chapters of the book of Joshua. The scores of the FIE students were higher than those of the other two groups. An analysis of answers showed that the FIE students had reorganized and transformed the information in the chapters. They had used spatial and temporal concepts to discuss the wars of the period. There was summation leading to categorization and the labeling of the participants in the wars, and the positions of the troops were described in relation to one another. "Joshua stationed some of his troops to the west of the Ai. His strategy was to attack from the front and from the rear."

Results similar to those in the above instance have been reported in other classes of FIE students on tests based on the exodus from Egypt and the travels of the children of Israel. FIE students described the journey according to direction, days, and sequence of events.

COMPARISONS

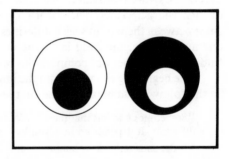

Among the first three instruments usually introduced in the Instrumental Enrichment program is one concerned with the development of spontaneous comparative behavior. We consider that comparative behavior is the most elementary building block of relational thinking and therefore a primary condition for any cognitive process that is to transcend mere recognition and identification.

Need for Spontaneous Comparative Behavior

Our basic contention, that the culturally deprived individual does not use comparative behavior spontaneously, does not imply that he is unable to compare nor that he does not do so in given instances. However, comparative behavior as a spontaneous manifestation is vital to enable him to become modified through direct exposure to sources of stimuli. Through clinical work, it has been found that the spontaneous use of comparison by retarded performers is limited to their most basic needs, which are not necessarily those that are relevant to academic achievement.

Comparative behavior is, therefore, one of the functions that must be corrected before the various other steps in development. Inducing comparison initially involves making the individual perceive two or more objects or events as the focus of his scrutiny. Inducing such perception is done not simply so that the individual will identify discrete entities but to facilitate the establishment of relationships between the objects of his scrutiny in terms of their differences and commonalities. The lack of spontaneous comparative behavior leaves the individual unaffected by the variety of experiences he has undergone. The success of any effort to produce a change of such a deeply ingrained pattern at the age of adolescence can only be ensured by providing a direct and systematic attack on this deficient function. The motivation of a retarded performer to compare must be enhanced through his insight into the meaning of this cognitive behavior for more pervasive adaption to academic and life situations.

The lack of spontaneous comparative behavior becomes evident with the introduction of the title page of the instrument. Students describe the figures in the symbol separately, with only a partial and imprecise enumeration of their characteristics. There is usually no attempt to project the relationships between them or to seek similarities and differences. In the rare case an attempt is made, the child lacks the verbal labels necessary to express his findings, or he does not compare the two objects on the same dimensions.

The beginning of insight into the importance of the process is illustrated in the following summary of the first lesson. The students are speaking:

> "Sometimes it seems that there is more that is alike and sometimes more that is different. It depends on how you look at it."

> "It depends on what is important at the moment."

> "Always at the beginning, it seems that everything is different."

> "No, that's not true. It always seems that everything is similar. But when you keep looking, you see how different things really are."

Comparison and Perception

Comparative behavior plays an important role in perception. To a large extent, it determines the nature of the perception, the acuity and sharpness of the perceived elements, and the precision with which various elements are registered. A wealth of details pertaining to a perceived object may be neglected if identification or recognition is the sole purpose of the perceptual process. However, when the individual compares spontaneously, he digs out and unravels the various characteristics of the object by an active volitional act.

We have worked with children who display great difficulty in describing the salient characteristics of an object unless they are required to contrast it with another object that is different in these dimensions. The relative nature of certain relational characteristics may also explain why an observer becomes conscious of certain attributes only following comparative behavior. Thus, *big* or *little* and *bright* or *dark* are only determined as one compares. If perceived in isolation, these particular dimensions will not be included in the description of an object.

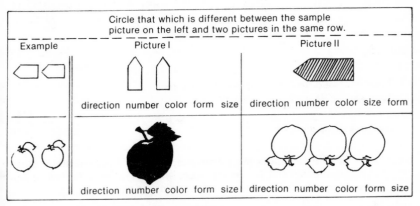

Comparisons (exercises 4 and 5, page 10)

The student is oriented toward the use of both stable and relative attributes in the comparison of items.

Process of Comparison and Its Concomitant Cognitive Functions

Comparative behavior is the abbreviation of a motor manipulation by which the two elements are superimposed, one on the other. In the process of seeking correspondence between two elements, each of the dimensions will be scrutinized thoroughly. Through this activity, there is a determination of whether the elements are identical. If they are not, there is a search for the locus and direction of the differences. Similarities and differences will be summed, and this will provide the basis for a statement describing the relationship between the two or more objects on a set of dimensions whose relevancy is directly linked to the goals set for the comparative behavior.

A number of cognitive functions are implied in the process of comparison. The first is a clear stable perception, which is not to be altered in the course of the operation. If one of the compared objects is altered, the constancies and invariants are conserved, thus ensuring the continuity of the perceived across the alteration incurred in the process itself. A second function is thorough and systematic exploration, which permits the exhaustive gathering of the data required for comparative purpose. Because systematic exploration is limited in the deprived individual, his input is apt to be poor and imprecise, and the data will depend on a random selection of elements rather than those produced by a scanning of the total field.

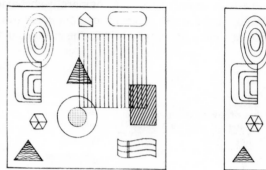

There are five differences between the two pictures.
Mark each difference you find with an X.

Comparisons (page 22)

Comparison requires a mental superimposition of two elements in order to ascertain similarities and differences. Successful completion of the task requires systematic search for the gathering of the complete data.

Precision

Without the need for precision, the comparing individual does not perceive an identity because his imprecise observations simplify the various dimensions of each object and produce a global, syncretic, nondiscriminating point of view that does not permit differentiation. An individual who has internalized the need for comparison has, of necessity, acquired certain strategies for gathering data that will assist him. The nature of experience and perception is far richer, more detailed, more precise, more subsumed, and more organized whenever spontaneous comparative behavior is present in either an implicit or an explicit way.

In a citizenship lesson, the teacher noted on the blackboard, at random, the characteristics of a good citizen. Her listing disturbed her students. They told her that in FIE they had learned to rank things according to their order of importance and asked her permission to use the same method in ranking the qualities of a good citizen.

Discrimination

Both stemming from and determining the nature of comparison is the process of discrimination, which permits the individual to perceive and then to formulate the differences between various objects. Many of the differences between objects are either overlooked or not perceived because the concepts necessary for such discrimination are either nonexistent or not readily elicited. This occurs because the concepts are not in current use or because no particular need to apply them makes them irrelevant for the comparative process. Thus *equal-unequal* or *similar-dissimilar* is rarely used spontaneously and is not readily elicited in these children. It is through the superimposition of the two elements to be compared that their relationship is constructed. Comparative behavior will depend on, as well as determine, the richness of the repertoire of dimensions used in a comparison.

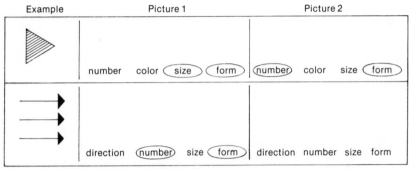

Comparisons (exercises 1 and 3, page 12)

Solution of exercise 3 entails conclusions based on hypothetical thought, inference, and logical thinking. If a picture must be drawn that is similar to the model only in the dimensions that are encircled, what should be drawn if there is nothing circled? What about dimensions that are not mentioned at all, like color? Through a logical process one may conclude that all that is not similar must be different.

In a history lesson, the teacher asked for the similarities between Islam and Judaism. The students were not willing to accept the task as presented. They insisted that a proper comparison included both similarities and differences:

"Both are religions. Both pray to one God whom the Moslems call Allah and whom the Jews call Hashem. Jews pray three times a day; Moslems five times. Both have Sabbath, but for Moslems it is on Friday and for Jews on Saturday. Both fast, but Jews fast only one day at a time, while the Moslems have a month-long fast. Moslems fast during the day and are allowed to eat at night while Jews must fast from sundown to sundown on important fasts."

Judgment of Similarity

Another element of this instrument concerns the judgmental process of the evaluation of *equal-unequal* or *similar-dissimilar,* which occur on a continuum. Such judgment must be adjusted to the specific context and basic purpose of the comparative behavior. The specificity of a culture, of a need system, or of familiarity with a particular area will determine the similarity that is perceived. For example, an uninitiated layman would perceive two rings as similar while they would not be considered comparable by a skilled mechanic because of his finer discrimination. The number of terms used by Eskimoes for designating various types of snow, as reported by Whorf (1956), is another example of refined discriminatory processes following, as well as leading to, comparative behavior. Refined discrimination forms the standards and criteria for similarity and dissimilarity.

```
┌─────────────────────────────────────────────────────────────┐
│                                                               │
│   Ugly  ⎫  _____      _____      │
│   Bad   ⎭                        _____      │
│                                                               │
├─────────────────────────────────────────────────────────────┤
│                                                               │
│   Lake  ⎫  _____      _____      │
│   River ⎭                        _____      │
│                                                               │
└─────────────────────────────────────────────────────────────┘
```

Comparisons (exercises 3 and 6, page 6)

> Intraclass differences are more difficult for the retarded performer to perceive and discriminate. In comparing a river to a lake or a pool to the sea, the commonality in both instances is defined as "water." The differences between them are expressed as "large" and "small." The student experiences no need for a precise differentiation and is content with gross differences.

In certain instances, the number of attributes by which things differ from one another will be used as the criterion for localizing them on a continuum ranging from identity to total difference. The dimensions on which elements are compared must be qualified and summed. Sometimes, however, a great valence is ascribed to a particular attribute so that it forms the basis for decisions as to similarity or dissimilarity between two objects, despite differences in a great number of less essential attributes. Here essentially is a function of the context within which and from which the comparative behavior stems.

> "The apple I'm thinking of is small, green, sour, and has a few spots on it that are rotten. Another is big, red, sweet, and absolutely perfect. In spite of the differences, they are both apples."

The process of judging, classifying, and establishing the relationship is an important determinant for, as well as an outcome of, comparative behavior.

Although we have stressed spontaneity, this does not mean that invoked comparative behavior does not have a role, specific to the immediate task in which the individual is involved, or that it may not be the product of a volitional, intentional, planned act. What is the energetic or dynamic factor that will provide the individual with the need for comparing and establishing relationships? The elaborational processes set goals for our perception, and, in so doing, they determine the nature of the comparative behavior.

The specific instruments designed to evoke comparative behavior establish a variety of prerequisites for relational thinking, and therefore they are preliminary to, and a preparation for, various other cognitive activities. Exercises in comparisons will have to precede those for categorization, classification, and seriation, as well as those dealing with syllogistic and transitive thinking. Emphasis on comparative behavior will appear throughout the program, but in this particular instrument the prerequisities for comparative behavior, the awareness of its importance and meaning, and the techniques for its proper use are fostered.

Content of *Comparisons*

Comparisons consists of 22 pages. The first unit introduces the concept of commonality and differences. In pictorial and verbal modalities, the exercises force comparison of two items on discrete dimensions, starting with size, form, number, and spatial and temporal concepts, and concluding with abstract attributes not immediately perceived, such as function, composition, and power. In these exercises, the student learns to seek the most relevant, most characteristic, most invariant attribute and to compare objects along the continuum of a single dimension.

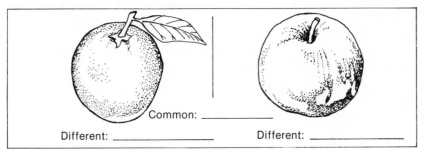

Comparisons (exercise 3, page 1)

In the above exercise, the choice of the leaf as the difference between the apple and the orange can indicate the use of an irrelevant dimension as the basis for comparison, or an impulsive response in which the input is the result of a superficial scanning. Whereas it is true that the orange does have a leaf, that characteristic is not an invariant, nor would it serve as a differentiator in all situations in which comparison between apples and oranges would be involved. Despite a superimposition of one object upon the other, and an identification of the two as belonging to the class of "fruit," there has been no attempt to define the differences in terms of membership of the same class.

A verbal modality raises the level of abstraction in the problem of finding and defining the commonality and differences.

Baby	*living things*	<u>*toothless*</u>
Old man		<u>*old*</u>

Typical error—*Comparisons* (exercise 7, page 2)

Two typical errors appear in the solution of the exercise above. "Living things" to express the commonality is too broad a class. Its overgeneralization is evidence of a lack of precision and no search for relationships which are not visually perceptible. The answers for the observed differences may indicate a lack of comparison along the continuum of a single dimension.

In answer to the question "Can we compare things we cannot see?", a student replied, "Yes, like in math. $158 + 158$ is the same as 158×2."

A girl added, "In my head I *know* exactly the kind of boyfriend I want. I compare every boy I meet with the model I have in my head. So far, I haven't found him, but I always hope that I will."

In the second unit of *Comparisons,* objects are compared to a standard along several dimensions simultaneously. Thus, the student is asked to create examples that are similar to and different from a given model according to a number of criteria, simultaneously applied (see Figure 6).

Exercises are introduced to help the student discriminate in his search for identities, similarities, and equivalencies.

A boy summarized the discussion of the difference between identity, similarity, and equivalency with the following notation on the blackboard: Identity $= 3 + 5 = 3 + 5$ Similarity $3 + 5 = 5 + 3$ Equivalency $1 + 7 = 3 + 5$.

The student is also asked to rank given examples in which similarities are gradually reduced according to their proximity to a model.

3

Comparisons (excercise 3, page 21)

In the exercises of the third unit, the learner establishes classes and class membership, using inductive and deductive processes. Superordinate concepts are used to describe both commonalities and differences.

Common: _____
Different: _____

Comparisons (exercise 3, page 17)

Additional Anticipated Errors

Many of the difficulties that arise may be anticipated. There may be a problem of inadequate vocabulary. A learner may say, "I know that this is a boy and this is a girl, but I don't know the one word which I can use to describe that difference." The retarded performer may be satisfied with the first similarity or difference he perceives. He may use association; he may describe each of the two objects, enumerating their characteristics without making any attempt to compare them along one dimension at a time.

In a nature class the children were asked to compare birds and fish. The lists made by the children who had not learned *Comparisons* were:

Birds	Fish
Fly	Cold-blooded
Feathers	Lay eggs. Some have live babies.
Beaks	Live in water
Wings	Gills
Build nests	Swim
Lay eggs	Fins
Lungs	

The children who had learned to compare were able to organize the same information so that points of similarity and difference were defined under superordinate headings and ascertainable at a glance.

Some teachers may reveal an inability to compare properly or a rigidity which does not permit the considering of alternatives. The following classroom exchange is an illustration:

The children have been asked to find the commonality and differences between milk and salt in one exercise, and between the sun and a flashlight in another:
Teacher: "The difference between milk and salt is that you can drink two or three glasses of milk because it is good for children, but you can't drink two or three glasses of salt."
Teacher: "What is the sun?"
Student: "The sun."

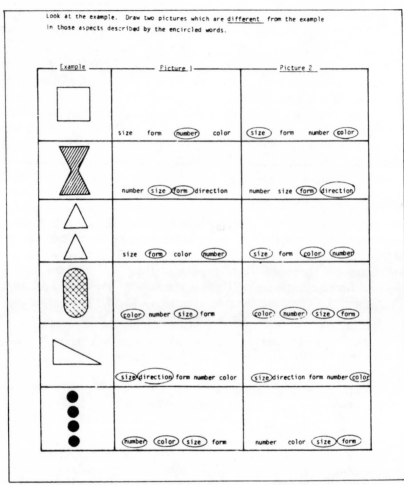

Look at the example. Draw two pictures which are different from the example in those aspects described by the encircled words.

Figure 6. *Comparisons* (page 14). To automatize the act of comparison, to provide the basis for classification, and to correct his episodic grasp of reality, the student learns to find similarities and differences between objects, events, and ideas. He learns to use concepts in his identification of the most essential or characteristic dimensions and to ignore the irrelevant. Among the functions treated are: blurred and sweeping perception; unplanned, unsystematic exploratory behavior; lack of verbal tools; inability to relate to two or more sources of information; narrowness of the mental field; and trial-and-error responses. The student actively creates two pictures, each of which differs from the example only in the aspects encircled, and is similar to the model on all other dimensions. The task is complicated and requires the ability to define the framework necessary for the solution of the problem, the simultaneous use of several sources of information, and a strategy for checking. Salient are the conservation of constancy and the need for planning.

Teacher: "What does the sun give?"
Student: "Light."
Teacher: "What else?"
Student: "Heat."
Teacher: "And the flashlight?"

Student: "Light."
Teacher: "That's the difference. The sun gives light and heat while the flashlight only gives light."

The teacher's replies may indicate a functional definition of the relationships. Perhaps another explanation of the teacher's responses in the above exchange is a passive-acceptant approach that reflects the teacher's belief in the inability of the child to accede to a more sophisticated comparative behavior. The teacher figuratively bends to the child's presumed level instead of attempting to raise the child's level of thought by appropriate questioning. The orientation toward seeking a single right answer is also detrimental. There is no way of knowing whether a correct answer is the product of reflection and the result of a consideration of possible alternatives or a product of an expression of a probabilistic approach. With the immediate acceptance of a single answer, there is not the necessary confrontation between, and the investigation of, divergent responses.

Spontaneous Use of Comparative Behavior

The need to compare becomes internalized and the process automatized. Students begin to compare without being directed to do so.

In a composition class, the teacher distributed pages for independent work. One of the FIE students compared the new assignment with pages he had previously done. In reply to the teacher's question of what caused him to compare, he said, "It just seemed natural that I should."

FIE students learned about Holland in geography class. They immediately compared it to the United States. Some of the parameters they used were size, population, location, natural resources, trade, and attitude toward Israel.

Both insight and generation of new information are evident in the following illustrations, which indicate that progress has been made in overcoming an episodic grasp of reality.

For social studies, students were required to watch a televised documentary series on different life-styles of different cultures. One morning an FIE student volunteered: "It seems to me that all cultures have had to face similar problems of getting married, raising children, and taking care of housing, clothing, food, and self-defense. If I compare them, I see that each has come up with his own strategy for solving the problem."

In a literature class, the teacher asked if the hero of a story was strong or weak. The students immediately began to define the problem: they were being asked to set criteria of strengths and weaknesses and then to see how the hero compared to these criteria. They then decided it all depended on the point of view of the reader and the actions of the hero in his relationships with other persons in the story. The students then concluded that the question was too broad because there were instances and events in which the hero was strong and others in which he was weak: "One simply can't balance these on a scale, because some actions are more critical than others."

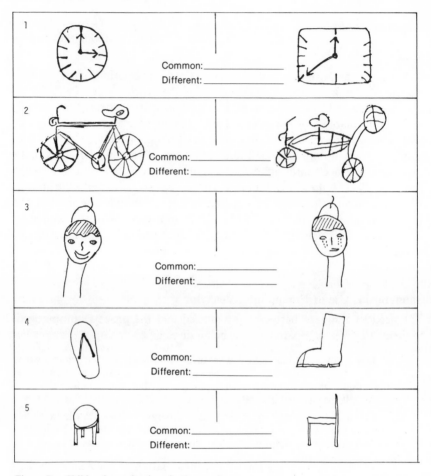

Figure 7.   Children's productions in *Comparisons*.

Their attack on the problem evidences transfer from their learning of *Organization of Dots, Orientation in Space, Analytic Perception,* and *Comparisons*.

Children's Productions

Children have been motivated to construct pages of *Comparisons* for the use of their friends and for reproduction by the Hadassah-Wizo-Canada Research Institute (see Figure 7). In exercises 1 and 2, intraclass differences are illustrated, with the necessity for summative behavior in the perception of the differences between the clocks. Exercise 3 brings in an affective element. In exercises 4 and 5, there is a requirement for a superordinate commonality in order to form the category.

CATEGORIZATION

o

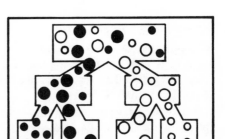

Categorization is designed to deal with the lack of, or impairment of, the ability of the culturally deprived child to elaborate the gathered data by use of hierarchically higher mental processes for the organization of the data into superordinate categories. This deficiency has been discussed previously in the section dealing with deficient cognitive functions at the elaborational and output levels. Classification is based on successful comparison, differentiation, and discrimination. With analytical perception and the projection of relationships, the process is not merely one of sorting but one of grouping objects or events according to underlying principles and subsuming them into appropriate sets. Sets can thereby be formed on the basis of commonality or the similarities that exist between objects or events. Because they are subject to various operations, sets can be broadened, reduced, or constructed anew by addition, subtraction, multiplication, and other mental operations.

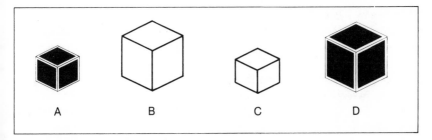

Categorization (model, page 13)

The universe of cubes can be reduced to a set of white cubes by subtracting the black ones; to a set of black cubes by eliminating the white; to a group of large cubes by excluding the small and ignoring color; and to a group of small cubes by subtracting the large ones. Four separate and new sets can be formed by multiplication so that there are sets of large black, large white, small black, and small white cubes. Other combinations are also possible. The criteria and principles of classification are determined by the individual himself.

Difficulties in *Categorization*

A cognitive style based on association, often encountered in the retarded performer, makes the articulation of a complex field very difficult. Kagan (1966) has found that, if pictures of a man, a watch, and a ruler are presented at the same time, a child with a cognitive style based on association will group the man and the watch together. The culturally deprived child is also apt to use incidental characteristics of the objects as the principle for their categorization, rather than their more stable or essential attributes. Reflective thinking is necessary to project between objects an existing relationship that is not based on purely sensorial perception or association.

Retarded performers are not oriented toward forming a set based on the most relevant criteria and, therefore, are unable to do so. They are also unable to relate to several sources of information simultaneously, as opposed to sequentially, in order to arrive at expanded classes. They do not display the flexibility or the divergency of thought that allows for the categorization and recategorization of the same universe of objects into different sets, as the principle and criteria differ with new objectives and needs.

If one of the attributes of learning is the ability to subsume new experiences and new stimuli within already existing schemata, then it becomes essential that the student extract the relevant information and find the rule that will enable assimilation into the appropriate cognitive categories. One cannot react to a tiger as one would to a mouse simply because both animals have tails. To be able to transform and generate new applications, the student must have the appropriate concepts.

Contents of *Categorization*

Categorization consists of 31 pages, divided into units and graded in complexity. The modality of the instrument's presentation is verbal, pictorial and schematic, and figural. It is based on skills and procedures learned in *Comparisons* and leads to the instrument *Syllogisms*.

The first unit arouses the need for categorization and introduces the concept of set membership. The child learns to label the universe of objects with which he deals and to seek relationships within that universe (see Figure 8).

Following is a fragment of a lesson in *Categorization* which is typical of the presentation of the subject:

Teacher: "What is classification?"
Students: "Organizing. Putting into order. Putting things to one side. Separating. Putting things into different groups."

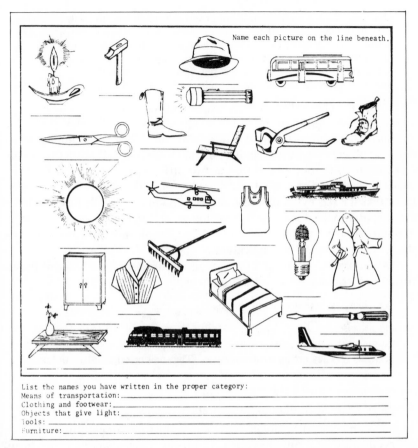

Name each picture on the line beneath.

List the names you have written in the proper category:
Means of transportation:_____
Clothing and footwear:_____
Objects that give light:_____
Tools: _____
Furniture:_____

Figure 8. *Categorization* (page 6). In order to assign membership to classes, it is necessary to be familiar with the invariant attributes of the given categories: It is important that the students gain insight into the underlying commonalities between objects that seem to be very different. Because the given sets are very distant from one another, there is little chance for error in attribution. There are difficulties, however, in labeling, in systematic work, and in using the two or more sources of information.

Teacher: "What do we ordinarily categorize?"
Student: "In school, we divide the kids into classes: according to their age and level; according to different teachers; according to the vocational subjects they take."
Teacher: "Other examples, not from school."
Student: "In the post office, they separate stamps into airmail and regular and according to their prices and the sets."
Student: "The mailman has to sort his mail into areas, and then into buildings and then into apartments."
Student: "When I worked in the kibbutz, we had to sort the tomatoes. At the same time we sorted for export and for local use; and for size, and color, and ripeness and for perfect ones and those with rotten spots."
Student: "Each kind sells for a separate and different price."
Student: "In my house, before my mother throws the clothes into the washing

machine, she sorts it into white things and colored things; into dainty things and coarse things; into what needs ironing and what doesn't. Then when they're clean, she divides the clothes into piles according to the person they belong to. Then we have have to put our own things away."
Teacher: "Into what pile does she put a red nylon blouse?"
Student: "Oh, she doesn't put that into the machine. She washes that by hand."

From the above discussion it is apparent that the students have only a vague, imprecise grasp of the nature and process of classification. There is a confusion between sorting and categorizing, and all of the examples are of concrete objects. There is no indication that there is a realization that no object can simultaneously be placed in two different sets, although it can be variously classified according to different principles. The student has yet to learn that the red nylon blouse could be sorted into the pile of the colored clothes, or into the pile of the dainty clothes, or into the pile of those that do not need ironing, and that the set of colored, fragile, non-ironed garments is the product of logical multiplication.

An imprecise definition of the set and insufficient knowledge of the attributes of its members also lead to errors.

Teacher: "Where do we put the snail?"
Student: "In the reptiles?"
Teacher: "No, it isn't a reptile."
Student: "In living creatures?"
Teacher: "They are all living creatures. The snail belongs to the molluscs."

Categorization According to Subject and Principle

In the second unit, the child learns to define the rules for categorization and to encode the operation, presenting his information in diagram form. In applying different principles of classification to the same objects, he becomes aware of the possibilities of grouping and regrouping according to objectives and needs. This is a major opportunity to provide the child with the experience and insight that he, himself, is the main determinant in the organization of the world. The understanding that the organization of the same stimuli is a matter of his own decision and act has an important bearing on his position vis-à-vis the world. This can be likened to the position attributed to Adam by the Bible in his act of labeling the creatures of the world:

> And out of the ground the Lord God formed every beast of the field and every fowl of the air, and brought them unto the man to see what he would call them; and whatsoever the man would call every living creature, that was to be the name thereof. And the man gave names to all cattle, and to the fowl of the air, and to every beast of the field (Genesis 2.19 and 2.20).

Through the act of labeling and classifying, Adam gained mastery of the creatures of the universe.

CLASSIFICATION OF PENCILS ACCORDING TO SIZE AND COLOR

A   B   C   D

1. Classification according to size:

   Classify pencils A, B, C, D according to the headings in the table. In each empty square write the appropriate letter.

   Subject of classification: PENCILS

   Principle of classification: size: (1) large (2) small

Categorization (part of exercise 1, page 11)

There is immediate practical application of the operations learned in this unit. A cosmetology teacher reported a reorganization of supplies according to categories. In carpentry shops, tools, nails, nuts, bolts, and screws are categorized into separate compartments and labeled. In language classes, children spontaneously classify words they encounter into the various parts of speech. In history classes, students classified the population of Rome, the guilds of Italy, and the estates of England.

There are still difficulties and errors, of course. The most common is that of distinguishing between the subject of classification and the principle of classification, or a confusion between the "what" and the "according to what."

In the third unit, objects are divided according to several criteria, simultaneously applied. In the beginning tasks of the unit, practice in the use of form, size, and color is provided. In later tasks, however, the principles for classification are not limited.

In the example on page 180, the student is required to discover the principle on which the classification is based, an act essential for functioning in a modern society.

"It isn't enough that I know how to classify; I have to figure out how somebody else did all the time. Every time I want to use the telephone book, the public library, the supermarket, or a department store I have to know according to what principles they are categorized."

In order to complete the exercises, the student must use the given solution as a starting point and reverse the usual process of classifying. He must decide on the points of similarity and difference. He must use the number of

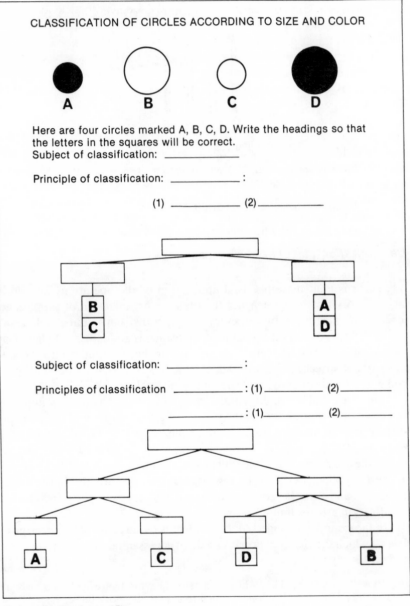

Categorization (page 15)

spaces available to him in the diagram as a cue and decide on the sequence in which his verbal description of the objects must be listed. In order to check his completed work, the student reverses the process, starting from the subject of categorization and following through with the principles according to which objects were categorized. The exercises require hypothetical thinking, the use of cues, and flexibility.

In the last unit, students are given an opportunity to categorize objects and events according to criteria and principles that they, themselves, establish. The student may be asked to plan a Sports Day for his school which will take into account all the activities, ages, sex, and competencies of the participants.

In the following example, the student is asked to build a zoo. He must determine the principles upon which planning and organization will be based. In order to complete the task successfully, he must be precise in his perception; work systematically, using a strategy that will ensure the inclusion of all of the creatures; seek the relationships between the creatures; draw conclusions regarding the type of enclosure necessary; and encode the information and present it diagrammatically. He must devise a method of self-criticism to check his work. It is obvious that there are several principles upon which he can categorize the creatures, and he will be confronted with divergent solutions in the classroom discussion. He must be ready to defend his selection of the criteria for categorization.

Categorization (page 19)

The child usually divides the creatures according to their habitat, their food, and the danger they present to man. He could just as well use other principles for categorization.

The spontaneous application of the principles of categorization and the presentation of information in the form of diagrams are reported by many teachers. The division of literature into fiction and non-fiction, with further subdivisions into classes, is fairly common. In a social studies class, the students diagrammed their society and categorized the population according to ethnic groups, with subdivisions of vocations, professions, sex, age, and the like.

> "We can categorize the kids in class according to many different principles. It all depends on the purpose of our categorization. If it's to march in a parade, we would use height. If it's to sing in a choir, they would have to be classified according to sex and type of voice. If it's for phys. ed., it has to be according to sex. But there is no limit to the number of categories we could divide them into."

Diagramming originally presents a problem for both students and their teachers. The usual error in the schematic presentation of a composite and diverse group is that of subdividing the universe according to principles individually applied, instead of first categorizing according to one principle, and then another.

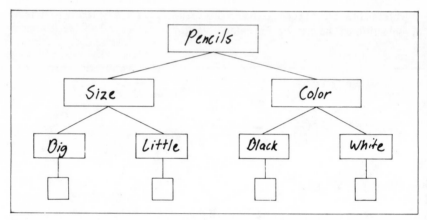

Typical error—*Categorization* (page 14)

There is no possible way to complete the exercise as shown above, since each pencil can be described in terms of both color and size. A correct solution would be as follows:

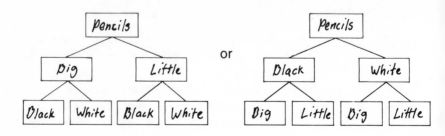

Throughout the *Categorization* instrument, there is an attack on the deficient functions in the phases of input, elaboration, and output. The student must be precise in his perception; must label, compare, and discriminate; must use only relevant information from several sources; and must restrain his impulsivity and convey his solution in the use of the code for the instrument. Repetition provides ample opportunity for reinforcement and automatization. The student learns not only to categorize, but also to recognize principles upon which given categories have been formed. The information implicit in relationships thus becomes available to him.

Spontaneous Categorization

The following anecdote illustrates the attainment of the various subgoals of the program through *Categorization:*

> The general science teacher took her class on a nature walk and asked the students to list what they saw. Upon checking the homework, she found that the lists of the FIE students were divided into three main categories: Animate, Inanimate, and Growing Things. Growing Things was subdivided into trees, flowers, and grasses. Trees were subdivided into fruit trees, evergreens, and deciduous. Flowers were subdivided into wild flowers, which was further subdivided into protected and nonprotected, and cultivated flowers. Grass was divided into lawns and weeds, with weeds subdivided into thorny and nonthorny. The other main categories were subdivided as well.
>
> The teacher reported, "I was shocked. The work of the FIE kids, the retarded performers, was well-organized, clear, and summarized, while that of the 'normal' students was an unorganized jumble. I can only hope that what was in their heads was not as mixed up as what was on their papers."

Categorization as a Prerequisite for Logico-verbal Reasoning

Both the subject of classification and the principles for grouping must be clearly and consciously enunciated. The sophisticated use of categorization demands a fine discrimination and recognition of similarities and differences. Classes based on similarities become the basis for syllogisms, while those based on differences are used in transitive thinking.

ANALYTIC PERCEPTION

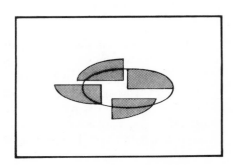

The instrument *Analytic Perception* uses the perceptual processes for the development, acquisition, and crystallization of a varied set of cognitive strategies in an individual in order to form attitudinal and motivational changes in his approach to reality. The articulation of one's internal field is dependent on the capacity of the individual to perceive differentiated parts in the external world. Such a differentiation involves behaviors that, even if they do exist, are not necessarily used spontaneously by the culturally deprived child.

In order to consider a whole as subdivided into its components, relationships must be established between the whole and its parts — parts that can be differentiated, identified, discriminated, enumerated, described, and ordered finally in their position relative to the whole. Definitions of the parts of a whole must be based on criteria that are adequate to a specific situation. These may be arbitrary decisions, based on specific needs or clear-cut extrinsic criteria for the subdivision of the whole into its parts.

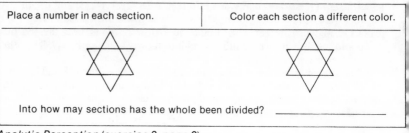

Analytic Perception (exercise 3, page 2)

The figure above can be considered as being formed by either a union of a hexagon and six triangles or of two triangles. It can also be perceived globally as the Star of David. How its parts are defined is contingent upon an arbitrary decision based on a specific need.

The articulation of the field is a direct product of an analytic process of topological relationships and their meaning and significance, and the nature of the whole to be divided, its contents, the language of its presentation, and its operations. The capacity to articulate an object or event in a great variety of ways, according to specific needs, induces a divergent approach. The whole and its parts are not viewed as rigid and stable but as entities that can undergo change while still conserving their constancies.

Each section which appears below the given design is composed of a number of parts. On the line beneath each section, write the numbers of the parts it contains.

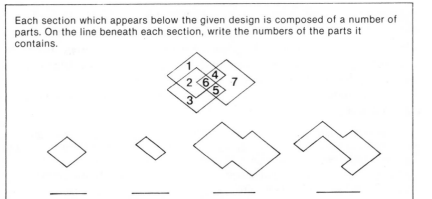

Analytic Perception (exercise 2, page 27)

The whole is subdivided into 7 parts, which belong simultaneously to different figures as well as to the total entity. Numbers 1, 2, 4, and 6 comprise one diamond; parts 2, 3, 5, and 6 define a second diamond; and parts 4, 5, 6, and 7 a third diamond. Each of the parts is a whole unto itself, however.

From the first exercises, the children learn that it is possible to divide a whole into parts and that the parts need not be equal in size:

"If I bake a cake, I cut it into the number of slices I need according to the number of people who will eat it. But I can cut a big piece for my brother, a little piece for my sister who is on a diet, a tiny taste for the baby, and grandma who has diabetes doesn't get any at all — maybe just an itsy-bitsy piece."

FIE students in sewing class talk about sewing a dress from a pattern with many parts. They start to assemble some of the pieces into a new whole called the blouse. In doing so they must know the relationships between the parts so that the right sleeve is not put into the left armhole and the yoke is in the back and not in the front:

"We have to know not only the way the parts fit together, but the order in which we have to sew them."

Systematic analysis is economical because it may involve multiplicative rather than additive processes whenever the whole is subdivided. There may be different criteria of analysis wherever overlapping subdivisions of the whole make it necessary.

An analytic process may be applied to a perception of the structure of an object or its graphic representation; to the location and definition of different parts of an activity or an operation; to a series of reasons through which an event or act is explained; or to a set of logical propositions. The common aspects of each of these processes are the breakdown of the whole into its parts and the seeking of the relationship among them. A structural analysis will involve an inventory of the parts, which are registered, labeled, counted, and summed. It will also involve a categorization of the parts in terms of specific criteria generated from the whole. In an operational analysis, the steps or stages are registered, labeled, enumerated, and summated. In many instances, analysis is of both content and process.

FIE student mechanics see the relevance of *Analytic Perception* to their vocation:

> "There's no need to take the engine apart if I know that all that's wrong is a flat tire. But if I got to take the engine apart to find out what's wrong with it, I got to know what the parts are, how they go together and the order in which I take it apart. So's when I go to put it together again I put it back in the right order with each piece *exactly* where it should be."

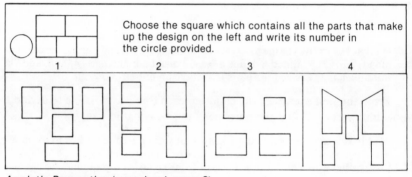

Analytic Perception (exercise 1, page 9)

> Solution of the above task involves the perception of the model in terms of categories and number, planning the strategy for the search for the appropriate frame, and devising a method for evaluation of success.

Content of *Analytic Perception*

Analytic Perception, 38 pages in length, introduces analysis into the cognitive repertoire of the culturally deprived child.

The first unit includes such tasks as subdividing a simple or complex whole into its parts, summing up the number of the components, and finding parts that are identical to the given standard within a complex whole (see Figure 9). In order to find a part, it is necessary to invest sufficient time for its complete and accurate perception, transport it visually or through interiorization into the field, and search systematically. Hypothetical thought and logical inference will assist in finding the part that is sought. Comparison to the model is the final step in the evaluation of success.

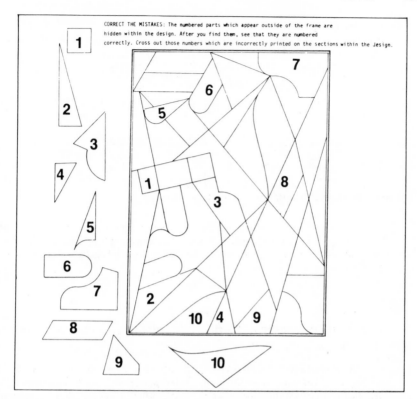

CORRECT THE MISTAKES: The numbered parts which appear outside of the frame are hidden within the design. After you find them, see that they are numbered correctly. Cross out those numbers which are incorrectly printed on the sections within the design.

Figure 9. *Analytic Perception* (page 8).The student must decide whether a part numbered within the frame is the same as the similarly numbered standard. If it is not, he must find the correct counterpart and number it appropriately. To solve the task, he must compare, search and work systematically, internalize the model or transport it visually, and think hypothetically. He must use space and lines as cues. He must define his strategy. Although size and form remain constant across variations in orientation, it is interesting to note that the standard seems to differ when it is placed within a new context.

In the discussion of finding a single part within a whole, students cite finding a part of speech within a sentence, the digestive system among the systems of the body, the Renaissance as a period in history, the introduction as a part of a total composition, one chapter in a whole book, and the short leg on a wobbly table.

"If I need to match a button, I have to know its color, its size, the number of holes it has, its shape, the material it's made of, and anything special about it."

In the exercises of the second unit, the parts of a whole are identified, categorized, and summated. Tasks involve seeking strategies for the recognition, registration, and inclusion of the relevant components of a whole.

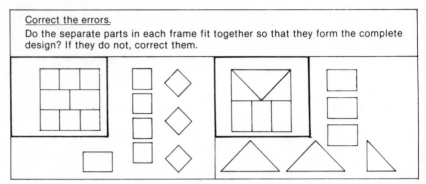

Analytic Perception (exercises 1 and 2, page 14)

Mistakes can be corrected by either altering the figures that are erroneous or by crossing them out and replacing them with the correct and necessary ones. Generally, in the correction of errors, the student must be taught to utilize an appropriate method.

A fragment of a lesson in which the students are speaking, unless otherwise indicated, is given below:

"In this unit we're supposed to figure out what the whole consists of, right? In our kitchen closet we have all kinds of things, rice, salt, sugar, flour, tea, coffee, beans, but I want to bake a cake. So the other things are not important to me. I need flour, sugar, salt, soda, eggs, butter, and milk."

Teacher: "Are there any other examples in which you must identify the relevant parts?"

"If you want to sew a shirt then you take out different things than if you want to iron a shirt."

"In paragraphs. You have to read it all, but only pick out the sentences you need to answer the questions."

"In the atlas, I only look at the map that deals with the country I'm interested in. And on that map, I really have to look carefully and see the parts and what their relationship is to one another."

In the third unit, tasks deal with the construction of wholes on the basis of identifiable parts and the closure of figures on a gestalt by deducing the parts that are missing and identifying them in another setting.

In the first half of the unit, the student is asked to draw the missing parts. In the second half, he is asked to complete the figures representationally. All of the tasks require a precise definition of the standard, comparison of the given part to the whole to determine what is missing, appropriate labeling of the missing parts, the use of two or more sources of information, and a comparison of the content of each frame to the verbal description of what is missing inasmuch as internalization of the standard is difficult.

To the left of each section you will find a design. Fill in each
of the drawings so that, when completed, each is the same as its model.

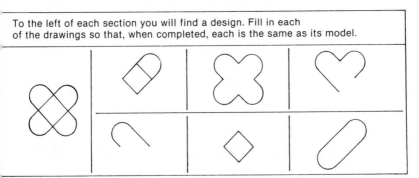

Analytic Perception (exercise B, page 16)

There are possibilities for error inherent in each of the stages. As the
standards become more complex, with a greater number of less familiar
parts, the tasks become more difficult.

Look at the design at the top of the
page. You are to choose one drawing
from the left and one drawing from
the right which, when combined, will
form the design at the top of the page.
Write both the letters and numbers of
the drawings you choose.

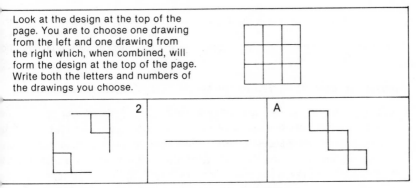

Analytic Perception (part of exercises 1 and 2, page 24)

Describing the standard design as a square divided into nine small squares,
instead of as a square with two horizontal and two vertal lines that are evenly
spaced, will make the missing parts impossible to find. The child is not seeking
six small squares in order to complete A, but parts of exterior and interior lines.

In the last unit, practice in construction of new wholes from the union
of some of the parts is provided. Tasks range from pure perceptual exploration to transpositions and transformations of the elements. They all require
the active participation of the individual involved in this process. Perception
is supported and reinforced by enacting and constant reconstruction of relationships involving comparative behavior, visual transport, and completion
of schemata through perceptual and logical inferences.

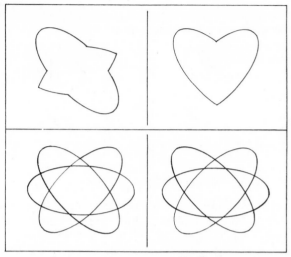

Analytic Perception (exercise A, page 31)

A strategy for search must be defined to find the simple figure within the complex whole. The orientation of the protuberances must be conserved. Blurred, sweeping perception will aggravate the problem caused by curved lines and lack of angles.

Analysis of *Analytic Perception* in Terms of the Cognitive Map

Content: The content of geometrical forms for *Analytic Perception* has been chosen only because it offers certain characteristics and possibilities that are more accessible to the low functioning retarded performer. The content, however, does not form the goal, *per se,* of the instrument. The goal is to teach the analysis of a whole into its component parts, to seek the relationship between the parts, to view each part as a whole unto itself, and to realize the possibility of uniting the parts into new wholes.

Modality: Figural, with minimal verbal elements; accessible to illiterates.

Phase: *Input:*   Blurred, sweeping perception; lack of labels; lack of constancy of form across variations in orientation; lack of spatial and temporal orientation; lack of systematic search.

Elaboration: Comparative behavior; summative behavior; planning; use of two or more sources of information; use of relevant cues.

Output: Interiorization of model; visual transport; projection of virtual relationships; restraint of impulsivity.

Operations: Discrimination; categorization; representation; hypothetical thought; logical reasoning.

Level of abstraction: Fairly low.

Level of complexity: From low to moderately high in latter part of the instrument.

Level of efficiency: With adequate preparation and intervention by the
teacher, students reach high level of efficiency quickly.

Anticipated Difficulties

The errors that appear in the following exercises are typical of those that may
be anticipated.

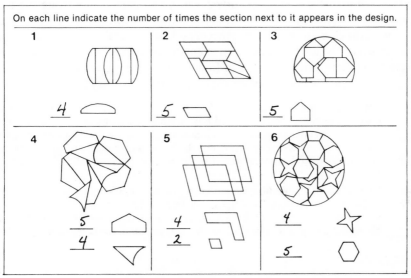

On each line indicate the number of times the section next to it appears in the design.

Typical errors—*Analytic Perception* (selected exercises, page 5 and 6)

Blurred, sweeping global perception without the articulation of the figure
into its separate parts is responsible for the errors in examples 1, 3, 4, and 6.

Problems in spatial orientation may account for the errors in examples 1, 2,
3, and 4.

Lack of hypothesis testing and no use of logical evidence may account for
errors in examples 2 and 5.

Problems in summation in 4, 5, and 6 may stem from inappropriate
strategies and unsystematic work.

Errors in example 6 may result from the unwarranted closure of the hexagons that appear at the edges.

Errors in all of the above examples may result from impulsive behavior,
a lack of precise interiorization, a lack of precision in output, a lack of comparison to the given standard, and differences in the appearance of the standard when it is shown separately and when it appears in the context of other
figures.

Use of Labels and Operations

An FIE vocational student discusses the need for labeling:

"I need to know the name of something when I ask for it or to understand when somebody else asks me for it. If a part on my bicycle is broken, I don't have to drag it downtown to show the repair man if I know the word 'pedal.' The same thing when I go to repair a blind. If they tell me a slat is broken and the size and material of the blind, then I know what to bring. Otherwise it means that I have to make a trip to see what is wrong and then another to bring the right part."

Insight

The role of the teacher in *Analytic Perception* is to demonstrate the real meaning of an analytic approach to life and to produce insight, thereby permitting the child to conceive of other areas in which analyses are possible and beneficial. The analytic approach is emphasized and illustrated as it is applied to other subject matter and to daily life experiences.

Vocational students see an application for what they have learned:

"If I'm gonna give a permanent, I have to figure out how much shampoo and cream rinse before and after, and how much solution and how much time I'm gonna be tied up. There's something else, too. You gotta figure in something for wearing out your tools and for rent on the place and for water and for electricity. Before I learned this instrument, I never stopped to analyze all the parts of the job."

"I worked for a guy who went bankrupt. Now I know why. He was a carpenter and he never figured out how much and what kind of materials he had to use and what they were gonna set him back, and how much time it was going to take him. He would just give a price without thinking about all the parts of the job."

In math,

"the recombination of the parts into different wholes is like in fractions: $2/3 + 1/4 = 11/12$."

In language,

"The direct object takes the action and follows the verb. You can't change its place in the sentence. It's just like in *Analytic Perception,* in the pages where the part has to be exactly the same and in the same direction."

Spontaneous Use of Crystallized Cognitive Behaviors and Generation of New Information

The example reported below illustrates the spontaneous use of cognitive behaviors developed through work on this instrument:

"Last night I helped my mother figure out how we're going to spend our welfare check. I did it just like we do in class in *Analytic Perception.* I took all the things we gotta pay every month and wrote them down, and we divided everything up and now we're gonna see how we come out by the end of the month."

A librarian reported on a visit to the library by an FIE class:

The children were supposed to write reports on Egypt. They went directly to the non-fiction section. There they eliminated everything but the geography and history sections. Within those two departments, they concentrated only on books dealing with the Middle East and the Mediterranean countries. They looked in the table of contents or the index of each book to see if there was anything in the book that they could use. I was interested because I had heard about the FIE program, but never had any contact with it. I asked them if I could be of help, and if there was anything else they could use that would assist them. I was, of course, thinking of the card catalogue. The children were quite pragmatic. They said that if they would use a World Book or Encyclopedia then everybody would have the same report, and that there was no point in looking at the file of cards because "they list everything the library has on the subject in individual books, but the books, themselves, may not be in. The other way, a couple of us can work together, and we can put together a little from each book, even if there is no single book on the subject." During lunch I sought out the classroom teacher to see if the children were following her instructions. She stated that she had given them no directions, other than that a report was due, and that if two or more students wanted to work together she would accept the group work, provided they submitted it under all of the names of the members of the group.

Motivation

Aesthetically *Analytic Perception* is one of the most satisfying instruments. Several of the exercises require coloring, and the students try to make their work as attractive as possible.

FAMILY RELATIONS

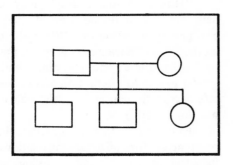

Family Relations provides the learner with the relational abstract elaboration of relationships experienced by him in his daily life. That such relationships are used and experienced by the retarded performer does not necessarily mean that he is aware of their conceptual nature so that he is able to detach the labels he uses in the specific context of his own experience and apply them more generally. This fact is only one of the many that provide evidence that sheer exposure to reality does not necessarily produce those dimensions of mental operations that we describe as related to abstract conceptual thinking.

Our findings that very limited traces are left by the encounter with stimuli and previous experience if the necessary schemata have not been established through mediated learning experience provide convincing evidence for the need for mediation. The culturally deprived child is vague and task bound in defining familial relationships if all he has been taught is to label specific people without deriving a relationship from the operation that can be generalized over a whole universe of persons. A volitional, reflective process provides the energetic determinant for the production and generalization of relationships. Comparative behavior is the prerequisite for the derivation and eduction of generalizable relationships.

Objective of the Instrument

Our goal in this instrument is not to teach relationships that exist in a family; nor have we selected the topic because of the familiarity of the subject to the retarded performer. To some extent, this familiarity with some family relationships may create stumbling blocks in reaching the goals we have set for this instrument. Children from enlarged families may not ascribe clear definitions to kinship nor accept the limitations set forth by such definitions. An "aunt," for example, may be any woman, from a mother's sister to a neighbor who has offered the child a cookie. The relationships among individuals in an enlarged or extended family are often undifferentiated, with the nature of such relationships defined by geographical proximity or by transactional determinants.

"How is he your cousin?" may bring forth a response, "Because he helps me." A child who is asked, "What makes him your brother?" may well persist in answering: "What else do you want him to be, my grandmother?" or "Because he sleeps in my room" or "Because he is good to me." All of these responses point to a utilitarian concept of the relationship, similar to a child's definition of an object by its accepted use rather than by references to its conceptual, relational nature (e.g., "What is a table?" "To put flowers on").

Familiarity with subject matter, therefore, is not always the best point of departure for understanding relationships and may be the source of established patterns of erroneous thinking. Nevertheless, we have chosen this content because it presents us with many different categories of relationships. The role an individual plays in a given kinship pattern is a relationship that leads to the question of relative to whom. Furthermore, there are a number of roles the same individual may fill simultaneously. An individual can be a son, husband, father, uncle, nephew, grandson, brother-in-law at the same time, with each of his roles determined and made possible by the existence of a partner, by virtue of whom each of his roles is ascribed. It is the mutual relationship between the two partners that defines the role of each. This permits the bringing of insight into the real nature of relation and relativity.

As an example of the multiple roles a person simultaneously fills, students cited Elizabeth II of England. She is, at one and the same time, Queen of England, head of the British Empire, protector of the Church of England, a mother, a wife, a sister, a sister-in-law, a grandmother, a mother-in-law, a daughter, a grandaughter, etc.

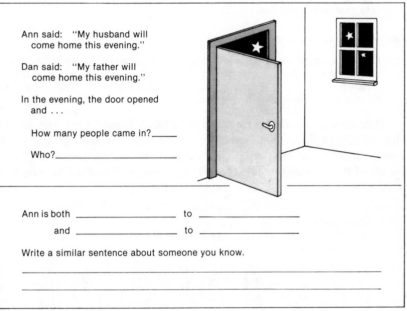

Ann said: "My husband will come home this evening."

Dan said: "My father will come home this evening."

In the evening, the door opened and . . .

How many people came in?____

Who?_____

Ann is both _____ to _____

and _____ to _____

Write a similar sentence about someone you know.

_____

_____

Family Relations (exercises 2 and 3, page 2B)

Definition of the role an individual plays is contingent upon the partner in the relationship.

Kinship can be used as a powerful tool to teach children, and especially retarded performers, to perceive and/or to project the relationship as a special link between two separate existences. Even more important, the child can be taught that the concept of a relationship is not fixed, not immutable, and not a one-time characteristic of a given object, but is, rather, a flexible phenomenon that will change according to the object with which it is related.

To celebrate the confirmation of their son, the Browns gave a family dinner party. They invited:

2 grandfathers	2 grandmothers
3 fathers	3 mothers
3 husbands	3 wives
1 son-in-law	1 daughter-in-law
2 fathers-in-law	2 mothers-in-law
5 sons	1 daughter
2 grandsons	

The Browns only had eight chairs, but everyone came to the party and all were able to sit down at the table at the same time, and each sat on a separate chair. How can you explain this?

Family Relations (exercise 2 and 3, page 23)

Children who did not learn *Family Relations* did not seek the solution in the multiplicity of roles the same person could play simultaneously. They answered, "They ate in shifts." "People brought chairs from home." "The host and the hostess were so busy they didn't have time to eat but served the others."

The need for logical evidence can be fostered through work with various kinds of relationships. What is the single condition for being a father? Is it to have a child? What are the necessary conditions that make one an uncle? Which of the various possible roles is the *one* that all individuals play?

5. What are there more of in the world:
   a. Sons or fathers? _____ Why? Because every _____ but not every _____.

Family Relations (exercise 5, page 15B)

Symmetrical relationships, such as those between siblings, are compared to asymmetrical relationships between parents and children, and relationships involving mutuality and hierarchy are contrasted with one-way ties. Thus, the differential nature of relationships is established. In this instrument, many other elements, such as grouping, categorization, summation, and representation, are also taught.

Content of *Family Relations*

Family Relations consists of 36 pages and uses verbal, symbolic, and graphic modalities. The first unit introduces the code that is used throughout the instrument to symbolize sex, role, and the horizontal and vertical relationships that exist in a family. To complete the exercises successfully, the student must work systematically, using two or more sources of information.

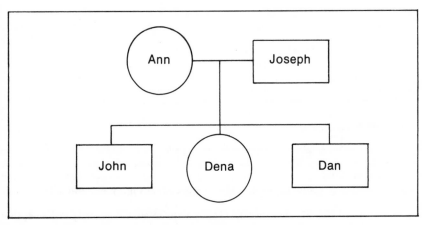

Family Relations (map of nuclear family, page 6)

The following is a segment of a lesson in which the students learn the code:

Teacher: "What do the lines show?"
Students: "Connections." "Ties." "Bridges." "Father and mother are always together. They go out together. They buy things together. They decide together."
Teacher: "From when are father and mother together?"
Students: "From always."
Teacher: "Always?"
Students: "From the time they are married."
Teacher: "So the tie is. . .?"
Students: "Marriage." "There are sons and daughters underneath."
Teacher: "Would it be possible to add to this family?"
The students agree that it would be.
Student: "In sex education, we studied impregnation. It is necessary to have both the sperm and the egg before there can be a child; so it is from the union of the man and the woman that the child would come. He would have to be below them, because he comes from them, but somehow we would have to show that he comes from both of them."

The original discussion of the tie between the male and female illustrates the previously mentioned functional definition of a relationship, which the teacher seemed to be quite willing to accept.

The exercises of the second unit deal with the multiple roles the same person plays and attributes that are essential to each of the roles. Completion of the tasks requires hypothetical thinking, logical evidence, and a conservation of constancy. In order to validate his answer, the student is forced out of an egocentric mode of communication and must use temporal concepts and logico-verbal reasoning, based on classes and class attributes. He communicates his answers verbally, with symbols and in charts.

Family Relations
(*left:* exercise 2, page 5A; *right:* blank genealogical map, page 8)

> A girl proudly announced, "Today I am an aunt." When questioned, she revealed that her sister had given birth to a baby boy the night before. A fellow student insisted, "Then you're not an aunt. You're an uncle."
> The teacher utilized this error to point out the lack of precision in the terms "uncle" and "aunt." She explained that some societies employ more differentiated terms to define family relationships. For example, the terms for uncle and aunt may indicate whether the relationship is one of blood or marriage ties, and whether it is paternal or maternal.

In the third unit, the concepts of symmetrical and asymmetrical relationships are presented, with opportunities first for recognition, and then for application. With the expansion of the family, new concepts are used and precisely defined. Hierarchical relationships are further developed. Summative behavior is elicited as is the search for relevant information and appropriate cues. There is a necessity for a constant redefinition of the problem from exercise to exercise, and impulsivity on the input and output levels must be restrained. (See *Family Relations* (page 9A) on page 199.)

The second half of the instrument stresses logico-verbal reasoning and provides specific practice in more and more complicated exercises. The need for planning behavior, representation, projection of relationships, and precision in data gathering is heightened. Spatial and temporal determinants are important in recognizing horizontal and vertical relationships and diagramming them (see Figure 10).

Analysis of *Family Relations* in Terms of the Cognitive Map

Content: Kinship as a vehicle for teaching conceptualized relationships.
Modality: Verbal, symbolic, and graphic.

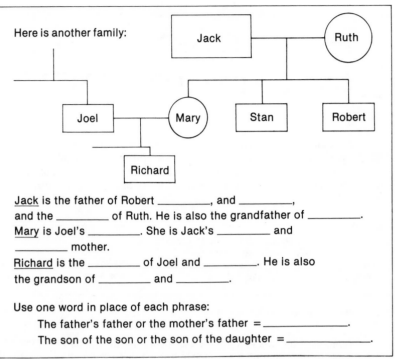

Here is another family:

Jack is the father of Robert _____, and _____,
and the _____ of Ruth. He is also the grandfather of _____.
Mary is Joel's _____. She is Jack's _____ and
_____ mother.
Richard is the _____ of Joel and _____. He is also
the grandson of _____ and _____.

Use one word in place of each phrase:
   The father's father or the mother's father = _____.
   The son of the son or the son of the daughter = _____.

Family Relations (page 9A)

Phase: Principally in *elaboration phase,* with the projection of horizontal,
   vertical, symmetrical, asymmetrical, and hierarchical relationships, as
   well as those of mutuality; use of two or more sources of information;
   summation; planning behavior; search for and use of relevant information; and definition of the problem.
   Input phase: Blurred perception; need for precise labeling; spatial and
   temporal relations; conservation of constancy; systematic search.
   Output phase: Egocentric communication; trial-and-error behavior.
   Restraint of impulsivity and verbal precision in all three phases.
Operations: Categorization; encoding and decoding; representation; hy-
   pothetical thought; inference and logico-verbal reasoning.
Level of abstraction: From medium to high.
Level of complexity: Low in first pages; higher with addition of more ele-
   ments, more relationships, and less familiarity with them.
Level of efficiency: Shows effect of practice; typical errors may be antici-
   pated.

Anticipated Difficulties
The samples on the following pages illustrate the errors that may be anticipated:

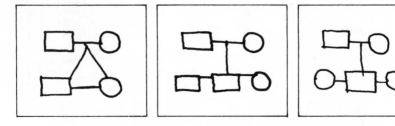

The above errors stem from the modality of presentation. They indicate difficulty in the internalization of the code. Even if the student is able to verbalize existent relationships, he is not able to encode them in the required language of the instrument. He experiences similar difficulty in encoding the direction of given relationships.

---

3. When Dan talks about Dena he says "my sister".
    When Dena talks about Dan, she says _____
    When _____ talks about _____ he says "my wife."
    When _____ talks about _____ she says _____.

Family Relations (exercise 3, page 3)

Solution of the task requires the use of cues, the determination of the referents, and the application of a principle learned in *Orientation in Space I*, the ability to decentrate and to represent.

Dena says, "I am one and a half years older than my mother."
Is that correct? *No*
Why? *because Dena can't be 1½ years older then her mother*

Family Relations (exercise 4, page 4)

Neither hypothetical thought nor logical reasoning is evidenced in this tautological reply.

---

1. If the sentence is not correct, place a line through the equal sign ($\neq$).
    Aunt = daughter's daughter.

Family Relations (exercise 4, page 4)

In this question and its reply, there is a correct output from a correct elaboration based upon improper input as the result of an incorrect definition of the problem. Children argue that every woman is the daughter of somebody's daughter and therefore that the statement defining an aunt as a daughter's daughter is correct.

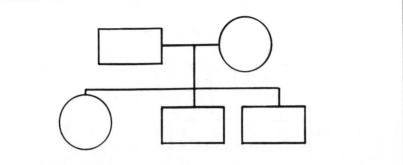

Place the names in the blank genealogical map, as indicated by the following sentences.
1. Arthur is Rita's father.
2. Simon and Jerry are brothers.
3. Jerry is Laura's son.
Answer the following questions with the help of the map.
1. Who is older, Arthur or Jerry?, *Arthur*
2. Who has two brothers? *Simon*
3. Who has a brother named Simon and one sister? *Jerry*

Family Relations (page 8)

The number of rectangles and circles is a cue that assists in the localization of the family members within the map. There is a need for inference, summation, and the projection of relationships. The wrong answer to the second question is a common error of the retarded performer who includes himself in the summation.

Children evince difficulty in discriminating between necessary and sufficient reasons and those that are possible. When exercises become more abstract and more complicated — with the use of letters instead of names and with the variety of relationships offered in expanded family situations — there is greater possibility of error.

Family Relations in Terms of the Subgoals of FIE

The following illustration indicates the spontaneous use of concepts and vocabulary acquired through the instrument:

A student asked his teacher to dismiss him early. The teacher declined. The boy persisted. "I know that the relationship between us is asymmetrical, but nevertheless I'd like you to dismiss me early." A supervisor overheard the exchange and asked the boy, "What is this 'asymmetrical' relationship?" The boy explained, "You see those two teachers? Their relationship is symmetrical. You are a supervisor, so the relationship between you and my teacher is asymmetrical, the same as the relationship between my teacher and me."

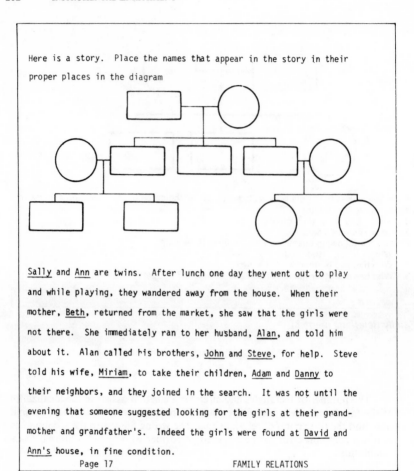

Here is a story. Place the names that appear in the story in their proper places in the diagram

Sally and Ann are twins. After lunch one day they went out to play and while playing, they wandered away from the house. When their mother, Beth, returned from the market, she saw that the girls were not there. She immediately ran to her husband, Alan, and told him about it. Alan called his brothers, John and Steve, for help. Steve told his wife, Miriam, to take their children, Adam and Danny to their neighbors, and they joined in the search. It was not until the evening that someone suggested looking for the girls at their grandmother and grandfather's. Indeed the girls were found at David and Ann's house, in fine condition.

Page 17   FAMILY RELATIONS

Figure 10. *Family Relations* (page 17).

Teachers of vocational and academic subjects cite the use of terms and operations of *Family Relations* in their classes:

> "A change in the status of one member of the family will result in a reciprocal change in other members," said an FIE vocational student. "It's like an electrical circuit. When somebody has a child, changes take place all along the line."
>
> "It's like adding a room onto a house, with one wall in common between two rooms," said a carpentry student, in discussing marriage as uniting two families through the one member they share in common.
>
> The hierarchy existing in the generations of family was transferred to the hierarchy in other social institutions, past and present.

There is strong motivation to apply newly learned operations:

In a history lesson, a teacher had intended to diagram the Hapsburg succession. A student volunteered, "But it would be more interesting to illustrate Abraham and his descendants." When asked why, the student replied that he had never tried to show the genealogy of a man who had more than one wife at the same time and children from each marriage.

In geography, a student exclaimed, "Working on this blind map is easy. It's just like in *Family Relations*. There I can just look at the figures and the connecting lines and figure out the relationships. Here, all I have to do is see the ocean on the west and the Sea of Galilee and the Dead Sea and I know I have a map of Israel and I can figure out the positions of the cities according to their relationships to those points."

The creation of insight into the concept of relationships was demonstrated in the following discussion of the diplomatic relations between countries:

Among the conclusions reached by the FIE students were that family relations were fixed by marriage or blood ties, while diplomatic relations were based on mutual self-interest. Blood ties could never be dissolved whereas those of both marriage and diplomacy could be. Even though marriages were dissolved, both partners retained their previous relationships as parents to their offspring, whereas, in diplomatic relations, former relationships were quickly forgotten in light of new alliances. They compared the changing relationships between the United States and Great Britain in 200 years, and the relationship between the Allied and the Axis nations during and between World Wars.

The above example also represents a shift in the FIE students from passive recipients of information to generators. They indicate an ability and readiness to unite and transform ideas so as to reach conclusions based on comparisons and analogies, through inference and logical thinking.

TEMPORAL RELATIONS

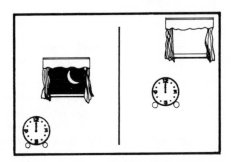

Temporal Relations is an instrument geared toward reorienting the culturally deprived child's perception of time and his capacity to register, process, and order temporal relationships. Lack of this orientation is attributable both to the generalized deficiency in perceiving relationships and to the more particular deficiency specific to orientation in time. As discussed in Chapter 4 (see pages 83–85), the fact that the temporal dimension cannot be perceived except through representation makes its grasp depend on a great number of functions that are known to be deficient in the retarded performer.

The measure of time, by definition, is a measure of intervals between two or more units. The fact that the units to be measured are totally devoid of material sensorial elements makes their manipulation even more difficult. Summative behavior and operations, such as quantification, ordering, and categorization of time units, are more complex because they deal with relationships rather than with the objects themselves.

> "When I waste a minute of the class' time, the teacher always says I wasted 35 minutes, a minute from every one of the kids in the class. I don't understand what she's talking about."

Temporal Relations is one of the few instruments in the FIE program that is not graded in difficulty, with later exercises based on the mastery of earlier ones. Instead, its 35 pages are divided into units, each of which presents, explores, and develops a different aspect of temporal orientation.

In the first unit, time as a measurable, objective, stable system of reference is defined, contrasted with distance, and then related to distance to form the concept of speed. Because velocity, or a space-time relationship, must also include the concept of elapsed time, any problem of relative speeds must also include a reference to the total duration of the movement. In varied exercises, students are taught to isolate each of the factors of time, distance, and velocity, and then to seek their interrelationship.

Bill and John rode home from school on their bikes. They traveled at the same speed yet Bill got home about half an hour later than John (without any problems or accidents en route).

Explain: _____

_____

_____

_____

Temporal Relations (exercise 3, page 3)

> In order to arrive at a definitive answer, two additional bits of information are necessary: the distance from the school to the home of each of the boys, and the exact time each set out from school.

It can be expected that the answer of the culturally deprived child to the above exercise would be that John, the boy who arrived home first, "won" or was faster. This is because the child would consider only one source of information, that of the relative final position of the two boys, without taking into account the distance each had to travel or the total time he was on the road.

Teachers, too, name John as the faster. However, their answer stems from another reason. Because of the similarity of the exercises to problems in mathematics in which there is always a single correct answer, teachers are apt to overlook the insufficiency of the data in seeking an answer to the problem and relate only to what is given.

In these exercises, the learner is taught to seek all of the relevant information, such as starting points, routes, distance, terrain, average speed, and so on, before attempting to compare and to summate. The difficulties the learner faces stem from his inability to add discrete units of time and to deal with multiple factors simultaneously. A more common error, however, is due to the imprecision with which speed or the time/distance relationship is usually expressed. One customarily computes the distance and divides it by the total number of hours *on the road,* or from door-to-door, to arrive at average speed, instead of calculating and perhaps adding the increments of time in which movement actually occurs. An amusing but true anecdote points to the potential fallacy in such computation:

> On one of the turnpikes a driver picks up his toll ticket, stamped with time and date as he enters. If the time punched as he exits is less than one hour it is clear that he has exceeded the speed limit, and he is fined for each minute less than the hour the drive should take. Consequently, a coffee shop near the exit is always filled with anxious travelers, sipping coffee and watching the clock to see when it is safe for them to resume their journey and exit from the pike.

The student is asked to use symbols to encode the problems, to seek the laws governing distance/time relationships, and to make inferences from the given data in order to anticipate and predict outcomes. Divergent thinking is forced in a search for possible reasons for discrepancies from the rule.

Solve the following problems and then indicate the solutions in the table on page 9.

1. A stork flew from Toronto to New York City. On the first day it flew a distance of 15 miles (24 kilometers). On the second day it flew at the same speed, yet covered a distance of 22 miles (35 kilometers).

Explain: _____

_____

_____

_____

Temporal Relations (exercise 1, page 7)

Problem	Distance	Table for the Problems	
		Speed	Time
1	A < B	A = B	?

Temporal Relations (exercise 1, page 9)

In the second unit, the various concepts of objective and measurable units of time, such as years, seasons, months, weeks, days, hours, minutes, and seconds, are presented. The student is asked to order series and to seek relationships between the units. He learns to distinguish between the hierarchies presented in *Family Relations* and the series in *Temporal Relations*.

Compare the items on the left with the ones on the right. Use the appropriate symbol from those listed below to indicate the relationship between each pair.

USE > FOR "GREATER THAN"   USE < FOR "LESS THAN"

USE = FOR "EQUAL TO"

one year	☐	11 months
60 seconds	☐	half a minute
a quarter of a year	☐	4 months
one month	☐	4 weeks
half an hour	☐	30 minutes
two years	☐	20 months

Temporal Relations (part of page 11)

The difficulty stems from translation from one system of reference to another when each has a different base.

The student is asked to classify various events according to different principles and to use the relationships existing between them for anticipation and prediction.

The concept of sequence is expanded in the third unit to include the relative aspect of the stable system of temporal reference, with the presentation of future, present, and past, and the flow from one tense to the other, which is dynamic, unidirectional, and irreversible. The student is then asked to link the events of the world with those in his own life.

There are past and future events which are related to general history.
The year 1980 belongs to the _____.
The year 1960 belongs to the _____.
The year 1971 belongs to the _____.
The flight to the moon belongs to the _____.
The flight to Mars belongs to the _____.

Past and future are related to individual history.
For me: the age of 20 is _____.
         the age of 10 is _____.
My present age is _____.
Write down things which belong to your past.

_____

Write down things which belong to your future.

_____

Temporal Relations (exercise 2, page 14)

The child is asked to compare the universal and individual conception of temporal order and to find the relationship between them.

The orientation of the culturally deprived child is basically to the present, with very little orientation toward the past or the future. Because of his limited representation and his feeling that things happen to him that are beyond his control, his anticipation extends only into the most proximal future. "After I drop out of school" or "Until vacation comes" are characteristic expressions of his limited future time perspective.

The FIE student has initial difficulty in coordinating the infinite, unceasing continuum of historical time with his own limited life cycle. This is apparent when he is asked to draw time lines. The present is shown in great detail and occupies a large space, while the millennia that precede it are shown in a tiny space. The FIE children are, however, able to reach a high level of abstraction as the result of insight gained in the instrument.

In a class discussion, a teacher asked if somebody was able to show how the relationship of past-present-future could be indicated. A boy volunteered and drew three circles, a large one for the past, a very small one for the present, and a very large one for the future. He then indicated the movement with arrows so that the present flowed into the past, with the future flowing into the present. He was troubled however by three things. The first was that a closed circle was not really appropriate for the future, which he described as infinite, and that maybe he should draw the more distant part of it with dotted lines. The second was that a static drawing did not sufficiently indicate the growth of the past, even in the time he was drawing it; and third, that there was no indication that there was no diminishing of the future despite its flow into the present.

Another student came to the board and demonstrated the same principle with the thickness of a line.

Another of the culturally deprived child's problems with the comparison and matching of the universal and his personal time frames is his idiosyncratic description of events. "When I had the measles," "When we lived on Main Street," "When my aunt visited with us" are of no assistance to him in linking with an objective system of reference.

The sequential nature of time and temporal order is presented in verbal, pictorial, and numerical modalities. Successful completion of the exercises requires comparison, systematic inquiry, the use of various sources of information and cues, the elimination of irrelevant information, an awareness of transformation and linkage between discrete items of information, the projection of virtual relationships, hypothetical thought, and inference. Impulsivity must be restrained in all three phases of the mental act. The exercises in Figure 11 demonstrate the sequential nature of time.

There are two possible sources of error in problem C shown in Figure 11. The first is probably attributable to cultural difference whereas the second is more typical of cultural deprivation. In Europe and Israel, dates are written so that the day is first, followed by the month and then the year. Thus February 7, 1978, would be written 7/2/78. The result is that children in these countries usually look at the day first in ordering of dates, instead of at the month.

The other problem is that of the opposition set up between the size of the number and its relative order. The reasoning of the culturally deprived seems to be: a person of less age (i.e., smaller number of years) is younger than one of greater age (i.e., a greater number of years). 1969 is smaller (younger) than 1979 (older); therefore 1979, which is older, must be earlier. The elaboration processes in this example are intact; however, the faulty conclusion is based on the original erroneous premise, the confusion between size and age.

The subjective view of an objective time span is presented in the next unit. The expansion of the idea of the relativity of time and the factors influencing the concept are explored. The student learns of the relationship between affective factors and perception.

Whereas in previous units there was an emphasis on time as an object that could be measured and quantified, time is explored as a dimension in the

A

a.	___to reap	___to plow	___to sow
b.	___it is raining	___the man is getting wet	___the sky is clouding
c.	___past	___future	___present

B

There are four dates in every row. Arrange the dates so that the earliest will be number 1, and the latest, number 4.

Example:

(2) 2/11/1970	(3) 7/4/1970	(4) 8/9/1978	(1) 12/1/ 1969
( ) 11/13/1969	( ) 8/30/1969	( ) 1/1/1970	( ) 12/31/1968
( ) 1/15/1540	( ) 2/12/1630	( ) 7/31/1611	( ) 2/4/1478
( ) 4/8/1830	( ) 5/26/1829	( ) 4/7/1830	( ) 3/19/1830
( ) 5/4/2001	( ) 7/4/1776	( ) 8/30/1976	( ) 4/12/1876

C

Figure 11.   *Temporal Relations. A:* exercise 3, page 17; *B:* part of an exercise, page 18; *C:* exercise 1, page 20.

exercises of this unit. "Early" and "late," "before" and "after" are illustrations of this aspect of temporal relations.

"My mother told me to come home early from the dance. I came home at 2 in the morning, way before anybody else left. But my father was waiting for me. Was he mad! I tried to tell him that 2 was 'early,' but for him it was late."

____has a date at 7:30.   ____has a date at 6:30.

Temporal Relations (exercise 1, page 27)

The last unit deals with synchronous and asynchronous events and the relationship between two occurrences that can be cause and effect or merely coincidental and the result of chance. The student learns to distinguish between necessary and sufficient factors and to seek precise information for temporal orientation. In this unit, he must frame hypothetical questions and infer logically to arrive at appropriate conclusions.

In each sentence two things are happening <u>at</u> <u>the</u> <u>exact</u> <u>same</u> <u>time.</u>

Next to each sentence, write

<u>M</u> if there <u>must</u> be a connection between the happenings.

<u>C</u> if there <u>can</u> be a connection between them.

<u>N</u> if there <u>cannot</u> be a connection between the two events and they just happened to occur at the same time.

____1. I turned on the radio. My door-bell rang.
____2. The girl fell off the chair. The mother was very frightened.
____3. The man took an umbrella. It was pouring outside.
____4. The bus stopped. Many people were waiting at the station.

Temporal Relations (exercises 1–4, pages 31)

The author recalls asking an adolescent to carry his briefcase to his car one afternoon when he had many things to carry. The next day he chanced upon the boy who said, "Don't ask me to help you any more." Upon inquiry, the boy revealed, "When I got home last night, my head ached and I had a temperature."

A sequence of events in time had been misinterpreted as a cause-and-effect relationship.

The instrument provides opportunities for the students to construct exercises similar to those presented that indicate mastery of the principles acquired. In addition, teachers in other subjects report the use of time in FIE students' descriptions of events and an orientation to the use of precise temporal concepts.

NUMERICAL PROGRESSIONS

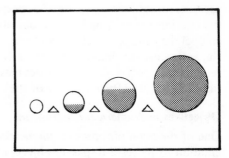

The major focus of the instrument called *Numerical Progressions* is the training of the culturally deprived child in the search for rules and laws that are the basis of certain experienced events by the eduction of the relationships existing between them. The order and rhythmic appearance of these relationships are formulated as rules, by help of which one can construct or predict the further sequence of events.

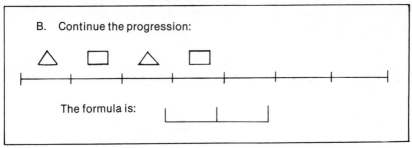

Numerical Progressions (exercise B, page 1)

In the classroom discussion of recurring cycles which enable prediction of the future based on the past, students usually speak of the rhythm in natural events, such as day and night, the phases of the moon, and the four seasons of the year.

"But there are man-made cycles, too. Like patterns in wallpaper or knitting, or traffic signals or the tempo in music."

"You have to distinguish between things that repeat over and over again like a busy signal on the telephone and things that you can know what's going to come next, but finally come to an end. Like when somebody says 'Get ready. Get set,' you know that 'Go' is next. Or you know that a person is born, is a baby, is a small child, is a teenager, is a man, and finally dies."

The episodic grasp of reality, which characterizes the culturally deprived child, makes him perceive events, objects, figures, or numbers as discrete, with little awareness of the relationships existing between them. His approach is probabilistic: if things are in proximity, they are juxtaposed by accident rather than by virtue of a specific rule or determinant. Even when the relationship existing between objects or events is grasped, nothing will compel the child to search for and perceive the more distant stable relationships, because this implies the search for, and perception of, second-order relationships, which describe the ties between relationships. This is an operation that is not in the repertoire of the culturally deprived child.

Objectives of *Numerical Progressions*

One of the main purposes of *Numerical Progressions* is to develop an orientation to perceive disparate objects and events as being linked by some kind of relationship that can be deduced. In certain cases, these links can be reduced to a common relationship that determines the changes and transformations, as well as the directions of such changes, according to certain rules. The process follows a sequence that includes the establishment of a relationship between two events; the establishment of the rhythm by which the relationship repeats itself in other events; and then the discovery and formulation of the rule by which the rhythm is produced in the universe of events regulated by it. In the particular task of a numerical progression, the application of the rule is evidenced in the construction of a new set of events on the basis of the given rule.

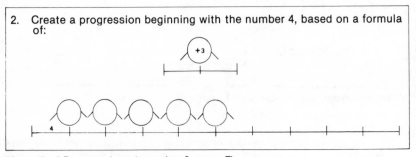

2. Create a progression beginning with the number 4, based on a formula of:

Numerical Progressions (exercise 2, page 7)

The relationship between relationships in a given order of events is the rule.

Students are familiar with formulas from mathematics and science classes. They know that there are rules and laws by which they must abide.

One boy, an expert in poker, was very definite in defining its rules. "A royal flush will always beat a straight flush. Although the spots and colors of the cards change with every deal, there is no question of which hand will win. The relationship is set: royal flush, straight flush, four of a kind, full house, flush, straight, two pairs, one pair. Not even a cheater can change that order."

A second and more general purpose of this instrument is to turn the learner into an individual who perceives himself as able to derive information from data that are presented to him. He sees himself as a generator of new information by the proper use of the rules that he has deduced through his active exploration of data offered him. His experience of his capacity to predict and representationally construct new situations and tasks by help of the generated rules gives him a feeling of mastery.

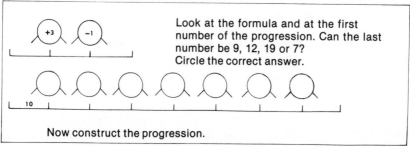

Look at the formula and at the first number of the progression. Can the last number be 9, 12, 19 or 7?
Circle the correct answer.

Now construct the progression.

Numerical Progressions (exercise C, page 11)

The question that is implied is whether the relationship between the positive and negative numbers will result in an ascending or descending progression.

Through hypothetical thinking and logic, the child is able to reach the correct solution of the problem. The convergence of data from multiple sources is required in the elaboration of the answer.

In the discussion of progressions in which there are both ascending and descending movements: "My meals are approximately the same each day. The calories I use up are about the same every day, too. The fact that I eat more (+ calories) than I use up in energy (– calories) is the reason I'm gaining weight."

It should be understood that the use of *Numerical Progressions* is not oriented toward the acquisition of arithmetic or numerical skills. Numbers are used because the relationships, which are based upon the perception of the interval between them, are relatively easy to extract and require only limited reading skills and verbal mediators. In order to render the relationships easily discoverable by the child, technical problems in this instrument are reduced to a minimum. Anyone who has the basic concept of numbers should be able to master the rather complex relationships and the rules derived from them without difficulty, provided that elaboration is produced and search is systematized and properly oriented.

Errors which may occur at this stage are usually due to blurred, sweeping perception, inattention to the signs, and impulsivity at the input and output phase. A failure to perceive the relationship in terms of intervals between numbers may also lead to mistakes.

> The following error illustrates that the child has grasped the principle that 3 must be added to 20. However, it is not clear whether his mistake is one of directionality, rigidity in the application of the rule, or ignorance of the mathematical concept that an inverse operation is necessary in order to find the number preceding the one given in an ascending progression.

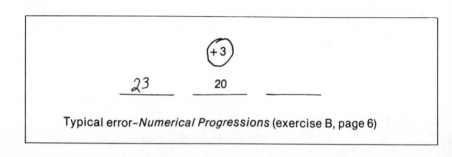

Typical error–*Numerical Progressions* (exercise B, page 6)

The transposition from sheer numerical progressions to other areas in which rhythmic relations are perceivable and organized according to specific rules is accomplished by bridging, by the use of graphs, coordinates, and the like. The child learns that each rhythm can be defined by a formula and that once this formula is extracted from the set of data it can be used for continuing the set or for producing a whole new universe based on the same rule. The insight that the children acquire can be illustrated by their applications of the acquired principles in widely diverse areas.

There are applications to daily life experiences:

> "If I know that the 20th of the month is a Monday, I know that the following Monday will be the 27th, and that the Monday preceding the 20th was the 13th."

> "If I save $2 every week, I can figure out how long it will take me to save up enough money to buy a motorcycle. Wow! It's really discouraging."

There is bridging to academic subjects as well:

Multiplication tables are cited as increasing according to a rule: "If I multiply or add, the answer has to be bigger than the number I started with."

In a music class, FIE students talked about a song sung by several different singers. "The notes are the same, and the relationships between them are fixed, but the song sounds different." They concluded that the difference was attributable to the signature key, i.e., the starting point.

Divergent thinking and flexibility are fostered by reflection about the possible alternatives in a unit that deals with causal relationships and the rules that govern transitions in a succession. The learner is encouraged to consider various possibilities and to seek evidence for the justification of the alternative he has selected.

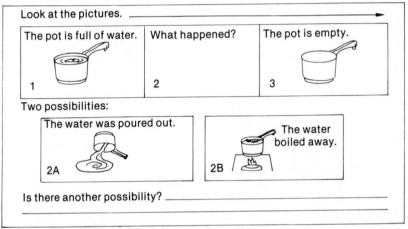

Numerical Progressions (exercise 1, page 4)

The student must learn that from a given cause it is possible to predict an effect, within limits. However, there can be any number of possible causes for a given set of events.

Students comment:

"If I come home and the jam jar is empty and there is jam all over my kid brother's face and clothes then I can be pretty sure that it wasn't ants that ate the jam."

"It's just like in a detective story. There are lots of suspects. The detective has to first find out all who have alibis, and from those who are left to find out who done it."

"It's like in history. We studied what caused the American Revolution."

The child acquires a sense of dynamism and directionality in a unit on ascending and descending progressions and learns to construct graphs based on the progressions.

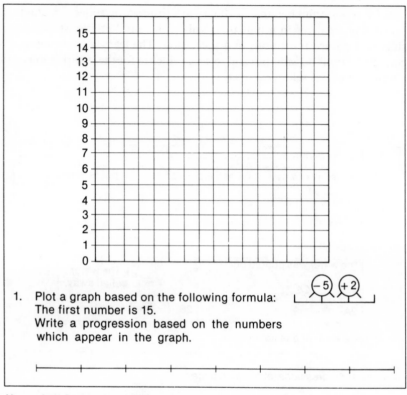

1. Plot a graph based on the following formula:
    The first number is 15.
    Write a progression based on the numbers
    which appear in the graph.

Numerical Progressions (exercise 1, page 14)

The unit on graphing becomes more complex, with plottings based on relationships rather than on absolute members (see plottings on graph in Figure 12). The student is asked to construct exercises, based on formulas and progressions that he has devised and that a classmate must plot. He is also required to plot graphs based on original formulas. In so doing, he must work within the constraints of the upper and lower limits of the space available on the graph and plan the task completely before starting.

Graphing is problematic for students and some teachers. In the error on the top of page 218, plotting the zero of the formula creates errors. The zero seems to have been conceptualized as a nothing, rather than as an event that has resulted in no change. A student's wryly humorous comment illustrates such an event: "Teacher tells us to shut up or to do our homework. His saying so don't result in no change in what happens or in what we do."

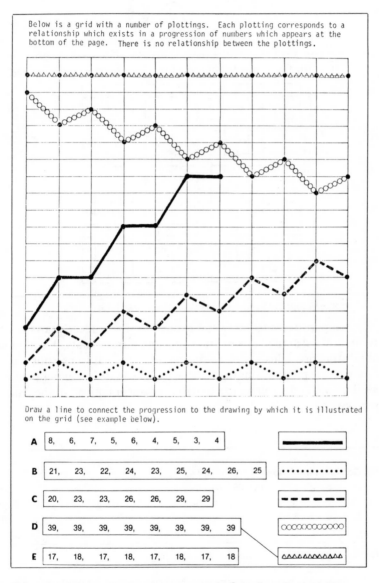

Below is a grid with a number of plottings. Each plotting corresponds to a relationship which exists in a progression of numbers which appears at the bottom of the page. There is no relationship between the plottings.

Draw a line to connect the progression to the drawing by which it is illustrated on the grid (see example below).

A	8, 6, 7, 5, 6, 4, 5, 3, 4	▬▬▬▬
B	21, 23, 22, 24, 23, 25, 24, 26, 25	••••••••••••
C	20, 23, 23, 26, 26, 29, 29	▬ ▬ ▬ ▬
D	39, 39, 39, 39, 39, 39, 39, 39	∞∞∞∞∞∞∞∞
E	17, 18, 17, 18, 17, 18, 17, 18	△△△△△△△△△△

Figure 12. *Numerical Progressions.* An exercise from the unit on graphing.

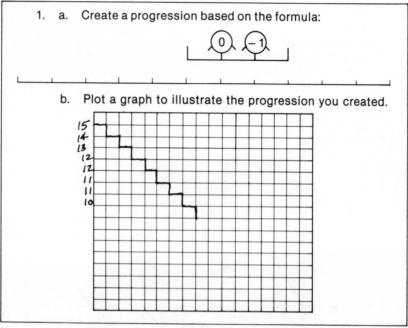

1. a.   Create a progression based on the formula:

b.   Plot a graph to illustrate the progression you created.

Typical error—*Numerical Progressions* (exercise 1, page 19)

By comparison, inference, and deduction, the student draws conclusions about the determinants of transition and directionality. He must surmount distractors in his search for a common rule that transcends the specific numbers in progressions that are highly similar. This requires precision, discrimination, and a willingness to defer judgment until all of the data has been processed.

Complete the following progessions:
J)   5   2   7 ___ 16   25   41.
K)   3   2   5   3   8   4 ___ 5   13 ___   ___
L)   6   2   8   2   10 ___   ___   ___   14.

Numerical Progressions (exercises J, K, and L, page 35)

Successful solution depends on breaking the set established in previous exercises and exploring alternative hypotheses.

Progressions become more complex as they reflect interlocking static and dynamic components. The student is asked to describe the process in words, in code, and on a graph.

Formula (in words)

Let us make a progression in which each number is the sum of
the two numbers which precede it.

The numbers which appear at the beginning of the row are 1 and 2.

A. Combine the two numbers and fill in the third number.

| **1** | **2** | | | | | |

B. In order to find the fourth number, you must combine the
second and third number. Combine and fill in.

Numerical Progressions (exercises A and B, page 26)

Finally, toward the end of this 35-page instrument, the student learns to recognize higher order relationships and to encode them. He must use several sources of information simultaneously and compare and draw conclusions, based on logical evidence, in order to find the stable, unchanging rules that serve to explain events that seem to deviate from the model of a progression with a fixed relationship between each of its members.

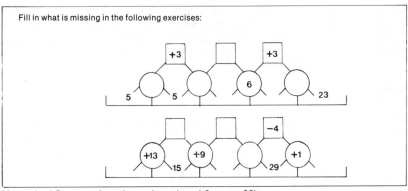

Numerical Progressions (exercises 1 and 2, page 30)

The student may be struck by a seeming incongruity in the second exercise above. The application of a negative superordinate relationship seems to result in an ascending progression.

Active Generation of
Information Through *Numerical Progressions*

The student is presented with many opportunities to construct complete exercises which he offers to a classmate for solution. In these interactions, the students, themselves, are responsible for recognizing errors and discovering their sources.

The change from a passive recipient to a generator of new information is illustrated, as well, in the following classroom exchanges. These anecdotes also provide evidence of insight and the crystallization of the rule-seeking process.

"Teacher, before you were talking about the shortest way as being the best way. That's not always true. When I walk my girl home, I look for the longest way."

"But, teacher, he can't say that just because the rule doesn't apply to the times that he walks his girl home, that it's not a rule. There are always exceptions to a rule, and then they make up a new rule."

"When you talk on the telephone, you have to hurry and say the important things first. Or, otherwise, your coin drops and you're through."

"In a job interview, the guy hasn't got a lot of time. You gotta talk right to the point, and fast."

"When you send a telegram you have to pay for every word. So you have to be stingy with your words."

"On a questionnaire or job application there isn't a lot of space to write, so you have to plan exactly what you say and write real small."

"Maybe we could just say that sometimes the shortest way is the best way. It all depends on the circumstances."

From a current events lesson: "It seems to be that the countries that have oil take out a certain amount of oil out of the ground every day, and they sell a certain amount every day. They take out more than they sell so they build up a supply on hand."

INSTRUCTIONS

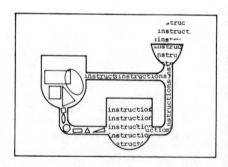

Instructions is one of the few instruments in the whole program in which verbal factors play an important and central position. Language is emphasized in this instrument as a system for both encoding and decoding processes on a variety of levels. These range from simple labeling following recognition (1), or enacting following decoding (2), to the use of inferred instructions derived from the interaction of given instructional codes and the presented stimuli (3).

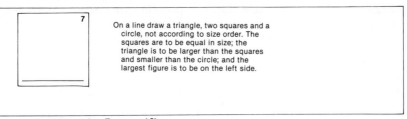

In the upper right of the frame is a _____ (1). In the lower right is a _____ (1). Draw a circle beneath the triangle and a square above the rectangle (2).

Draw a square beside the rectangle (2). Be sure that the square is not above the triangle (3).

Instructions (left: exercise 4, page 3; *right;* exercise 7, page 3)

In the exercises above, (1) indicates the demand for labeling, (2) enacting following decoding, and (3) the use of inferred instructions.

This instrument, which requires the individual to read an instruction and to carry it out, uses the three phases of the mental act in a systematic and ordered way. Input (i.e., the gathering of the data), elaboration (i.e., ordering the object in the required relationship, such as "upper left" or "lower right"), and output (i.e., carrying out the instruction by the drawing of the required figures) are organized so that each phase is controlled. Feedback is a built-in part of the task through comparison between the emitted instruction and the motor performance. The instruction capitalizes on and strengthens previously acquired and corrected functions, such as the perception of objects and the establishment of spatial relationships. Instructions are presented in a way to compel planning behavior and to counteract impulsive responses, and make a superficial scanning or partial reading of an instruction or a task unit ineffective. Consider the example below against the well observed incapacity of the retarded performer to refrain from starting to act on an instruction before it is completely given.

| 7 | On a line draw a triangle, two squares and a circle, not according to size order. The squares are to be equal in size; the triangle is to be larger than the squares and smaller than the circle; and the largest figure is to be on the left side. |

Instructions (exercise 7, page 13)

The child must read to the end in gathering his data and defining the problem. He must then order the figures in the required relationships and the sequence in which they must be drawn. After the completion of his drawing, he checks the instructions, item by item, to see if his product complies with them.

The following spontaneous student applications to other areas of material learned in FIE have been reported by teachers:

In a classroom discussion of the input, elaborational, and output phases in the carrying out of an instruction, a student volunteered, "Just like in a word problem in math. I have to read it through a couple of times to see what I'm supposed to do. When I figure out whether I'm supposed to add or subtract or what, I have to decide what to do first and what next. After I finish, I got to read it again, step by step, to see if I covered everything and did what it says.''

"Sometimes they don't tell you right out in a math problem. Like, if I get $3(4 + 6) - 8 =$, I know I got to add 4 and 6 first before I times it by 3 and take away 8."

"In sewing, I have to read the instructions to the end before I start and then I figure out what parts go where and what goes with what and in what order. If I'm not careful I can finish the garment and have pieces of interfacing left over that I forgot to put in."

Labeling of objects and relationships is introduced in a progressive way, making the instrument accessible even to children who have little experience and still less orientation in carrying out an instruction properly, even if it is presented to them in concrete and familiar situations.

The constant confrontation of various sources of information within the instruction itself, and between the instruction and other parts of the task, such as the drawing offered, makes the perception active, the exploration focused, and certain characteristics of the perceived object and/or the instruction relevant, as contrasted with others that are irrelevant and, therefore, not to be considered. For instance, the verbal labels for three geometric figures, their size, orientation, color, and their location in relation to one another and to the frame in which they must be drawn, are elements that must be considered for the successful completion of a task. Planning behavior becomes essential because parts of the information needed to fulfill the tasks are offered only at the end of the instruction or require the representational execution of certain other parts and inference before the learner is able to decide upon and execute the rest. In the illustration below, functions such as spatial orientation, comparative behavior, and precision are essential in the planning.

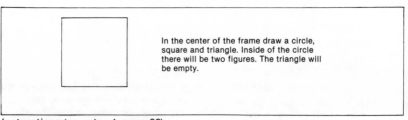

In the center of the frame draw a circle, square and triangle. Inside of the circle there will be two figures. The triangle will be empty.

Instructions (exercise 4, page 22)

Without preliminary planning there is the possibility of making an error in the relative positions and sizes of the three figures.

Inferential processes are fostered by providing the individual with partial instructions, which, once combined with stimuli in the given reality, lead to an unambiguous, compelling solution. The learner then has to infer the

ɔlution from the given data and perform accordingly. In the instructions
ɨven in the example below, it is only by combining the two statements and
ɪe given perceptual cue that the learner is able to solve the problem properly
ɪnd draw a line that meets the requirements.

In the trapezoid, there is a vertical line on the
_____ side.
Draw a horizontal line which will not intersect
the vertical line.

ɪnstructions (exercise 3, page 25)

Within the confines of the space above the vertical line, or perpendicular to
it but not intersecting it, the student has several alternatives in the drawing of the
horizontal line.

Illustrations of bridging by the students are numerous:

" 'Do not walk on the grass' means you can walk on the path or any place that is
not grass."

" 'No swimming in this area' means I can swim any place there is no such sign."

" ' Take one after every meal' means I have to eat before I take it but it doesn't
say what or how much."

" 'Answer the questions at the end of the chapter' means I better read the chapter first, even if the teacher doesn't say so!"

ɒescription of the Instrument

ɪnstructions consists of 41 pages, with exercises increasing in complexity and
ɨfficulty. It uses a verbal and figural modality. There is an emphasis on the
ɼrocess of encoding visual stimuli and decoding verbal instructions. The
ːacher plays an important role in the expansion of the instrument to other
ɼeas and the use of other modalities.

Hypothetical thought and representation are required, as well as a read-
ɪess to defer activity until all the relevant information has been gathered
ɪnd elaborated. An egocentric mode of communication is discouraged while
ɪere is an emphasis on the restraint of impulsivity.

The necessity for deferring action until one has all the available infor-
ɪation engendered the following remarks:

"Sometimes you can find a short cut if you read to the end, first. Like in cooking
class. I read all the recipes for what I want to make. If I need melted margarine
for two or three things, I melt it all at once. If some things take longer to cook
than others, I start with them first."

"In shop, you better check that you have disconnected the electricity before you
stick your hand under the power saw to see why it won't work."

"Just think of the mess old Noah would have been in if he had started to build
the ark right off. He wouldn't have paid no attention to the size and it wouldn't

have been big enough to hold all the animals.'' The reference was to the passage in the Old Testament (Genesis 6.14), ''God said to Noah, 'Make thee an ark of gopher wood with rooms, and pitch inside and out. And this is how thou shalt make it; the length of the ark 300 cubits, the breadth of it 50 cubits, and the height of it 30 cubits.' ''

The first unit of *Instructions* reinforces the concepts learned in *Orientation in Space I* and *II, left, right, center, between, above, below, upper,* and *lower,* and their combinations, as characterizing the relationships between geometric figures and their location within the frame. The student is asked not only to describe but also to actively produce drawings in accordance with the instructions.

The rectangle is in the _____ of the frame. Above the rectangle there is a _____ , and below the rectangle there is a _____ .	○ ▢ △
In the lower part of the frame there is a _____. Above the line, draw two squares. Below the line, draw a rectangle.	_____
In the upper left side of the frame draw a circle, and in the lower left side, a triangle.	

Instructions (exercises 1, 2, and 3, page 3)

Initial tasks reinforce previously acquired concepts and are of a low complexity.

Draw two squares in the frame so that one is on the upper right side and the other is on the upper left side. Below the square on the left, draw a circle	▢ ▢ ○

Instructions (exercise 6, page 3)

The completion of the task in the above manner may indicate a rigidity of thought.

Typical errors that may be anticipated in this unit would include: a lack of appropriate labels for geometric figures; a lack of differentiation between the terms ''center'' and ''middle''; an inability to use the terms ''right, "left," "upper," "lower," "above," and "below" operationally and as opposites; an inability to divide the frame into four quadrants so that the horizontal median divides upper from lower, while the vertical median divides right from left; and a lack of flexibility which does not allow alternative placements of the required figures. This last error is illustrated in the example above by the placement of the circle in the lower left corner. While this is certainly correct, the retarded performer does not consider the possibility that the circle could be drawn in numerous other places within the frame and still fulfill the criterion of being "below" the square on the left; and that the words "directly beneath and below" would more adequately describe and delimit the area in which the circle is to be drawn. This same lack of flexibility is demonstrated by the student who exclaims that he cannot draw a straight line because he does not have a ruler.

In the second unit, an analytic approach both to the frame and to the required operations is taken. Parts are coded, and following instructions entails the use of the code and a sequencing of operations.

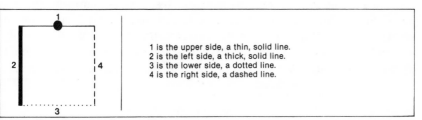

1 is the upper side, a thin, solid line.
2 is the left side, a thick, solid line.
3 is the lower side, a dotted line.
4 is the right side, a dashed line.

Instructions (exercise 1, page 7)

In employing codes beyond FIE exercises:

The students easily bridge to the use of codes in the differentiation of postal zones and telephone areas. Vocational students speak of identifying automobile and machine parts by their numbers. They stress the necessity of ordering typewriter ribbons, fixtures, paint, hair dyes, and knitting yarns by the precise manufacturer's code. From numbers, the discussion moves to other codes such as those used in maps, in police calls, and even in ordering items from the menu of a sandwich shop.

The necessity of following a sequence of instructions becomes apparent to the students:

Examples range from math problems to daily life experiences. "First you put in your coin. Then you listen for the dial tone. Then you dial the number you want." "On your mark, get set, go" is another common illustration.

The third unit presents size-order. Instructions are indirectly given through the relationships between the figures. There is reinforcement of the concept of acceptable divergency in exercises in which the relationship among three circles of varying size is expressed in different ways while varying instructions lead to similar results (see Figure 13).

The fourth unit deals with vertical, horizontal, and diagonal lines and their combination. These are then presented as parallels. New geometric figures, such as trapezoids, rhombi, hexagons, and parallelograms are introduced, as are new concepts, such as bisect, intercept, and commonality. Solution of the problems requires processing all of the information and planning before starting to carry out the instructions. Exercises are complicated because of the novelty of the figures; the number of units in each instruction; the necessity of gathering the information indirectly; and the requirement to defer activity until the material is elaborated, a starting point determined, and a plan for action devised.

The following example illustrates a format that appears in each unit of the instrument. A student is asked to look at the model on the left side of the page and write its description in such a way that it can serve as an instruction for the duplication of the model. After the models have been described, the page is folded to conceal the given models, and, after a short interval, it is given to a classmate who follows the written instructions in drawing the figures. When he finishes, both students review the finished production. In the event that the completed drawing differs from the model, they decide together on the source of error and try to determine how the mistake could have been avoided. These tasks are highly motivating and encourage peer interaction and communication.

Instructions (exercises 1, 2, and 5, page 35)

A description of the tasks on page 226 will have to include figures, number, orientation, relative size, relationship of one to the other and localization within the frame. In indicating relative size and position within the frame, additional cues must be given.

In discussing the need for precision in giving and following directions:

"Like once I made a date to meet my friend in front of the supermarket on the avenue. It was only after I waited an hour that I realized that there were two supermarkets on that avenue, two blocks apart."

"My uncle works for a landscape gardener. He told me a funny story. His boss told him to tear out all the plants on the left side of a house on Front and Main Streets. When he was all finished and admiring how he had cleaned everything out, his boss drove up. He started yelling and screaming because he meant the house across the street."

"Both of those mistakes could have been avoided if they had only used a name or address."

The last unit introduces the concept of depth, expressed in terms of "beneath," "under," "between," "above," and "on top of." Successful completion of the tasks requires representation in order to determine the relationship between several figures, partially superimposed one on the other. A temporal orientation is necessary to determine which lines are to be drawn first. Success is also contingent upon arriving at the rule: the uppermost figure is seen in its entirety and it conceals portions of the objects beneath it.

Darken the lines so that the smallest square will be underneath, and the largest square will be uppermost.	
With a pencil, go over some of the lines so that the largest square will seem to be on the bottom, and the smallest square uppermost.	
Darken the lines so that the center square will seem on top of the other two squares.	

Instructions (exercises 6, 7, and 8, page 40)

On the line, draw a square, a rectangle and a triangle in size order.

The square should be bigger than the triangle, and the rectangle the biggest of all.
The smallest figure should be on the right side.

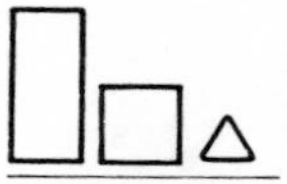

Draw three circles in size order on a diagonal which begins at the upper left corner.
The smallest circle should be the top one.

The rectangle which is on the _____ side is the _____ of them all.
The triangle which is on the _____ side is the _____ of them all.
The square is in between the _____ and the _____.

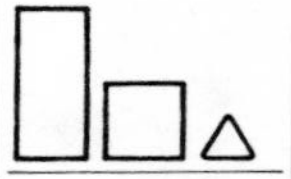

On the diagonal which starts from the upper _____ corner, there are three circles arranged according to size:
The biggest circle is the lowest.

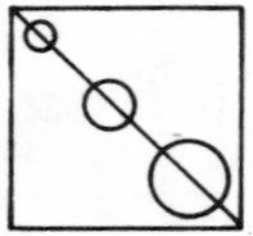

On the line there are a triangle, a square and a rectangle, arranged according to _____.
The _____ is the _____ and is on the _____ side.
The triangle is the _____ of them all.

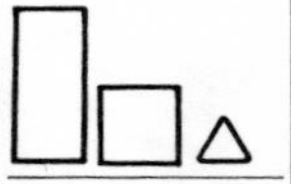

The three circles are arranged according to _____:
The smallest is on the _____ left side.
The medium is on the _____ of the square, and the biggest is on the lower _____ side.
A _____ line passes through the three circles.

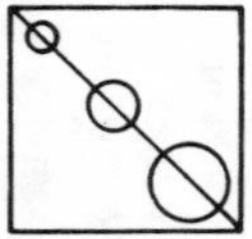

The forms are arranged on the line in size order:
The square is bigger than the _____ and _____ than the rectangle.
The biggest one is on the _____ side.

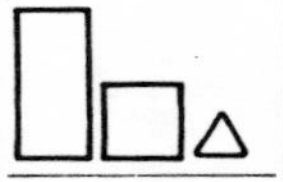

A diagonal starts from the lower _____ corner, and on it there are three circles, according to _____.
The circle in the right corner is the _____ of them all.

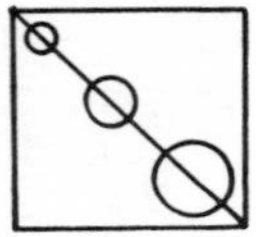

Look at all four exercises. All the pictures are the same, although the instructions are _____.

Look at the four exercises. All the pictures are _____ although _____.

Figure 13. *Instructions* (page 12).

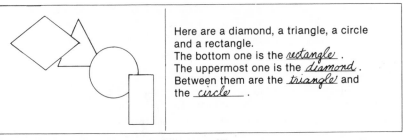

Here are a diamond, a triangle, a circle and a rectangle.
The bottom one is the *rectangle* .
The uppermost one is the *diamond* .
Between them are the *triangle* and the *circle* .

ypical error—*Instructions* (exercise 1, page 37)

The error in the above exercise is caused by a misunderstanding of the words "top" and "bottom" in the context of the exercise. The student is obviously referring to the frame as two-dimensional so that the rectangle is the "bottom" figure inasmuch as it is closest to the lower edge of the frame.

This problem appears again in the exercise below. There is no attempt to seek positional relationships between the figures themselves. The referent is the frame.

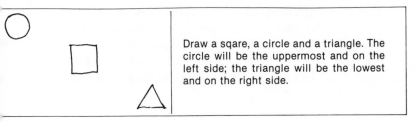

Draw a sqare, a circle and a triangle. The circle will be the uppermost and on the left side; the triangle will be the lowest and on the right side.

ypical error—*Instructions* (exercise 3, page 37)

Analysis of *Instructions*

t is neither the content, nor the modality, nor the level of abstraction that makes this instrument difficult. Whereas the complexity of some of the instructions, in terms of number of items and their unfamiliarity, may give rise o problems, it is the parameters of the deficient cognitive functions and operation that cause the most errors.

The students soon gain insight into their difficulties in giving and receiving instructions. They learn to look for key words like "*After* you have finished..." or "Find *one* word...." More important, they start to ask the necessary questions to remove imprecision, to clarify instructions, and to eliminate any ambiguities.

The effect on the students can be illustrated by this verbatim report on a segment of a lesson:

Student: "Now when I get sent out on a job interview, I ask who I got to see, because I know he's the only one who's going to know anything about it. I ask where I can find him and what is the best time to see him. Then I ask for the ad dress, and the exact name of the company, and how to get there.''

Student: "Don't you care what the job is and how much it pays?"

Student: "Sometimes that's not the most important thing."

Teacher: "Is there a time when the 'how much' is important?"

Student: "Sure. I need to know exactly how much glass I'm gonna need to fix broken window, because it's gotta fit exact in the frame."

Student: "I think how much when I buy something."

Student: "How much is important any time you're baking or cooking."

Student: "Is 'why' important?"

Teacher: "What do you think?"

Student: "I do things all the time, at home, at school, without knowing why They tell me and I do them, if I don't want to get into trouble."

Student: "If I ask 'why?' I get 'Because I said so!' That's no reason."

The teacher reports that the students all agreed that there should be a reaso "why" behind any instruction but that they are not yet sure that they hav the right to question.

There is spontaneous application of the strategies and approach of *In structions* in other subject-matter areas. Teachers report hearing, "Now let's see. What do the instructions say I'm supposed to do?" They also repor that FIE students ask them to be more precise and more explicit in giving in structions. "It's like having 25 'Philadelphia lawyers' in my class," com mented one teacher, ruefully.

ILLUSTRATIONS

Illustrations is similar to the other instruments in the FIE program in its un derlying objectives. It differs, however, in its mode of presentation. It is no taught sequentially, from beginning to end, but as separate pages inter spersed among those of other instruments. Its pages are a collection of situa tions that present the learner with problems that must be perceived, rec ognized, and solved. As such, they represent an opportunity to apply th acquired prerequisites of thinking in the phases of input, elaboration, an output.

Pages are not necessarily presented in order, but are selected by th teacher on the basis of need. The decision for presenting one or more page may be dictated by the need for the correction of a specific function o operation, or the attainment of a special educational goal. Use, howeve may also be decided upon by technical reasons, such as a shortened period the necessity to unite two classes for the day, or a particular event that affect the usual climate of the classroom.

The tasks in *Illustrations* have been constructed on the basis of the nee to produce in the learner an awareness of the existence of a problem, leadin to the disruption of equilibrium and a search for a solution. The humor, absurdity, or incompleteness that reflects the disruption of equilibrium may then become the solution of the perceived problem. "It is funny because it is impossible." The solution for some of the tasks may depend on the proper decoding of details and relating them to others in the field or known from previous experience. "It is funny when we understand the reason which doesn't show in the picture but we have to understand it anyway to solve the problem."

An awareness that a problem exists is possible only through the use of the prerequisites of thinking, including a sharp perception of details, comparative behavior, and a search for the transformations that occur from one frame to the next. The concept of transformations implies that some elements of previous events are kept constant but appear changed as a result of the application of operations. The learner is therefore required to reconstruct the operation that has produced the transformation.

The tendency of the retarded performer is to perceive the frames episodically without any relationship between them, with neither sequence nor order to the depicted events. He has no need to preserve the unity of the successive frames. Unless he can perceive the sequence of events as linked, he cannot perceive the transformation that occurs. This can be exemplified in *Illustration* 4 (Figure 14).

The learner must perceive that the same man and the same suitcase appear in all of the frames. He must be aware that a change has occurred in the man, however, and seek the cause for the transformation. In order to solve the problem, the learner must perceive important details. He must learn that the information upon which he must act is all given in the illustration. He must not consider any facts external to the illustration itself.

The child must compare the first frame and the last. In the first frame, it is evident from the details of his whistling, his jaunty walk, the flower he is holding, and the single finger on which he is balancing the suitcase that the man finds the case easy to carry. In the last frame, however, from the discarded flower, the man's expression, the perspiration streaming from his brow, his posture, and his way of carrying the suitcase, it is apparent that it is indeed a heavy burden.

The student usually attributes the transformation to a change in the weight of the suitcase ("The man added something heavy to the suitcase"), to a change in the suitcase ("This is another suitcase"), or to a change in other conditions ("After you carry something for a long, long time, it begins to feel heavy"). The child must be able to say that neither the weight, nor the case, nor the length of time is different because no such change has been depicted. It is only after he perceives these conditions that he is able to phrase the question, "Why has the man changed?" By extrapolation, the learner must conclude that the weighing of the suitcase and the realization that it is heavy affect the man who is carrying it. It is the knowledge of the objective

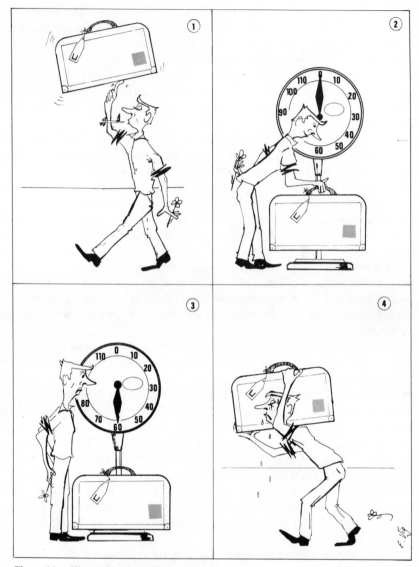

Figure 14.   *Illustrations* (page 4).

reality that has caused the transformation in the man's perception of the weight of the suitcase. When this principle has been grasped, the students provide many examples of its application:

"I don't really feel hot until after I've heard on the radio that we're having a record-breaking heat wave."

"It's not until everybody tells me how awful I look that I start to feel really sick."

Figure 15.   *Illustrations* (page 11).

After the students have applied the necessary cognitive functions for the solution of this illustration, the same principle is presented, with situational variations, in *Illustrations* 11 (Figure 15), 12 (Figure 16), 13 (Figure 17), 19, and 21. The same linkage, attention to details, use of relevant cues, and comparisons are required to understand the transformation occurring in each.

In *Illustration* 11, the weight lifter is obviously proud of his achievement in lifting weights that are extremely heavy for him. The information in

Figure 16.   *Illustrations* (page 12).

frames 1 and 2 must be linked to perceive the situation. When he is confronted with a scrawny youth, half his size, effortlessly carrying a much heavier weight, he is sad and dejected. The lack of social merit for his achievement leads to his negative motivation. The FIE student empathizes with the weight lifter. Unfortunately, too often, he himself has undergone a similar transformation.

The events in *Illustration* 12 (Figure 16) depict positive motivation as the result of comparison. The drayhorse can barely pull his load until he sees a more miserable horse pulling a larger, heavier load. The result of his per-

Figure 17. *Illustrations* (page 13).

ception is the incentive for the transformation that occurs between the first and last frame. To grasp what has transpired, the child must reconstruct the operation by comparing:

Horse 1		Horse 2	
Stronger	versus	Weaker	⎫ Change in the nature of Horse 1's
Lighter load	versus	Heavier load	⎬ perception of the weight of his
			⎭ load and his incentive to pull it.

In *Illustration* 13 (Figure 17), the diner's obvious relish and enjoyment of his meal are destroyed as a result of the waiter's telling him what he has eaten. Again, the learner must link the frames, define the problem, and extrapolate the reason for the transformation.

In all four of these illustrations, there is a change as a result of combining affect and cognition in which there is a balance between reality and one's perception of it. In *Illustration* 4, the element of cognition is prime; in *Illustrations* 11 and 12, the interplay between cognition and motivation is demonstrated; and, in 13, the emotional aspects are the most important. The other illustrations in this particular series demonstrate the changes that occur in one's attitude, motivation, and feelings as the result of knowledge.

In eight illustrations, ingenuity and the behavior of "detour" are used to solve problems whose solutions are inaccessible by a direct approach. In this set, the student must be taught to look for the source by which he can establish the goal, to define the reasons why a novel approach is necessary, and to seek the strategies that have been used for the attainment of the goal. He must learn to disassociate the goal from the means used to achieve it.

In *Illustration* 5 (Figure 18), the fox covets the haunch of meat that belongs to a large, ferocious-looking dog. A direct attack is impossible because the dog seems ready to fiercely defend his meat. So the strategy of the wily fox is to circle the tree, confident that the dog will follow him. Then when the dog has circled the tree so many times that his twisted rope restricts his movement away from the tree, the fox is free to grab the meat without danger. The strategy implies planning by the fox, as well as an anticipation of what will happen to the rope and, consequently, to the dog, as a result of his behavior. The learner must perceive the details that are depicted, and recognize the solution as novel and ingenious.

There are nine illustrations in which the depicted situations are either humorous or absurd. A house that is pulled from its foundations (*Illustration* 28) when the housewife adds one sock to the skimpily laden clothesline that is attached to it is funny because it carries "the straw that breaks the camel's back" to an impossible extreme. In *Illustration* 10 (Figure 19), the torrent of water streaming from a seascape accidentally hit by a janitor's broom is patently absurd because it contradicts all that is known about paintings. The humor in all of these illustrations stems from the unanticipated and impossible denouement.

The instrument includes three illustrations of ingenious solutions that do not really solve the problem but make one feel better because the implicit humor is totally unexpected. There are three illustrations in which the lack of planning behavior leads to unanticipated results. Three other illustrations are more difficult to classify because they combine several elements. Many of the illustrations teach values and point a moral without preaching. Because the modality is pictorial, the instrument is accessible to illiterates.

Figure 18. *Illustrations* (page 5).

Both students and teachers very much enjoy *Illustrations*. However, teachers must be cautioned against turning the pages into psychotherapeutic sessions or formal language lessons. They must bear in mind that the goals of *Illustrations* are those of the other instruments of the FIE program. There must be the same attention to the correction of deficient cognitive functions, to the teaching of concepts and vocabulary, and to creation of intrinsic motivation and insight to maximize the effect of *Illustrations* on the retarded performer.

Figure 19.   *Illustrations* (page 10).

REPRESENTATIONAL STENCIL DESIGN

Representational Stencil Design represents an advanced level in the Instrumental Enrichment program. It capitalizes on functions acquired through other instruments (e.g., *Organization of Dots, Analytic Perception, Comparisons, Categorization, Spatial Orientation,* and *Temporal Relations*) and permits their application in situations that require rather complex levels of representational internalized behavior.

Representational Stencil Design consists of tasks in which the learner must construct mentally, *not* through motor manipulation, a design that is identical to that in a colored standard. Colored stencils, some of which are solid and some of which are cut out, are printed on a poster, and the student re-creates the given design by referring to the stencils that must be used and specifying the order in which they must be mentally superimposed on each other. *Representational Stencil Design* is based on Arthur's Stencil Design Test (1930), but by its demand for representation, rather than motor manipulation, and by the complexity of its tasks, it differs essentially from its predecessor.

The completion of these tasks requires a complex sequence of steps. In terms of the task itself, first the student must analyze a complex figure, constructed of shapes and colors that, in themselves, are the product of an interplay produced by the segregation and integration of lines of the different stencils. The identification of the various components, the shapes of which are transformed by superimpositions, is a rather difficult task because it must take into account the outcome of the superimpositions as transformations of each one of the disparate stimuli.

3 Cut out tilted cross and triangles in black stencil

18 Cut out center circle in white stencil

1 Solid black

4 Cut out center cross and peripheral triangles and arrowheads in black stencil

2 Cut out large center square in black stencil.

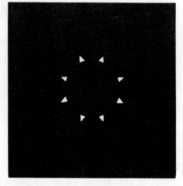

Representational Stencil Design (design 24, page 16A)

The circle cut out of white stencil 18 is totally unrecognizable once the black stencils 3, 4, and 2 are superimposed upon it. Only eight small triangles remain of the white circle. The only way to recognize the presence of Stencil #18 is to perceive the circular ordering of the triangles.

The identification of the whole through its transformed parts requires representation and an active construction of reality with the help of the available cues.

A second important step is to identify the order in which the superimposition of stencils determines the specific shape that emerges. Perceptual reality is never really reversible; therefore, the order of the perception of events makes a strong difference and will determine the nature, shape, and quality of the perceived. A simple example of the effect of ordering is the perception of the temperature of water if one has first immersed one's hand in a pail of ice water and then in a pail of warm water or reversed the order.

By virtue of their intellectual realism, children and retarded performers may often confound what they perceive in reality and what they know. This is exemplified in a child's drawing of a tree in which he carefully draws its roots because he knows they exist, in spite of the fact that they generally are not seen in reality. In *Representational Stencil Design,* the child may choose two solid stencils from the poster and believe that, in their superimposition, the solid covered one will be seen simply because it is known to be there.

Defining the order of the superimposition of the stencils necessitates the segregation of lines and the location of cues. This requires the identification of stimuli present in each of the stencils, in terms of color, shape, size, and orientation, and the use of a number of specific cues such as angles, corners, and holes. Stencils will be accepted or rejected according to their specific attributes and their role in the production of the final designs. Additive operations are needed in order to produce an octagon. For example, the white frame shown in the design on page 244 can only be produced by the superimposition of two cutout shapes (a square and a diamond) of the same color.

The appreciation of size requires an adaptation of the proportions from the size of the stencil, as printed on a poster, to its size as it appears in the smaller printed design. There is a reduction of 38.5% in the size of the stencils from one source to the other. Such representation and reduction require conservation and constancy across change in size, a function that is not always present in the retarded performer.

The operation by which the individual is asked to represent, rather than to manipulate, to produce and to observe the change, is a highly complex task because, in addition to the representation itself, it requires a continuous internal feedback of the consummated transformation, and then an anticipation of the changes that still must be produced to accomplish the task. In other words, not only does one have to anticipate the task itself, but, once this anticipated task is produced representationally, one has to consider it as an existent state — perceptually and physically — and act on it to produce another transformational process. The individual must bear in mind, "What have I already done so that I have this image design? What is correct or what is not and needs change?" It is not difficult to imagine how many functions, perceptual, inferential, and logical, are involved in these tasks.

The *Representational Stencil Design* instrument is composed of three separate parts: 1) one printed poster (70 cm × 100 cm) of 18 colored stencils (each 12 cm × 12 cm), 2) 29 pages of exercises that are to be completed by the students, and 3) four reuseable booklets containing 55 complex designs (each 7.5 cm × 7.5 cm).

The student is introduced to the 18 stencils on the poster and learns to distinguish between them, initially on the basis of their color — white, black, red, blue, green, and yellow. Then he must use shape to discriminate between the stencils which are cut out in the forms of crosses, circles, diamonds, squares, and triangles. He must compare and differentiate between the cutouts according to the parameters of shape, size, orientation, and position on the stencil. Completion of these exercises requires systematic observation, comparison, categorization, and summation.

In the exercise that follows, the child is asked to compare the numbered stencils on the page with the colored stencils on the chart. After identifying them, he is asked to classify them and present the information in diagram form.

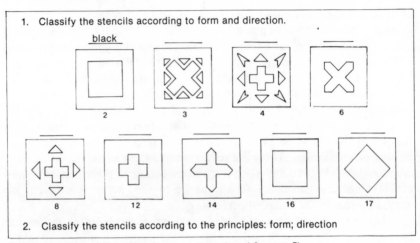

1. Classify the stencils according to form and direction.

2. Classify the stencils according to the principles: form; direction

Representational Stencil Design (exercises 1 and 2, page 5)

The objective of the second unit is to recognize the designs that result from superimposing stencils by separating given simple designs into their components and by assembling designs from specified stencils. Both temporal and spatial orientation are necessary in ordering the stencils in the design.

"It's like when I get dressed in the winter. First I put on my undershirt, then my shirt and then my sweater. You can't see my undershirt because my shirt covers it, and all you can see of my shirt is its collar."

The student starts to use the code, symbolizing each stencil with a number. In addition to planning and comparison, hypothetical thought and logic assist him in his representation. He must conserve the constancy of the attributes of the stencils during their transport from the poster to the booklets. The student becomes increasingly active as he is called upon to construct designs and fill in missing stencils. He is asked to correct errors, noting the source from which they stem.

Define the nature of the error in each in each of the following three answers. Choose the correct definition for every error from those listed below and put its letter on the line provided next to the answer to which it applies.

$$7 - 14 - 12 - 6 \qquad \underline{\qquad}$$
$$7 - 14 - 12 - 16 \,^- \, 6 \qquad \underline{\qquad}$$
$$7 - 14 - 12 - 6 \,^- \, 17 \qquad \underline{\qquad}$$

a. Stencil correct in form but not in color.
b. Stencil correct in color but not in form.
c. Sequence of stencils is not correct.
d. One stencil is missing.
e. One stencil is extra (superfluous).

STENCIL NUMBERS
left to right

Representational Stencil Design (exercise A4, page 9)

The student is asked to analyze Design A4 with an orientation toward the discovery of the error in each one of the given answers. It should be noted that hypothetical thought and inference assist in the solution.

The basic premise is that there is only one error in each answer. The first answer has only four stencils whereas the other two have five, so the error in that answer must be that one stencil is missing. The order of 7-14-12 is shared by all three answers with stencil 6 in the fourth place in two of the answers. This leads to the conclusion that the error in the second answer is that the sequence of stencils is not correct. Therefore, the error in the third answer must be that the wrong stencil has been used, and that it should be 16 and not 17.

In discussing the application of the above exercise, students give examples of where a source of error is the same as those given in the exercises:

"In the shop window I see a blue blouse that just matches my skirt. In stock they have similar blouses, but not in the blue color I want, or they have other blouses, not as pretty, in the color but not in the style."

"In typing I make mistakes by switching the letters. The letters are right but they are not in the right order. Sometimes I leave out a letter in a word."

"In math, in solving problems in which I have to clear the parentheses sometimes I don't do it right. $3(5 + 8) =$ means I have to add the 5 and 8 first before I multiply by 3."

"Sometimes when I take a matching test, I get to the end and see that there is one answer that I haven't matched up. I know that I've made a mistake, either by skipping or by using one answer twice."

Rules that govern the construction of the design, such as that the bottom stencil must be solid and is that which is seen in the center of the design, are induced through logic and verified. Concurrently, the student learns of the dangers of overgeneralization: not always is the order in which the colors appear in the design an indication of the order of assembly of the stencils. The student analyzes the sources of possible errors by reversibility and representation.

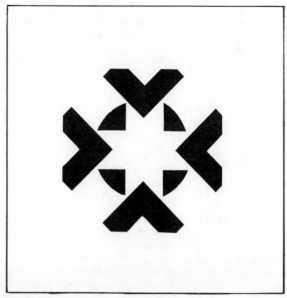

Representational Stencil Design (design 47, exercise 2, page 25)

The creation of this design requires the merging of two white stencils and the use of only parts of two black stencils.

As the instrument progresses, the student projects virtual relationships by mentally filling in parts of the design so that he can determine which figures were used. He seeks his answer by affirmation, by negation and elimination of what is a logically impossible choice. He reasons hypothetically and seeks substantiation.

In discussing mergers, the students differentiate between those in which the parties lose their separate identities and those in which they do not:

"When two companies merge, they become a new one, usually with a new name or with both their names linked. But when a man and woman marry, they merge, too, but they don't lose their identities, and the woman, unless she's a 'libber,' takes the man's name."

With the convergence of two or more stencils, the student must rely more heavily on representation. Inasmuch as there is no possibility for manipulation, in case of error the student must be able to reverse his operation and still conserve the partial design that is the result of correct positioning. He must extrapolate from the known to the unknown and depend on logical evidence for support.

Representational Stencil Design (design 51, exercise 1, page 26)

This instrument is particularly attractive and challenging. It best illustrates the gradation of exercises in order of difficulty. The mastery of early stages is required for successful completion of the later exercises. Although the more difficult tasks of the last two booklets contain cues, it has been found that students are so highly motivated that they prefer to solve the problems independently, using the given information to check their work rather than as an aid in coping with the tasks.

Analysis of *Representational Stencil Design* in Terms of the Cognitive Map

Content: Complex geometrical forms.

Modality: Figural, numerical, and verbal. Accessible to functionally illiterate with the teacher's reading of instructions.

Phase: *Input:*   Systematic observation and precise perception; labeling; seeking spatial and temporal relationships; conservation of constancy; restraint of impulsivity; systematic work.

Elaboration: Comparison; use of two sources of information; use of cues; categorization; hypothetical thinking; use of logical evidence.

Output: Use of code; restraint of impulsivity; internal feedback.

Operations: Segregation; differentiation; representation; anticipation of transformation; encoding and decoding; generalization.

Level of abstraction: High.

Level of complexity: From medium to extremely high.

Level of efficiency: Errors are generally caused by the high level of complexity or any of the deficient functions. Errors may be classed according to types: the use of stencils of the correct color but incorrect in cutout forms; the use of stencils of the correct cutout but incorrect colors; the correct stencils, but incorrect in sequence; the use of too many or too few stencils.

Insight: Both the student and the teacher acquire important insight as a result of this instrument.

The author has long contended that not only is the retarded performer capable of representation but he also will be more successful in solving certain problems by representation than by motor manipulation. Contrary to the notion long held by special education teachers, the author holds that manipulation impedes rather than assists the retarded performer in the grasp of principles that will permit generalization to tasks differing in novelty and complexity.

Recent work by Neifeind and Koch (1976) has attempted to study this contention of the author. Neifeind and Koch have found that, whereas the normal adolescent performs better by manipulation than by representation in the performance of these tasks, the retarded performer who has received training performs significantly better when he uses representation than when he manipulates. When he manipulates his score falls below that achieved by his normal peers, while when he uses representation he does better than his untrained normal peers.

It will be recalled from the discussion of the lack, or impairment, of cognitive functions that the retarded performer is described as having an episodic grasp of reality (page 102) which makes trial-and-error motor manipulation of very limited efficiency in his learning process. It is only by forcing an orientation toward seeking relationships and a requirement for representation and anticipation of transformations that the difficulties of the retarded performer are overcome.

The ability of the retarded performer to represent the outcome of an imagined act usually comes as a surprise to the teacher trained in special education. The emphasis on motor manipulation of concrete material that is used in the teaching of young children has been carried into the work with the retarded performer as a result of generalization of a theoretical assumption that holds that the mental age of the retarded performer can be equated with the chronological age of a young child. The theory presented in this book contends that retarded performance is the result of deficiencies in cognitive functioning because of a lack of mediated learning experience, and considers as inappropriate excessive emphasis on motor manipulation for the retarded performing adolescent. The author would stress those activities in which interiorized representational behavior is the sole modality by which the student can solve the problem at hand.

With the awareness of the student and teacher of the ability of the student to cope with the tasks of *Representational Stencil Design,* there is an increase in the level of expectations of the teacher and a readiness on the part of the student to engage in an increased reliance on modalities of presentation that are not limited to sensorial and motor interaction with the environment.

TRANSITIVE RELATIONS; SYLLOGISMS

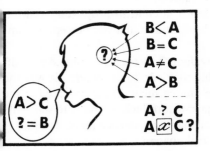 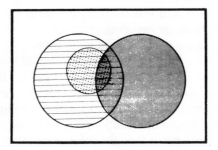

The instruments *Transitive Relations* and *Syllogisms* deal with formal operations and logico-verbal reasoning. These instruments both require and foster higher level abstract and inferential thought for which the student has been prepared by his mastery of earlier instruments. Some of the prerequisites for operational thinking, such as the projection of relationships and the perceived relation between a whole and its parts, have been provided by *Organization of Dots* and *Analytic Perception.* The recognition of classes and the attributes of their members have been taught in *Comparisons* and *Categorization,* while symmetrical, asymmetrical, and hierarchical relationships have been presented in *Family Relations.*

In both *Transitive Relations* and *Syllogisms,* the student learns to infer new relationships from existing ones through deduction. Deductive inference involves the use of a rule and its application to a variety of situations. The retarded performer's passivity, reflected in his attitude toward himself as incapable of generating new information, impedes his readiness to make inferences and draw conclusions. In addition, his episodic grasp of reality, his inability to project relationships, and his lack of spontaneous comparative behavior beyond his limited need system make for a lack of orientation to generalization or rule seeking.

Developmentalists contend that the acquisition of logical thought is gradual and proceeds in well defined stages. They say that failure to infer is based on an inability to use an external frame of reference to connect and categorize.

Bryant (1974), however, claims that inferential thought processes are accessible even to young children under specified conditions. He demonstrates that errors can be plausibly accounted for by the extent to which the child is able to remember the information upon which the inference is based, and/or the child's ability to gather the appropriate information for active, spontaneous inference. Bryant also attributes difficulties in inferential thinking to the limitations of a relative code, which is adequate only for direct comparison between objects presented simultaneously or to connect separately presented objects through their common relations within the same framework, and to the use of external frameworks.

The difficulty of the culturally deprived child in projecting relationships, in encoding perceived relationships, and in analytic perception contributes to his inability to infer.

Gibson (1969) argues that all individuals only take in a limited amount of information at any one time and that they select in a systematic way the dimensions to which they attend. The limited mental field observed in the retarded performer, as well as the impairment or lack of ability to select the relevant information, is responsible for the inappropriate input that makes inferential thought either nonexistent or impaired.

Transitive Relations

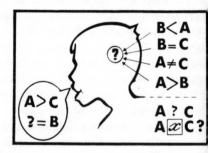

Transitive Relations, 23 pages long, deals with the inferences of new re tionships from those existing between objects and/or events that can be scribed in terms of "greater than," "equal to," and "less than." In the fi five pages of the instrument, the student is introduced to the concept of dered sets and the signs used to designate relationships. In the first exerci he is offered strategies for ordering his data and encoding them in such a v as to have the coded information present in his visual field.

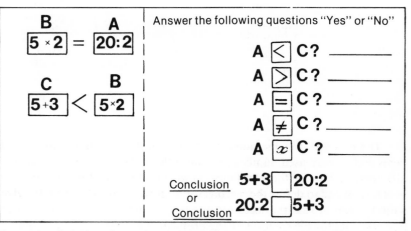

Transitive Relations (exercise 1, page 4)

Encoding the given numerical data is taught first. The relatively simple mathematical operations make the relationship between A, B, and C easy to grasp. Through substitution and the use of implication, the student arrives at the alternative conclusions.

The student is then introduced to the rules governing transitive thinking and taught to connect separately presented statements through a common reference point. Perhaps, just as important, he learns when transitive thought processes are inappropriate for the solution of a problem.

The student is introduced to problems for which there is no solution available because of insufficient information. Although the retarded performer is quite accustomed to saying "I don't know" because he is unable to supply the information, he learns that there are situations in which nobody can know the answer. He is taught to systematically explore the given data to ascertain if they are sufficient to enable him to arrive at a conclusion.

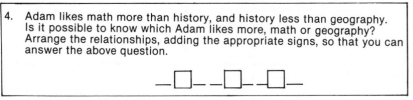

Transitive Relations (exercise 4, page 6)

Adam likes both math and geography more than history. Because his love for geography can be greater than, less than, or equal to his love for math, no definitive answer is possible. The student learns the rules for arriving at such a conclusion.

5. I am taller than my brother. My brother is shorter than my sister.
   Is it possible to know who is taller, my brother or I?
   _____

Transitive Relations (exercise 5, page 6)

The exercises become more complex with the association of multiple items and an increased number of relationships. The student is required to differentiate between those instances in which transitive thinking is or is not operational and to define the reasons for his inability to infer from the given data. He learns to ask the necessary questions in order to obtain the information essential for his solution of the problem.

3   Every day Joan bought a tuna sandwich and a cup of coffee for lunch.
    She usually ate at Joe's Cafe, but one day she decided to eat at Tip's Tea
    Room, a place that had just opened. The total bill for her egg sandwich
    and cup of tea was exactly the same as it usually was at Joe's for her
    regular lunch; however, she noticed that the price of the sandwich at Tip's
    was higher than at Joe's. She immediately concluded that:

    The coffee at Joe's   ☐   The tea at Tip's Tea Room

    When A + B $=$ C + D
    And   A $\leq$ C
    Then   B $\geq$ D

Transitive Relations (exercise 3, page 13)

Throughout the instrument, the student is given opportunities to learn rules and apply them. He engages in highly abstract application in his translation of verbal problems into signs and in his decoding of the relationships described in signs and applying them to verbal problems.

In an apartment house, the tenants in apartments A, B and C each had a party one Saturday night. The noise coming from apartment A added to the noise from apartment B was more than twice the noise from apartment C. The tenant in apartment C called the police and claimed that the noise coming from apartment A was greater than the noise from his own apartment and was disturbing his party. The tenant of apartment A claimed that this was not so and argued that the noise from his apartment was less than that coming from apartment C.

Who was right:
A _____?
C _____?

What additional information would have helped the police and us to find the solution?

_____ ☐ _____ , _____ ☐ _____

When the only given is A + B $>$ C + C, there is not enough information to find the relationship

A x C   B x C

Transitive Relations (exercise 2, page 14)

The sign $\boxed{x}$ is used in this instrument to designate, "It is impossible to know." The student learns to look for key words and to ignore irrelevancies in his encoding of the data and application of the rules for transitive thinking.

Transitive Relations offers a genuine challenge to students. A teacher who has had no specific training in logic finds the exercises difficult as well. Thus, the tasks are an example of the equilateral triangle that exists in FIE among teacher, student, and material, with teacher and student struggling together to master the tasks.

Syllogisms

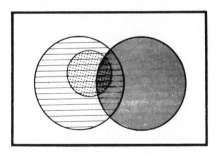

Syllogisms deals with formal propositional logic. In the first unit of this 60-page instrument, the student expands the concept of sets, originally acquired in *Categorization*. He learns the laws governing sets and their members, and the implications of these laws. He learns to construct new sets by various operations, such as logical multiplication.

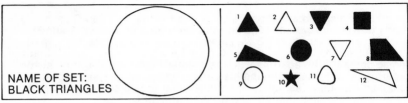

Syllogisms (exercise 2, page 3)

The set, black triangles, is the result of logical multiplication. Each member must be simultaneously black and a triangle.

The second unit deals with mutually exclusive sets in which no member of one set can, by definition, be a member of the other.

3.   **No midgets are giants.**

Tom Thumb is a midget.
Conclusion: _____ is not a _____ .

Syllogisms (exercise 3, page 13)

The student learns to apply the rule that if no A is B, then any member of set A cannot be a member of set B. This implies that no member of set B can be a member of set A.

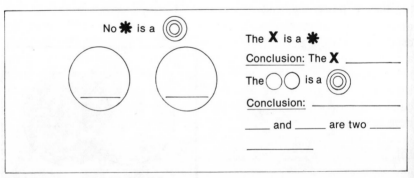

Syllogisms (exercise 2, page 54)

In the third unit, there is a presentation of identical sets. In this unit, as well as in the second, the student learns of the dangers of overgeneralization, which leads to stereotypes, to the inappropriate ascription of attributes, and to erroneous inclusion in sets.

Subsets and intersecting sets are then introduced, with the implications of set membership and the valid inferences that can be made from them. This then leads to syllogisms. Exercises are presented verbally and pictorially, with an effort to make the logical operations as abstract as possible by using symbols and signs in place of words. The student is asked to use Venn diagrams and signs to present his conclusions.

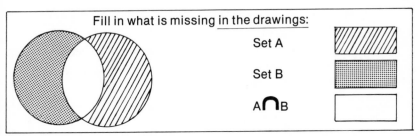

Syllogisms (exercise 1, page 45)

In addition to formal syllogistic thought, there is an effort to make the student critical in analyzing propositions and premises for their truth. In his propensity to deal with the "here and now," the culturally deprived child has been described as experiencing difficulty in the use of representational or hypothetical thought and lacking the need for logical evidence. All of the exercises of the last unit are geared toward the correction of these deficient functions (see Figure 20).

In this instrument the student learns propositional logic. He gains an awareness of all the possible alternatives and, through valid inference, discriminates between possible and true alternatives. This particular instrument aims at producing in the learner a sense of the compellingness of inferential thinking and a need for logical evidence. Logico-verbal and inferential thought processes are used as a modality of communication between the child and his environment, once the input and elaborational phases have been oriented in this way.

Syllogisms and *Transitive Relations* are the last two instruments in the FIE program, and their mastery indicates an ability to engage in inductive and deductive reasoning under highly abstract conditions.

There is spontaneous application by the student of the principles and processes learned in these two instruments. A "square" becomes a "subset of four-sided figures" and an "exclusive set" to "rectangles." There are constant demands to "prove it." Both the insight and orientation to logical thinking gained through *Transitive Relations* and *Syllogisms* lead to an awareness of common errors in thinking.

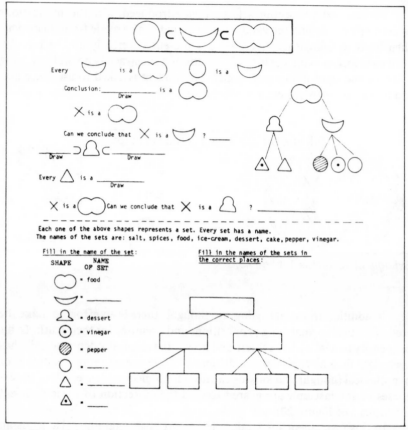

Figure 20. *Syllogisms* (page 30). This exercise demonstrates the high level of abstraction and complexity of the tasks in *Syllogisms*. The same problem, if presented verbally, would be easier. For instance, if the student were asked to describe the relationship between trees, fruit trees, and an orange tree, he would have no difficulty in describing the more inclusive sets.

A student stormed into FIE class. "That math teacher don't know nothing. The problem was if a farmer decides one year to plant his field every 4 feet instead of every 6 feet and he needed 120 plants before, how many would he need now. The teacher kept saying he'd need less, because that was the answer in the back of the book. I told him to forget the answer and to use his head! 'Man, if you'd just use your head you'd know it's logical that you gotta have more trees.' I told him, 'It's what we learned in FIE is a reciprocal relationship.' I tried to go to the board to show him, but he got mad and told me to get to my seat and shut up. He didn't want to hear nothing more from me."

A girl member of a minority group said, "It got so that I hated to give my last name to people. I could almost hear them thinking to themselves, 'Oh, she's one of those!' Now I know they have a problem in using stereotypes and overgeneralization and using false premises. It's their problems and not mine!"

During elections, the following conversation took place in an FIE class:
Student: "Just because he's a movie star doesn't mean that he knows more about politics than I do, necessarily!"
Teacher: "Why do you say that?"
Student: "He's a member of the set of 'movie stars' so he has the attributes of movie stars. Knowing about politics isn't necessarily one of those attributes. He may or may not be a member of a set of those people who know about politics, but there's no way of knowing for sure. Just because he's good in one thing doesn't mean that he's good in the other. They are not two identical sets. One could maybe be a subset of the other, or may be an intersecting set. But just because some A's are B doesn't mean that all B's are A, if A is movie stars and B is people who know something about politics."

SUMMARY

In this chapter, we have presented the instruments regularly used in the 2-year classroom FIE program. The emphasis has been on the objectives of each instrument, with illustrations and anecdotes to demonstrate how the goals are achieved. Whereas the format and modality of each instrument may vary, the same elements have received attention in the construction of the material of the whole program.

With each of the instruments, there is an attempt to arouse the need of the student to engage in the subject and to increase his motivation to do so. The basic concepts, codes, and symbols of the instrument are presented and described, followed by tasks to ensure recognition and reproduction. The exercises then demand an interiorization and a search for relationships. Representation, elaboration, and transformations are elicited in problems that require the generation of new information on the basis of what has been previously acquired. Finally, the student is active and autonomous in constructing new sets of events in which he demonstrates his mastery of the functions and operations of the instrument.

The material of each instrument is graded in difficulty. The difficulty, however, is not merely one of increased complexity. It may be engendered by any one of the parameters of the cognitive map and, as such, may be anticipated by the teacher. Care has been taken not to overload a series of exercises with too many problematic elements or to make the tasks too easy. A balance has been sought to ensure sufficient novelty and complexity to maintain a challenge and a high level of motivation for the student without leading him into the blind alley of frustration.

Material has been sequenced so that the student is not asked to engage in tasks for which he is not adequately prepared. Any factual knowledge that is a prerequisite for an exercise is presented to the student on the page itself, or by the teacher in accordance with the instruction of the author. Although the demand for prior knowledge is minimal, there nevertheless are tasks in which the teacher must be sure that the student understands what he is being asked to do and that he has the tools with which to comply.

The use of operations, too, has been taken into consideration in the sequence and gradation of the instruments. For instance, no student is asked to find intraclass differences before he has learned how to compare and discriminate those differences existing between classes. Once he has mastered the basic operation, however, demands for its application are explicit and then implicit in progressive tasks.

In the following summary chapter, we return to the subgoals of the programs, briefly presented in Chapter 6. With a few illustrations and anecdotes, we demonstrate the interinstrument cohesiveness in the attainment of the objectives of the FIE program.

8

INSTRUMENTAL ENRICHMENT
SUBGOALS: HOW COGNITIVE
FUNCTIONS ARE FOSTERED

In the preceding chapter, the 15 instruments of the FIE program were described and analyzed in terms of their specific objectives. The deficient cognitive functions, the parameters of the cognitive map, and the part played by the subgoals of FIE were discussed and illustrated, in the presentation of each instrument, by examples of exercises and anecdotes. In this chapter, an attempt is made to analyze the program horizontally and demonstrate how the attainment of the individual subgoals constitutes an underlying motif that can be traced throughout all of the instruments.

A few exercises and bits of classroom discussions have been selected to show the inter-instrument cohesiveness in the attainment of the FIE goals. It should be noted, however, that each task is not necessarily directed toward achievement of only one subgoal or to one cognitive function. Completion of the exercise may require a definition of the problem, adequate perception, labeling, spontaneous comparison, precision, planning, systematic work, spatial and temporal orientation, the use of two sources of information, a broadening of the mental field, the use of hypothetical thought, the need for logical evidence, and the restraint of impulsivity in all three phases of the mental act. That same task may offer specific practice for the application of previously acquired schemata. Its mastery may be highly motivating and lead to insight. Illustrative of such an exercise are the two examples from *Organization of Dots,* page 14, that appear below. Although they have been chosen to demonstrate an attack on blurred, sweeping perception because that is a primary source of failure, they could also have been selected as an example of many other subgoals of the FIE program. This element of the meeting and merging of many, if not all, of the objectives of the program in the construction of each task must be borne in mind in the analysis that follows.

SUBGOAL I: CORRECTION OF DEFICIENT COGNITIVE FUNCTIONS

The foremost subgoal of FIE is, of necessity, the correction of the deficient functions that are characteristic of the cognitive behavior of the culturally deprived individual. FIE uses diverse approaches and modalities to attack the deficient cognitive functions. The great number and variety of tasks included in the program provide ample opportunities to exercise and develop each individual function appropriately, thereby producing possibilities for the generalization of cognitive schemata to diverse areas and enabling transfer.

Blurred, Sweeping Perception

Although the correction of blurred, sweeping perception is the primary concern of *Analytic Perception,* it is the subject of tasks in all of the instruments. A few examples should suffice to illustrate:

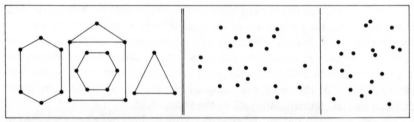

Organization of Dots (exercises 8 and 9, page 14)

Successful completion of the task requires complete input data which are contingent upon sufficient investment. The figures and their parts must be precisely and completely defined. To discriminate properly between the two six-sided figures requires a perception not only of the number of sides, but of their relative length. The orientation of the hexagon within the square serves as a cue in the search for the small triangle on top of the square.

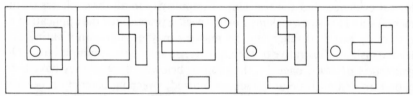

Comparisons (exercise 7, page 8)

A rich input is necessary to find and mark the two identical frames. This necessitates dividing the whole into its parts and perceiving details in terms of the relationship of the three component figures, one to the other.

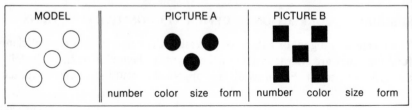

Comparisons (exercise 4, page 9)

The task at the bottom of page 258 is to circle those characteristics in common to the model and each of the two pictures. Global perception results in an inaccurate and imprecise definition of the borders of the figure so that B is perceived as similar in form to the model in the above exercise.

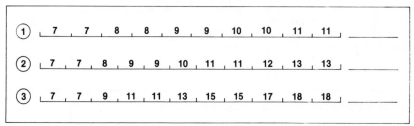

Numerical Progressions (exercise 3, page 15)

Limited focusing on only the first two numbers of each progression and an insufficient investment in terms of time and scanning will result in a sweeping perception of similarity between the progressions. The identity of the first two numbers of each progression will lead the student to the erroneous conclusion that the formula for all three progressions is the same.

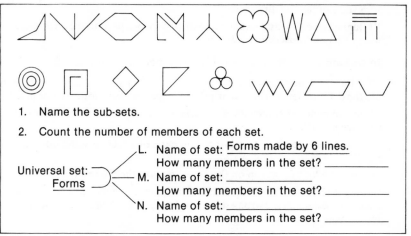

Syllogisms (exercise 3, page 25)

A precise definition of the boundary of each set is necessary in order to appropriately assign members to it. Sweeping perception prevents the adequate discrimination necessary for completion of the task.

4. In the warm days of summer, many birds from many lands congregate around the fish ponds. According to a survey of the Audubon Society, it was found that there were more pelicans than storks, but there were the same number of pelicans and cranes as there were storks and wild geese. Because of bad weather, the survey was stopped before there was time to count the number of cranes or wild geese. By using the information at hand was it possible to find the relationship between cranes and wild geese? _____

Place the data in the above story in the spaces next to the appropriate letters.

Write the formula and the conclusion.

A_____ B_____ C_____ D_____   ____ + ____ = ____ + ____

_____ ☐ _____

Transitive Relations (exercise 4, page 13)

The task requires clear and complete input data. The four classes must be delimited and defined as to their relationship, one to the other, in order to form a basis for transitive thinking. Thus, A (pelicans) + B (cranes) = C (storks) + D (wild geese). Given A is more than C, are there more, less, or the same number of cranes as wild geese, or is it impossible to know?

In classroom discussions of blurred, sweeping perception students used the following examples:

"Twins look alike if you look at them fast. But if you look carefully, you see that they are really different."

"Jewelers have a little glass that they look at jewelry with. They need it to tell the fake from the real stuff. You have to look at it real close and for a long time before you can tell the difference."

"I flunked an exam last week because there were two parts to the question, and I didn't do one 'cause I just didn't see it."

In seeking strategies for focusing, students have commented:

"To draw your attention to something important in a book, they underline, or use those funny letters (italics) or print it bigger, or use another color ink:"

"When someone says something important, they say it louder or softer or kind of space it out."

"In art, we learned how to make certain parts of a picture stand out from the rest."

"Girls put a lot of makeup on their eyes to make them stand out."

"You got to look at the shop teacher real good in the morning to see how he feels. If he got up on the wrong side of the bed, you don't open your mouth. You just do your work and shut up."

The requirement for proper input is pervasive throughout the instruments. Students find that a superficial familiarity with certain forms and configurations is not sufficient for the efficient handling of the tasks. The repeated need for proper input sharpens the awareness of the individual and thereby produces in him the necessary perceptual vigilance.

The Need to Use Two or More Sources of Information

Threaded through the tasks of all of the instruments is the need to use two or more sources of information in order to solve a problem. The two sources may be close to one another in time and space. For example:

> "In English when I have to find out what the words in a story mean, I have to use both a dictionary and the book with the story."

More often, however, one source is remote from the other, either spatially or temporally. Distance in space requires interiorization or visual transport, while that in time requires retrieval from memory.

> "It's not enough just to see the number of a subway train. You gotta know if it's going uptown or downtown, and if it stops where you gotta go."

In *Organization of Dots,* the model is close to only a few of the frames and is further and further away as the tasks move down and across the page. Solution of the task requires the use of at least two sources of information.

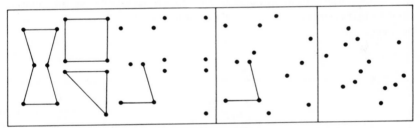

Organization of Dots (exercises 2 and 18, page 6)

> Both the size and the form of the figures in the standard are interiorized or transported visually to the field of dots. In the absence of any other cues, the two dots in the center of the hourglass assist in the projection and orientation of the figure.

The tasks in *Orientation in Space I* involve moving back and forth across the page in order to gather all of the necessary information and write the answer in the place set aside for it. For example, the position of the boy and the four stationary objects in the field must be coordinated to arrive at a conclusion about relative orientation (see page 157 and Figure 4 in Chapter 7).

> "In a trial, the people on the jury have to listen to the prosecutor and to the attorney for defense, and to all the witnesses, and to the accused, and then hear the law from the judge, and put them all together to reach a decision of whether the guy is guilty or not guilty and recommend punishment."

> "When I cut a garment from material there's all kinds of things I gotta pay attention to. Some I can see, like if the material is big enough for the part I have to cut, or if it's the right sleeve or the left sleeve. Some I have to know about, too, like corduroy or velvet, have to be cut going in one direction or else the light hits them wrong and it looks like the dress has been cut from different material. So I

have to pay attention to the direction of the material, and the place of the selvage.''

The task in *Comparisons,* illustrated below, requires that the class and the attributes of color be considered in finding two citrus fruits, one of which is yellow and the other orange.

___ yellow

___ orange

citrus fruits

Comparisons (exercise 1, page 13)

Unlike earlier exercises in *Analytic Perception,* the following task requires the conservation of the orientation of the parts within the whole. The size, shape, orientation, and direction of lines must all provide information for the identification of the parts of the model that have been united to form the new whole.

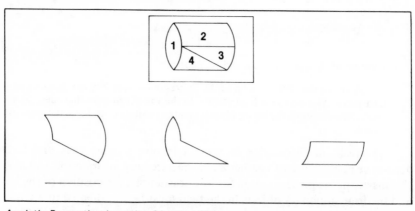

Analytic Perception (exercise 2A, page 25)

The student's comment below shows an attention to two sources of information, fostered through work in *Analytic Perception:*

"In attaching an electric wire to a round three-prong plug, you have to pay attention to the colors in the strand of wire and get those parts right, *and* to the position of the ground. Otherwise you have made a new whole like in these exercises, but it's all wrong.''

In the example below from *Numerical Progressions,* the various sources of information are separated physically on the page, as well as in the operations required for the solution of the task.

---

1. a.   Look at the formula.

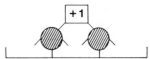

b.   Create a progression based on the above formula in which the first relationship is +2, and the first number is 1.

Numerical Progressions (exercise 1 and 2, page 24)

The student must relate to the relationship between relationships, and transport it to the relationship that exists between two successive numbers. Based on the resulting changes in the relationship between the successive numbers, he will be able to construct the numerical progression. In the actual activity, he moves from level to level, and from one source of information to another.

In another instance,

"When I want to watch TV, I see what's on in the listing in the paper. I gotta look up the day, the hour, and the channel. They're all in different places on the chart. Then at the point they all meet, I can see what programs are on and what channel I want."

To discover the components of a design in the *Representational Stencil Design,* the position, size, and orientation of the cutout stencils, their color, and the order of their placement must be considered simultaneously. There is a physical distance between the chart on which the stencils are shown, the small booklet in which the design appears, and the pages of the instrument in which the problems are presented and answers written. The elements of anticipation and representation require the ability to work with several sources of information simultaneously and to organize them according to sequence.

The exercise on page 264 in *Transitive Relations* requires the use of four modalities: verbal, pictorial, numerical, and symbolic. For mastery, the student must move from one source of data to another and from the top of the page to the bottom and back again.

Robert and Simon are twin brothers.
George is younger than Simon and younger than Robert.

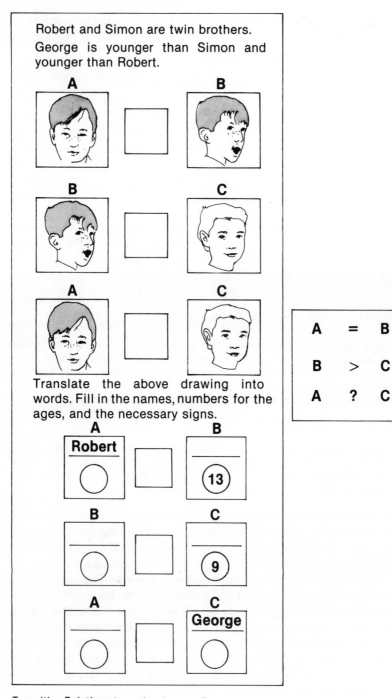

Translate the above drawing into words. Fill in the names, numbers for the ages, and the necessary signs.

A	=	B
B	>	C
A	?	C

Transitive Relations (exercise 1, page 4)

From these examples from seven instruments, it should be apparent that the use of two or more sources of information is required by exercises throughout the FIE program.

Impulsivity and the Lack of Planning Behavior

The impulsivity of the retarded performer is often corrected operationally by the introduction of planning behavior into his repertoire. Therefore, impulsivity and the lack of planning behavior are discussed together and illustrated by examples that relate to both of these deficient cognitive functions.

Impulsivity is reflected in the retarded performer's probabilistic use of stimuli and his tendency to use either a salient element or the first he encounters. Correction of this deficiency involves the explicit need to gather all the information necessary for elaboration. The input of data must be sufficient to enable their enumeration, comparison, and summation. In addition, there is the need for imposing a delay between the input and output phases of the mental act. Changing the cognitive style of the retarded performer will result in a change in his cognitive tempo. The introduction of reflective thinking represents an attempt to create a distance between input and output.

Planning behavior involves being aware of both the goal, or end product, which is located at both a temporal and spatial distance, and of the strategy through which it can be obtained. A plan requires that the steps toward the goal be detailed, ordered, and judged as to their desirability and efficiency. The lack of readiness to anticipate and predict the outcome of a behavior and the lack of awareness that alternative strategies are available will seriously impair the retarded performer's planning behavior.

It is through the reflection over and evaluation of alternative strategies in reaching the goal that the cognitive tempo is altered; it is through planning behavior that the delay between input and output is imposed.

In the drawing are a rectangle, a circle, a triangle and a hexagon.
Go over the lines with a pencil so that the circle and the hexagon will seem on top of the rectangle, and the triangle beneath it.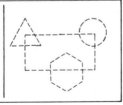

Instructions (exercise 7, page 38)

The starting point and the sequence of drawing each figure must be determined in order that the end product conform to the written instructions. Inasmuch as the uppermost figures are those seen in their entirety, the student must first complete the circle and hexagon, then the parts of the rectangle that are not covered by those two figures, and finally the parts of the triangle that are not covered by the rectangle. All motor activity must be deferred until the data are gathered and a plan devised.

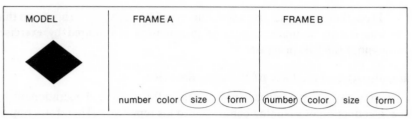

MODEL	FRAME A	FRAME B
	number color (size) (form)	(number) (color) size (form)

Comparisons (exercise 6, page 72)

In the above exercise the student is asked to complete each of the frames so that his drawings are similar to the given model in only those dimensions that are circled. Thus, in frame A, more than one diamond of the same size as the model must be drawn and it can be any color except black. In frame B, one black diamond either larger than or smaller than the model must be drawn.

Impulsivity and trial-and-error behavior lead to errors and erasures. The strategy for successful completion of the exercise entails complete elaboration of the data prior to output, and a detailed plan of operation. A method of evaluation must be decided upon to ensure that the solution will match the demands of the task.

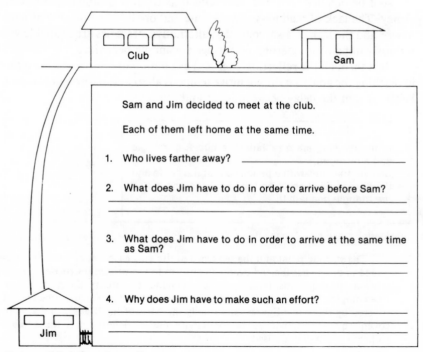

Sam and Jim decided to meet at the club.

Each of them left home at the same time.

1. Who lives farther away? _____

2. What does Jim have to do in order to arrive before Sam?
_____

3. What does Jim have to do in order to arrive at the same time as Sam?
_____
_____

4. Why does Jim have to make such an effort?
_____
_____

Temporal Relations (page 4)

On the *Temporal Relations* page presented here on page 266, the second and third questions orient the student to the need for planning. In the process, he must consider various alternatives, part of the reflective thinking that imposes a delay between input and output.

An FIE consultant was present at a lesson on the above page from *Temporal Relations*. Following is his report:

The teacher read the instructions and asked the students to complete the page. Afterwards, the class went over the answers orally.

Student 1: "He has to be speedy."

Student 2: "He has to leave earlier."

Teacher: "No. Both of them leave at the same time. Read the instructions."

Student 3: "Jim could ride his bicycle."

Teacher: "Perhaps."

The teacher wanted to go on to the next page. There was no summary, no reference to the necessity for planning and coordination between the two boys, no reaction to an unwarranted assumption by the student who suggested that Jim ride his bicycle. Nothing. I asked permission to intervene.

"Until now you have learned about Jim and Sam. On the basis of what you have learned, is somebody able to generalize and give me the rule?"

The girls had difficulty in verbalizing so I asked for more examples.

Student: "Two people are going on trips. One wants to go to a place that is close, the other to a place that is further away. They leave from the same place at the same time, so the one who has to go further has to go faster."

In this answer there is already the beginning of generalization, and this was the reason for my intervention. The teacher's expectations are very low; she does not believe that her students have the capacity to do anything so she stays in the realm of the specific task. In order to sharpen the contrast between the expectations of the teacher and the capacity of the students, I continued:

"So you are saying, it depends on the distance. What is the factor, then, that is responsible for covering more ground or less ground, if the time is the same?"

Student: "The speed."

I continued: "Now tell me the rule."

Student: "If a person wants to cover more distance, he has to increase his speed in order to arrive in the same amount of time as a person who has to travel less distance."

"Now let us apply the rule to our page."

Student: "If Jim wants to arrive at the same time as Sam, he must plan to run real fast."

I hope that the teacher was convinced that the students are able to achieve a great deal more than they are being asked to do because the teacher, too, has the potential of achieving a great deal more.

The reading of the questions to be answered prior to starting on an assignment becomes an important technique of the student in all of his academic work. The defining of the ultimate objective of a task orients him in his work so that he pays the necessary attention to the key elements in his work, and can efficiently plan his strategy. The following FIE example is illustrative:

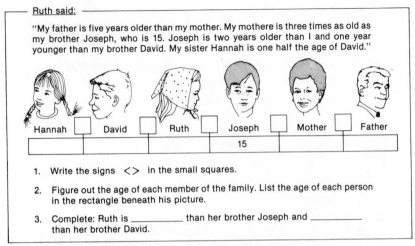

Ruth said:

"My father is five years older than my mother. My mothere is three times as old as my brother Joseph, who is 15. Joseph is two years older than I and one year younger than my brother David. My sister Hannah is one half the age of David."

Hannah   David   Ruth   Joseph   Mother   Father

15

1. Write the signs < > in the small squares.

2. Figure out the age of each member of the family. List the age of each person in the rectangle beneath his picture.

3. Complete: Ruth is _____ than her brother Joseph and _____ than her brother David.

Transitive Relations (exercise 2, page C)

Joseph is the referent, and his age the starting point for the solution of the task. Using Joseph's age as the source of information, first the age of the mother and then that of the father can be easily computed, as can the ages of Ruth and David. From the age of David, one can easily find the age of Hannah.

To orient oneself toward the gathering of the appropriate data and the planning of the detailed strategy for solution, the entire problem must be read first. It is only after the completion of the second question that one can answer the first.

The need for planning is implicit in these exercises in *Representational Stencil Design,* in which the child is asked to color the stencils according to the given numbers.

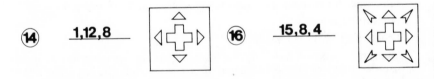

Representational Stencil Design (left: exercise 14, page 8, *right:* exercise 16, page 8)

In exercise 14, stencil 1 is solid black, number 12 is green with a cross cut out of its center, and stencil 8 is red with an identical cross cut out of its center and triangles cut out of its periphery. After assemblage in the given order, there should be a red surface with green triangles and a black cross. The plan, therefore, must include a representation of the transformations and an analysis of the order of applying the colors.

In exercise 16, stencil 15 is solid white, stencil 4 is black with a cross cut out of its center and triangles and arrowheads in its periphery, and stencil 8 is as described above. The colored design, therefore, is black with red arrowheads and white triangles and a white cross.

An impulsive student, who does not gather all of the data and plan his work before carrying it out, will make mistakes.

In the following task in *Numerical Progressions,* the student is asked to compose a formula, construct a numerical progression, and plot it on a graph. His first step must be to count the number of available spaces on the given graph. Obviously, the range of his progression, its starting number, and the number of items it contains will be limited by the space in which he must plot it. The number of elements in the formula he devises, and the direction and magnitude of change he decides upon, are also contingent upon the boundaries imposed by the physical structure of the graph.

An impulsive student, who starts work immediately and without a plan, is apt to find that he is unable to plot the progression he has constructed because he has not paid attention to the interrelating elements of the problem.

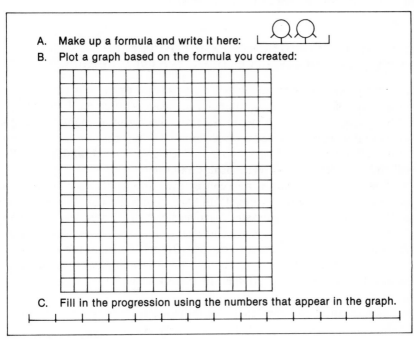

A. Make up a formula and write it here:

B. Plot a graph based on the formula you created:

C. Fill in the progression using the numbers that appear in the graph.

Numerical Progressions (page 15)

Planning, which involves an analysis of both components and operations, becomes part of the repertoire with which FIE students face their everyday problems. The following two fragments of students' conversations demonstrate the detailed strategy by which the goal is reached.

"If I want to go to the movies, I have to find out what is playing. Then I have to find out what time it starts and what time the bus leaves in order to get there in time. Then I have to invite a girl and find out where she lives. Then I have to plan what time I have to leave in order to pick her up. But first of all, I have to be real helpful around the house, so when I ask my dad for money he don't say no.''

"During the summer, I worked with a contractor, and he *really* had to plan. He had to have the frames for the windows put in before the glass was delivered and installed. He had to have the electricians come before the walls got painted. And he had to have the walls painted before he oiled up and finished the floors. One time things got screwed up and the stove got delivered before they were ready to install it and I had to sit beside it all night so it wouldn't get 'ripped off'.''

Summary

In the interest of brevity, we have limited ourselves to the description of the correction of only blurred, sweeping perception; the use of two sources of information; and a lack of planning and impulsive behavior. The examples that have been given should illustrate to the reader the inter-instrument approach to the attainment of the first subgoal.

SUBGOAL II: ACQUISITION OF BASIC CONCEPTS, LABELS, VOCABULARY, OPERATIONS, AND RELATIONSHIPS

Instrumental Enrichment involves a repertoire of operations that are the components of adequate cognitive behavior. An operation has been defined in this context as an activity by which we mentally organize, manipulate, and act upon information gained from external and internal sources. Through formal operations, the adolescent is able to leave the concrete and sensorially real and consider abstract relationships and rules.

Operations, vocabulary, and concepts (as opposed to specific subject-matter areas) provide the "content" of the program. Because this content is taught primarily to enable the student to master the FIE exercises, there is no attempt to be exhaustive. The instruments themselves are essentially content-free; their content is treated as a vehicle to the major goal of the acquisition of the prerequisites of thinking. The selection of the content to be taught is dictated by the needs of the student, in accordance with the requirements of the total program.

Conservation and constancy, for example, are concepts introduced in *Organization of Dots,* expanded in *Comparisons* and *Family Relations,* illustrated in *Analytic Perception,* applied in *Representational Stencil Design* and *Illustrations,* and evoked in all of the other instruments.

Categorization is explicitly taught in the instrument of that name, but the need for the operation is implicit in exercises in *Syllogisms, Comparisons, Transitive Relations, Temporal Relations, Family Relations,* and *Representational Stencil Design.*

Numerical Progressions provides ample opportunities for the application and reinforcement of the operation of seriation, but tasks requiring ordering in a series also appear in *Comparisons, Instructions, Categorization,*

Temporal Relations, Transitive Relations, and *Representational Stencil Design.*

Encoding and decoding are repeatedly invoked, and a variety of modalities are used in addition to the verbal. Whether it is by use of numbers in place of positions or by arrows in place of a human figure, as in *Spatial Orientation I,* by circles, rectangles, and horizontal and vertical lines in *Family Relations,* by signs in *Temporal Relations, Categorization,* and *Transitive Relations,* or by Venn diagrams in *Syllogisms,* the action is that of translation from one modality to another.

Inference and logical reasoning are elicited by tasks in each of the instruments. Examples from the first instrument and the last can illustrate the prevalence of the need for these operations.

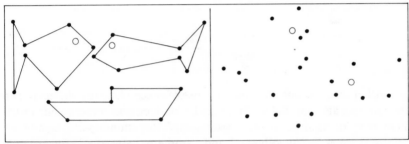

Organization of Dots (exercise 3, page 16)

Inasmuch as the eye, given as a cue, does not assist in discriminating between the two fish, a new strategy must be determined. There are two dots, close together, in front of each tail that can serve as a point of reference for locating the tail. By inference, it is possible to conclude to which fish the particular tail belongs. Then, by use of the tail and the eye, one may logically arrive at the orientation of the fish one has found.

2. Mel's weight was identical to Roger's when each boy was weighed wearing his winter coat. When the boys removed their coats and the coats were weighed, it was found that Mel's coat was heavier than Roger's.

(1) Use letters in place of the information:

    Mel ☐   Roger ☐

    Mel's coat ☐   Roger's coat ☐

(2) Write the equation

_____ ☐ _____

_____ ☐ _____

Conclusion:

_____ ☐ _____

Transitive Relations (exercise 2, page 13)

The two boys can be encoded with A and C, while their coats are respectively B and D. The formula $A + B = C + D$ expresses the original situation. Then, if B is heavier than D, one can infer that A is lighter than C.

Sets based on logical multiplication, in which membership implies the possession of the attributes of each of the intersecting sets, are explicitly presented in *Syllogisms;* however, the operation is also required in many of the earlier instruments. An example or two will suffice to illustrate.

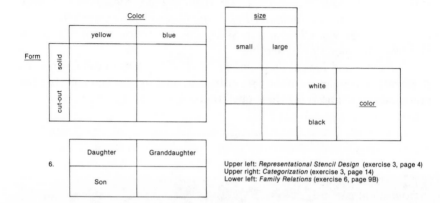

6.

Upper left: *Representational Stencil Design* (exercise 3, page 4)
Upper right: *Categorization* (exercise 3, page 14)
Lower left: *Family Relations* (exercise 6, page 9B)

All of the instruments require the use of precise labeling although there are concepts and vocabulary that may be more characteristic of one instrument than of another. Thus, "strategies," "relationships," "symbols," "signs," "cues," "hypothesis," and "frame of reference," for example, are repeated throughout the program, while the concepts of kinship, hierarchical, symmetrical and asymmetrical relationships, and mutuality are introduced in *Family Relations.* Through *Comparisons,* the students learn the precise meaning of "identity," "similarity," "equivalency," "attributes," "characteristics," "dimensions," and "commonality." In *Orientation in Space I,* there is the first differentiation between "relative" and "constant," the first distinction among "position," "side," and "direction," and the first use of the term "relationship."

Teachers who are new to the FIE program may protest the teaching and use of terms such as "synchronous," "interiorization," or "visual transport" to their retarded performing students. "Why, these kids can hardly put two words together and don't have the terms for far more basic concepts. Why not teach them easier words? They won't remember them anyway." It is the author's contention that words are neither "hard" nor "easy" in and of themselves. Inasmuch as there is no term for a concept or operation in the retarded performer's vocabulary, there is no reason why the most correct, most precise word should not be taught to him. His retention of the word will ultimately be determined both by the frequency of opportunity that he has to use the word and the strength of his need to do so.

The result has been a facile use of terms acquired in the learning of the instruments by retarded performing adolescents. Roger Simon, in a personal communication, has described the process as the forging of a "linguistic community." The concepts, operations, and labels become an integral part of the FIE student's repertoire and are readily applied in academic, vocational, and interpersonal situations.

SUBGOAL III: PRODUCTION OF INTRINSIC MOTIVATION THROUGH HABIT FORMATION

Habit has been defined earlier (page 116) as an internal need system, the activation of which has become detached from and independent of the extrinsic need that initially produced it. To a very large extent, our cognitive functions are ruled by the habits that have been formed and crystallized throughout our experiences and are referred to as "cognitive schemata," "cognitive style," and so on. That our perceptual activity is almost automatically accompanied by comparative behavior, to the extent that we seldom perceive without simultaneously comparing, is the result of habits established during early childhood and fostered by mediated learning experience.

It is therefore of the greatest importance that many of the acquired modes of functioning be crystallized and solidified as cognitive habits. Habits are produced by redundant, repetitive exposure to, and activity upon, certain stimuli that can be depended upon to elicit the same behaviors over periods of time. Thus, the formation of habits is heavily contingent upon the amount and the nature of the opportunities to actively repeat a specific behavior.

Such redundancy and repetition have their drawbacks and difficulties, however. The first is boredom. A young child is not only willing to repeat the same activity or to hear the same story ad nauseum, but will protest the slightest change or deviation in it. In contrast, an adolescent or young adult is bored by repetition and seldom motivated sufficiently to sustain the repeated activity.

The second drawback is the danger of producing rigid habits that will not necessarily generalize to activities that require higher levels of flexibility. Characteristic of a habit is that once it is set into motion it continues unchanged. Therefore, the necessity has been to create behavioral schemata that will be crystallized in the mode of their application but will, at the same time, be flexible enough to permit generalization and transfer.

Even the need for the flexible application of certain otherwise automatic and crystallized behavior can be internalized as habit. Thus, confronted with a novel situation, the individual will be oriented toward those characteristics of the task that require from him a known and familiar form of behavior or will recognize those that indicate instead a change in the previously established pattern of response.

In FIE we have solved this problem of repetition versus boredom and rigidity by using redundant rules applied to situations and tasks that never repeat themselves. The learner is required to repeat the same schemata over and over, but each time in new situations that change in the level of their complexity and/or the modality of their presentation. Repeated presentations of the same principles and prerequisites of thinking are offered within each instrument and across the various instruments.

Intra-instrument repetition has been demonstrated in the discussion of *Orientation in Space I* (see page 160), where the system of reference is presented to the learner in 15 different situations, levels of complexity, languages of presentation and modalities of response. The inter-instrument elicitation of schemata acquired in *Orientation in Space I* is illustrated below.

The instrument starts with the articulation of space according to a personal system of reference, with changes in relationships resulting from movement. However, decentration and detachment from the concrete soon occur, and representational space becomes a vehicle for the development of relational abstract thinking. In relating two elements to one another, or in coordinating different views, the student learns to consider the relative positions hypothetically and representationally. He is able to "step into the shoes" of the other. The required flexibility and generalization are produced by variations of the task in which the rule is applied.

The principle of change in orientation resulting from movement remains invariable, although it appears in a different content and modality in *Organization of Dots,* as shown in the example below.

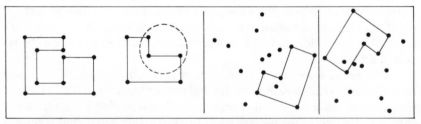

Organization of Dots (line 3, exercises 1 and 2, page 11)

The encircled configuration on the upper right of the asymmetrical figure in the right of the model will appear on its lower left, upper left, and lower right as the figure is revolved in space.

The use of spatial orientation as the relevant attribute is elicited by many tasks in *Comparisons*. One illustration follows:

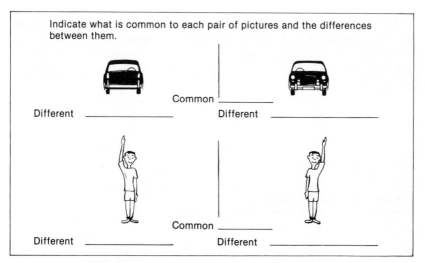

Indicate what is common to each pair of pictures and the differences between them.

Common _____

Different _____   Different _____

Common _____

Different _____   Different _____

Comparisons (exercises 4 and 5, page 4)

Directionality is also explicitly defined as an attribute in *Stencil Design:*

ANSWER THE QUESTIONS

How do you know that the black stencil closest to the center is 4, and not 3?   (Use the word direction.) _____

_____

Define the two errors: 13 — 12 — 4 — 18 — 3 — 17

Representational Stencil Design (exercise 1, page 19)

The use of orientation as a strategy applied automatically for the proper solution of the task is evident in *Analytic Perception.*

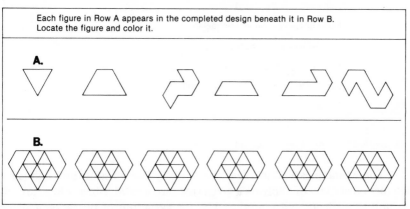

Each figure in Row A appears in the completed design beneath it in Row B. Locate the figure and color it.

A.

B.

Analytic Perception (exercises A and B, page 32)

In order to place the part within the whole, attention must be paid to the direction of the protuberances.

In *Instructions,* there is repeated application of the concepts learned in *Orientation in Space I.* In early tasks this is directed. In later ones, the schema is elicited by the nature of the task in which the child is asked to look at a given frame and to describe it verbally so that it can be duplicated from his description.

The hexagon is in the _____ of the frame. Draw a square to the right of the hexagon. Draw a triangle to the left of the hexagon.

The hexagon is _____ the square and the triangle.

Instructions (left: exercise 3, page 4; *right:* exercises 3 and 4, page 39)

The schema undergoes a process of enlargement and is invoked in situations more remote and more complex than those in which it was originally acquired.

In *Family Relations,* the student must take the role of the speaker in order to project the required relationship.

"I am Esther's cousin. Esther is my _____."

"I am Joseph's father. Joseph is my _____."

"I am Herb's uncle. Herb is my _____."

"I am Michael's brother. Michael is my _____."

"I am Sarah's sister. Sarah is my _____."

"I am Jim's grandson. Jim is my _____."

"I am Jim's granddaughter. Jim is my _____."

Family Relations (exercise 1, page 19)

These examples are but a few among many that illustrate how habits for the mental activity of applying a given rule can be established, while flexibility and generalization are produced by the variations of the tasks in which these rules can be applied. Achievement of a blanket, automatic response that is unidirectional and irreversible is not the goal of crystallization. Rather, the aim is that the schema which is crystallized remains fluid so that its use is not blind but is a strategy that is the result of reflection when the situation requires it. On the other hand, the situation should invoke use of the appropriate schema whenever it is applicable.

Another important reason for the crystallization of cognitive habits is our concern with the efficiency of mental processes. The use of higher mental processes is a volitional act, generated by a need and specific motivation. To be elicited the mental act must respond to the criterion of economy in the organism confronted with that need. If the act requires too great an effort, its use may be abandoned in favor of lower types of responses that require less mobilization of energy and are in the immediately available behavioral repertoire of the individual. The less crystallized a behavior, the more mental effort it will require, with a resultant delay in response. The less automatic an act, the less economical will it be in the sum total of the behaviors of the individual; therefore, there is less likelihood that it will be used spontaneously and efficiently. The reduced need to use higher mental operations combined with the increased effort required by them explains to a large extent the minimal use made by the cognitively deficient individual of even those mental operations that are readily available to him. This is even more apparent when we refer to mental operations that he has acquired only recently. By virtue of their novelty and high fluidity they are weak and vulnerable; thus the impact of any change in the conditions and physical and emotional states of the individual might interfere with his capacity to use the cognitive processes. The inefficiency and vulnerability of recently acquired behavioral patterns are a well known phenomenon (Konrad and Melzack, 1975).

Redundancy and overlearning have been banned from modern pedagogy because rote learning is considered the antithesis of creative and productive discovery learning. Many of the curricular and enrichment programs developed by current pedagogic streams have avoided the use of repetitive, redundant learning. In doing so, little harm has been done to those individuals whose cognitive processes have been crystallized into patterns of behavior through mediated learning experience in their past. However, failure has been the consequence for those children who, in order to function, had to first produce the patterns before being able to use them as instruments for further learning.

In constructing FIE, our major goal has been to develop a means for producing learning schemata in children, while simultaneously constantly enlarging these schemata by introducing novel situations into them. This double process of accommodation and assimilation, described by Piaget as the dynamic principle of the development of intelligence, is used by us for the specific purpose of crystallizing the prerequisites of learning while rendering them flexible enough to enable generalization and constant adaptation of their application in new and varied situations.

The degree of our success can be measured by the spontaneous use of concepts and schemata in areas other than Feuerstein's Instrumental Enrichment.

A student reports: "Since I started to learn FIE, I have felt a need to be precise in the gathering of data. It really bothers me when I am not precise."

A student talks of the necessity to see an object or event from various points of view: "I feel that I am beginning to understand things better. When people talk, I try to understand their points of view. I find that when two people argue, I get involved and try to get them to understand the feelings of one another."

One of the home economics teachers reported that her girls who had learned FIE were able to set a table, while they stood in one place: "In placing the silverware correctly, the girls used to walk around the table, from place to place; otherwise, the knives and forks ended up on the wrong side of the place setting. Now they can work quickly and without errors, without having to face each place in turn."

A history teacher reported: "I have had no personal experience with FIE, but I thought you might be interested in what happened in my history class. We were discussing Athens and Sparta, when suddenly one of my 'weak' students spoke up: 'Let's not do it this way. It isn't clear at all. Let's do it like we do in FIE.' I asked how he did it in FIE. He replied: 'We look for how they are alike and how they are different. There, we used things like color, size, number, direction. But that's not good here. We have to find the right dimensions on which we can compare Athens and Sparta.' He then went to the blackboard, drew columns for Athens and Sparta, and asked for suggestions for the parameters for comparison, which he wrote on the side. 'Now, it's clear and we can compare properly,' he said. I must admit that he was right."

SUBGOAL IV: PRODUCTION OF REFLECTIVE, INSIGHTFUL PROCESSES

Insight, previously defined (see page 142) as the orientation of the learner toward establishing the relationship between his specific behavior and a given outcome, has a very important bearing upon the capacity of the individual to single out those strategies and behavior patterns that have proved successful in reaching an anticipated goal, as compared with those that have led to failure. An individual who does not understand the relationship between a given act performed by him and its specific outcome will continue his randomized, chance behavior for a much longer period than one who uses reflective thinking. Thus, lack of insight is one of the primary reasons for the culturally deprived's very limited learning through trial and error.

Insight implies an awareness not only of the functions that must be used in order to produce a given mental act and solve a problem, but also of the specific needs generated by situations that elicit the successful use of such mental operations and cognitive functions. When does one have to inhibit impulsivity? Where is maximal precision in output necessary, and where can one do with less? When can one not proceed without planning behavior? In what situations is representational hypothetical thinking a vital condition for success? Will emotionally loaded arguments or logical evidence best persuade one's partner? What has caused failure in a given task and what has led to success?

FIE is constructed in such a way as to make reflective thinking not only possible but also necessary. Its tasks pose many questions and make the results visible immediately. Basically, reflective thinking and insightful processes represent a search by the individual for internally generated feedback by relating behavior to specific outcomes and to certain determinants. However, the cognitively deficient may bypass such needs if there is no mediation by an initiated and oriented adult. One of the most important roles of the teacher in FIE is, therefore, to involve the individual and the group in a process of reflective thinking.

Insight is produced by the teacher in discussions that deal with the following:

1. An analysis of the various functions involved in the proper completion of a task
2. An investigation of the types of errors produced and the specific reasons for their appearance
3. A development of an awareness of the changes or modifications occurring in the cognitive processes following exposure to the learning experience
4. A search for and formulation of the most efficient, as well as the most economic, strategies for successful mastery of the task
5. Creation of an awareness of the role played by the cognitive functions, strategies, planning behavior, and insight dealt with in the instruments in a variety of other life situations

The activity and interchange of the group, which are oriented by the teacher to divergent thinking, confront the individual with a great variety of responses to a given question, thereby making him reflect on the possibility of the co-existence of diverse explanations for, and determinants of, given conditions.

Insightful behavior is also the means to achieve transfer of training by a volitional, conscious, and purposeful use of rules, principles, strategies, and habits acquired through the learning process of FIE. Such insight is vital for the generalization of the acquired behaviors to other areas for successful adaptation. One of the reasons for the selection of adolescents as the target population for FIE is their accessibility and ability to derive insight from their actions. Once properly oriented, adolescents can use their unorganized and task-bound experiences to produce the appropriate links.

One of the major ways to produce insight in the FIE learner is to continuously demonstrate that the goals of FIE and the functions it teaches are prerequisites for the mastery of specific tasks with which he is confronted and for his successful adaptation to life at large. Thus, the meaning of categorization, summative behavior, anticipation, planning ahead, inhibition of impulsivity, and the use of logical evidence are stressed and illustrated by examples brought by the learner and teacher. An awareness of what the students have learned in FIE has been expressed explicitly by many students themselves:

> In the report on her practicum, a young woman who is learning the program in a teacher-training seminary incidentally reports: "I find that since I started learning FIE I am much more tolerant of the kindergarten teacher with whom I work. I can see the source of some of the mistakes she makes and some of the things she says."

> "The minute I started to cut the material, I knew I had made a mistake, and that I hadn't left enough room for seams. I remembered what I had learned in FIE and sat down and thought about everything I had to take into account and remembered how we talked about correcting mistakes. I moved the pattern over so I was able to save the piece I had started to cut, and with the other I didn't have any trouble at all."

The orientation of the teacher toward the development of insight is demonstrated in the sample lessons in Chapter 9.

SUBGOAL V: CREATION OF TASK-INTRINSIC MOTIVATION

Task-intrinsic motivation, or the readiness to perceive the performance of an activity as a goal in itself, solely for the pleasure inherent in its performance, is very limited in the culturally deprived adolescent. There is ample evidence from research by Berlyne, Switzky, Hunt, Friedman, Keinka, McCall, Haywood, and others to demonstrate a differential motivational orientation and its effect upon learning. Relatively efficient learners are characterized by a preference for novel, complex, incongruous, and surprising stimuli, while the inefficient learners prefer the familiar. In their discussion of the development of individual differences in motivational orientation, Haywood and Burke (1977) claim that extrinsic motivation is the result of a failure to find satisfaction in novelty and in task orientation. If a child has been unsuccessful in his attempt to explore and gain mastery, his failure is experienced as punishment; he then withdraws into a pattern of avoiding dissatisfaction by concentrating on the nontask aspects of the environment. Haywood (1968) has argued that mentally retarded persons are more likely to develop a primarily extrinsic motivation orientation.

Haywood and Weaver (1967) found that differences in motivational orientation had significant effects upon motor performance of institutionalized retardates when differing incentive conditions were employed. Strongly extrinsically motivated subjects punched more holes under a 10¢-per-hole incentive condition than in a task-incentive condition. Weakly intrinsically motivated subjects punched more holes under a task-incentive condition than under a 10¢-per-hole extrinsic reward.

A commonly observed phenomenon in the culturally deprived adolescent is the premature shrinking of his fields of interest to the most specific and purposeful goal-oriented behaviors. The questions "What for?" "Why should I do it?" "What will it bring me?" and "How much will I get paid?" reflect his lack of readiness to do something that does not respond to an immediately perceived need and the means for its satisfaction.

The autotelic principle is lacking even in the play activities of these children and adolescents. In sports activities, for example, their motivation is oriented toward a goal extrinsic to the playful and sportive, a goal that involves gain or remuneration of some kind.

The lack of representational behavior and the limited future orientation of the culturally deprived adolescent cause an even more stringent limitation of his fields of interest, restricting them to the most elementary needs, the immediate gratification of which is perceived as most important. It is only understandable that gratuitous behavior, which is not perceived as leading to immediate gratification, is eliminated from the repertoire of activities. The same is true for any activity in which there is an imbalance between investment and return.

Thus, in the construction of FIE materials, there has been great emphasis on the generation of task-intrinsic motivation. Exercises of a high level of complexity and difficulty, the solution of which requires an elaborative effort, preceded by accurate input and followed by an output that offers immediate feedback, have been developed. Such tasks, once mastered, have an important meaning. Frequently the student becomes aware — and, if not, he must be made aware — that such mastery is difficult not only for him, but for initiated adults as well.

Teachers who experience difficulties in the solution of the tasks during FIE workshops are usually convinced that their students will be unable to cope with the exercises. "Look. It's hard for me. How can I expect my retarded performers to do what I can't do?" Such teachers are asked to communicate to their students the problems they themselves had in their initial confrontation with the tasks of FIE. The students are also aware of the difficulties classroom visitors have in solving the tasks. On one occasion, a learner patted a supervisor on the shoulder: "Don't feel bad if you can't do it right away. It was hard for most of us at the beginning. Just think for a few minutes about what you are supposed to do."

In contradistinction to content learning and transmission of information to the student as a passive recipient of knowledge that is novel to him and familiar to the teacher, mastery of FIE requires investment by both teacher and student. This produces a very different relationship among student, teacher, and material. The usual relationship between the three is characterized by the close proximity between the teacher and the material that is taught, with a relatively great distance separating them from the learner,

who is far away from both. In many cases, this makes the learner feel alien-
ated from both the content and the teacher, especially in those instances in
which a strong need for mastery and equality is present in the child. Such instances, mainly observable in the adolescent, are often exacerbated in the
culturally deprived adolescent, whose feelings of estrangement and alienation arise from his general condition and his position in the school.

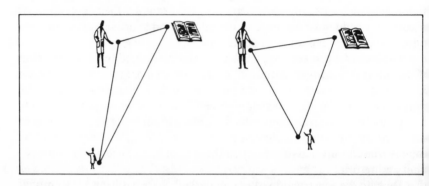

In FIE, with its high degree of novelty and complexity to both teacher
and student, in its initial phase at least, we have the almost unique feature of
an equilateral triangle. The teacher, who must correct an error or help the
student solve a problem, is not able simply to retrieve the correct answer
from his memory. In order to arrive at a solution, the teacher must do exactly what the child must do. Although it is easier for the teacher, the experience makes the student-teacher relationship much more of a partnership.
This is even more apparent when, in the presentation of the tasks to the
child, the teacher makes a more or less serious error through inattention, imprecision, or because of the complexity of the task. Such errors are immediately picked up by the children or by the teacher himself, and may reinforce the feeling of a cooperative effort. This relationship, if properly applied, reinforced, and made apparent, may add a corrective dimension to the
usually oppressive learning situation and the potential for the conciliation of
"natural enemies."

It should be noted that, in teacher-training workshops, teachers are intrigued by the instruments and show the need to reach mastery in the more
complex tasks after success with the less difficult ones. Teachers react very
much as do the students in the classroom in their confrontation with the material. There is great difficulty in gaining the attention of the participants for
theoretical discussions in face of the attraction of the material. Because of
the lack of readiness of the teacher to leave the solution of the tasks and shift
his role to that of analyzing the objectives and didactics of their presentation, it has been found necessary to separate the sessions and to allow the

teachers to gain mastery of an instrument first, and only at a later period to participate in a discussion of the theory and didactics.

The motivation that grows out of an equilateral relationship or one of cooperation will offer immediate gratification to the status-seeking behavior of the child. It may also enable him to perceive himself as capable of acceding to similar functions as the teacher, in the future.

The pervasive difficulty of most FIE exercises makes the cognitively deficient retarded performer perceive himself as able to master tasks in which others have similar, and sometimes even greater, difficulties. It is this complexity and the relatively high level of difficulty to which the adolescent is most responsive. It is the feeling of the author that, in many cases of remediation, the lack of motivation on the part of the learner is attributable to his feelings that what he is being required to do does not really reflect his capacity.

The FIE program may change the usual ranking order in the class as established by the relative academic achievements of its members. Many of those students who are less successful than their peers in academic subjects may out-perform them in the FIE activities. The teacher may resist the fact that students who do not participate in lessons in other subjects and "sit like lumps" are suddenly able to achieve more than their more verbal and successful peers. The meaning of this phenomenon is usually not questioned by the more enlightened teacher, who is willing to change a preconceived attitude toward the capacity of the retarded performer. In some instances, however, a teacher resists and attributes the new success to a fluke or denigrates its meaning.

Usual intervention programs may be resisted by the failing child because of his negative self-image, especially if he has been placed in homogeneous classes, such as "special schools," "special groups for slow learners," and the like. Many of these children equate each program offered especially to them with programs for the retarded. This sensitivity creates animosity toward such programs since a readiness to perform would imply their acceptance of their low self-image. Therefore, many of the teaching programs that represent reduction or simplification of normal curricula to accommodate a lower level of functioning are rejected by the children or are dealt with in an inadequate way. Such resistance is rarely encountered in the FIE program after the retarded performer becomes acquainted with the material and the degree of complexity it represents.

The above mentioned resistance was encountered quite dramatically in the first year of FIE's implementation. In Hebrew, the initials for "Research Unit" are the same as those for "Retarded Children." Despite their previous enthusiasm for the program, the students in one class rejected the pages as soon as one child pointed out the initials and his interpretation of them. This reaction spread throughout the school by the next day. Students who had heartily enjoyed the program refused to participate in FIE lessons. "We are not retarded. These pages are not meant for us," they said. Not until there were explanations of the meaning of the initials by members of the Institute staff were the children ready to resume the program. Needless to say, the offending initials were immediately removed from the balance of the pages.

The complexity of the tasks produces in the learner a state of disequilibrium, which is reflected in a positive valence of the task in form of curiosity, interest, and a desire for mastery for the sake of mastery. This, however, may not be sufficient to sustain motivation during the length of the program; therefore, social reinforcement is built into the system to ensure the continued interest of the child in FIE activities. One step that has been taken to ensure the continued motivation of FIE students is to create a total FIE atmosphere in a school, with all the classes participating in the program.

Too frequently the culturally deprived student is removed from his heterogeneous group to participate in an intervention program. Because it is felt unwise to have him miss lessons in academic subjects, he is usually sent out when the class as a whole has art, music, or physical education. To the stigma of being set apart from the group is added the indignity of not being allowed to participate in a "fun" subject in which he could probably do as well as or better than his peers. With FIE, the heterogeneous groups as a whole are offered the program on the premise that cognitive functions are universal and that even the most successful student will show positive changes as a result of his participation in the program.

In order to help the FIE student overcome the teasing of others in school, in the neighborhood, and at home, he is given copies of the most difficult pages he has successfully mastered to distribute to those who taunt him. It is soon apparent that the FIE tasks are genuinely hard for the teasers. Respect, albeit reluctant, is offered in face of the FIE student's achievement.

The student's success in FIE is also rewarded and reinforced by other methods. The original pages that he has constructed are reproduced and distributed to other classes and other schools. Students become aides and assist the teacher either in their own classes or in others.

It should be stressed that the student does not receive a grade or any token for participation in the FIE program. Requests for grades, and there have been some, are usually explained by, "It's the only subject I do well in and I'd like to have at least *one* good grade on my report card."

High motivation for FIE is demonstrated by objective data. Some schools report a decrease in absences on the days FIE is taught. There are students who come to work-learn frameworks only on those days and remain in class only until after the lesson. In at least one school, the period of the FIE lesson was changed from immediately before lunch after the complaint of the cafeteria supervisor. Some students had refused to leave the classroom until after they had completed their work. "We can eat any time, but we only learn FIE three times a week." Teachers report that when a lesson is canceled for any reason, students claim the teacher "owes" them one and must make it up.

> A teacher arrived late for an area meeting. She apologized for her tardiness and explained that her class absolutely refused to let her leave until she had given the lesson in FIE.

One teacher reported that students came to him during their free hours and asked for more pages. The secretary in the same school stated that many students who had to wait for their homeward-bound buses asked for FIE exercises instead of going to the gym or lounge.

A decline in motivation may be associated with the inability of the student to solve the problems and his subsequent frustration. Difficulties may be associated with the content, modality, level of complexity, level of abstraction, or the functions and operations elicited by the material. With the teacher's assistance and subsequent mastery, the level of motivation is restored. Tasks that are too easy or pacing that is too slow can also have an effect on the willingness of the students to engage in the program.

The approach, methodology, and attitude of the teacher are also potent factors in the initiation and maintenance of motivation. The attitude of the school administrators and of the other members of the staff to the FIE program is important as well.

In summary, the FIE program has been constructed so as to initiate and sustain task-intrinsic motivation. By the anticipation of problems and by proper classroom management, the teacher is a potent factor in the maintenance of a high level of motivation.

SUBGOAL VI: AROUSAL OF THE RETARDED PERFORMER FROM HIS ROLE OF PASSIVE RECIPIENT AND REPRODUCER OF INFORMATION TO A ROLE OF ACTIVE GENERATOR OF NEW INFORMATION

The culturally deprived retarded performer perceives himself as a recipient and reproducer of information rather than as its generator. An example of a child's overdependence on outer sources is his reply to the question "In what year were you born?" His answer will be, "I don't know. I've never seen my birth certificate, but my father knows." Despite the fact that the child knows his age, the current year, and the operations of addition and subtraction which he uses under specified conditions, he is not oriented to operate on the information available to him to generate an adequate response.

In a similar instance, the author asked a girl how long it took her to travel to school in the morning. She replied that she did not know. Questioning revealed that she did know at what time she took the bus, the time that the bus arrived at school, and the operation of subtraction necessary to arrive at the answer. However, her negative answer demonstrated an attitude toward herself reflective of the basic attitude of the retarded performer to the world.

Things happen to the culturally deprived child and events overcome him, rather than his experiencing them actively. Objects are not summated; events are not defined; and there is a limited spontaneous subsuming behavior, *in sensu* Ausubel (1963). An episodic grasp of reality is one illustration of this attitude. It indicates a lack of readiness on the part of the retarded performer to assume an active position toward the world, especially in the area of cognition, in that he does not try to organize and articulate his experience of the environment. He does not try to change and transform it in view of and according to his needs. He experiences himself as one who, at best, can perceive the stimuli and receive information and reproduce it, but who cannot produce new information by himself by using inferential thought processes in elaborating the data available to him.

This passivity is also often observed in the lack of readiness of the individual to invest in order to re-evoke memory. In many cases, when the child is asked about something which must be retrieved, his response is "I can't remember." The reason for this reply is that the cognitively deficient learner does not have the awareness that one can actively and at will reconstruct past experience. He therefore makes no attempt to delve into memory storage and retrieve from it *mnema* that are not accessible to him in more direct ways.

The associative thinking often ascribed to the culturally deprived is actually a kind of passive attitude toward cognitive processes. Only those components of thought that arise on their own, without the volitional orientation of the individual, become available to him. Unhappily, all too often this attitude is accepted by those in his environment as well, since few people believe that if a person does not spontaneously remember he can still make the desired information available by a proper, active reconstruction of the experienced past.

FIE places a great emphasis on the organized, purposeful, active behavior that turns the individual into a generator of new ideas based on previously gathered information. It does so in such a way as to produce in the learner a strong and clear awareness of the active volitional nature of the cognitive processes. It stresses the operations and the production of structured material, as well as well defined and precise tasks, rather than the stimulation of associative thinking which is found in the so-called creative methods.

The concept of locus of control can be interpreted as a function of the capacity of the individual to perceive himself as a generator of information. The culturally deprived child's incapacity to so perceive himself makes him strongly dependent upon extrinsic factors, including other individuals, as the determinants of both his behavior and destiny, while he plays a primarily passive role. What is often referred to as "externalism" (Frankenstein, 1966), typical of many of these youngsters, is evidence of this attitude. Although information-seeking behavior is observed, the necessary investment in order to elicit the information is often limited.

FIE has made an active attempt to change this attitude in two major ways. The first is by providing the learner with ample opportunities for generating information, ideas, and materials. The second is by providing him with immediate feedback of his mastery and the proper interpretation of the active role played by his own self in producing units of information, inferences, and conclusions.

Almost all of the instruments provide an opportunity for the student to utilize acquired principles to construct complete exercises similar to those he has been given. From *Orientation in Space I,* in which he is given totally blank spaces and asked to create exercises based on principles learned in the instrument for his classmate to complete, through *Temporal Relations,* in which he is asked to construct sentences with necessary and/or sufficient reasons for an event he makes up, the student is given a chance to apply what he has learned in situations that he himself creates.

In the exercises that follow, the student is asked to provide the basic information to a classmate for solution.

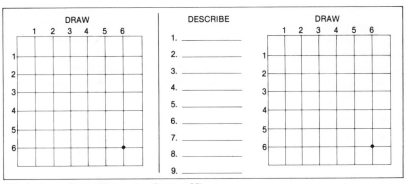

Orientation in Space III (exercise 2, page 20)

In *Orientation in Space III,* the student draws an itinerary, which is described by one of his peers, and the itinerary is redrawn from the description by another classmate. The "author" and the two students evaluate the results together and determine the source of errors, if there are any.

b. Copy some of the numbers, some of the relationships, and some of the relationships between the relationships from your progression (2a) and give it to a friend to complete.
(Fold the page on the broken line.)

c. Open the page and check if your friend filled in the numbers as they appear in your progression.

If not, why?

(1) My friend made a mistake. _____

(2) I did not fill in enough numbers. _____

Numerical Progressions (exercise 2A, page 17A)

After the student has filled in a progression, a relationship between numbers, and the relationship between relationships, the exercise continues as above.

The following example should suffice to demonstrate the FIE student's capacity to apply what he has learned to entirely new situations, generate new information, and work independently.

One day the teacher announced: "As you know, we are going on a three-day camping trip and we must start making plans about what we plan to study on this field trip, and what to take in camping equipment, supplies, food and clothing. Let's start with food."

The FIE class asked that they be allowed to try and plan the food themselves. In the following description of the ensuing discussion, there has been no attempt to note which student is speaking, but the conversation is entirely that of the students.

"We have to organize the food. We can do it in two different ways: In the first way, we can put all the food for breakfasts in Box A; all the food for lunches in Box B; all the food for dinners in Box C, and all the food for snacks in Box D. In the second way, we can use Box A for all the food for the first day; Box B for all the food for the second day and Box C for all the food for the third day.

"What are the advantages of plan one? It's easy to pack. We won't eat for breakfast what somebody else planned for lunch. We can keep the same kinds of foods together so we won't waste time looking for things."

"The advantages of the second plan are that we can use up the leftovers from one meal for the next. We can take along cooked food from home and eat it all on the first day so it wouldn't spoil without refrigeration. We only have to keep one box out for every day instead of three."

The teacher said, "It seems to me that there is another way, too, that hasn't been mentioned."

The children: "If you mean that we could keep the different kinds of food together, separated according to their categories, it wouldn't be at all efficient. It would mean that for every meal we would have to drag out several boxes. No. That's not good at all.''

The students continued their discussion of pros and cons. What they ultimately decided is less important to us than the method by which they analyzed the components of the problem and the justifications for the proposed alternatives.

The above case illustrates in microcosm the application of the products resulting from the attainment of the subgoals of the FIE program, as well as the change in FIE students from passive recipients to active generators of information.

SUMMARY OF CHARACTERISTICS OF INSTRUMENTAL ENRICHMENT

I. 1. Instrumental Enrichment is based on a systematic utilization of functions that are the prerequisites of proper cognitive operations. Each instrument focuses on a specific cognitive function, but simultaneously addresses itself to the correction of many others that may be deficient.

I. 2. Instrumental Enrichment involves the cognitive operations considered as the components of adequate cognitive functioning. These are of varying levels of complexity and novelty.

I. 3. Instrumental Enrichment assigns tasks to the learner that require from him the use of higher mental processes. Even though there are exercises in the instrument that involve more elementary cognitive processes, they are prerequisites for, rather than the essential goal of, the activity.

I. 4. Instrumental Enrichment places stress on the development of intrinsic motivation through formation of habits by manifold and varied repetition of the different target functions. However, the emphasis of the repetition is not on the tasks themselves, but on the function that is invariant within the divergent activities elicited by the task. This facilitates flexibility, shift, and transfer.

I. 5. Instrumental Enrichment attempts to elicit two distinct types of motivation. The first is task-intrinsic. Tasks are shaped in a way that makes them a target for curiosity and arouses a need in the learner for active mastery, a need which increases with the progressive complexity of a task. Success at earlier levels engenders a potent need to cope with and master the more difficult tasks.

   The second type of motivation is the reinforcement of the social meaning of the task. There is a need to achieve not only in relation to the peer group but in relation to the teacher as well. The teacher in Instrumental Enrichment shares more of a partnership relationship with the student than in most other instructional interactions.

   Both types of motivation are fostered by the challenge presented by the tasks, which are genuinely difficult, even for an experienced and achieving adult.

II. 1. Instrumental Enrichment is designed as a content-free set of tasks, in the sense that the content of an instrument does not serve as its goal *per se* but is, instead, a carrier for the more direct goals of the instrument. Content is not chosen by virtue of its specificity, but because its special characteristics permit the acquisition of the prerequisites of thinking.

II. 2. Despite its deliberate content-free design, Instrumental Enrichment provides for easy bridging to specific subject-matter areas because its dimensions are those necessary for content learning. Such bridging is enhanced by the activity of the teacher whose goal is to produce insight in the student.

II. 3. Instrumental Enrichment is designed to stress the nature, structure, and complexity of the tasks themselves and the effects produced through the child's confrontation with them. Its structure ensures the attainment of the majority of the program's subgoals. The efficiency of FIE is highly enhanced, however, by the mediation of a well trained teacher.

III. 1. Instrumental Enrichment implies a level of consciousness and awareness of the partners involved in the training process: teacher-student-material. This awareness involves both the global goal of Instrumental Enrichment and the specific meanings of each task for the development of efficient use of cognitive processes and adaptation to new situations, in general.

III. 2. For performing its tasks, Instrumental Enrichment includes and requires a variety of transformational, elaborational processes, with the performer actively contributing to the organization and restructuring, and the discovery and reapplication of the produced relationships. Mastery of the tasks in Instrumental Enrichment is never a matter of rote learning or the mere reproduction of a learned skill. Accomplishment of the tasks always involves the learning of rules, principles, or strategies underlying the task, rather than the task itself.

III. 3. Instrumental Enrichment materials are constructed to produce the conditions of a responsive environment. As such, the materials elicit in the student a need for mastery of the task with the criteria for mastery established by the materials themselves; and thus, feedback is built into the tasks and the student is constantly informed of his performance.

III. 4. Instrumental Enrichment is accessible to, and useful for, a wide range of populations in terms of levels, ages, and skills. Its content-free nature, and the progressive difficulty and challenge of its tasks, make it appropriate for all cases in which improvement in cognitive functioning is sought. Of particular importance is that it avoids stigmatizing, or reinforcing a low self-image in, individuals who engage in the program by avoiding the frequent practice of simplifying "normal" curricula to accommodate lower levels of functioning.

IV. 1. The principles and didactics of Instrumental Enrichment are useful in changing the attitudes and techniques of educators, psychologists, social workers, and counselors toward the target populations. The methodology of Instrumental Enrichment is transferable to other subject matter and treatment areas.

9
TEACHER TRAINING, THE ROLE OF THE CONSULTANT, AND CLASSROOM IMPLEMENTATION

TRAINING

The training of teachers for Instrumental Enrichment poses a multifaceted problem because FIE is composed of materials and techniques that are based on a theory, all of which must be mastered for the successful implementation of the program. Therefore, any model for teacher training involves at least four goals: training for the understanding and acceptance of the underlying theory of FIE; mastery of the instruments themselves; training in the didactics of FIE; and training for insight, bridging, and application of the acquired processes.

Rationale for Differential Emphasis in Training

Teachers for FIE are not specially recruited, and they represent a wide range of academic training, experience, skills, and orientation. It might be argued, however, that there is a natural selection involved, in that those who enter training are dedicated teachers who feel that they currently lack either the materials or the methods for working with the pupils they teach. Furthermore, of those who investigate the program, only teachers who are sufficiently motivated will continue in the face of the additional time and effort that training in FIE involves.

The emphasis placed on any one of the four above-mentioned areas of training is a function of the needs of the particular teacher. For example, a veteran teacher, with years of experience with retarded performers, may have consciously or subconsciously concluded that these students have a very limited capacity. His view is overtly reflected in the low level of his expectations and in his passive acceptance of the manifest level of functioning of his students. In light of his experience and training, this veteran teacher can scarcely be blamed for his attitude. After all, he reasons, the curriculum and texts have been selected by experts; he himself is conscientious, devoted, and unsparing in his efforts. Yet, his students still perform at second- or third-grade level, despite 8 or more years of schooling. Since he has decided that it can be neither the material nor the teaching, he reasons that it must be the child who cannot learn. For such a teacher, training must start with and stem from an introduction to the theory of cognitive modifiability. Only after an understanding of the theory and its implications will this teacher become proficient in the use of the program and appreciate the nature and extent of its intervention.

For another teacher, the effect of mediated learning in the consequent development of cognitive behavior provides the explanation he has sought for the varying exceptionalities of the students in his classroom. However, his training in special education has emphasized that retarded performers cannot learn through abstraction and representation, but only through concretization and motor manipulation. For such a teacher, emphasis in training will be on the FIE instruments, the complexity of the tasks, and their use of internalized, representational, and conceptualized modalities of functioning.

Still another teacher emphasizes content. If he does not receive the single correct answer he seeks, he views any other response as an error and his failure in teaching. He reacts with little enthusiasm to his students' accomplishments, either because he considers them minimal and insignificant or because he views them as "normal" and "natural." At best, his lesson is a frontal presentation of information and task-bound techniques. There is yet another type of teacher. Neither the theory nor the materials are difficult for him to master and to accept. However, he practices a passive-acceptant approach and does not enter into dialogue with the child. He does not want to produce stress so, rather than rephrasing the question or waiting for a reply, he skips the child who does not immediately respond. For both of these teachers, training must emphasize the didactics of FIE.

Finally, there is the teacher who can describe the low level functioning of his class, yet is unable to recognize, understand, or interpret appropriately the meaning of the changes that do occur in his students. Even when confronted with children's achievements in areas previously "known" to have been inaccessible to them, he reacts by minimizing the meaning of such success, either by denigrating the performed task or by diminishing its value because it is the product of teaching. He sees himself as the teacher of a subject rather than of children. His emphasis is on the output, which he measures by the number of completed pages and correct answers, instead of on the input and elaboration phases of the mental act and the ability to apply the learned principles and strategies. The training of this classroom teacher in FIE must be oriented to the recognition, registration, and appreciation of the micro-changes that occur in the child's cognitive behavior, which he must then communicate and interpret to the child. The child's insight into the meaning of his performance must be engendered and cultivated by the trained teacher.

Considering the interdependence between the teacher's awareness, skills, and attitudes and the progress of the learner, a well planned program for teacher training takes on the utmost importance. Although the instruments have been constructed to involve the student in active coping and to minimize the teacher's formal role, there are certain subgoals of Instrumental Enrichment whose attainment is strongly contingent upon the teacher's knowledge, didactics, methodology, motivation, and attitudes (see Chapter 8). It is the teacher who must help the child acquire the concepts, vocabulary, and operations. The production of insight depends upon the teacher's capacity to turn the child's attention toward those functions that are required for the mastery of the task. It is through the teacher's knowledge and creativity that the child is originally oriented toward bridging from Instrumental Enrichment exercises to broader areas of behavior in school and everyday life activities. The amount and nature of the child's motivation to continue his work, both in FIE and other areas, are determined by the teacher's interpretation of the child's success or failure and the ascription of the proper significance to specific behaviors. It is only through training in insight and bridging that such a teacher can function autonomously and successfully as a teacher of Instrumental Enrichment.

Understanding the Underlying Theory of FIE

Theoretical training centers on the concept of the cognitive modifiability of the retarded performer at the age of adolescence. The lack of mediated learning experience as the proximal etiology of cultural deprivation and the description of the students' failures in terms of deficient cognitive functions represent a radical departure from some teachers' well established systems of beliefs. Repeated confrontation with, and elaboration of, both theoretical and empirical data are necessary to accomplish a change in the teachers' conceptualizations. However, without a belief in modifiability and an active-modification approach, there can be little hope for progress in the classroom.

In his attempt to know the child, the teacher must become thoroughly familiar with the deficient functions and their effects upon the child's cognitive behavior. In addition, he should recognize the non-intellective and behavioral concomitants of cultural deprivation. During training, there must be an orientation toward the process of functioning, as opposed to a focus on the product, and an attention to the peaks of the child's performance, rather than to his failures. Only by knowing the child, his strengths as well as his weaknesses, can the teacher utilize appropriate modalities, plan the course of intervention, and evaluate the child's progress.

The FIE teacher should become adept at the analysis of material according to the parameters of the cognitive map (see Chapter 5). With knowledge of the components of the mental act, he is able to anticipate difficulties and devise the appropriate strategies for either overcoming or bypassing them.

Theoretical training also includes elements introduced to sensitize the teacher to the kinds of difficulties that may be experienced by some of the children in his class. Motivation, self-image, the role of teachers' expectations, and the nature of peer interactions are among the background subjects presented. Although the classroom situation does not always offer opportunities for prescriptive teaching, Instrumental Enrichment, used flexibly, enables the sensitive teacher to vary strategies and investments according to the specific needs of particular children. It is through theoretical training that the teacher develops the skills to monitor, record, and evaluate even the short term progress of his students, thus assisting him in the better planning of his teaching.

Mastery of the FIE Instruments

The second goal of the training program is the mastery of the instruments by the teacher through direct experience. Teachers often experience considerable difficulty in solving FIE tasks. It may seem strange that teachers themselves require concerted effort to master the exercises of an intervention program for retarded performers. In fact, some of the initial resistance stems from, "If I can't do it, my class certainly won't be able to." A great deal of tact is required to convince the teacher that his students will not experience much more difficulty than he did. Because of the specificity of certain tasks, they may be difficult for many "normal" individuals. For instance, various exercises are saturated with spatial factors that may result in differential efficiency, irrespective of the level of intellectual functioning. Yet, the fact that the teacher who had difficulty is able to gain mastery should prove to him that, even without natural "endowment" in a specific area, one can succeed in the tasks by increasing the amount of cognitive investment.

Another reason for difficulties in mastery of the instruments is that many teachers have not been oriented toward operational thinking, either as a subject for teaching or as a part of their own training. Intuitively, they have reached valid conclusions requiring syllogistic or transitive thinking; however, when they are forced to analyze an argument for its validity or teach someone else to do so, they lack the tools. Similarly, teachers may be familiar with the terminology that has to do with specific operations but have never been called upon previously for their precise definition.

The direct experience in reaching efficiency with the instruments, especially when there is difficulty, is a valuable part of training for at least three reasons. First, it highlights the author's view that there is no discontinuity or sharp demarcation between normal and retarded performance; and that cognitive functioning should be viewed not as an all-or-nothing phenomenon, but along a continuum. Second, it helps the teacher to adjust his expectations of both the retarded performer's difficulties and the extent of modifiability that may be achieved in overcoming them. Third, it helps to create the "equilateral triangle" among teacher, child, and material (see page 282). The teacher can say quite honestly, "I had trouble there, too. Let's see what helped me. Maybe it will help you, too."

Didactics

Our experience in training hundreds of teachers has shown that there must be an interval between mastering an instrument and learning how to teach it. The teacher who has had to struggle to meet the challenge of the exercise is unable to shift back immediately into the role of a teacher, who must objectively restructure the material and find the methodology for its presentation.

Didactics in teaching training are both general and specific. Although teachers have usually taken methodology courses before their certification, approaches and techniques must be reformulated to make them appropriate for the culturally deprived, and, even more important, specific instruction in the art of the presentation of the FIE materials is necessary.

General Didactics   Training in general didactics includes a broad variety of topics that may be just as appropriate for teaching normal children as for work with the culturally deprived. Discussions range from classroom management to the treatment of the exceptional child; from the optimal way to frame a question to the use of students' answers as a source for further learning; from the encouragement of creativity to the restraint of impulsivity; as well as many other topics of interest to the classroom teacher of both regular and special classes.

Thus, the general didactics do not differ radically from those that are desirable for teaching all children, but there are many instances in which certain techniques must be intensified, altered, or eliminated in dealing with the retarded performer. As an example, impulsivity may be reduced by imposing a latency period between asking a question and receiving a response. The FIE slogan, "Just a Minute. Let Me Think," is one that should be adopted for all students, but it is even more apt for the retarded performer whose impulsivity in the gathering of data is a prime cause of his failures.

Learning by discovery is appropriate for normal children but is obviously not effective for those who suffer from an episodic grasp of reality. With a deficiency in the identification and projection of relationships that are required for inductive reasoning, there is initially very little spontaneous discovery of the rule by the retarded performer. In the early stages of FIE, it is the teacher who must help the child to generalize from the rule, once established, and orient him to its application.

In trial and error, repeated trials lead mostly to errors by the culturally deprived child, who is prone to repeat his mistakes in each additional attempt and is unable to represent the outcome of his act. He must be restrained from acting until he has formulated a hypothesis that he can then subject to proof. However, the teacher should be trained so that, when an error is made, he reacts appropriately to it. Error cannot be viewed solely as failure; rather, its source must be sought. In doing so, the teacher demonstrates his respect for the child as a thinking being who has arrived at a response through reasons that may not correspond to the task, but which, nonetheless, exist and must be explored.

That positive reinforcement and feedback are effective mechanisms in the learning process is well established. For the culturally deprived child who has little positive regard for his accomplishments, the effects of reinforcement and feedback are even more potent. Although many of the instruments are constructed to provide the child with immediate feedback of his success, it is the teacher who must be taught to interpret to the child the real meaning of his achievement. A teacher's reaction to the functioning of students whose initial performance level was very low must convey a positive emotional evaluation and not merely an objective assessment of the absolute results of the performance. The teacher should be trained to provide his students with an interpretation of their cognitive behavior, evidenced in the successful completion of the tasks, in terms of the progress made from the initial levels of functioning. To do so requires an awareness of the meaning of the minimal changes in the child's use of the prerequisites of thinking, in the mastery of operations, and in his efficiency. The understanding teacher then becomes the amplifier of the micro-changes occurring in the child's behavior and interprets the promise that can be derived from the changes for the future activity of the child. The interpretation of changes, measured on a very refined scale, will make the child aware of the meaning of his work for other activities and will present him with the social meaning of his success, thereby reinforcing it and ensuring its continuation.

Among the micro-changes that the teacher must be oriented to recognize are the following: a readiness to read directions before starting; decreased need for additional questions in the definition of the problem; decreased dependency on the teacher; an increase in the spontaneous use of vocabulary, concepts, strategies, and principles learned in FIE in coping with other work; an increase in the number of spontaneous corrections; an increase in the demand for precision on the part of self and others; a lengthened concentration and attention span; an increased self-confidence; a more relevant response to questions; increased detail in describing objects; increased curiosity and questions about concepts and relationships between objects and events previously not noticed; a willingness to defend opinions on the basis of logical evidence; a pride in performance; and a wish to generate new problems based on Instrumental Enrichment.

The author has compiled a long list of changes that may not be dramatic but do indicate meaningful progress. The neutral, cold, and distant teacher who ignores them and only offers objective feedback does not consider the structure of the child's motivation, his need for reinforcement, and the real significance of such minute changes for the future development of the child's cognitive behavior.

The above examples should serve to illustrate how general didactic considerations must be altered so that they will be appropriate for teaching Instrumental Enrichment to retarded performers.

Specific Didactics   Didactics specific to FIE concern the methodology and techniques by which to achieve the six subgoals of the program. They include the theoretical analysis of the FIE material and the practical aspects of how to implement the program with various populations. Having become familiar with the instruments during the mastery phase of training, the teacher now learns to analyze pages, units, and instruments according to the subgoals of FIE and the parameters of the cognitive map. In planning a lesson, he seeks the relationship between the specific page and the total unit as well as the instrument or program as a whole. He determines which objectives and principles are appropriate for the page, although his selection of a specific goal and ordering of priorities will come only later, after he knows his class members and their needs.

In workshops, the teacher explores the various possible alternatives, modalities, and formats of presenting the page. He seeks teaching aids and investigates techniques. He learns to critique lessons that have already been given and to offer suggestions for their improvement. He himself plans and gives lessons in front of his peers.

The teacher learns to serve as a model for his students. If he insists on precision, he too must be precise. Even his errors may be valuable if utilized correctly. The teacher should be able to admit that he has made a mistake and analyze the source of his error with the class. "Why did I make a mistake? I was impulsive and jumped at conclusions before I had all of the facts." One teacher ruefully told the author that she had interrupted a child who was overly long in giving an answer. Another student remarked, "Teacher, you just tromped all over his mental space." She admitted her impatience and apologized. This incident not only demonstrates effective modeling but the atmosphere of interaction in the FIE lessons. The prevention of frustration in those students experiencing difficulties, the encouragement of participation, and making the child feel that he is a partner in the process of his redevelopment are among the important elements in the teacher-pupil interaction and specific didactics of FIE.

There are practical things that must be taught as well, the "how to's" of the program: How to keep students from starting to work before the preliminary explanations and definition of objectives; how to pace the lesson and divide the period between independent work and discussion; how to make the correction and evaluation of independent work lead to self-criticism; how to assist children who have been absent; how to summarize a lesson; how to reinforce the students' motivation without grades; and many other questions.

Training for Insight and Bridging

Of all the components of an FIE lesson, it is the development of insight and the bridging to content and experiential areas that are most difficult for the teacher and require the greatest investment in ongoing in-service training. The production of reflective, insightful processes is the fourth subgoal of

FIE, and the reader should refer to the earlier discussions of insight in this context in Chapters 6 and 8.

Only through an awareness of the objectives of the activities required by FIE is insight gained into their significance for the modifiability of the retarded performer. The goal of insight is to provide the adolescent with the ability to recognize the factors that are responsible for his success and to ensure their spontaneous application to tasks in other areas, when appropriate. Insight is achieved through an understanding of the demands of a task and an analysis of thought as a process. There must be an understanding of the functions and operations that are fundamental to the particular problem that must be solved. The creation of insight is accompanied by the child's recognition of his deficiencies, the limitations imposed by his current level of functioning, and the gap that exists between his manifest cognitive behavior and that to which he aspires. It is not sufficient to make the child aware of his failures; he must also be convinced that the proposed intervention will, in fact, lead to increased efficiency and skills in problem solving. It is not that the culturally deprived adolescent is not well aware of his failure, but he usually ascribes it to external sources, to the teacher or to the material, and not to his own inability or incapacity. In many cases, he has constructed his defenses so effectively that a negative motivation is established so that he either avoids those experiences in which he feels he has little chance of success or denigrates them as having no value for him. The end result is the child's avoidance of any confrontation that might lead to an inner conflict and the disequilibrium that is the energizing element of human activity.

How can a teacher breach the defense wall the child has constructed to mask his failures and force the child to look into himself and the task objectively, without affecting the child's self-image? How can the teacher make the child aware of his specific deficiencies without producing in him feelings of incompetence or insufficiency? How can the teacher imbue in the child a willingness to cope and a belief in the ultimate success of any investment he makes?

The training of teachers in the creation of awareness and insight aims at raising the cognitive functions and operations to a universal level required by all mankind for its adaptation. The teacher should demonstrate that the development of adequate cognitive behavior is a common and generally accessible goal for all. The quality of thought, rather than the quantity of immediately available information, should be shown as essential for man's successful adaptation to the demands of the modern world. The teacher learns to orient the student to reflective thinking, usually absent from the repertoire of the culturally deprived child.

Insight can be achieved by analyzing experiences and showing the child which functions play a role. Not only successes, but failures, too, should be analyzed in terms of their components. Each activity should be evaluated according to its relevance in achieving certain goals. The child's own experience should be utilized to generate his understanding of his past performance for its contribution to his future accomplishments.

In FIE, the teacher requires creativity, flexibility, and knowledge to match the content-free material to the needs, capacities, and curricula of the class. To apply the gained insight and to extract the function, operation, or principle from its task-bound context is a skill that must be practiced. To arrive at the generalization of operations that enables transfer to other situations, the child must be assisted. Difficulties in this type of bridging may stem from the teacher's experience with prescribed programs in which he has been explicitly instructed not only in the methodology but also in what to say.

Only through a relevant, actual illustration, or the rephrasing of a verbal statement expressing a new idea, can meaning be gained. "By these activities, one is forced to assimilate one's own particular illustration to the same structure to which one assimilated the new idea" (Furth, 1970, pp. 45–46). It is the teacher who leads the way in moving from the realm of the immediate task to the abstract and orients the students in their search for understanding and application. The teacher must therefore be equipped with experience and strategies for the transfer of the methodology and principles of FIE to other content and nonacademic areas.

Training Models

Training models currently used in Israel to qualify certified teachers in the implementation of FIE include both in-service training in the field by the FIE consultant and participation in workshops during vacations, and in area workshops in the course of a school year. Participants acknowledge the benefit they derive from the group in the learning of theory and the instruments. There is a "cross-pollenation" during the exchange of ideas and a supportive interaction. During centralized workshops, various modalities of training, including lectures, discussions, videotapes, written protocols of lessons, modeling, and simulation, are used.

The program of the half-day workshops, which are held approximately five times a year, consists of a classroom observation with a demonstration lesson given by one of the teachers, followed by a critique by his peers, sharing of experiences, and additional work on bridging and transfer from the instruments.

Practicum keeps pace with the training. It has been found desirable that teachers start to teach the instruments immediately as they learn. In-service training is usually continued through biweekly classroom visits and consultation until the teacher has taught the entire series of instruments.

Another Israeli model of training in FIE consists of teaching the theory and instruments in academic settings both at universities and teachers' colleges. At universities, participants in the seminars on cognitive modifiability and Instrumental Enrichment are graduate students who may not be directly associated with classroom teaching. Although the instruments are demonstrated and analyzed, the emphasis is on theory. In fulfilling the university course requirements, the participant may implement Instrumental Enrichment with an individual student or group in practicum, or present a paper on a selected aspect of the FIE program. A course in FIE is part of the student teacher's curriculum in many of the teachers' colleges. After graduation, he may participate in an intensive workshop in the subject for certification as an FIE teacher.

In the United States and Canada, there have been adaptations of both of the Israeli teacher-training models. Short, intensive workshops during vacations are followed by area workshops or participation in graduate seminars at universities. However, the assistance of FIE consultants and training in the field are accepted practice across all of the sites where the program is implemented.

FIE CONSULTANT

The ultimate goal of training is to render the teacher independent and fully equipped to teach Instrumental Enrichment. To further this objective, the classroom teacher is assigned an FIE consultant, or master teacher, during the first 2 years of the implementation of the program. In addition to providing in-service training to supplement introductory seminars and workshops, the consultant also works with individual children in the class who experience difficulties with the material because of absences or causes that require diagnosis and strategies for overcoming.

The term "consultant" has been selected as the most appropriate to describe a relationship that is nonhierarchical and based on mutual trust and confidence, and whose ultimate goal is to enable the teacher to function independently. If the consultant is to be effective in encouraging and assisting the teacher, his biweekly presence in the classroom should be welcomed by both teacher and students and perceived as nonthreatening. His first task, therefore, is to convince the teacher and students that he is sincere in his desire to contribute and that what he has to contribute is desirable. The teacher should feel sufficiently at ease so that he can call upon the consultant for advice and support at times other than the regular visits.

The nature of the interaction between the consultant and teacher is determined by the latter's personality, training, skills, attitudes, and needs. The teacher's needs and weaknesses, if any, determine the nature of the consultant's major input. The consultant must have an in-depth knowledge of FIE on theoretical, technical, and practical levels. In addition, he should be familiar with the academic and vocational curricula of the class so that he is equipped with a wealth of examples to facilitate bridging of the FIE processes and with knowledge of the relevant contexts in which the students can apply what they are learning. The consultant must also be aware of the nature of the teacher-class relationship since a negative class attitude toward the teacher can expand to include a negative attitude toward the subject he is teaching. The general level of the students and the nature of the peer relationships become important elements in the dynamics of a group in which there may be sudden shifts in roles, with weak students displaying previously unrevealed ability and reaching mastery before the "proficient" students.

More specifically, the consultant is present in the classroom at the time of the lesson and intervenes, upon request or spontaneously, according to a prior agreement with the teacher. After the lesson, there is a discussion of what transpired, with positive reinforcement and suggestions for improvement, which are of value only if they can be applied to future lessons. The consultant will often model and present the lesson at the request of the teacher. If necessary, the consultant assists the teacher in the systematic planning of future lessons.

Consultants report that one of the tendencies they must initially combat most often is the low level of expectation of the teacher and the reluctance to offer abstract thinking to the child or elicit it from him. Often there is an apparent lack of flexibility which does not permit digression from the lesson plan to fully exploit the students' answers in the progress of the lesson. The tendency of the teacher to "hit and run," to touch upon a variety of subjects without exploring any of them fully and without summarizing the discussion, is also a recurring problem.

The consultant reinforces the motivation of the student and teacher to engage in FIE by providing feedback of success and recognition of identifiable advances and changes. Motivation is contingent upon an awareness of the long range objectives and immediate utility of the program.

Students may reject the program, even if they enjoy it, when they feel that participation in FIE is stigmatizing or removes them from other activities they like and in which they can perform; or they may be deceived by its deceptively easy format, or consider it of no value because there is no homework or grade. Still others may feel the scarcely hidden bias of their peers, or even of some members of the staff. There may be resistance because of the way the teacher presents the material, or because the instrument itself focuses on particular deficiencies that make it too difficult for mastery. It is the consultant who has the task of restoring the initial level of motivation by analyzing the situation and interpreting it. Experienced teachers, convinced of the contribution of FIE, have no difficulty in overcoming any initial student resistance, should it occur, and are able, even without the assistance of the consultant, to utilize the task-intrinsic motivation usually elicited by the program.

CLASSROOM IMPLEMENTATION

There is neither a set script for an FIE lesson nor a single approved model. There are, however, general guidelines in planning and implementing FIE lessons. Instrumental Enrichment should be taught at least three times a week, on alternate days, in periods of at least 45 minutes, as an adjunct to the regular curriculum. If, however, FIE is not an addition to the curriculum, but replaces an academic subject, it is recommended that the hour of the lesson vary from day to day, if possible, so that it is not given at the expense of the same core subject each time.

Preparation for the Lesson

The teacher is urged to plan the lesson in advance to allow for the most effective use of the time available. Planning should include an analysis of the page or pages according to the parameters of the cognitive map in order to ascertain the focus of the exercises and decide upon appropriate didactics and the strategies necessary to prevent or circumvent any difficulties the students might have. The teacher must clearly define and *limit* the objectives of the lesson, determining the principle he wants to develop and seeking examples of its application in academic and vocational subjects, daily life experiences, and interpersonal relations.

Placing the students' desks in a semicircle or U facilitates easy movement and enables eye contact. It also encourages the students to listen to and interact with one another instead of engaging in the usual "ping-pong" of teacher-student-teacher. The informal seating arrangement contributes to the friendly, relaxed attitude that should mark FIE lessons.

Presentation of the Lesson

Introductory Discussion   This stage, which normally should not exceed 10 minutes, is appropriate for definition of problems and objectives and arousal of interest and motivation. The definition of the problems and the specific objectives of the page should ultimately rest with the students. At the beginning of the program, however, this identification may still be a joint effort by students and teacher. Without making a frontal presentation, the teacher must make sure that the students thoroughly understand the instructions and the concepts, terms, and vocabulary of the exercises. The students should be oriented toward gaining insight into the nature of the problems and their relevance to themselves.

Independent Work   Students should work independently for at least 25 minutes in each lesson. The teacher goes from student to student, offering individualized assistance and encouragement, reinforcing successful mastery, and preventing frustration or the repetition of errors. He investigates the process with the student and the specific source of difficulty. He initiates student-student confrontation and discussion of problems. The ultimate aim of the teacher is to develop independence and self-confidence on the part of the student. To do so, the student must be taught to check and evaluate his own work and that of his peers.

It has been found helpful to enlist as an aide the student who finishes his work quickly. Peer tutoring is beneficial to both learners involved. The tutor should be taught, however, that to assist effectively is not to solve the problem of his neighbor, but to teach process and strategies. It is interesting to note that, because of the differential modalities and emphases of the exercises, it is not always the same child who becomes the aide.

Discussion and the Development of Insight   When most of the students have completed their independent work, the class as a whole is gathered for a discussion of the various solutions that are offered by the students. Following this, the teacher and students explore divergent thought processes and alternative responses. Although different solutions may be correct, the students should take time for reflection and decide on the most appropriate one. The teacher and students analyze the difficulties that were faced and how they were overcome. There is a review of the vocabulary, concepts, and operations that were used. The principles that may have been presented in the introductory phase are developed, elaborated, and applied. The classroom climate should be such that students can initiate questions and participate in discussions, confident that they will not be ridiculed.

Summary   The summary at the end of the lesson should not exceed 5 minutes, but should not be overlooked. The summary should include a restatement of the goals set at the start of the lesson and an evaluation of the degree to which they were achieved. It should make the students aware and conscious of the particular areas addressed by the lesson. Initially, the teacher summarizes the lesson. Later, this conclusion becomes the responsibility of the students. It may be a simple statement of what was learned or a review of the lesson.

Flexibility

The teacher must be willing to digress from a lesson plan according to the needs of the students and the classroom situation. The students' responses should play a major role in the construction of the lesson, with the teacher serving as a guiding and orienting force. The optimal pace of a lesson is the teacher's concern.

There need not be a set pattern for FIE lessons, although all of the above-mentioned presentation components should be included. For instance, if the independent work, discussion, and summary are completed before the end of a period, the teacher may introduce a new page, which need not be finished within the remaining time. On the following day, the student could continue with his independent work. However, teachers must be cautioned against reducing the time spent on actual work on the pages.

Individualized, Remedial Work

Although all of the elements of an FIE lesson should be included in individualized, remedial work, the time allotted to each will necessarily vary. With only one or two youngsters, there is no problem in interrupting independent work to discuss a point (something very difficult to achieve in a group setting) so process can be explored and insight into the task created while the student is still working on it.

From our experience, we have found it both more interesting and beneficial to conduct clinical remedial lessons in groups of at least two. There is a dynamic interaction in which each learner benefits from the questions and comments of the other. With two or more children, the possibilities of reducing teacher-initiated input and increasing cooperation, in which each child builds on the response of the other, are enhanced.

In remedial work, only certain instruments may be selected in an effort to correct the specific cognitive deficiencies of the participants, or the entire program may be taught. In providing phase-specific mediation, attention must be paid to the sequence of the instruments. Selected instruments should be taught in their entirety, however.

SAMPLE INSTRUMENTAL ENRICHMENT LESSONS

Each of the following lessons demonstrates actual classroom occurrences from FIE classes of culturally deprived students in Israel. The students' achievement measures in math and language on standard school tests had been 2–5 years below the norm. While each lesson has been constructed in accordance with FIE principles, they differ in objectives, a difference partially attributable to the nature of the material, the stage in the FIE program at which they are taught, the needs of the children themselves, and the style of the teacher.

Organization of Dots

The objectives of this lesson in *Organization of Dots* were to introduce the instrument, to arouse the need of the students to work on it, and to create insight into the relevance of the cover page. Specific subgoals included the introduction of the projection of virtual relationships and the role of mankind in organizing the universe.

Because this lesson is one of the first lessons in the FIE program, its presentation is more frontal than that of later ones, with the teacher not only directing the discussion, but doing most of the talking. The students are seventh-grade vocational students engaged in their second FIE lesson.

JUST A MINUTE ...
LET ME THINK !

After distributing the cover page (above) and finding its similarity to the other cover page the children have seen in their first lesson, the teacher begins. (T = Teacher; S = Student. Unless otherwise noted, it is not the same student who responds each time.)

T: What is different in this page? Take a moment to think.
S1:   The sky.   S2: The stars.   S3: The picture in the box.
T: Yes, the difference is in the rectangle on the left side of the page, where we find the symbol for this particular instrument. What about the stars in the rectangle?
S: They are connected by lines.
T: Right. Now, if we were to go out at night and look at the sky, would we see this constellation as it is here?
S4:   Yes.   S5: No.
T: S4 says yes and S5 says no. First, S4, tell us why you say yes, and then, S5, tell us why you said no.
S4:   Well, I think that's the Big Dipper and it's up in the sky.
S5:   There are no lines in the sky.
T: You're both right. It *is* the Big Dipper and there are no lines in the sky. Why do you suppose it is called the Big Dipper?

S6:   'Cause it looks like one.

T: Yes, the ancient Greeks who originally organized the stars into the constellation saw that if you drew an imaginary line from star to star you
would get a figure that looked just like a dipper. Why do you suppose that
was important to them?

(No answer. Students are unaccustomed to hypothesizing or generating information.)

T: In order to find the North Star (pointing) they found that if you take this
distance between these two stars (pointing) and come up five times that
distance, there is Polaris, the North Star. Now perhaps you can think of
the reason that man found it helpful to connect stars with imaginary lines.
Who might need to know the location of the North Star?

S: Sailors.   S: Travelers in covered wagons.

T: Yes, travelers on land and sea, all through the ages, drew these imaginary
lines and connected the stars into constellations. They organized them
and gave them names, and used them in order to know directions. Just as
travelers without a compass use them today. For any of you who are interested, there are star books on my desk. You may look at them during
the break, and we'll talk about the constellations during science. Now,
can you think of anybody else today who uses imaginary lines?

S: Airplane pilots.

T: Yes, the flight plan of a pilot is an imaginary line from one place to
another.

S: On the ocean there are no lines.

T: True. To navigate on land and sea, one must connect the point from
which one departs and the point to which one arrives with imaginary
lines.

S7:   On maps.

T: Very good. Tell us what you mean.

S7:   I can't remember what you call them. They're the lines that go this way
and that way (drawing horizontal and vertical lines in the air).

T: Very good. The lines of longitude and latitude. Let's see what else there is
on the map (pulls it down).

S8:   The borders.

T: Yes, there are boundary lines between the states. Have any of you ever
crossed the state line? The city line? Is there anything that makes you
know that you've crossed it?

S: The sign.

T: Yes, there is usually a sign that welcomes you.

S: The reason they need the sign is that there is no way of knowing that you
crossed it. It usually looks the same on both sides.

T: A very good conclusion. There are lines drawn on maps that do not appear in reality. Are there any others?

S: The lines on a weather map.

T: Good. And we could go on and add lines that divide the time zones, and
others; but let's leave maps. Any place else that you or somebody else
draw imaginary lines as a strategy, a way of reaching some goal?

S: (tentatively) In sewing, I baste on an imaginary line to keep it straight.

T: Excellent.

S: When I write on paper without lines, I draw an imaginary line to keep my
writing even.

T: Good.

S: When my dad is building something and wants to see if it's straight, he drops a line with a weight on it.

T: That's called a plumb-line and most good carpenters use one. But we're looking for imaginary lines.

S: I just look and see if it's straight.

T: Then you are drawing an imaginary line instead of using a plumb-line.

S: When I pitch, I draw an imaginary line between the hitter's knees and shoulders.

T: Good for you.

S: When I add, I use an imaginary line to keep one number right under another.

T: That's very good. Is there a reason for that?

S: If I didn't, I'd add the wrong numbers together.

T: So you have a need to organize the numbers.

S: Teacher, sometimes you say "I draw the line at that."

T: When do I say that?

S: When somebody is doing something you don't want them to do.

T: In other words, I draw an imaginary line and say, "Up to this line, behavior is acceptable. Past it, it is unacceptable." We could go on and try to find more examples of imaginary lines that are drawn to connect things, to separate them from other things, but let's stop here. If these lines do not exist in nature, why do you suppose man finds it necessary to use them?

S: Well, people drew imaginary lines to connect the stars.

T: You're right. My question is *why*. (No answer). Well, let's imagine we are looking up at the sky on a clear night. What do we see?

S: Lots of stars. Maybe the moon.

T: A lot of stars, each one separate. I can't tell one from the other. But I do know what a dipper looks like. I know what a W looks like. I can close my eyes and see them. And now when I look up into the sky, I have a picture of an upside down W in my mind. I look for five stars that are so located that if I drew an imaginary line (on board) to connect them, I'd have an upside down W, and then I know that I have found the constellation Cassiopeia, and from there I know I can also find the North Star. I have *organized* the stars so there's no longer a big jumble. Just as when I draw a map with borders between states, I organize the land. I look for the connections, the relationships between things. I put things into order. And then, when I want to find one specific thing, it is easier than if everything is disorganized. Let's say it's during recess and I want to give John here a message. How will I find him?

S: Look for Susan. (General laughter.)

T: Don't laugh. Maybe it's a good idea. Why would I look for Susan?

S: Because they're always together.

T: So you are saying that if I look for one, I'll find the other. A good strategy. Are there any other ways? Remember how many students there are in the school and how big the grounds are.

S: I wouldn't look for him. Recess is only 15 minutes. So I'd wait until he was back in class and get him. It would be easier.

T: I agree it would be easier. With your strategy, what have you done?

S: I guess I looked for him in the place he usually is.

T: Yes, by using the organization of the class, you've made it easier to find John. You've narrowed the field of your search. Now, is the class a natural organization? Were you all born into this class?

S: Of course not. The principal and counselor put us here.

T: Yes, once again we have an example of an organization made by man. Before, with the stars, the organization was based on form: of a dipper or of a W. Is this class made up on the basis of form, of your shapes?

S: No. We're all in here because we're in the seventh grade.

T: Seventh grade, good. Anything else?

S: Well, we're all vocational students.

T: Right. This class is organized on the basis of grade and vocation. So if we want to find a seventh-grade vocational student, we'd look for him here. Is there any other way that things can be organized? We've talked about organizing according to form, like the stars, or what they are, like the class.

S: When we do the laundry, we do the white clothes separate from the colored.

T: Very good, according to color. For our next lesson, I'd like you each to think of examples of things that are organized and the principle of their organization, the rule according to which they were organized. All right, now what have we talked about today?

S: We've talked about imaginary lines.   S: Organizing.

T: Yes, we have talked about the way man organizes the things in his world and the imaginary lines he draws around them to keep certain things together and apart from other things. This instrument is called *Organization of Dots* and the symbol on the cover page will give you a clue as to what we are going to do in it.

S: I guess we're going to connect the dots with lines.

T: Yes, we're going to connect dots with lines in order to form a figure that looks like the one given to us in the model. But that is for the next lesson. Please put the cover pages in your folders.

Temporal Relations

The above lesson may be contrasted with the following transcript of a lesson (pages 311–313) in *Temporal Relations,* an instrument taught in the second year. In this lesson, the teacher calls for hypothetical thinking, inferences, and critical analysis. In orienting the discussion, the teacher is flexible and builds the lesson on the students' responses; however, he succeeds in developing with the class the goals he has set for the lesson. The reader should note that the three pages were handed out simultaneously and that independent work preceded the introduction, discussion, and summary. The students are culturally deprived eighth graders.

T: Please read the directions at the top of the pages quietly to yourselves. Are there any questions? Do you all know what to do? Are you sure? If you are, please start to work. I'll circulate among you and answer any questions that you may have.

(When all the students have completed or are close to completing the exercises on pages 7 and 8, the teacher stops them.)

T: Before you go on, I have a question. Why do you think I distributed page 9 at the same time that I passed out pages 7 and 8?

S1:   You're supposed to fill out the table on page 9 after you've finished 7 and 8. The answers from 7 and 8 go on 9.

Solve the following problems and then indicate the solutions in the table on page 9.

1. A stork flew from Toronto to New York City. On the first day it flew a distance of 15 miles (24 kilometers). On the second day it flew at the same speed, yet covered a distance of 22 miles (35 kilometers).

   Explain: _____

   _____

   _____

2. Two joggers are competing. X jogs faster than Y. Who gets farther after two hours of jogging?

   _____

   Explain: _____

   _____

   _____

3. A small car and a big car left Chicago at 9:00 o'clock in the morning and reached Springfield at 10:30 o'clock. Which of them drove faster?

   _____

   Explain: _____

   _____

   _____

4. Now arrange the following data in the table and solve the problem with the aid of the table:
   X and Y rode motor scooters from New York City to Albany without stopping en route. X left at 8:00 o'clock in the morning. Y left at 10:00 o'clock in the morning. Who left earlier?

   _____

   At 12:00 o'clock both arrived at the same place.

   Explain: _____

   _____

   _____

   _____

Temporal Relations (page 7)

5. Ellen and Bess work in the garden. Ellen hoes quickly. Bess hoes slowly.

Ellen started at 7:00 in the morning.

Bess began at 9:00 in the morning.

Which of them had hoed more flower beds by noon? _____

Explain: _____

_____

_____

6. Two turtles were walking in the field. Both started off from a certain rock and walked to a well. Turtle A walked 35 feet (11 meters) in half an hour. Turtle B walked 35 feet (11 meters) in one hour.

Which of them reached the water first? _____

Explain: _____

_____

_____

Temporal Relations (page 8)

Table for the Problems

Problem	Distance	Speed	Time
1	A < B	A = B	?
2	?	A > B	A = B
3	A = B	?	A = B
4			
5			
6			

Now solve the problems in the table below with the help of the data given in the table.

Example	A = B	A > B	B > A
1		A = B	B > A
2	A = B	A = B	
3	A > B	A = B	
4	A < B		A > B
5	A < B		A = B

Temporal Relations (page 9)

T: Do you all agree?

S2:   Well, that's what the instructions say. "Solve the problems on these pages and then write the solution in the table."

S3:   No, I don't agree. Page 9 has to be divided into top and bottom. We write the answers from 7 and 8 on the top part of the page. On the bottom part it says, "Solve the problems with the information given in the table."

T: S3 is right. We must divide the page for purposes of our discussion. But nobody answered my question. I could have waited until you finished 7 and 8, and then given you page 9.

S4:   You wanted to save time.

S5:   You wanted to give the kids who work fast enough to keep them busy.

T: Those are both good reasons, but in this case I had another reason. Does anybody have another idea?

S6:   I do, but I'm not sure it's right. I looked at all three pages before I started. Then I saw that the chart on the top of page 9 was just another way of giving the information on the problems of the other two pages. It used letters and signs instead of all the words. So I used the table to help me solve the problems on page 7 and 8. I worked on both.

T: So instead of using the table to encode the answers you had already found, you used the table as an aid in solving the problems. Do you all understand what he did? Why don't you come to the board and show us?

S6:   (at board) Well, like in all the other pages we've done in the instrument, there are three things we have to know about. The distance, the speed, and the amount of time altogether. . .

T: The total interval.

S6:   The interval. So I looked at the examples, and then I said to myself: What about the distance? Well, it says the distance on the second day was greater than on the first (writes $B > A$). The speed was the same on both days ($B = A$). The only thing I don't know from reading the questions is how long the bird flew (writes a ?). So then I answered the other questions at the same time that I filled in the chart on page 9.

T: Thank you. You worked very efficiently. I hoped that some of you would use that strategy when I passed out the pages. (Notices S20.) Yes?

S20: But teacher, that's not what the directions say to do.

T: S6, do you have an answer for S20?

S6:   Well, if I know how to do something, it's not necessary that I follow the directions exactly. For instance, if somebody tells me how to get to his house, I don't need to follow his directions if I know a short cut.

S20: But, in *Analytic Perceptions,* when we wanted to take a short cut, we decided that we weren't working just to get the answer, but to learn how to do something, so we should follow the directions exactly as given.

S6:   Well, now I've learned how, and following the directions doesn't teach me anything new.

T: OK? OK. The only thing is that you must be sure that your strategy is appropriate under the conditions of the new task. What did this kind of work require from S6 before he started?

S7:   He had to think.

S8:   He had to plan.

T: S6 told us how he worked. What did you do, S6?

S6:   I looked at all three pages before I started and I saw how they were related. Then I saw that there were letters and signs instead of words, so I translated the words into signs.

T: Before he started, S6 defined the problem, looked for relationships, and planned a strategy for his work. Yes, the letters and signs are abstract ways of presenting the specific data. What do I mean when I say "abstract"?

S9:   Just like in *Family Relations,* when we use a circle, a rectangle, and a line connecting them to show a man and his wife. It doesn't make any difference who they are.

S10:   Just like 2A + 2B is the perimeter of a rectangle.

T: You've given me good examples, but you haven't told me what "abstract" means.

S11:   It's the opposite of concrete. It means the opposite of something we can see or touch or feel.

T: That's good enough. We have moved away from specific cases and made it a general rule. By using letters and signs in the first problem, we are no longer thinking about a particular bird, but about any instance in which there are these relationships between distance, speed, and time. Now what is the difference between the upper part of page 9 and the lower part?

S12:   They're both the same.

T: It's true that they have many things in common, but are they identical?

S12:   The chart is the same. The headings are the same. We use A's and B's and the signs for "equal to," "more than," and "less than."

T: The code or the language is the same. But I asked if they were *identical.* Remember when we studied *Comparisons,* how did we compare?

S12:   We looked for similarities and differences. They're different, too.

T: If there is a difference, are they identical?

S12:   No, because to be identical is to be the same in every single detail. Here they're different. On the top there are lots of question marks and on the bottom there are no question marks but empty spaces.

T: What do the question marks mean?

S13:   They mean I can't fill it in because I don't know.

T: You don't know? Or there's not enough given information to know?

S13:   There's not enough information.

T: Yes. Is the fact that there are question marks in the top part a meaningful difference, or is it just by chance?

S14:   No, it's important. In the bottom part, any time that two things travel the same distance at the same speed, they'll take the same amount of time.

T: Does that relationship always hold true?

S14:   Yes, any time. It's always the same. It's a rule.

T: Do you all agree? Yes, it is a rule, a law that says that there are fixed, constant relationships between the three factors. The example says that if the distance is the same, and A goes faster than B, then A will take less time. (Writes on board: Distance: A = B; Speed: A > B; Time: A < B.)

S15:   It's the same in all kinds of races.

S16:   They always give the winner's time in races.

T: Why do they only give the speed?

S16:   Because the track is the same for all the horses, and the one who goes fastest has the least time.

T: And speed is what?

S16:   The time a certain distance is covered.

T: Excellent. Why is there a difference between the top part and the bottom part of the page? Look at number 6 on page 7. There the distance is the

	same for both turtles.
S:	From the rock to the water hole.
T:	We know the speed.
S:	Turtle B goes faster than turtle A.
T:	What did you write for an answer?
S:	A question mark.
T:	Why do we have to write a question mark? Why couldn't we apply the rule we just mentioned?
S15:	They didn't tell us when both turtles set out and if they kept going without stopping.
T:	What difference would that make?
S15:	We don't know the time they spent.
T:	What was the question that we were asked to answer?
S15:	Who arrived first.
T:	When I see the word "first," what can I infer? What conclusion can I reach?
S16:	That there was a second. S17: That there were others.
T:	Yes, "first" is a relative term. It implies a comparison between two or more, with one reaching the goal ahead of the others. Do I have enough information to answer that question?
S:	No.
T:	Are there any questions that I *can* answer from the available information?
S18:	Yes, which turtle traveled faster.
T:	Good. What additional information do I need in order to answer the question that is asked?
S19:	What time each turtle arrived at the goal.
T:	S15, you said we had to know the time they each set out and if they kept going without stopping. Do you still feel that is important?
S15:	Yes, from that information, I could get the answer.
T:	Yes, you could *infer* that if the distance is the same, and one is faster than the other, it would cover the distance in less time, and therefore be the first. S19, could you *fill in the chart* if you were given the time each turtle arrived at the goal?
S19:	Yes.
T:	S15, do you agree?
S15:	No, because he wouldn't know if one set out earlier than the other, or if one rested along the way.
S19:	I guess he's right, because I really wouldn't know about the amount of time each spent walking. I could just answer the question of who beat who.
S20:	But, teacher, everybody knows that if the track is exactly the same and one horse is twice as fast as the second that the first horse is going to come in first.
T:	Yes, that is what one could expect according to the law. But if what you say is true, there would never be any horse races. The one with the best record would always win. Is that what happens?
S1:	No, the horse could fall down. S2: He could have an off day.
S3:	The track could be muddy and the horse couldn't run fast in the mud.
T:	With your reasons, what have you done?
S6:	Those are reasons why the horse *isn't* the fastest at the time of the race.
T:	Yes. I don't want you to think that laws exist but cannot be applied in reality. It is the same law, but there are changes that occur in real life

situations that affect the application of the law. Let's leave the track. Do you have any examples of laws and their applications, circumstances under which it seems like the law changes?

S4:   The law says you have to drive slow in the city, but an ambulance, they put on their siren and go whoosh....

S19:   I was thinking just the opposite. It's only supposed to take 15 minutes to get home by bus. But sometimes there's a lot of traffic and a lot of people so the driver has to stop at every station and it takes twice as long.

T: The rule is?

S: Fifteen minutes from school to home.

T: Things do not occur entirely by chance. There is a rule, but when we try to apply it in certain circumstances, as you have pointed out, those circumstances cause changes.... (Intends to summarize, but is interrupted.)

S6:   I think it's like the law. The judge knows the law, but when he passes sentence, he takes all kinds of other things into account: Is it a first offense? Is the kid a juvenile? Did he do it alone or did somebody make him?

T: Yes, when law is applied, the judge takes into account all the things you mentioned and others beside.

S: In citizenship, we learned that everybody over 18 can vote if he is a citizen and has not been convicted of a felony.

S5:   In my house, there's a rule. No noise when my uncle is sleeping. When I make a sound, I get walloped. When my sister does, all they do is shush her. It's 'cause she's the favorite.

T: Could there be another reason?

S5:   No. She's the favorite.

S: It's because she's the baby. She doesn't know any better.

T: I think you're right. S5, does she go to bed at the same time that you do?

S5:   Of course not, she's a baby. She goes to bed earlier.

T: Well, the day may come very soon, that she thinks you're the favorite because you go to bed later than she does. I started to say that in some circumstances there may be changes so that the law is inappropriate. We cannot apply it. But, let's find some laws that are fixed and unchanged in application.

S: The sun always rises in the same place and sets in the same place.

S: Summer always follows spring.

S: An even number can be divided by two without leaving anything over.

T: Physical and mathematical laws are not changed in their application. And, if we think, we can find many other relationships that remain constant, like black is the opposite of white, or the relationship between mother and child, that we discussed in *Family Relations*. But let's summarize our discussion. First the relationship between page 9 and pages 7 and 8, and then the comparison between the upper and lower half of page 9. Who will start?

S: On pages 7 and 8, we had to answer questions about specific cases. We couldn't answer some because we didn't have enough information.

T: Very good. Would somebody like to add something to what he said?

S: Yes. All the questions had to do with speed, distance, and amount of time.

S: What about number 5? There's no distance there.

S6:   Yes there is. The number of rows they hoe is the distance.

T: Remember *Orientation in Space?* We talked about the concept of distance and the ways it could be measured. But we will come back to your question when we summarize the first unit in the next lesson. Now what about page 9 and the relationship between its two parts?

S: On page 9, letters and signs are used to show the relationships between distance, speed, and time.

S: On the top of page 9, we write the information from pages 7 and 8; on the bottom of the page, we write the relationships according to the law.

S6: We can also use letters and signs to help us solve the problems.

S7: We talked about the laws and how they are in real life.

T: Very good. Your summaries are getting better every day. Now one last question before we put the pages away. Think for a moment before answering. Is it easier to gather the data and see the relationships in the verbal questions or in the table?

S: In the table. There we get down to the "nitty-gritty."

T: Yes, in the table the information is organized and we can see the relationships at a glance. We don't have all the extra words to contend with. Please put your work into your folders. We'll start the next lesson by completing these pages. Then we'll go over your answers and discuss them, and any problems that gave you some trouble. Then I'll ask you to summarize the first unit before we start the next one.

Illustrations

The following transcript illustrates the development of a lesson (page 319) in the dynamic classroom situation. The teacher's objective was to teach transformation and the strategy of detour; however, the needs and comments of the students determined the course of what actually transpired. It should be noted that, even in a page as free of content as page 3 of *Illustrations,* the subgoals of the program, especially the correction of deficient cognitive functions, are evident. The class is of seventh-grade culturally deprived slow learners.

T: I'll give you a few minutes to look at the page and then we'll discuss it. ...All right. Who would like to start?

S1: In the first picture, the rat is looking at the thing on the table; he wants it so bad, he's crying.

S2: He's not crying. He's drooling.

T: Why do you say "crying," S1?

S1: I looked at it too fast. I can see now that he's drooling.

T: S1 said that the rat wanted the thing on the table so badly that he was drooling. Does one usually drool when one wants something? I saw a new book I wanted very badly....

S3: (interrupting) No. Your mouth waters when you see something delicious that you want to eat.

T: Only when you see it?

S3: No. Sometimes when you smell it cooking and you're hungry.

T: All right. When you smell it. Anything else? (No answer.) Sometimes when I hear somebody describe a good dinner, my mouth starts to water. I begin to salivate. We'll discuss the reasons for this in our next general science lesson. But now, what is it that makes the rat drool, or salivate?

S4: The cake.   S5: The cheese.

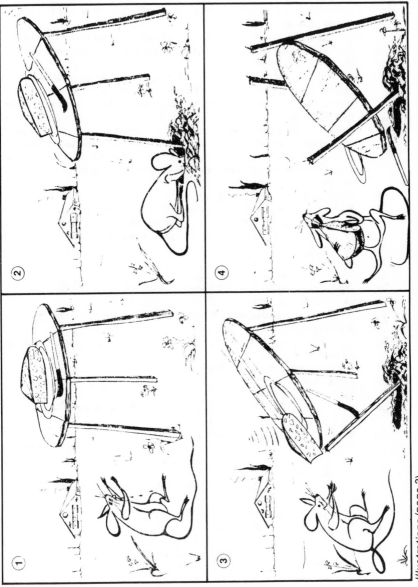

Illustrations (page 3)

T: Which shall it be?

S4:   It looks like a piece of fruit cake.

S5:   The only reason it looks like a piece of cake to him is because it's shaped like a piece of cake. But I never heard of a rat liking cake. I know mice and rats like cheese because that's how you catch them. My father puts cheese on a trap and...

T: Let's not wander too far from our subject. (To S4) Has S5 persuaded you? If so, what are those little things that you thought were fruit?

S4:   Holes. Like in Swiss cheese.

T: Yes, I think so. I'm not an expert on rats and don't know if they like cake or not. And in this case it isn't really important whether it is cake or cheese, but we want to learn to be precise and gather all the available information. So let's see how we arrive at a conclusion. There were two possibilities. Because of its shape and size, the object could be either a piece of cake or a piece of cheese. In order to decide, we have to put together what we see and what we know. We do know that rats really like cheese, and we see the rat's mouth watering. Is there anything else that shows us that the rat really wants the object?

S6:   The way his hands are lifted up.

T: Right. So we have additional evidence that he wants the object. Now, we must decide, on the basis of what we know, which of the two, the cake or the cheese, would cause the rat to act the way he does. Our conclusion?

All: Cheese.

T: What is the problem?

S7:   It's too high up for him to reach.

T: When something is too high to reach, what do we usually do?

S8:   Get a chair and climb up.

T: All right. We stand on something that will bring us up to the height of the object.

S: My mother uses a ladder in the kitchen because she can't reach the dishes on the top shelf.

T: Are there any other alternatives?

S9:   Get a stick.

T: Yes?

S9:   Get a stick. You know. Like the grocer. He can't reach the toilet paper on the top shelf so he gets a stick and knocks it down.

S10:   The janitor closes the transom with a pole.

S11:   When I can't reach the fruit on a tree, I get a stick and hit the branch.

S12:   No, it's better to throw something at the fruit and knock it down. That way you don't break the branches.

T: Let's see what you have been saying. When something is too high, we have two alternatives. (Writes on the board.) The first is to raise oneself up. (Writes: *Up: ladder, chair.*) The second?

S13:   To bring the thing down. (T writes on board: *Down: stick, rock.*)

T: Are there any other possibilities?

S14:   You can try to jump up and reach it, or stand on tiptoes.

T: In which of the two categories would you place that? Or is it a new category? (S14 writes *jump* under *chair.*)

T: Right. Now let's see which of these strategies the rat used to solve his problem. Let's look at the next picture.

S15:   He's digging a hole.

T: Just a hole any place?

S15:   No, he's digging a hole around the table leg.

T: What do you think that will do?

S16: It will bring the front part of the table down so that the cheese will slide off.

T: You've thought of a good cause and effect relationship. Do you think the rat expects the cheese to slide off?

S17: Yes, in the third picture, he's standing there with his hands stretched out to catch it.

S1:   The rat thought about it beforehand. "Just a minute. Let me think."

T: Let's be a bit more specific. He thought about what?

S1:   His plan.

T: What did we call such a plan in *Organization of Dots*?

S18: A strategy. He planned his strategy.

T: Good. Do you all remember what a strategy is?

S15: A strategy is the steps I take to solve a problem. Like in checkers, when I make the other guy jump me so I can jump two of his men.

T: That's right. A strategy is a plan, method, or series of steps for reaching a specific goal or result. Did you know what the rat's strategy was when you looked at picture 2?

S3:   No, I only thought of it when I saw the third picture.

S14: That's some smart rat!

T: Do you all agree? Let's look at the board and see the alternatives we offered.

S19: He couldn't use any of them because they weren't around.

T: How could we classify the strategy he did use?

S20: Under the heading, "to bring the object down."

T: Because he couldn't get to the cheese directly, he used a detour strategy. Do you know what "detour" means?

S: Yes, when you close the road, you can't get directly to where you want to go, so you have to go off on a side road and go around to get there.

S14: (interrupting) He used his imagination.

T: What do you mean?

S14: Well, he thought of all the possibilities in his head and saw that he couldn't use them and that he would have to come up with something new.

T: In other words, if we explore the various possibilities in our head before we start, we can save time, effort, and make fewer mistakes. The rat was certainly ingenious. Have you heard the word before? (On board, writes *ingenious*.) Look it up.

S: "Characterized by cleverness or originality of invention or construction. Cleverly inventive or resourceful."

T: S14 said that the rat was *clever* and thought of a *new strategy*. So we can agree that the rat was ingenious. Do you remember any other pages with an ingenious solution?

S: Yes, the mother dog and her puppies.

T: I'd like you to compare the two pages, in both of which there were ingenious solutions to the problems. How did the mother dog get her puppies across the stream?

S: She was a dachshund kind of dog. So she just lay across the water and the puppies walked across her back.

T: Is there any difference between that kind of solution and the one the rat used? I know it's a hard question, so I'm going to start and then let you carry on. The dog used a direct solution. She had a goal and her solution led directly to it, while the rat...?

S: The rat had to do something first. He had to dig a hole first.

T: You're right. The rat had to use a detour, to reach the goal only by stages. It requires a plan. You know animals are quite clever. A rat who wants to steal eggs lies on his back and holds the egg with his four legs. Another rat pulls him along by his tail until they get back to the nest. Can you think of something where you reach the goal indirectly, and must do something else first to achieve your goal?

S: Do you mean something like this: If I want to make potato salad, first I have to peel my potatoes, then boil them, and then wait until they're cool before I cut them up.

T: Very good, although in your example you are working on different steps of the process.

S: If I want to add fractions, first I have to find the least common denominator and change them all into the same thing.

T: Excellent. OK. Then the rat's ingenious solution was an indirect way of reaching the goal. It was a strategy of detour. S20, something is troubling you. Don't you agree the solution was ingenious?

S20:   I guess so.

T: Then what is bothering you?

S20:   I don't know how to say it. But look at the table!

T: What about the table?

S20:   The leg is broken...

T: Yes?

S20:   The table belongs to somebody else and so does the cheese. The rat stole the cheese...

S1:   He did not! He worked hard to get it.

T: Let's let S20 finish.

S20:   Well, even if he worked hard, the cheese didn't belong to him and to get it he broke somebody else's property.

T: S20 is saying something very important. Until now, we've been seeing the situation only from the rat's point of view. It seems there is another point of view in the situation. S20 is...

S4:   Putting herself in the shoes of the person who owns the house.

T: Yes. Is it reasonable for us to infer that it is the property of someone?

S4:   Yes, there's a house in the background of the first picture.

T: Yes, it's likely, though we can't be positive. All right. Let's return to what S1 said. The "rat worked hard to get it." Does anybody want to comment on this?

S: Wait, I want to say something else. It's his own fault! He shouldn't have left the stuff laying around.

T: I'm going to write *worked hard* on the board, so we won't forget it, because S1 has brought up another point that is worthy of discussion. What do you mean, S1?

S1:   I mean that anybody who leaves something lying around takes the chance of having it stolen! I remember when last year somebody stole my money off my desk. The other teacher said I should have put it away.

T: Did you agree?

S1:   Not really. It was on *my* desk. Whoever took it just stole it.

T: It seems to me that what the other teacher was saying is that by leaving your money out you put temptation in the path of somebody who was unable to resist it. But let's separate the two instances: the rat who stole the cheese and the "rat" who stole S1's money. Are they the same or is there a difference?

S18:   Animals don't know any better.

T: You're right. I remember once before Thanksgiving I put a turkey out to defrost. A cat ate a whole drumstick before I discovered her!

S21:   My mother got mad at my puppy because he chewed her good shoe. He didn't know the difference between a new shoe and an old shoe.

T: So what you are saying is that the difference in the two instances is whether you could expect the thief to exercise judgment and to know right from wrong.

S1:   The kid who stole my money knew right from wrong. He just didn't care.

T: I stand corrected. The difference is whether you could expect the thief to know right from wrong or care about it. . .

S18:   The rat doesn't know right from wrong. He doesn't think of it as stealing. He sees something good to eat and he wants it.

T: Let's take what you are saying one step further. Is an animal capable of saying this is right and this is wrong? No. That is what separates man from other animals. Our problem here is that we are using man's standards of property ownership and good and bad, and expecting the rat to know them too. . . . Now what is similar in the two instances of the rat who stole the cheese and the "rat" who stole the money?

S: Taking something that doesn't belong to you.

S: Stealing.   S: Temptation.

T: Can we arrive at a general rule based on these examples?

S: Well, if what you have is tempting to those who don't know or don't care about who it belongs to, then it is better to put it away or protect it somehow.

T: Very good. S1, do you understand now what the other teacher was trying to tell you? (S1 nods.)

T: We only have a short time, and I want to get back to S1's earlier statement. "He worked hard to get it." Do you want to explain it, S1?

S1:   Well, the rat saw something he really wanted and he was willing to work hard to get it. He didn't give up. He kept digging even though it was hard work.

S20:   Oh, teacher, that's stupid. On TV last night, I saw police digging up counterfeit money. The crooks that made it had to work hard to make it, and then work some more to bury it, but that didn't mean that what they were doing was right!

T: It seems we have a dilemma (writes *dilemma* on the blackboard), a difficult and perplexing problem, because what S1 says is true and what S20 says is true. Let's think for a moment and see if we can resolve it.

S: I think that what S1 means is that "God helps those who help themselves."

T: Yes?

S: Well, if you really want something you shouldn't sit around and wait for somebody to hand it to you. You should go out and work hard to get it.

S20:   I still say that hard work alone isn't the important thing. It's what you're working hard at doing.

T: Let's see if this is the answer. S1 means that being willing to work hard to get something you want is a good trait, but S20 says merely working hard is not the main criterion on which to judge an act. Sometimes it is not even relevant. I'll talk to your English teacher about our discussion this morning and perhaps there will be further opportunity to explore the dilemma. But now, it's nearly time for the bell. Who would like to summarize this page?

S: A rat wanted some cheese that was out of his reach. In order to get it, he came up with (looks at the board) an ingenious solution that was a detour strategy.

T: Well done.

The digression from the prepared plan in the above lesson demonstrates the sensitivity of the teacher to the needs of his students, poorly expressed as they may be, and his flexibility in meeting those needs. The legitimacy of a tangential discussion, or the extent to which it should be explored, is judged by the teacher who must weight its relevancy to the lesson and the achievement of the objectives of the program. In many instances, the pace of the program has been appreciably slowed by apparently aimless and rambling deviations from the planned course of the lesson.

In the above transcript it should be noted that, except for the interaction with the student who complained of favoritism at home, all of the issues, even those with strong affective overtones, were treated on a cognitive level in which universal rules were sought. No matter how far afield the discussion seemed to range, it was brought back to the page and used for the development of insight.

It should be apparent to the reader that the above lessons are merely examples of classroom implementation. FIE material, content-free as it is, is equally appropriate for widely divergent populations, and the lessons will differ as a function of the population to whom the material is being taught.

SUMMARY

In this chapter, we have discussed the training and support system for teachers of Instrumental Enrichment. Protocols of typical lessons were selected to illustrate the nature of the classroom interaction and the centrality of the teacher in conducting the FIE lesson. The next chapter is concerned with an extensive study of the effects of Instrumental Enrichment on a large population of socially disadvantaged, culturally deprived adolescents. Chapter 11 considers the current status of implementation and research in both Israel and North America, with the full knowledge that by the time the pages reach the reader changes will already have occurred, and takes a look at future directions for FIE.

10

EXPERIMENTAL EVALUATION OF INSTRUMENTAL ENRICHMENT

In the preceding chapters, the theory underlying the cognitive modifiability of adolescents was presented, followed by a description of the materials, techniques, and didactics of Instrumental Enrichment. FIE was presented as a focused intervention for the modification of the cognitive structure of the retarded performing adolescent. The goals set for this program transcend those of conventional content-oriented curricula, which are usually limited to providing the retarded performer with content, information, and basic school skills. In contrast, the Instrumental Enrichment program attempts to sensitize the culturally deprived adolescent to make better use of learning opportunities presented to him both formally and informally. This program aims at affecting modifiability itself, so that the individual develops the ability to elaborate on stimuli impinging on him through direct exposure from internal and external sources and to become modified by this process. In this chapter, the results of a research project designed to evaluate the modifiability of the low functioning, culturally deprived adolescent, under a variety of treatment and placement conditions, are presented in broad outline. (For a detailed account of the research project, see Feuerstein and Rand, 1977.)

RESEARCH OBJECTIVES AND HYPOTHESES

The major objective of the research project was the comparison of the effectiveness of two strategies, Instrumental Enrichment versus General Enrichment, for the cognitive redevelopment of low functioning adolescents placed in residential and day center settings. "General Enrichment" (GE) is the term used to describe strategies that attempt to close the gap between low functioning and normal adolescents by providing an enriched and supplementary input of content and curriculum-oriented experiences. Although attitudinal and motivational factors are considered, the essential strategy of General Enrichment is the provision of additional information or specific skills. GE programs are contrasted with Instrumental Enrichment (FIE), which aims at producing changes in the overall cognitive *structure* of the individual, rather than changes only at the *level of performance*. Consequently, the following hypotheses were formulated.

Hypothesis 1

Disadvantaged and culturally deprived adolescents in residential and day centers who are exposed to Instrumental Enrichment show greater gains on intellective and non-intellective measures than do those who are exposed to General Enrichment.

The GE and FIE programs were conducted with adolescents placed by Youth Aliyah in residential and day centers. This provided a further research objective, because the performance of the adolescents in each setting could be compared and the possible differential effects of the programs within each setting assessed.

The residential setting is conceived of as a powerful total-care environment, providing the retarded performer with a great variety of intellectual and social stimuli under controlled conditions. It is therefore considered to facilitate the redevelopment process better than the day-center setting in which more limited contact with caregiving personnel and narrower educational goals are more likely to continue to expose the retarded performer to the very same depriving factors initially responsible for his condition. The day center emphasizes the training of specific vocational and occupational skills that may be profitably used from the start of the training provided in the program. This approach leads to a curriculum that emphasizes those aspects that are of immediate benefit and meaningfully limits the investment necessary to achieve structural changes in the adolescent's cognitive functioning. The residential center, on the other hand, offers a broad scope of educational and instructional goals. There is less emphasis on the immediate training of specific skills, and an attempt is made to direct and encourage the adolescent toward developing and pursuing academic interests. The educational process in the residential setting is conceived of as a preparatory stage necessary for the reintegration of the retarded performer into a normal educational framework. Repeated studies preceding the present research have invariably shown the favorable effects on the development of retarded performers of the more academically oriented program as contrasted with programs restricted to direct training of manual skills (Feuerstein, 1970). These differences between the two types of settings are the basis for the second hypothesis.

Hypothesis 2

Participation in the Instrumental Enrichment program produces better performance on criterion measures in residential centers, where intervention is administered in the context of a total-care program, than in the day centers, where care and educational programs are relatively limited.

Consideration of the differential effects of the General Enrichment and Instrumental Enrichment programs in the residential and day center settings produced the next hypothesis.

Hypothesis 3

There is an interaction effect between treatment (FIE versus GE) and setting (residential versus day center), with the Instrumental Enrichment program and the residential setting having a mutually reinforcing impact.

If Instrumental Enrichment produces changes of a structural nature, as hypothesized, then its impact should not be limited in time to the period of actual intervention. If the intended modifiability is achieved, then new modalities of functioning produced by the program should enable the individual to benefit cumulatively from nonmediated and direct exposure to experiences. As a result, a measurable divergent effect should occur with the passage of time from the inception of the intervention program. Thus, hypothesis 4 was formulated.

Hypothesis 4

The long term effects of Instrumental Enrichment are divergent such that, over time, there is a progressive increment in the differences of the performance of subjects exposed to this program compared to that of subjects receiving General Enrichment, and also with respect to the course of their own performance.

The above hypothesis relates to the follow-up study now in progress. Although only part of the data is currently available, some preliminary findings relating to this crucial hypothesis are presented below, following the discussion of the results.

In order to validate the above hypotheses, two residential and two day centers were selected as research sites. Instrumental Enrichment was implemented in one residential center and one day center, and General Enrichment was taught in the other residential and day centers, which served as comparison groups.

THE TARGET POPULATION

In this section, the demographic, socioeconomic, and other relevant characteristics of the research population are presented. Unless otherwise indicated, the data describe the total research population ($N = 218$). The main sources of information were parent interviews, subject questionnaires, and Social Welfare Agency and Youth Aliyah files. Wherever possible, there was cross-validation of the data from different sources, and all inconsistencies were re-checked through institutional records and in home visits.

Family Background and Country of Origin

Ethnic Background: Parents' Country of Origin   Our subjects and their families belong to the general category of "Oriental" communities in Israel. This term applies to groups of ethnic diversity, including almost all immigrants to Israel from Eastern, non-European countries. More than 90% of our subjects' parents were born in Asia or Africa, although the representation of Oriental groups in the whole Israeli Jewish population, age 35 and over, in 1970 was only 34.5% (*Statistical Abstract of Israel,* 1971). Almost 55% of the parents came from North Africa (Morocco, Algeria, Tunisia, Libya, and Egypt), and over one-third came from Asian countries (Iraq, Iran, Yemen, and India).

Educational Level of Parents   The general level of formal and informal education, including vocational training, of the subjects' parents was rather low. Only 26.3% of the subjects' fathers and 19.2% of their mothers received any education beyond the primary level, as compared with 56% of adult males and 49.5% of adult females in the total Israeli Jewish population (*Statistical Abstract of Israel,* 1971). The average number of grades of schooling was 5.72 for the fathers and 4.44 for the mothers, significantly lower than the 9.36 and 8.37 grade averages for Israeli males and females, respectively, in the adult Jewish population (*Statistical Abstract of Israel,* 1971). Assessment of literacy was based on reports by the parents themselves: 71.3% of the subjects' parents were literate (fathers, 83.8%; mothers, 58.7%). This compares unfavorably with the total Jewish population in Israel born in Asia and Africa (76.4%) (*Statistical Abstract of Israel,* 1971), but is superior to the general literacy levels in their countries of origin, in Asia and Africa. According to UNESCO estimates (*Alphabetization,* 1969–1971), the literacy rates in the Arab world in the 1960s ranged from 13.8% in Morocco (ages 15 and over) to 27.8% in Iran and India. Nearly all of the parents in our research population received their education before their emigration.

We also examined the literacy per family unit, in order to describe the familial educational environment and identify the proportion of our subjects who were raised in families in which one or both parents were unable to read or write in any language. We found that one-half of our subjects (50.5%) were from families where both parents were literate, and nearly one-fifth were from families without even one literate parent. Families with one illiterate parent, usually the mother (26.5%), comprised 30.6% of the sample.

Both education and literacy were higher for the parents of subjects in the residential settings than for those in the day centers. The trend is similar, although to a lesser and statistically not significant extent, in the comparison between the parents of FIE and GE subjects.

Immigration and Family Status in Israel

Immigration   The year of immigration is an important variable because of the lengthy period needed for assimilation into Israeli society. For children it is particularly critical, determining the extent of their socialization within the Israeli educational system. During certain periods, complex economic and social factors affected the ability of the country to provide for and absorb newcomers.

Only 4.3% of our subjects' parents came to Israel before May, 1948, when the State of Israel was established and the country opened its gates to mass immigration. In only 2 years, from 1948 to 1950, the size of the population doubled. By 1960, the population had tripled, presenting the new state with tremendous social and economic problems. These were years of war, economic hardship, joblessness for many, and lack of adequate housing. Immigrants were housed in special transit camps, and many were unemployed or, when fortunate, employed in work subsidized by relief funds. Many of our subjects' parents arrived in these periods: 24.8% from 1948 to 1951, and 31.95% from 1952 to 1961. Only 9.2% came after 1967, when the State was well established and conditions for absorption were easier. Although by 1971, when our experiment began, most families in our sample had been in Israel for a considerable period of time, with 49% over 15 years and 61% over 10 years, most had immigrated to Israel during the period of the early childhood of their children (our subjects).

The comparison between the four research groups shows that there were no meaningful differences between them regarding the year of parents' immigration. Although the GE groups were comprised of more "old timers" than the FIE groups, it should be noted that in our population early immigration did not necessarily, or even generally, mean better absorption or higher social and economic status in Israel.

Place of Settlement in Israel   Only 9.5% of our subjects' families settled in metropolitan areas. Twenty-four percent lived in small towns that were established before the great wave of immigration, but the majority (64%) lived in development towns. These new towns were established during the 1950s in accordance with a twofold policy: 1) to prevent the creation of slums and shanty towns in the metropolitan areas that were adjacent to the transit camps, and 2) to promote the dispersion of population throughout the country. However, this policy created new problems. Most development towns were built and populated before the provision of sufficient infrastructures and community services. Many inhabitants were initially employed on relief projects. Because few attractive or higher paying jobs were available, the better educated and more enterprising people left these towns, leaving behind the more disadvantaged segment of the population.

The schools located in the development towns and new immigrant neighborhoods reflected many of the problems typical of these areas, including lack of facilities and a dearth of professional and experienced teachers, with a great turnover in teaching staff. Furthermore, because there was only a very small, and sometimes nonexistent, representation of long time Israeli residents in these new towns, children of new and older immigrants had almost no opportunity to mix socially or in the classroom with children whose parents were integrated into Israeli society and its dominant Western culture.

Socioeconomic Status (SES) of the Family in Israel   The SES of the family after immigration to Israel was assessed by analyzing data on housing density and the father's occupation and income. (Other factors usually considered as indices of SES, such as education, have already been discussed.) Two main findings emerged from an examination of our subjects' fathers in Israel. First, the large majority belonged to lower income and lower occupational status groups. Second, for many of the fathers (51.8%), immigration to Israel resulted in a change in occupation.

The low SES of the subjects' fathers may be gauged from a comparison of the occupational distribution of the study population, compared to the distribution for the entire Israeli Jewish labor force and to Israelis born in Asia and Africa. Although professionals and white collar workers constituted 29.4% of the total Israeli population (*Statistical Abstract of Israel,* 1971), and 15.5% of the African and Asian-born labor force (*Statistical Abstract of Israel,* 1971), only 6.6% of our study population fell into these categories. The percentage of artisans and workers in industry and construction in our study population was 75.2%, nearly twice as high as the rate for the total Israeli labor force (38.9%) (*Statistical Abstract of Israel,* 1971). Of the fathers, 5.8% were unemployed, compared to 1.6% for the total Israeli Jewish population in 1970 (*Statistical Abstract of Israel,* 1971).

Fathers' Occupations and Changes after Immigration   The non-Western economic structure of the countries of origin and the occupational character of certain Jewish communities in Moslem countries are reflected in the occupational spectrum of the fathers. Before emigration, the majority of our subjects' parents lived in small communities in the countryside and were engaged in traditional occupations. If they emigrated to metropolitan areas, they remained physically, economically, and socially on the fringe of society. Nearly two-thirds of the fathers were cobblers, tailors, tanners, weavers, craftsmen, metal workers, or silversmiths; 27% were engaged in trade as merchants in textiles, clothing, oil, and nuts.

Table 1 presents a comparison in percentages of the distribution of fathers' occupations in their countries of origins and their occupations in Israel at the time of the experiment. The table clearly illustrates a transition from commercial and craftmanship occupations in their countries of origin to positions in Israel as workers in industry and construction, at all levels of skilled and unskilled work.

Although institutions of modern industrial society, such as trade unions and on-the-job training, may have cushioned the transition from the country of origin to Israel, we assume that for this particular segment of the popula-

Table 1. Distribution of fathers' occupations in their country of origin and then in Israel in adjusted percentages for total study populations, and net changes in occupational categories between distributions

Occupation	Country of Origin (%) (N = 246)	Israel (%) (N = 423)	Change in %
Professionals, executives, clerks	5.7	6.6	+0.9
Commerce	27.2	6.6	−20.6
Service workers	11.4	6.6	−4.8
Artisans	33.7	11.1	−22.6
Skilled workers in industry and construction	9.4	25.6	+16.2
Unskilled workers	9.8	38.5	+28.7
Agricultural workers	2.8	5.0	+2.2

tion from which our study sample was drawn the change from a traditional to a technological society posed serious barriers to successful absorption.

Income Although many of the manual occupations are well paid in Israel, labor market fluctuations in these fields reduce the overall income potential. Furthermore, parents working in construction and industry reported considerably lower incomes than the national average for their occupations. The large size of the families, many with five or more children, also considerably reduced their relative economic status. According to our estimate, obtained through social agencies and reports of the subjects' parents, the great majority of the families fell far below what is considered to be the national "poverty line."

Housing Density More than one-third of our sample lived under highly crowded conditions (3 or more persons per room), with a median of 2.5 persons per room for the total study population. Although this density is only slightly higher than that reported for Israelis born in Asia and Africa, it was found in only 7.8% of the total Jewish population in Israel (*Statistical Abstract of Israel,* 1971). No significant differences were found between the four research groups of the study in regard to housing density.

Family Characteristics

Family Composition and Intactness Almost all of our subjects grew up with their own families. Most of the families consisted of only two generations, parents and children, with only 10% comprising extended families, including grandparents and married siblings living together. Seventy-six percent of the families were intact with both parents present; in 24% the parents were separated, divorced, or at least one parent was deceased. This indicates a rather high degree of family disorganization as compared with the 3% one-parent families with dependent children in the general Israeli population

(Statistical Abstract 1971/2). Furthermore, according to welfare agency files (42.7% of the families in the total research population were welfare clients), a considerable number of technically intact families actually suffered from symptoms of sociofamilial disorganization due to chronic illnesses, drunkenness, breakdown of marital relationships, child abuse, and delinquency, suggesting that the term "intact" should be regarded with caution.

Family intactness was similar for the research groups. Although there were relatively more intact families in the FIE groups than in the GE groups (80.6% and 69.8%, respectively), these differences were not found to be statistically significant.

Number of Children in the Family   The majority of our subjects were members of large families. The mean number of children per family for the total research population was 6.02 (range, 1–11), as compared with only 2.1 children per family for the total Jewish population in Israel in 1969, and 3.5 children per family for Israelis born in Asia and Africa (*Statistical Abstract of Israel,* 1971). There were no statistically significant differences between the research groups in the pattern of family size.

Age of Parents   Close to 75% of the subjects' fathers and about 90% of the subjects' mothers were younger than 51 years at the beginning of the experiment. The average age of the fathers was 47 years, and, for the mothers, 41.5 years. The averages for each of the four groups were close to the averages for the total research population. Only in the residential center FIE group were the fathers and mothers a little younger (fathers, 44.5 years; mothers, 38.4 years).

Working Mothers   Seventy-seven percent of the subjects' mothers were housewives and did not work outside of the home. However, considering the very large size of their families and the many tasks required in the home, the percentage of those who did work (23%) was relatively high. Almost all the working mothers were employed as unskilled manual workers.

Welfare   Of the subjects' families, 42.7% of the total research population were welfare recipients, receiving some special assistance, such as special medical care, child care, job placement, or provision of basic household equipment, regularly or occasionally, over and above the services and allowances available to all Israeli citizens. Although there was no difference in the proportion of families on welfare between the two treatment research groups (FIE, 42.1%; GE, 32.3%), there was a significantly higher percentage of parents on welfare in the residential settings (51.9%) than in the day centers (37.4%).

The above finding was consistent with the fact that social workers referred many more of the children of the welfare clients to residential centers (27%) than to day centers (6.5%). The pattern of referral was quite distinct for the two types of settings: day center students were referred primarily by

Table 2. Average age of subjects: means by settings (RC and DC) and treatments (FIE and GE) in total research population ($N = 218$)

	RC		DC		RC + DC		FIE + GE		
	FIE	GE	FIE	GE	FIE	GE	RC	DC	Total
Mean	13.2	13.31	13.82	13.99	13.55	13.75	13.20	13.90	13.64
SD	0.76	0.67	0.85	0.59	0.89	0.69	0.72	0.74	0.81
N	44	35	70	69	114	104	79	139	218

RC, residential center; DC, day center; FIE, Instrumental Enrichment; GE, General Enrichment.

schools and related psychological services (78%); referrals to the residential centers were made almost equally by parents (36%), welfare agencies (27%), and schools (37%).

An analysis of data in welfare agency files indicated that this segment of our population was in particular distress with respect to poor health, family maladjustment, and delinquency. Sixty-four percent of the population reported sick family members, of whom 14.3% needed chronic hospitalization. There were records of juvenile delinquency and arrests in 24.3% of the families. Of these, 83% were siblings with records of minor misdemeanors or truancy. Chronic maladjustment, with marital problems, chronic unemployment, compulsive gambling, or drunkenness as its source, was reported for 42.2% of the families. In addition, for the total study population, 50.3% of the adolescents had a sibling other than our study's subject in a residential institution. The placement of two children from the same family in a residential setting indicates the extent of distress of our subjects' families.

Characteristics of Subjects

Age   Subjects in the total study population ranged in age from 12 to 15 years ($\overline{X} = 13.64$) at the beginning of the experiment. The data for each setting are provided in Table 2. Subjects in day centers (DC) were significantly older ($p < 0.001$) than their counterparts in the residential centers (RC). Modal ages for the four settings ranged between 13 and 14 years. The average age of subjects in the day centers was older than that in the residential settings. This is at least partially linked to the differential goals of the settings. The day centers are essentially trade schools providing vocational training for elementary school graduates or dropouts. In contrast, residential centers offer placement for younger adolescents, and their program is oriented accordingly (see Birk and Eflal, 1971; Feuerstein, 1971; Kashti, 1974; Kashti and Arieli, 1976).

Sex   The total research population was comprised mainly of boys. At least 75% of our subjects in all four settings were male, and in the day centers this figure was higher (88%). This proportion is unusual, given the relatively equal distribution of boys and girls of the age of 13 to 14 in the general Israeli educational system, and may be explained by the fact that the subcultures from which our study population was selected attach less importance to the education of girls for financial and cultural reasons. Girls are perceived as able to function satisfactorily in their traditional roles at home without education, while boys who need to become economically self-sufficient are viewed as needing vocational training.

In addition, more typically for boys than girls, cognitive problems are accompanied by serious behavioral problems that disrupt the classroom and produce conflicts both at school and at home. Thus, there is a greater readiness to refer and place the boys in special educational settings than is the case for girls with similar cognitive and academic difficulties.

Country of Origin and Age at Immigration

Country of Origin   In contrast to their parents, of whom 99% were foreign-born immigrants to Israel, the majority of the subjects in the research population were born in Israel (54.8%). Of the remainder most were immigrants from Asia and Africa, and only 3.7% were of European birth, an exceptionally small proportion for the Israeli educational system. When analyzed differentially by treatment, significantly more ($p < 0.01$) Israeli-born subjects were found in the GE groups (72.1%) than in the FIE groups (38.9%), and those in the GE group born outside of Israel had immigrated at an earlier age. Only slightly more Israeli-born subjects were in the residential settings (61.5%) than in the day centers (51.1%), and this difference was not statistically significant.

Immigration   Of our subjects, 69.1% were residents in Israel before the age of 6 years, when formal schooling begins. Thus, we concluded that our subjects were largely first generation Israelis who had been in the country at least 6 or 7 years before the experiment began. Nine percent of the subjects arrived in Israel during the 4 years preceding the experiment, having had substantial educational experience outside of Israel, assuming that they had been attending school in their countries of origin since age 6. Only 3.2% were very recent immigrants, arriving a year or two before the experiment, who could be expected to experience language difficulties. In fact, even though most of their parents had arrived in Israel as adults speaking in a foreign language, 63.2% of the children reported speaking Hebrew in their homes (13.0% spoke Arabic; 14.4%, European languages; and 9.3%, Persian and other languages).

The residential versus day center comparison revealed only a slight difference in the age of subjects at immigration, with residential center subjects arriving earlier than the day center subjects but not significantly so. Of the FIE subjects, 16% were very recent immigrants (arriving in Israel between the ages of 9 and 12), as compared with less than 2% of subjects in the GE group. In the FIE/DC setting in particular, a large group of subjects were recent immigrants (17.1%). To the extent that long term residence in Israel contributes to the resolution of various problems of adjustment for the immigrant (family, school, etc.), these findings favored, at least initially, the performance of the GE groups over the FIE groups in the present experiment.

Educational and Social History   A substantial portion of the subjects, although still formally enrolled in regular schools, had in practice become dropouts, with sporadic and highly irregular school attendance. When present in school, they tended to present behavior problems, and teacher intolerance of their disruptive school behavior, coupled with low expectations for their academic achievement, made positive learning experiences unlikely. Nearly 25% of subjects interviewed at a later stage for follow-up purposes reported repeating classes while still in regular schools. More than twice as many residential center subjects as day center subjects (RC = 36.4% versus DC = 17.5%, $p < 0.05$) repeated classes, which is an indication of the lower level of cognitive functioning of RC subjects. No differences were found in this respect between the FIE and GE groups.

In addition to school problems, our subjects frequently had adjustment problems in their community, as was also the case for their families. In the total study population, 15.4% of the subjects reported having been on probation at some time. As these were self-reports, we may assume that this is an understatement of the probation problem. Obviously, probation is only one outcome of delinquent behavior, occurring at the end of a legal and administrative process. We may assume that the actual amount of delinquency was greater, perhaps much greater, than the reported probation frequencies. There were only slightly more subjects on probation in the GE (16.3%) than in the FIE programs (14.6%), but more than twice as many in residential centers (22.2%) compared to day centers (11.0%). This finding was highly consistent with the general definition of the residential group as more dependent, maladapted, and socially and behaviorally disturbed than day center subjects.

Psychometric Characteristics

In order to complete the description of our study population, the results from a variety of tests obtained on the pilot study at the pretest level of the experiment are briefly presented below. Before considering the results of any particular tests two points should be emphasized. First, IQ measures are typically employed in the placement and treatment of children from the population from which the experimental sample was drawn. Furthermore, the global IQ score has a considerable influence on the manner in which these children are perceived. Second, contrary to the generally accepted approach, it is our contention that the population with whom we were concerned and whom we have described as culturally deprived manifests specific deficient functions at the peripheral level (input and output phases of the mental act) rather than a general inability to function at the elaborational level. Thus, it is a reduced need for precision or impulsive, inappropriate, and unsystematic exploratory behavior at the input level, for example, that leads to poor test performance, rather than an inability to grasp and execute the necessary logical operations implicit in various assessment tests. A theoretical account of the factors that produce the syndrome of cultural deprivation and its nature has been provided in previous chapters. This account may now be supplemented by some empirical data concerning the level and nature of functioning of our study population.

Two sets of IQ data were collected. In the initial pilot study the MILTA IQ test (Ortar, 1966) was administered to 248 subjects. The MILTA test was developed in Israel and consists of four subtests: vocabulary, sentence completion, concept formation, and numerical problems. All the subtests involve considerable verbal ability as apart from the vocabulary and sentence completion subtests, the concept formation tasks require the elimination of two words from a group of six, and the numerical problems require comprehension of the written problems. The percentage of correct answers for each subtest was as follows: vocabulary, 32%; sentence completion, 30%; concept formation, 24%; numerical problems, 45%. The total mean IQ score was 67 (SD = 11.4), placing the subjects within the EMR and borderline range. Virtually the same results were obtained on a comparable sample of 498 culturally deprived subjects (see Feuerstein, 1978, p. 7), both with respect to total IQ score and the percentage of correct answers for each subtest (IQ, 67; vocabulary, 35%; sentence completion, 32%; concept formation, 28%; numerical problems, 47%). Much the same picture was obtained from the results of the Primary Mental Abilities (PMA) test (Thurstone, 1965) administered to the experimental subjects at the pretest level. Distribution of IQ scores derived from the PMA is provided in Table 3, and the mean percentage of correct answers for each subtest of the PMA is provided in Table 4. The total mean IQ for the PMA ($N = 218$) was 80. From Table 3 it is clear that more than half of the sample fell below the 85 IQ cut-off point. Israeli norms for the PMA scores indicate that the experimental subjects at ages 13 and 14 years were performing lower than children 3 and 4 years younger.

The superior performance by the subjects on the PMA as compared with the MILTA appears to be attributable to the inclusion of nonverbal subtests in the PMA. Tests that require verbal skills, particularly reading comprehension, place the culturally deprived child at a clear disadvantage. This is reflected in the subtest scores of the PMA in Table 4. The lowest percentage of correct scores was obtained on the vocabulary subtest (47%). In comparison, the pictures subtest, which is a measure of receptive vocabu-

Table 3.   Distribution of IQ scores in percentages derived from Primary Mental Abilities (PMA) test scores at pretest level ($N = 218$)

PMA IQ	%	Cum%
−55	0.5	0.5
56–60	2.8	3.3
61–65	2.8	6.1
66–70	5.1	11.2
71–75	14.2	25.4
76–80	15.1	40.5
81–85	13.7	54.2
86–90	12.4	66.6
91–95	16.9	83.5
96–100	9.6	93.1
101–105	5.0	98.1
106+	1.4	99.5

Table 4.   Mean percentage of correct answers for Primary Mental Abilities (PMA) subtests and PMA total

PMA subject	%
Vocabulary	47
Pictures	69
Numbers	69
Addition	56
Spatial relations	48
Figure grouping	67
Word grouping	67
Perceptual speed	63
Total	59

lary, yielded the highest score (69%). The same trend is evident with respect to the word (57%) and figure (67%) grouping subtests. Also, on the PMA test, the numerical problems subtest yielded a higher score (69%) than the addition subtest (56%), again suggesting that the overall low performance of the subjects was less a product of elaborative difficulties and more a consequence of peripheral deficiencies, such as a diminished need for precision. The results obtained on the Minnesota Perceptuo-Diagnostic test (MPD) lend further support for the view that the low level of functioning of the subjects should not be attributed solely to deficient elaborative processes. The MPD provides a measure of the degree of rotation of a copied figure. Fuller and Laird (1963) maintain that the MPD is culture-free and that, within limits, education, intelligence, and reading ability do not influence the results. According to the cut-off scores established for the MPD, 24% of the subjects scored in the normal range (<20), 68% in the range designated "emotionally disturbed" (21–54), and 8% in the "schizophrenic" range (>54). Fuller and Laird point out that children with IQ scores of less than 80 often rotate the figures more than subjects in the 80–110 IQ range and that caution should be exercised when interpreting their results. However, irrespective of whether the results are interpreted in terms of emotional or perceptual problems, they indicate a deficiency in functioning that does not appear to involve elaborational processes in any direct way.

Achievement levels of our population were assessed by means of a specially designed instrument, the Project Achievement Battery. This test is described later in this chapter. For the present purpose the results of two subscales, reading and arithmetic, are considered. Reading was assessed by means of three progressively more difficult tests. At level 1, the test was based on the identification of written labels from drawings of familiar objects with a few brief and simple instructions. This level is characteristic of the reading achievement of grade 1 and mid-grade 2 pupils. At level 2, simple comprehension is introduced. Subjects have to choose between four alternative answers to questions based on simple statements expressed in one or two sentences. At level 3, more complex comprehension is required and the questions are based on short paragraphs.

Seventy-five percent of the questions were answered by 92% of the subjects at level 1; by 29% at level 2; and by only 5% of the subjects at level 3. At the other end of the scale, less than 25% of the questions were answered by 2% of the subjects at level 1; by 8% at level 2; and by only 30% at level 3. Thus, it is evident that many of the subjects were barely literate and the vast majority were functioning well below the accepted levels for their age.

On tests of mastery of the four basic arithmetic operations, the subjects achieved a mean of 87% in addition, 60% in subtraction, 55% in multiplication, and 34% in division. These tests consisted of items that required only a knowledge of techniques without any problem solving and are usually mastered by fourth-grade regular pupils. Clearly, only addition had been mastered by the subjects, accompanied by marginal performance on subtraction and multiplication and clear failure in division.

Summary

Our subjects and their families were at a very low socioeconomic level. Occupational status, income, education and literacy, housing density, and place of residence were not only low when compared to the general Israeli Jewish population, but were also low in comparison to their reference group of immigrants from Asia and North Africa. A special Prime Minister's Committee on Children and Youth in Distress (1973) defined social distress by the following three criteria: 8 years, or less, of education for the father; housing density of 3 or more persons per room; and an average income per person of under IL 140 (about $30) per month in 1968/1969. They found that 9% of all the children in Israel fulfilled all three criteria, while 53% of all the children were in "social distress," based upon one or more of these criteria. By these standards, the majority of children in our total research population were socially distressed.

In Israel, low SES was combined with the stress of immigration and absorption, and a considerable number of the families manifested poor adjustment, such as dependency on welfare institutions, chronic poor health, and delinquency. Social disorganization, however, had apparently already set in abroad for our study population, when the larger and more disadvantaged segments of the population were caught in the process of rapid social change. Internal migration, urbanization, and impoverishment, together with an uncontrolled encounter with western colonial culture (especially French culture in Morocco), led to alienation from traditional values, norms, and social institutions (see Chapter 2; see also Feuerstein and Richelle, 1963). Old close-knit communities and extended family networks were disrupted. The traditional patterns of socialization and cultural transmission were obstructed. Yet no new patterns of socialization compatible with the demands imposed by a society dominated by western culture had been established in the North African or Asian countries where most parents grew up, or in Israel where the majority of the subjects were born. Many parents apparently lived in a "culture of transition" in which old values were no longer valid or, at least, were not supported by the social structure. Thus, for example, although a large family was still religiously and socially meaningful, the economic and educational implications were sometimes too difficult to cope with under the existing conditions. New values were superficially adopted with the emphasis only on their external manifestations.

All of these elements of social disorganization may lead, even in the absence of material poverty, to the syndrome of cultural deprivation, as defined and explained in Chapter 2. Thus, conditions of rapid social change, cultural shock, poverty, and stressful experiences may eventually drain parents' resources to act meaningfully as educators and agents of mediated learning.

It should be emphasized that the difficulties manifested by the families of our study population illustrate the syndrome of low modifiability typical of the culturally deprived individual, once he is exposed to conditions requiring from him a change in order to adapt. From this point of view our study population differs meaningfully — as is reflected in psychometric tests, school achievement, and other behavioral parameters — from the majority of culturally different immigrants from the same or similar countries whose adaptation was much more successful.

THE EDUCATIONAL SETTINGS: EDUCATIONAL IDEOLOGY AND PRACTICE

The experimental and control settings consisted of residential centers and day centers. This choice was made in order to study the differential efficiency of Instrumental Enrichment in settings that varied from both a theoretical and a practical point of view. The second of our hypotheses, predicting superior performance in residential centers, was derived from earlier observations of these settings.

Residential Center

The residential center along with the kibbutz movement provided the original frameworks into which Youth Aliyah has absorbed more than 140,000 children over the past 45 years. The youth village, as it is called in Israel, represents an outgrowth of the communal, self-governing, group-oriented lifestyle produced by the kibbutz movement. The majority of youth villages in Israel were founded by members of kibbutzim, often adjacent to kibbutz land in order to prepare youngsters to join the kibbutz movement after their graduation. This relationship has strongly marked not only the geographical and architectural structure of the residential setting, but has generated a set of goals that has an impact on three major aspects of life: in the youth village's group life, with the individual oriented toward becoming a part of the group and adhering to the superordinate group goals during the period of his residence in the youth village and, in many cases, afterwards; in academic achievement, in which group goals, rather than individual needs, are emphasized; and in work, which entails the active participation and contribution of the individual to the upkeep of the community. Although youth villages have been established with many minor variations, common to all are these three main goals.

General Approach   The underlying philosophy of the residential center included in the study, is the active-modification approach, which, in essence, considers the individual, even at adolescence, as amenable to significant change. The goal, therefore, is to produce the necessary changes in his structure of thinking and behavior that will render him more adaptable to his environment. Neither the manifest level of functioning, nor personal characteristics, nor, particularly, the behavioral repertoire of the individual, are considered immutable for the purpose of setting educational and instructional goals. Rather, they are all targets for intervention in order to produce the desired changes for better adaptation.

Change in Environment   The youth village (residential setting) placement involves a detachment from the familiar and habitual framework of life that is normally provided by the family, extended family, neighborhood, and community institutions. This detachment has important implications, some of which are negative but many of which are positive, because it constitutes an attempt to produce an environment very different from the one familiar to the individual. In the case of the culturally deprived and socially disadvantaged child, it means removing him from the locus of deprivation which, for many adolescents, is a *sine qua non* for a significant shift in their cognitive structure, level of functioning, aspirations, and social adaptation.

Care Program   The youth village, by virtue of being a total-care program, produces a powerful environment in which value systems, attitudes, and ways of thinking are not only taught formally, *ex cathedra,* but applied immediately in all aspects of the adolescent's life (see Bloom, 1964). The youth village provides unusually great consistency and carryover from one area of life to another with each activity permeated by similar values. Life in the youth village is mainly organized around group care programs. In contrast to many residential settings, in which groups are formed because of the geographical proximity of its members, in the Israeli Youth Aliyah village group-care programs are an expression of a specific philosophy. This philosophy is grounded in the belief that the best way to reach the adolescent educationally, morally, and even in terms of instruction, is through the mediation of the group. The guided and controlled group acts as a transmitter and amplifier of the values held by the educational body. For a large portion of the time spent in the residential setting, the group experience supplants the more typical environments of adolescence and becomes the primary socializing agent.

Induced Regression   The youth village provides an optimally isolated and protective environment that permits a process we refer to as "induced regression" to occur. Briefly, this term refers to the need of the individual, who behaves in a quasi-adult way, to indulge in a state of socially acceptable and encouraged regression to an earlier stage of social behavior and development. When the adolescent, who regards himself as an adult, is confronted in a school situation with the need to enter into a relationship typical of a considerably younger child, a state of tension and internal conflict is created that may prevent him from learning. Thus, in order to learn to read and write, the individual must accept a state of relative dependency on the teacher. This role is totally at variance with the needs of the adolescent to assert himself as an independent, self-determined individual. Although the culturally deprived adolescent functions at a low cognitive level and performs poorly at school, he nevertheless regards himself as similar to an adult in terms of needs, aspirations, rights, and life-style. One may even define the need of the adolescent to perceive and assert himself as an adult as inversely proportional to his level of cognitive functioning and his academic achievement. The lower he performs, the older and more independent will he try to appear. The cognitive deficiencies provide the motive for his search to compensate for his low performance level by indulging in adult-like pleasure-seeking behavior. Thus, the adolescent is unable to inhibit or delay immediate gratification in favor of pursuing long term goals to improve his performance level. The perceived levels of maturity, independence, and assumed adult roles of the adolescent conflict with those of the elementary school pupil, which are imposed by entering a program aimed at redevelopment. The conflict produced by these discrepant roles can only be reduced by the adolescent indulging in more childish and immature behaviors. In order for this to occur, induced regression is necessary. The framework of the youth village permits the individual to adopt social roles that conform with his low level of functioning, and, hence, he is able to take advantage of the learning situation. Induced regression serves to remove the role conflict that is particularly stressful in the culturally deprived adolescent because of the disparate levels of social as opposed to cognitive functioning.

Day Centers

The active-modification approach, typical of the residential setting, is replaced, to a large extent, in the day center by a passive-acceptant approach. This is basically reflected in the attempt to use the current level of functioning of the individual as the best predictor of his future development. Rather than trying to induce meaningful changes in the individual, the day center tends to accept his level of functioning and motivation, and this serves as the major determinant of the choice of activities and types of investment in his education. Academic activities are given limited emphasis in day center programs, both quantitatively in terms of hours, and qualitatively in terms of the nature of teaching and pressure exerted on the individual to achieve proficiency. The emphasis is removed from the academic activities to vocational training. This approach is reflected both in the completely open admission policies, with a minimum standard required, and in terms of a greater readiness to accept absenteeism, often the result of temporary employment opportunities. The passive-acceptant approach is also manifested in the encouragement given to the individual to grasp and accept his limitations in order to establish for him more realistic goals. One example is the fact that no procedures exist and no encouragement is offered the individual to strive for reintegration into regular schools or to prepare himself through appropriate training for further academic experiences.

In contradistinction to the residential center, the day center represents an attempt to help the socioculturally deprived and low functioning adolescent dropout, without radically and totally changing the environment in which he was reared, and provides him with a program that corresponds to his current manifest level of functioning. The establishment of educational facilities within the community was for many families a response to the immediate and practical need to prepare their child for employment.

Unlike the programs in the residential setting, in which there is intense group pressure to follow common goals, and even to maintain close contacts after graduation, the day centers stress individual goals. Knowing that he will be referred directly to his work site, and having many ties and daily involvements outside of the day center, the individual is less inclined to identify with or invest in group-oriented activities. As a consequence, there are fewer superordinate group goals to take priority over individual goals. This lack of common goals leaves room for self-generated aims that are more likely to emanate from the street culture than from the value system of the school.

The concept of induced regression, which we described as a process inherent in the residential center, is not likely to occur as easily and naturally within the day center. The need of the adolescent to become, as soon as possible, proficient and productive in a vocation consistent with his current level of functioning is promoted and encouraged. The greatest investment of effort is in vocational training, and behaviors that reflect earlier stages of development, such as dependency and play, are considered inappropriate by both students and staff.

Membership in an adolescent peer group, in which the need for assuming quasi-adult roles is very strong, does not facilitate induced regression toward the levels of functioning needed for the redevelopment of the deficient academic functioning. The "tough guy" on the street will not easily give up his image at school by adopting that of a submissive child ready to fulfill the role of the student who identifies himself with the low level of activity required by the program offered to him.

It is interesting to note that previous studies (see Arieli, 1974; Feuerstein et al., 1976; Kashti, 1974), comparing residential centers and day centers for the culturally disadvantaged, revealed that the students in the day centers start off at an *advantage* with respect to criteria of psychometric performance, achievement, and demographic conditions. At the end of their training, however, they emerge at a disadvantage with respect to the criteria of language, achievement, IQ scores, and the like. One way to explain the differences observed in the development of the two groups is by invoking the divergent characteristics of the two settings (Kashti and Arieli, 1976). Thus, we reached our hypothesis that Instrumental Enrichment would be less effective in the day centers than in the residential centers.

EXPERIMENTAL IMPLEMENTATION OF
INSTRUMENTAL ENRICHMENT IN THE CLASSROOM:
A CRITICAL, QUALITATIVE EVALUATION

Research Design for Implementation
of the Instrumental Enrichment Program

The research design for the experimental groups required the teaching of Instrumental Enrichment in residential and day centers (RC/FIE and DC/FIE) for 5 hours weekly, over a period of 2 school years. To this end, teachers in both settings were to be trained in the theory and practice of Instrumental Enrichment. Both preliminary and basic training, with an emphasis on the underlying theoretical framework and mastery of the actual instruments, were to be conducted in intensive workshops. Ongoing in-service training was to be provided in weekly classroom visits and bi-weekly staff meetings devoted to didactics (see Chapter 9).

The design entailed the provision of a supervisor at both research sites, who would also function as a participant-observer; an Instrumental Enrichment master teacher, who would visit each research site twice a week to assist individual students and enable them to keep up with their respective classes; and a rapporteur, whose role would be to report the entire project. Full records were to be kept by each member of the Hadassah-Wizo-Canada Research Institute project staff to provide material for ongoing evaluation of the program.

Teachers engaged in the research would be asked to maintain contact with the Hadassah-Wizo-Canada Research Institute through two regular reports: one weekly, evaluating the Instrumental Enrichment material and its effect on the cognitive functions of the students; and one monthly, describing classroom occurrences, problems encountered in the course of teaching, and evidence of changes in performance and behavior.

The total intervention program, in the course of 2 school years, would consist of 14 instruments: *Organization of Dots; Orientation in Space I, II, and III; Categorization; Comparisons; Analytic Perception; Family Relations; Temporal Relations; Numerical Progressions; Instructions; Illustrations; Representational Stencil Design;* and *Syllogisms*. It was estimated that students would complete seven instruments in each school year.

Implementation of Instrumental Enrichment with Teachers

The actual implementation of the intervention program did not vary essentially from its design. However, because of the dynamic nature of the study, its protracted period, and its setting in established educational institutions, a number of predictable, as well as unanticipated, divergences and problems occurred and are described in the qualitative evaluation of the project.

Teacher Selection   The research design required that homeroom teachers teach Instrumental Enrichment to their own classes. There was, therefore, no selection on the basis of classroom experience, familiarity with the material, teaching ability, personality, or attitudes regarding the potential for modifiability of retarded performers. In fact, there was a wide range of diversity with respect to these parameters among the teachers who taught Instrumental Enrichment in the experimental settings.

FIE Teacher Training

Objectives   The objectives of the teacher training for the research project were essentially similar to those formulated previously for classroom implementation of FIE (see Chapter 9). In addition, however, because of their participation in a research-oriented program, teachers were trained in assessment procedures and in the essentials of reporting for feedback and critical analysis of classroom occurrences and student behavior.

Workshops   Seven teachers from the DC/FIE group and seven teachers from the RC/FIE group participated in a 10-day workshop in Instrumental Enrichment during the summer of 1971, immediately before the implementation of the FIE program. The inclusion of neophytes to both general teaching and Instrumental Enrichment necessitated expansion of the planned training to include subjects in psychology and education, in addition to the theory and materials of FIE. During the first year, there were 3 additional days of intensive workshops. There were 12 days of intensive workshop during the second year. Because only four of the original seven teachers at each site returned to their respective schools at the start of the second year, it was necessary to train two new FIE teachers at the DC/FIE site. Those teachers who were unable to participate fully in workshops were individually taught instruments by the supervisor in the field.

Biweekly Meetings   The Hadassah-Wizo-Canada Research Institute staff of supervisor, rapporteur, and master teacher met biweekly after school with the principal and FIE research teachers at each site. The agenda always included reports by the teachers of the work in progress, discussions of any problems encountered with the material, with the didactics of their delivery, or with classroom management. Instruments were reviewed and taught.

Reports of the Institute staff indicate that the atmosphere of the meetings changed in the course of the 2 years as staff members and FIE teachers became better acquainted with each other and with the material. Teachers became more outspoken, active, and open, increasingly taking the initiative in discussions. They became more objective in their analyses, reflecting increased self-confidence and ease with the FIE material. Discussions of problems of classroom management, didactics, and techniques were replaced by anecdotal descriptions of changes in student attitudes and behavior and spontaneous student use of FIE-related principles, strategies, and concepts in other areas.

In-service Training at Research Sites   Training was continued in-service by the supervisor at each research site. The supervisor visited each FIE class once weekly, intervening upon request, and offered guidance based on the post-lesson critique. In order to ascertain if observed teacher-student interactions were a phenomenon unique to FIE, the supervisor also observed both the FIE teacher instructing other subject matter and the class with other teachers in vocational and academic subjects.

The dependence on the Institute staff decreased as the teachers' experience with the material grew. Increased feelings of competence were reflected in the teachers' final evaluations of the program, in which the majority agreed that a weekly classroom visit was unnecessarily frequent during the second year of the program. There was unanimity, however, in their expressed desire for a continued liaison with the Hadassah-Wizo-Canada Research Institute as a source to which to turn for assistance in diagnosing the deficiencies in cognitive functions specific to some of the retarded performers in their classes.

Teacher Training at the Comparison Sites

At the comparison (General Enrichment) sites, there were three meetings annually between the Hadassah-Wizo-Canada Research staff and the site personnel in order to explain the nature of the study and the basic philosophy of the Instrumental Enrichment program. General in-service training, organized by the institutions themselves, took place frequently, however. These sessions were devoted mainly to methodology, fostering motivation, and general improvement of classroom interactions.

Explanation of the Instrumental Enrichment program at RC/GE was facilitated by the presence in that comparison site of three people who had previous experience and training in FIE. Using them as teachers of General Enrichment aroused the fear of confounding the results of GE exposure. However, our agreement to use the regular homeroom teachers for the whole research population precluded a negative selection and their elimination from the program. Their participation was neither planned nor desirable, but a fact of *in vivo* research.

Implementation of Instrumental Enrichment in the Classroom

Instrumental Enrichment was introduced into seven classes at the RC/FIE site and into 11 classes at the DC/FIE site at the beginning of the 1971 school year, immediately after the subjects were pretested. In addition to those who were present for the entire 2-year period, the target population also included students who were not eligible for inclusion in the final evaluation because they were to graduate at the end of the first year and those who entered the school during the second year of the research. (These students received FIE, but they are not included in the research data.) With the graduation of two classes from RC/FIE and three from DC/FIE sites, the research program continued in four classes of RC/FIE and six of DC/FIE during the second year.

Sequence of Instruments   All the research classes received *Organization of Dots, Orientation in Space I,* and *Comparisons* as the first set of the program. The second set of instruments, presented simultaneously, were *Orientation in Space II* and *III, Analytic Perception,* and *Categorization.* The third set consisted of *Numerical Progressions, Family Relations,* and *Illustrations. Instructions, Temporal Relations,* and *Representational Stencil Design* comprised the fourth set. *Syllogisms,* although not listed in the preliminary design, was introduced into some of the classes at the end of the second year. In order to provide a variety of modalities and minimize frustration in cases of specific deficiencies, the students worked on the three instruments of each set, in rotation.

Pace in the Study of Instruments   The total number of instruments completed in the course of the experiment differed from class to class. At the end of the first year, all classes had completed at least five instruments; by the end of the second year, the majority of classes had completed most of the instruments, except for *Representational Stencil Design.* The number of instruments completed was contingent upon four interrelated factors: the initial class level; the actual number of hours of FIE; the pace maintained by the teacher and students, and the experience of the teacher.

Initial Class Level   Classes in which there were illiterates were able to work on nonverbal instruments without undue difficulty. However, in other instruments, teachers were required to read the instructions aloud and to provide individual assistance in writing the answers, which slowed the pace appreciably.

Cancellations of FIE Lessons   There were both scheduled and unscheduled deviations from the design caused by institution-centered and extracurricular activities and teacher absences. In distinction from other subjects for which substitutes are easily available in the event of an absent teacher, the scarcity of trained FIE teachers at the time of the experiment made substitution difficult. With sufficient notice, FIE teachers filled in for one another or the lesson was conducted by the master teacher; otherwise, lessons were canceled. Both pregnancies and reserve military service raised the anticipated number of teacher absences during the course of the project.

Absenteeism   The overall absenteeism of students was generally low, although relatively higher among the DC/FIE learners, especially in the winter. One technique for eliminating differences caused by absences or by slower performance was to periodically set aside a lesson for completion and "catching up." Another was to send the student to the master teacher for individual work. Only 10% of the students needed repetitive help; the rest were able to proceed with their regular classes after one session with the master teacher.

Student Mobility   Pace was also affected by student mobility during the course of the school year. Some students were shifted from one class to another; others, newly enrolled, were admitted into ongoing classes. The admission of new students into an FIE class was usually a disruptive factor. Although the newcomers were not included in the research, they required individual aid from the master teacher in the acquisition of the basic FIE skills and/or sufficient familiarity with the material to permit their participation in the lessons without impeding the progress of the class. Students in the experiment were also used to tutor the newcomers, a valuable experience for strengthening their self-image.

Pace in Teaching   Supervisor reports indicate that some teachers had difficulty in balancing the time spent in work on the instrument pages against time devoted to class discussions, and time spent in review against time given to the presentation of new material. Even veteran teachers sometimes succumbed to tangential discussion, and, although their lessons were "lively" and "interesting," the pace was slowed appreciably.

Second Year of the Experiment

Regrouping   At the start of the second year of research, classes were reorganized on the basis of various emerging factors, including vocational choice (DC/FIE), language and mathematics achievement (RC/FIE), and local criteria. The regrouping introduced new students without prior FIE experience into FIE groups, and new teachers (DC/FIE) who had never before taught the material into veteran classes. Not all of the experimental classes had proceeded at the same pace and completed the same instruments during the first year, and not all of the students within each class had attained the same level of mastery. These factors created difficulties in finding a single entry point with the second-year classes after regrouping. It was necessary to start certain instruments anew if the majority of the class had not completed them, and to omit others if too many of the class had been exposed to them in the first year.

Classroom Management   To the extent that there were difficulties in classroom management, their source differed from the first to the second year of the experiment. Reported behavior problems at the start of the program were partially attributable to the general inexperience, unfamiliarity with FIE, and the personal teaching styles of the teachers. Students new to the institutions had not yet internalized the norms of acceptable behavior, and students unfamiliar with FIE took advantage of the relative freedom of the lesson. By the end of the first trimester of the program, such management problems had abated.

Teachers did not complain of behavior problems at the start of the second year of the program, but of management problems *per se*. Classes were generally more difficult to teach because of the varied FIE experience of the students. Again, various strategies had to be used to achieve homogeneity of a sort. These included individual lessons with the master teacher, peer tutoring, and class review of key pages of some of the instruments. With the completion of the first set of second year instruments, problems in classroom management directly attributable to the FIE program were rare.

Qualitative Evaluation of FIE in the Classroom

The qualitative evaluation of the FIE program in the classroom is based on weekly and monthly teacher reports, daily annotated logs of the participant-observer and rapporteur, weekly reports of the master teacher, questionnaires and interviews with both students and teachers, and transcripts of biweekly staff meetings and of the final joint meeting for evaluation in which all the research teachers and Hadassah-Wizo-Canada Research Institute staff members participated.

Despite the aforementioned problems, over which we had no control, that are typical of any educational experiment executed within an institutional framework, the Instrumental Enrichment program was deemed successful by its participants.

Student Participation

Students and teachers alike reported that the atmosphere in FIE lessons was different from that in other classes. Without the pressure of grades and fear of failure, students were more relaxed. With the acceptance of their ideas and comments as an integral part of the fabric of the lesson, they were more willing to express themselves verbally and to contribute freely to discussions. Self-criticism and independent work became more and more evident. The teachers reported that the students showed increased self-confidence which, in turn, led to a willingness to cope with more difficult problems.

Students "surprised" their teachers by their prolonged concentration and absorption in their work. They also began to read critically and to analyze material. Each time they found a typographical error in one of the instruments — and, at that stage of the experiment, there were still many — they did not hesitate to notify the Research Institute by phone or letter. They were also alert to any contradiction or error of the teacher — a less welcome surprise for the teachers — and were no longer ready to accept passively all that was said to them. Teachers also reported that students were bridging from other areas into FIE lessons and vice versa.

Teacher and Student Attitudes toward FIE

The reported evaluations should not be interpreted to imply that either teacher or student attitudes and motivation were uniform and unanimously positive during the entire course of the experiment.

Teacher Attitudes toward Instrumental Enrichment Initially the teachers expressed ambivalence toward the FIE program. Although willing to give it a "fair try," they expressed a number of reservations. Most of these revolved around the fact that the FIE program required five periods out of the total devoted each week to academic subjects (day center, 16 hours; residential center, 24 hours). They felt that the time could better be devoted to improving basic skills in reading, writing, vocabulary, and mathematics, and to learning the academic curriculum. Some of the teachers were skeptical, not only regarding the transfer of FIE principles to other academic subjects, but of the ability of the students to master the exercises as well.

Three months after the start of the experiment, much of the original teacher resistance had decreased overtly. They reported a restraint of impulsivity, the spontaneous use of concepts previously not in the repertoire, and a general enthusiasm for FIE on the part of students. However, there was still evidence of teacher ambivalence and conflict. A great part of the first year's work by the supervisor and the Hadassah-Wizo-Canada Research Institute staff addressed itself to trying to change the original attitudes, preconceptions, and didactics of the teachers.

Much of the attitude change that occurred was the result of the achievements of the students. Teachers reported increased student motivation, alertness, and intellectual curiosity, a readiness to work independently, and an increased sense of personal responsibility. Similarly, teachers were impressed by the students' ability to define problems and plan ahead, and to compare spontaneously. However, many of the teachers missed traditional tests and grades as a basis for evaluation of mastery and progress. They needed the constant reinforcement of encouragement and assistance in recognizing the changes occurring within the target population.

As desirable actions and reactions on the part of the students were gradually internalized, the teachers seemed often unable to recognize that they represented a modification of the students' initial behavior, having lost sight of the original performance levels. This became more pronounced at the start of the second year of the experiment, when second-year teachers, unfamiliar with the initial baselines for behavior and academic achievements, were unable to evaluate the true progress of their students.

In addition, teachers' expectations underwent a pronounced shift. Transcripts of teachers' meetings indicate that at the beginning of the research they argued that the instruments would be too hard for their students. In the middle of the second year, they maintained that the instruments were too easy, despite the actual increased difficulty and complexity of second-year instruments. At the start, the teachers had underestimated their students' potential for modifiability. Later, after observing substantial changes in some of the cognitive functions, they had difficulty in evaluating the nature and extent of the remaining deficiencies.

In their final evaluations, the research teachers claimed that they had worked harder in FIE than in other subjects they taught, but that they felt "greater satisfaction" in their work. Some teachers indicated that they were using the FIE methodology in their teaching of other subjects. All felt that their students had benefited from participation in the program. They expressed a willingness to continue to teach FIE in nonresearch settings in the future. The validity of this attitude of overall satisfaction is supported by the continuation to date of FIE in all four of the institutions of the study and the continuation in the program of the research teachers in the period that has elapsed since the cessation of the study.

Attitudes toward and motivation for FIE initially differed between the RC/FIE and DC/FIE classes as a result of the teachers' differential experience with the program. In the DC/FIE group, teachers were more ambivalent. The more difficult and content-free instruments triggered doubts, anxiety, and open resistance. However, the students' ability to reach a level of abstraction resulted in increased optimism about the capacity of the children to undergo the desired changes. When students who had participated in the research program did well on entrance examinations to other institutions of learning, and more were accepted than in any previous year, the principals and some teachers attributed this success to the effects of FIE. These teachers, the first to implement FIE, did not have the benefit of previous experience with the success of the program and therefore experienced a longer period of doubt and ambivalence than do the FIE teachers of today.

Student Attitudes and Motivation   Motivation levels fluctuated and differed both between students and within the same student as a function of insight, particular instrument, period in the research program, and teaching approach.

The DC/FIE population was oriented to vocational subjects, which they saw as the *raison d'être* of their schooling. They were interested in learning a trade and tolerated the academic subjects only to the extent to which they could see a direct connection between the subject matter and their immediate needs. Mathematics and language were considered "important." Although they enjoyed Instrumental Enrichment, they regarded the program as taking time from their immediate and primary goal. With insight into the contribution of FIE to the more successful mastery of topics related to their vocational needs, they became more enthusiastic.

The RC/FIE population was less vocation oriented, but they were concerned about being accepted at other educational institutions upon graduation from the residential center. They also attributed great importance to mathematics, language, and traditional subject matter, and had to gain insight into the relationship between the FIE material and their personal needs in order to enhance their original positive motivation for the FIE program.

Paradoxically, the less an instrument resembled traditional subject matter (which despite its importance in furthering immediate goals was strongly associated with failure), the more immediate attraction it had. When the instrument or the methodology with which it was taught resembled a "regular" lesson, there was a decline in motivation. There was also a tendency among the students to react to such lessons with anxiety, aggressiveness, reduced concentration, and copying (see Yando and Zigler, 1971).

The opinions of their neighborhood peers attending regular schools also had an influence on the students' motivation and attitudes. "Why us?" was a question often repeated by RC/FIE students who returned from their leaves at home. There was an implicit stigma attached to being singled out as a recipient of an intervention program. Yet they were ambivalent because they enjoyed FIE. The conflict was partially resolved when they confronted their taunting so-called "normal" peers or siblings with the more difficult pages they had mastered, and the so-called normals failed to solve the tasks.

By the middle of the first year of the experiment, the teachers and participant observers reported that the students "saw value in the program," and felt they were "being helped by the program." When teachers were absent, students were distressed about missing FIE lessons and requested that the substitute teacher provide the lessons. There was a reported decline in absenteeism among students at the DC/FIE site, who claimed they had come to school, even if not well, because they did not want to miss FIE. Some students voluntarily came to their teachers or to the master teacher during recess or free periods to ask that they be allowed to work on pages.

At the start of the second year, there was a brief but general decline in student motivation. Because of the redistribution of classes (discussed above), it was necessary to teach pages of instruments that a portion of the class had completed during the first year. The veteran students saw a lack of progress in the enforced repetition. The motivation level was restored by using some of these students as aides, by pointing out how much more rapidly and correctly pages were completed, and, eventually, by progress into new material.

By the middle of the second year, with *Syllogisms* and *Representational Stencil Design,* the supervisor and teachers reported that the motivation level of the students was high. The instruments were perceived as challenging, and the students felt that they were able to cope. Positive attitudes were also reinforced when the students applied for admission to other educational institutions. They reported that the interviewers had told them that they knew "how to analyze a problem and to think."

In the years subsequent to the research program, and with the widespread introduction of Instrumental Enrichment into the Israeli school system, the original "Why me?" has changed into "Why not me?"

CRITERION MEASURES (INSTRUMENTATION)

In order to test the impact of Instrumental Enrichment in the two educational settings (residential center and day center), both intellective and nonintellective measures were used. Performance measures included assessments of general intellectual functioning, and special cognitive aptitudes and achievement in a number of academic areas. Changes in personality characteristics were monitored by pre- and postassessment of self-concept and adjustment at school. All criterion measures were administered to the total study population ($N = 548$) for purposes of determining validity and reliability, but the research hypotheses were tested on a total research population ($N = 218$) and on matched pairs ($N = 2 \times 57$) drawn from the residential and day centers for separate and combined evaluations of Instrumental Enrichment versus General Enrichment.

Assessment Instruments

The intellect-related criteria were not addressed directly to specific cognitive structures, such as Guilford's structure of the intellect (1967). Nevertheless, it was considered desirable to apply criterion measures of cognitive growth that assess both general functioning and specific aptitudes because the hypotheses related to an experimental program that may differentially affect various cognitive functions and overall intellectual development. The instrument chosen for this purpose was the Thurstone Primary Mental Abilities (PMA) test, version 4 to 6 (1965), which provides separate subtest scores on verbal, numerical, spatial relations, reasoning, and perceptual speed factors, as well as a total score from which an estimate of tested intelligence can be derived. Thus, it was possible to test the major hypotheses on the effects of treatment (FIE versus GE) and setting (RC versus DC) on the cognitive functioning of the target population by comparing experimental and control subjects on the total score and on the subtests. (For a more detailed discussion of the reasons for selecting this and other tests, and their reliability and validity with the Israeli sample, see Feuerstein and Rand, 1977; Feuerstein et al., 1979.)

The only other performance measure administered both pre and post level was a specially constructed battery of achievement tests in basic scholastic areas, the Project Achievement Battery. The tests in this battery were adjusted to the level of functioning of our target population and consisted of twelve subtests: general knowledge, nature, antonyms, Bible, geography, part-whole relationships, geometry, reading comprehension, addition, subtraction, multiplication, and division. Although Instrumental Enrichment was scrupulously kept content-free, in the sense that it did not contain any formal school subjects, we were interested in determining if the cognitive prerequisites, principles, and skills developed with the help of the Instrumental Enrichment program would enable the adolescents to improve their achievement in the content of their school curriculum. Results on these tests would provide a further dimension to the results obtained on the PMA and other measures, which are related primarily to the more general aspects of intellectual functioning.

In addition to the tests of scholastic aptitude and achievement, two non-intellect-related measures were administered before and after the intervention. One was the Tannenbaum and Levine (1968) Classroom Participation Scale (CPS), which enables teachers to evaluate adolescents' behavior at school. This instrument is divided into two parts; the first (CPS I) is a simple checklist of traits denoting various kinds of desirable and undesirable personality characteristics, and the other (CPS II) is composed of single-sentence descriptions of adaptive and nonadaptive classroom habits, with each description captioned by an adjective or adjectival phrase. The teacher rates the child on a Likert-type scale, with scores ranging from high to low agreement. Both the trait checklist and behavior description sections were subjected to factor analyses, and each yielded three strong factors: for the trait checklist, *acting out behavior, unsocialized behavior,* and *immaturity;* for the behavior descriptions, *interpersonal conduct, self-sufficiency,* and *adaptiveness to work demands.*

Another non-intellect-related measure, the Levine and Katz (1971) Levidal Self-Concept Scale, is designed to tap self-perception relating to the following areas: social and academic competency, feelings of independence and autonomy, mobility aspirations and occupational expectations, self-control in goal attainment, openness to experience, and physical attractiveness. The instrument is constructed as a Likert-type scale using five response categories from 1 to 5 with 3 indicating no opinion, and the higher numerals indicating increased disagreement. A factor analysis produced three factors: *failure at school, motivation for learning,* and *confidence in personal success.*

Apart from the above-mentioned tests and non-intellective measures, seven tests were administered only at the post level. The purpose of their administration was to assess the differences between treatments and settings on some dimensions relating to specific cognitive functions that receive emphasis in the Instrumental Enrichment program. The dimension of global versus analytic cognitive style was tested by means of Witkin's Embedded Figures Test (EFT) (Witkin, 1950) and by Marlen's Sophistication Scale on the Human Figure Drawing (HFD) test (Witkin et al., 1962). Spatial orientation was measured by an expanded version of the Kuhlmann-Finch Postures Test (Finch, 1953), which requires the conservation of the model figure across changes produced by its rotation. The rapidity-precision complex was tested by the Lahy Test (Zazzo, 1964). Three nonverbal intelligence measures were also administered at the post level only: the Porteus Maze Test (Porteus, 1965), the D-48 Test (Gough and Domino, 1963), and the Terman Test (Terman, 1942). The reason for administering the additional intelligence measures was the relatively low performance observed in the experimental population on the pre level PMA verbal factor.

The Embedded Figures Test (EFT) and the Human Figure Drawing (HFD) test both measure global versus analytic cognitive style, the former by tasks of perceptual discrimination and the latter through the production of drawings that are considered a function of internalized body image and self-concept.

One of the basic assumptions of the EFT is the central cognitive role assigned to the individual's capability of articulating a whole by taking its component parts into account and, subsequently, the individual's capability of identifying a given part within the whole. The EFT was employed to evaluate the impact of Instrumental Enrichment on the learner's capacity for articulation, which should be positively influenced by the experimental program leading to a greater level of psychological differentiation and integration of components into a harmoniously functioning self.

The HFD test is a simple paper and pencil test. The subject draws figures of both sexes and the drawings are scored for sophistication and detail. Among the several scales available, the drawings obtained for the present research were evaluated using the five-point scale developed by Marlens and Witkin (Witkin et al., 1962). This scale was developed by taking into consideration elements centering on level of form, level of identity, and sex differentiation, in addition to the level of detail. Therefore, a score on this test reflects psychological differentiation rather than purely developmental or cognitive functions. (Interjudge correlations were about 0.75. The drawings obtained from our population were rated independently by two raters who consulted with a third rater in the approximately 10% of cases in which a lack of agreement was indicated.)

The Postures test, which is a non-timed group test of spatial orientation, was administered as a composite instrument. It consists of the entire Kuhlmann-Finch test (Finch, 1953) plus an additional set of tasks independently developed along the lines of the former. A test item consists of a model human figure next to which similar but rotated figures are presented. The subject selects by inspection the figure identical to the model, taking rotation into consideration. The test calls for preservation of the image of the model figure and hypothesis checking by comparison of the rotated image against the model figures provided. The items of the original Kuhlmann-Finch test contained variations limited to the arms of figures, and this test could not, on its face value, be assumed to discriminate sufficiently in our population. Our addition represents a more complex task and contains simultaneous variations of arm and leg positions.

The Lahy test of the rapidity-precision complex (see Zazzo, 1964) consists of eight simple figures that are created by the rotation of a protruding bar from the angles and midpoints of a small square. Three of the eight figures are model figures, and the subject has to mark the tokens of these types. The test becomes difficult because of timing (300 seconds) and the large number of figures (1,000) presented on one large sheet of paper. The figures are presented in random order, and the test yields scores of the proportion of correct and incorrect inclusions and exclusions derived from the total number of figures attempted during the allotted time. The test requires rapid and precise analysis of the figures and calls for quick comparison of types and tokens. In this respect, the Instrumental Enrichment program, which seeks to emphasize analysis and comparative behavior, gives a priority rating to rapidity only after precision is guaranteed.

The Terman nonverbal intelligence test (Terman, 1942) is a timed group test in which intelligence is measured by concept formation tasks. A test item consists of five simple drawings of familiar figures of geometric designs, and the subject has to select that which does not conform to the grouping principle governing the remaining figures or designs.

The D-48 Test (Gough and Domino, 1963), which has a high level of complexity because of spatial components, is an individually administered timed test of general intelligence employing analogies and progressions in relationships among dominoes. The problems vary from simple addition to subtraction, identities, subtraction with progression, double progression, and others.

The Porteus Maze Test (Porteus, 1965) is an individually administered nonverbal test that emphasizes the purposeful and planning aspects of intelligence. It uses a series of mazes to evaluate the ability to execute, in the prescribed fashion and correct sequential order, the steps necessary to achieve the goal. The test requires planning capacity and foresight, sustained attention, and persistence in the face of fatigue, as well as manual dexterity.

Sampling Procedure and Data Analysis

The research was conducted in four settings, two residential centers and two day centers, with the total population of each participating in the study. One residential center and one day center were exposed to Instrumental Enrichment; one residential center and one day center were exposed to General Enrichment and constituted the comparison group.

The criterion measures were administered immediately prior to the beginning of the school year (pretest) and again immediately following the completion of the program at the end of 2 years (posttest). The total study population consisted of 548 subjects and included subjects who would complete their schooling after 1 year and, consequently, would not be available for the posttesting. These subjects, however, were included in the study since, with only 1 year of exposure to an intervention program, they provided an interesting comparison for the follow-up study. After the 2-year duration of the experiment, complete data were available for 218 subjects. Results were analyzed for those subjects and also for a sample of matched pairs. Unless otherwise indicated, the data presented refer only to the sample of matched pairs. This sample consisted of 57 pairs of subjects matched separately within settings for contrasting treatments. Each pair consisted of a subject from the FIE group and a subject from the GE group within the same setting (RC and DC). It was decided to restrict the matching to a sample of Instrumental Enrichment versus General Enrichment subjects, paired on the basis of comparable PMA total prescores, age, sex, and ethnicity. Scores on the Project Achievement Battery and non-intellect-related measures were not used for matching purposes because the reliability coefficients of these measures were only moderately high. Additional matching variables and extension of the matching across both treatment and setting would have critically reduced the sample size. No meaningful statistically significant differences were found between the groups on the matching variables (see Feuerstein and Rand, 1977; Feuerstein et al., 1979).

Since both treatment and setting were hypothesized as critical in determining the outcome of the experiment, 2×2 analyses of covariance (Instrumental Enrichment versus General Enrichment and residential center versus day center) were conducted on posttest scores for each of the criterion variables, both for the total research population and for the matched pairs group. For tests administered at the post level only, the PMA total prescore was always employed as the covariant. For most of the criterion measures, appropriate PMA subtests were included as additional covariants on the basis of their face validity with respect to each given measure. The experimental design also facilitated a test of the interaction effects of treatment and setting.

RESULTS

A two-way analysis of covariance of postscores on each criterion variable yielded main effects of treatment (Hypothesis 1) and setting (Hypothesis 2) as well as their interaction effects (Hypothesis 3). (For a detailed presentation of the results, see Feuerstein and Rand, 1977. Hypothesis 4 is discussed in the concluding section of this chapter.)

Hypothesis 1

Hypothesis 1 predicted that subjects receiving Instrumental Enrichment would score higher on criterion measures than subjects receiving General Enrichment. Table 5 presents the results for the PMA total and separate subtest scores. It is clear that this hypothesis was confirmed for the PMA total score, the only criterion test variable on which Instrumental Enrichment and General Enrichment samples were matched. The result indicates that the main effect of Instrumental Enrichment was demonstrated in overall performance on the PMA, which is regarded by Thurstone (1965) as a measure of general intelligence. Table 5 reveals that there were significant differences at the 0.05 level or better, favoring the Instrumental Enrichment groups on four out of eight PMA subtests (numbers, addition, spatial relations, and figure grouping). On the other hand, the General Enrichment sample did not show any significant improvement over the Instrumental Enrichment sample on any of the PMA subtests at the end of the 2-year period, although all four groups improved considerably on their own initial performance level established before the onset of the experiment.

Additional results supporting the first hypothesis were obtained on the measures administered only as posttests, as indicated in Table 6. Subjects from the Instrumental Enrichment sample scored significantly higher than their General Enrichment sample counterparts on two of the three general intellect-related measures, the Terman test, and the D-48 test. Although the experimentals were also better than the controls on the Porteus IQ test, this difference failed to reach the accepted level of significance.

Confirmation of the first hypothesis was also obtained on all four of the tests of specific cognitive performance, which were administered only at the posttest level (see Table 7). The data on the Embedded Figures Test (EFT) indicate that, although experimental subjects on the average spend considerably less time working at the tasks of this test, they have more correct responses, and both differences are significant at the 0.01 level. Results on the

Table 5. Primary Mental Abilities (PMA) test: Adjusted means, standard deviations, and results of analyses of covariance test

PMA subtests		RC FIE ($N=24$)	RC GE ($N=24$)	DC FIE ($N=33$)	DC GE ($N=33$)	RC+DC FIE ($N=57$)	RC+DC GE ($N=57$)	FIE+GE RC ($N=48$)	FIE+GE DC ($N=66$)	F ratios FIE vs GE	F ratios RC vs DC	F ratios Interaction
Vocabulary	M	16.04	17.07	16.85	16.48	16.94	16.34	17.03	16.36	NS	NS	NS
	SD	5.40	2.97	4.19	3.78	4.76	3.45	4.41	3.97			
Pictures	M	23.92	24.17	23.91	24.51	24.21	24.07	24.61	23.79	NS	NS	NS
	SD	3.54	3.45	2.93	2.40	3.17	2.86	3.46	2.67			
Numbers	M	17.54	16.50	17.79	16.88	17.83	16.57	17.75	16.80	15.34[a]	7.60[a]	NS
	SD	1.98	2.59	2.41	3.15	2.22	2.91	2.34	2.82			
Addition	M	23.54	21.67	22.88	22.39	23.45	21.79	23.88	21.70	4.22[b]	6.38[a]	NS
	SD	5.41	4.85	5.50	5.37	5.43	5.12	5.17	5.40			
Spatial relations	M	17.92	14.96	18.33	14.67	18.04	14.90	16.82	16.22	22.02[b]	NS	NS
	SD	3.88	4.79	4.30	4.43	4.10	4.55	4.56	4.71			
Figure grouping	M	21.62	19.50	21.24	20.64	21.25	20.31	20.78	20.78	3.79[a]	NS	NS
	SD	2.04	2.72	2.70	3.56	2.43	3.25	2.61	3.15			
Word grouping	M	17.67	17.79	18.79	17.57	18.43	17.55	18.01	17.98	NS	NS	NS
	SD	3.76	2.62	2.86	3.73	3.28	3.29	3.21	3.35			
Perceptual speed	M	32.12	31.58	33.82	31.51	32.59	32.26	32.44	32.41	NS	NS	NS
	SD	5.90	6.41	5.16	6.23	5.50	6.25	6.10	5.80			
Total	M	170.37	163.33	173.61	164.67	172.68	163.92	172.04	165.38	13.66[a]	6.90[a]	NS
	SD	15.21	17.13	17.28	21.79	16.38	19.81	16.41	20.03			

RC, residential center; DC, day center; FIE, Instrumental Enrichment; GE, General Enrichment.
[a]Significant at the 0.01 level or better.
[b]Significant at the 0.05 level.

Table 6. Terman, D-48, Porteus: Adjusted means, standard deviations, and results of analyses of covariance tests

Tests		RC FIE (N=24)	RC GE (N=24)	DC FIE (N=33)	DC GE (N=33)	RC+DC FIE (N=57)	RC+DC GE (N=57)	FIE+GE RC (N=48)	FIE+GE DC (N=66)	F ratios FIE vs GE	F ratios RC vs DC	F ratios Interaction
Terman	M	35.39	36.86	42.79	34.12	39.39	35.27	36.10	38.21	6.57[a]	NS	9.17[a]
	SD	11.43	6.40	5.94	9.75	8.67	8.51	9.25	9.13			
D-48	M	57.72	45.85	62.71	55.18	60.31	51.07	53.05	57.87	22.89[a]	5.15[b]	NS
	SD	9.47	8.00	9.31	10.86	9.61	10.73	10.57	10.72			
Porteus IQ	M	105.55	99.26	97.00	98.40	100.47	98.43	103.52	96.16	NS	5.61[b]	NS
	SD	8.73	15.98	16.16	14.45	13.97	14.96	13.20	15.15			

RC, residential center; DC, day center; FIE, Instrumental Enrichment; GE, General Enrichment.
[a]Significant at the 0.01 level or better.
[b]Significant at the 0.05 level.

Table 7. Embedded Figures Test (EFT), Human Figure Drawing (HFD), Postures, Lahy: Adjusted means, standard deviations and results of analyses of covariance tests[a].

Tests		RC FIE (N=24)	RC GE (N=24)	DC FIE (N=33)	DC GE (N=33)	RC+DC FIE (N=57)	RC+DC GE (N=57)	FIE+GE RC (N=48)	FIE+GE DC (N=66)	F ratios FIE vs GE	F ratios RC vs DC	F ratios Interaction
EFT												
Average Time	M	76.86	107.14	58.81	100.26	68.30	102.37	85.87	85.22	28.75[a]	NS	NS
	SD	42.07	27.64	38.33	33.47	40.72	31.09	38.37	41.54			
Total Correct	M	10.05	7.27	10.26	8.84	10.10	8.17	8.84	9.29	16.68[a]	NS	NS
	SD	1.91	3.05	2.25	2.60	2.04	2.72	2.89	2.53			
HFD	M	2.45	2.95	2.59	3.13	2.53	3.03	2.68	2.87	5.07[b]	NS	NS
	SD	1.18	0.90	1.32	1.02	1.26	0.97	1.07	1.20			
Postures	M	28.83	26.12	28.85	24.82	28.65	25.63	27.64	26.74	13.38[a]	NS	NS
	SD	3.87	3.78	4.33	4.82	4.14	4.41	4.03	4.98			
Lahy												
Total number attended	M	248.17	231.26	276.41	267.31	265.12	249.18	249.31	264.73	NS	NS	NS
	SD	73.40	113.49	83.57	84.22	79.93	98.19	94.48	83.35			
Proportion correct	M	0.926	0.887	0.929	0.884	0.930	0.890	0.920	0.900	7.51[a]	NS	NS
	SD	0.072	0.120	0.061	0.083	0.065	0.099	0.099	0.076			
Proportion wrong	M	0.004	0.040	0.007	0.025	0.010	0.030	0.020	0.020	4.41[b]	NS	NS
	SD	0.006	0.119	0.016	0.062	0.013	0.090	0.084	0.046			

RC, residential center; DC, day center; FIE, Instrumental Enrichment; GE, General Enrichment.
[a]Significant at the 0.01 level or better.
[b]Significant at the 0.05 level.

Human Figure Drawing (HFD) test likewise indicate scores in favor of the experimental groups. (Lower scores indicate higher levels of sophistication.) Although the data for the Lahy test, for the rapidity-precision complex, do not yield any significant difference on the number of items attempted, the experimental groups had significantly higher proportions of correct, and lower proportions of incorrect, responses than the control groups.

Additional support for the first hypothesis, although less dramatic, was obtained with the results on the Project Achievement Battery (see Table 8). Significance differences at the 0.05 level or better in favor of Instrumental Enrichment occurred on only 2 out of the 12 subtests (i.e., Bible and geometry). However, the control groups did not prove significantly better than the experimental groups on any of the remaining 10 subtests.

The tendency toward more positive development of the experimental groups was confirmed by results on some non-intellective criteria. Classroom Participation Scale (CPS) II is an indicator of school behavior, and all three factors extracted from this instrument indicated significant differences at the 0.05 level or better in favor of the Instrumental Enrichment sample (see Table 9). Instrumental Enrichment seems better suited to the adolescent's development in the areas of interpersonal conduct (factor A), self-sufficiency (factor B), and adaptiveness to work demands (factor C). The higher score of the controls on Factor A indicated that subjects receiving General Enrichment were more likely to be seen by their teachers as developing or maintaining such negative behavior characteristics as aggressive interaction with classmates, disruptive behavior, and lack of deportment in class than were their Instrumental Enrichment counterparts. As perceived by their teachers, the Instrumental Enrichment groups were also much more likely to start and finish work independently and to show persistence in work (factor B). Similar results favoring the experimental sample were obtained for factor C and included such behaviors as helping others and sharing materials safely.

The other non-intellective criterion measure on which pre- and posttest scores were obtained was the Levidal Self-Concept Scale. The results showed no significant differences in improvement for the two groups over the 2-year period. Thus, there were no meaningful differences between experimental and control samples in self-ratings dealing with questions of failure at school (factor A), motivation for learning (factor B), and confidence in personal success (factor C).

In short, the results showed that the changes in cognitive performance and general behavior over the 2-year period favored the Instrumental Enrichment group, thereby confirming the first hypothesis.

Hypothesis 2

Hypothesis 2 predicted higher scores on criterion measures for subjects studying at residential centers than for subjects at the day centers, irrespec-

Table 8. Project Achievement Battery (PAB): Adjusted means, standard deviations, and results of analyses of covariance data

Achievement subtests		RC		DC		RC + DC		FIE + GE		F ratios		
		FIE (N=24)	GE (N=24)	FIE (N=33)	GE (N=33)	FIE (N=57)	GE (N=57)	RC (N=48)	DC (N=66)	FIE vs GE	RC vs DC	Interaction
General knowledge	M	9.00	7.85	8.25	7.86	8.63	7.75	8.56	7.99	NS	NS	NS
	SD	2.52	2.46	2.96	2.86	2.79	2.68	2.53	2.90			
Nature	M	8.35	9.05	8.06	8.52	8.43	8.52	8.85	8.19	NS	NS	NS
	SD	2.50	1.60	2.44	2.74	2.44	2.34	2.12	1.58			
Antonyms	M	10.57	12.10	10.81	11.57	10.85	11.62	11.45	11.06	NS	NS	NS
	SD	3.69	1.51	3.81	2.54	2.72	2.18	2.94	3.25			
Bible	M	13.96	14.38	14.36	11.13	14.23	12.20	14.39	12.50	6.98[a]	5.70[b]	NS
	SD	5.11	3.63	4.06	5.32	4.48	4.95	4.42	4.96			
Geography	M	10.39	12.38	10.25	9.75	10.93	10.28	11.48	9.76	NS	10.19[a]	NS
	SD	4.14	3.46	3.47	3.72	3.73	3.81	3.92	3.57			
Part-Whole	M	7.96	8.00	7.98	7.65	8.06	7.69	8.00	7.80	NS	NS	NS
	SD	1.36	1.90	3.62	1.89	2.86	1.84	1.62	2.92			

Geometry	M	5.70	4.48	5.47	4.86	5.58	4.75	5.31	5.11	5.28[b]	NS	NS
	SD	2.12	1.72	1.83	2.12	1.94	1.95	2.01	1.98			
Reading comprehension	M	8.43	11.20	10.58	9.34	9.88	9.82	9.74	9.92	NS	NS	11.37[a]
	SD	3.86	2.26	2.74	3.74	3.38	3.35	3.47	3.30			
Addition	M	21.58	20.61	20.48	20.25	20.87	20.51	21.40	20.22	NS	4.88[b]	NS
	SD	2.04	2.66	3.28	2.77	2.86	2.71	2.39	3.02			
Subtraction	M	19.04	21.00	18.13	21.07	18.92	20.77	20.32	19.47	NS	NS	NS
	SD	4.67	2.94	5.56	11.82	5.18	9.11	4.00	9.19			
Multiplication	M	33.00	34.09	29.69	32.58	31.78	32.47	35.99	29.42	NS	16.23[a]	NS
	SD	7.85	7.32	10.93	9.41	9.79	8.56	7.53	10.24			
Division	M	26.48	29.52	23.26	22.87	25.14	24.90	29.54	21.85	NS	36.15[a]	NS
	SD	5.54	5.21	7.58	7.64	6.85	7.46	5.54	7.55			

RC, residential center; DC, day center; FIE, Instrumental Enrichment; GE, General Enrichment.
[a]Significant at the 0.01 level or better.
[b]Significant at the 0.05 level.

Table 9. Classroom Participation Scales (CPS) I and II: Adjusted means, standard deviations, and results of analyses of covariance tests

CPS factors		RC		DC		RC + DC		FIE + GE		F ratios		
		FIE (N=24)	GE (N=24)	FIE (N=33)	GE (N=33)	FIE (N=57)	GE (N=57)	RC (N=48)	DC (N=66)	FIE vs GE	RC vs DC	Interaction
CPS I												
A	M	2.57	2.50	1.82	2.66	2.21	2.55	2.63	2.21	NS	NS	NS
	SD	2.06	2.01	1.67	1.88	1.85	1.91	2.01	1.81			
B	M	3.81	3.30	1.85	2.31	2.56	2.69	3.47	2.07	NS	17.23^a	5.09^b
	SD	1.57	1.75	1.77	1.55	1.94	1.69	1.66	1.67			
C	M	3.05	2.80	2.58	3.06	2.83	2.95	2.94	2.85	NS	NS	NS
	SD	1.50	1.28	1.21	1.37	1.36	1.33	1.39	1.32			
CPS II												
A	M	6.76	7.90	7.30	8.44	7.26	8.17	7.48	7.86	3.77^b	NS	NS
	SD	1.92	3.13	2.47	1.95	2.27	2.45	2.61	2.28			
B	M	10.57	9.90	11.79	9.16	11.60	9.52	10.77	10.42	22.45^a	NS	NS
	SD	1.43	2.25	1.97	2.73	1.77	2.56	2.03	2.70			
C	M	10.29	9.70	10.97	9.58	10.78	9.65	10.14	10.25	10.92^a	NS	NS
	SD	1.45	1.26	1.36	1.21	1.42	1.22	1.38	1.46			

RC, residential center; DC, day center; FIE, Instrumental Enrichment; GE, General Enrichment.
Factor A, interpersonal conduct; factor B, self-sufficiency; factor C, adaptiveness to work demands.
^{a}Significant at the 0.01 level or better.
^{b}Significant at the 0.05 level.

tive of their programs of intervention. The hypothesis was confirmed for the PMA total score and the numbers and addition subtests of the PMA (see Table 5). On the additional intellective measures (i.e., the Terman, the D-48, and the Porteus IQ), the residential center proved superior only on the Porteus IQ (see Table 6). A significant difference in the direction opposite to that hypothesized was found for the D-48 test. No significant differences were revealed on any of the tests of specific cognitive dimensions (i.e., the Embedded Figures Test, the Human Figure Drawing test, the Postures test, and the Lahy test). These tests were primarily administered in order to assess the impact of Instrumental Enrichment on specific cognitive functions. Consequently, they were not expected to be highly influenced by differences in the educational settings.

On the Project Achievement Battery, significant differences at the 0.05 level, in favor of the residential setting, were obtained on five subtests (i.e., Bible, geometry, addition, multiplication, and division) (see Table 8). Furthermore, the day center subjects showed no significant improvement over their residential center counterparts on any subtests of this battery or on any of the subtests of the PMA.

The non-intellective measures generally did not distinguish between the two settings. However, one significant difference was found on factor B (unsocialized behavior) of the trait checklist of the Classroom Participation Scale (CPS) I (see Table 9). This result indicated that subjects in the residential settings were more likely to be regarded by their teachers as developing or maintaining such traits as depression, tension, and withdrawal over the 2-year period.

Hypothesis 3

The expected interaction effect between treatment and setting, formulated in Hypothesis 3, which was intended to show that Instrumental Enrichment would be especially potent in a residential setting, did not materialize to any meaningful extent. No interaction effect was found between treatment and setting on the PMA total score or on any of the PMA subtests. No confirmation of this hypothesis was found on any of the additional intellective measures except for the Terman test (see Table 6). The results on this test, however, were reported for subjects receiving Instrumental Enrichment at day centers and not, as hypothesized, for subjects receiving the experimental program in the residential setting. On the Project Achievement Battery, an interaction effect was observed on the reading comprehension subtest (see Table 8), but, again, the mutual reinforcement was not in the anticipated direction. Contrary to expectation, instead of Instrumental Enrichment being particularly effective in a residental setting, it proved more successful in the day center environment, although the opposite was true for General Enrichment. A third interaction effect was obtained on factor B (unsocialized behavior) of the trait checklist of the Classroom Participation Scale (CPS) in support of the hypothesis. Instrumental Enrichment yielded more salutary results on this factor in the residential setting, although General Enrichment produced similar results in the day center settings (see Table 9). These limited and inconsistent interaction effects could not support a general acceptance of the third hypothesis.

In conclusion, the results from the matched pairs group indicated that adolescents participating in the Instrumental Enrichment program in the residential and day settings obtained significantly greater gains on most of the intellective and some of the non-intellective measures than did General Enrichment groups in similar settings. At the same time, both residential center groups, representing the two different kinds of treatment, outperformed their counterparts in day centers on some of these measures. There was only a significant interaction on one subtest of the achievement battery and on one of the postmeasured intellective tests, and, even in these cases, the interaction was not in the expected direction. Instead of Instrumental Enrichment being more effective in a residential setting, it proved more successful in the day center environment; the opposite was true for General Enrichment. However, this was the case for only 2 of 31 criterion measures in the intellective test batteries. In contrast, the main effects supporting Instrumental Enrichment were found on 15 of these measures. Residential facilities proved significantly more effective on 9 of the 31 intellective variables tests. Apart from one isolated instance, main effects were always in the expected direction.

Compared to tests of cognitive performance, the non-intellective measures did not show clear support for the study's major hypotheses, except for the three behavior description factors of the Classroom Participation Scale (CPS) II. These factors (interpersonal conduct, self-sufficiency, and adaptiveness to work demands) refer to the personal requisites for competency at school, primarily the volitional characteristics that tend to accompany success in achievement.

DISCUSSION

The results of the experiment conducted with a population of socially disadvantaged and culturally deprived low performing adolescents confirmed that Instrumental Enrichment was more beneficial for the target population than was the General Enrichment program to which the comparison subjects were exposed. Overall cognitive functioning and growth in particular scholastic aptitudes, achievement skills, and classroom behaviors were all influenced positively in the experimental (FIE) groups. The evidence is consistent enough along intellective and non-intellective dimensions to suggest that Instrumental Enrichment merits adoption in programs that aim at modifying the cognitive structure of low functioning adolescents.

The conclusion that may be drawn is that a phase-specific substitute for mediated learning, such as that exemplified by Instrumental Enrichment, can have an impact on the cognitive development of retarded performers even after they have reached adolescence. There is no need to withhold special services for this age group and to place our hope almost entirely in early intervention on grounds that once a child has graduated beyond his preschool years it is too late for an equitable return on investments in mediated learning. Results of the present study should lead to a far more optimistic view of the responsiveness of the older child to educational stimulation. Our research results challenge the conception that low functioning adolescents are not accessible to significant changes in their cognitive structure, and that any changes that do occur are most likely attributable to compensatory efforts that are remedial in nature and focus largely on specific content areas. The Instrumental Enrichment program, which emphasizes the prerequisites of thought processes rather than their specific content, appears to bring about important changes in cognitive development, perhaps even more important than those facilitated by tutoring in school subjects, as suggested by the weaker showing of the comparison General Enrichment subjects in this study.

Instrumental Enrichment enabled the adolescents to cultivate more efficiently those cognitive operations that are usually tapped in tests of general intelligence. The noteworthy posttest results obtained on the Primary Mental Abilities test by experimental subjects matched with controls suggest a much broader base of efficient cognitive functions for the experimental groups than would traditionally have been attributed on the basis of the pretest measures. The FIE subjects' performance on all administered measures of general intelligence was almost universally superior. These measures, which included the PMA, the Terman, the Postures, the D-48, and the Porteus IQ, sampled a wide range of intellectual skills and their requisite operations and cognitive processes presented in different modalities including verbal, numerical, and figural. The superior results obtained by the experimental groups on all of these measures (except for the Porteus IQ where the advantage of the experimentals fails to reach accepted levels of significance) leave little room for doubt that the Instrumental Enrichment program was successful in redressing the deficiencies of a multitude of cognitive functions. The results obtained from the measures administered exclusively at the post level of testing indicated that the Instrumental Enrichment program enhanced performance on such varied functions as multiphased elaboration of numerical relations (D-48), the capacity to store and recognize the details of basic data relationships through their transformation (the Postures), and the employment of higher order principles of data organization and abstraction (the Terman).

The impact of the Instrumental Enrichment program may be further assessed by close inspection of data obtained on the five-factor Primary Mental Abilities test. The results of experimental subjects, matched with controls on the pretest PMA performance, indicated that the scores on the numbers, spatial relations, and reasoning (figure grouping and word grouping) subtests were the most likely to contribute to the superior results on the total score, in confirmation of the main hypothesis. On the spatial relations factor, the Instrumental Enrichment groups scored higher than their General Enrichment counterparts than on any other subtest of the PMA, the difference reaching well beyond the 0.01 level of significance. On the reasoning factor, for both figure grouping and word grouping, the experimental groups scored higher than the controls, but differences were significant only for the figure grouping subtest. These results of the PMA test suggest that Instrumental Enrichment exercises are particularly effective in improving numerical and figural concepts, and relatively less efficient with respect to verbal modalities of presentation. These findings are not surprising, considering the limited use of verbal modalities in FIE and the relatively greater difficulties encountered by the children when confronted with tasks requiring efficient reading and reading comprehension.

There is no doubt that general cognitive ability influences performance on a wide variety of tasks. The presence of a greater degree of psychological differentiation in the experimental subjects was substantiated by the performance of these subjects on all post measures administered to test a variety of indicators of differential cognitive styles (Embedded Figures Test and Human Figure Drawing test) and on tasks measuring sustained attention in the rapidity-precision complex (the Lahy test). The results on both the EFT and the HFD test revealed that the experimental subjects were more analytical in their cognitive style and more sophisticated in their degree of articulation. Likewise, these subjects were found to be able to preserve a mental image through transformations and to grasp and execute distracting allocation-of-symbols-to-groups tasks (Postures and Lahy) to a greater extent than the control subjects. These findings suggest that the benefit gained from working on the Instrumental Enrichment exercises goes beyond the strengthening of general intellectual powers and extends to those aspects of cognitive competency that are commonly regarded as representing the more stable characteristics of the individual's cognitive style and problem-solving strategies. The Instrumental Enrichment program deliberately attempts to limit impulsivity. This deficiency impairs the functioning of the culturally deprived individual by excluding longer response latencies and preventing him from even attempting, in an adequate fashion, to engage in efficient problem-solving behavior. In the program, speed is constantly discouraged, and every Instrumental Enrichment booklet has on its coversheet the cautionary note "Just a minute. Let me think." This is intended to remind the child to be careful in solving problems and to sacrifice speed for precision. It is within this context that one has to interpret the insignificant differences between FIE and GE on the perceptual speed subtest of the PMA and on the rapidity-precision test of the Lahy. On the latter test, although Instrumental Enrichment subjects were superior on precision, no differences in their favor were found for the rapidity component. Although all of the subtests of the PMA and the Lahy were timed, and the subjects were told that their scores would depend on speed and accuracy, in the case of the perceptual speed subtest, and the Lahy, rapidity of response was even more important because the tests are built around relatively rudimentary matching or assignment tasks that become difficult only when they have to be completed rapidly.

It is clear, then, that Instrumental Enrichment has a beneficial effect on both general intellective capacity and on aspects of style and precision in intellectual and cognitive functioning. From the results of the experiment, it appears that Instrumental Enrichment cannot replace content learning, a purpose for which, of course, it was never intended. Instead, it should be considered an efficient device for complementing content learning. As such, it enhances the student's capacity for more efficient absorption of school subjects and facilitates a more suitable approach to any intellectual challenge. This conclusion is suggested by the presence of significant results in favor of the experimental subjects on the Bible and geometry subtests of the Project Achievement Battery. These findings suggest that Instrumental Enrichment has some impact even on achievement-type learning.

The results of the Project Achievement Battery, however, should be interpreted in the light of the fact that the research design allocated about 300 hours more of curriculum learning, such as reading skills, writing, general information, and arithmetic, to subjects receiving General Enrichment. This was because Instrumental Enrichment was administered to the experimental groups as part of the regular school-day program. A more accurate comparison, therefore, would be between subjects receiving the Instrumental Enrichment program and others receiving the General Enrichment program, minus 300 hours of curriculum learning. Thus, our experimental groups, by not receiving the same amount of exposure in the achievement areas, were at a considerable disadvantage. Nevertheless, the outcome of the experiment showed FIE subjects' performance to be equal to or better than that of GE participants on the achievement tests, and there was no instance in which the GE subjects performed significantly better than the FIE subjects on any of the subtests in the battery. This may be interpreted as evidence of the power of Instrumental Enrichment to accomplish the same effect as curriculum enrichment, but in considerably less time, as well as simultaneously producing superiority in other vital areas of cognitive functioning. The Instrumental Enrichment program also seemed to have a beneficial effect on the more general areas of personal development and adjustment. Although no change in self-concept was recorded by the Levidal Self-Concept Scale in favor of either FIE or GE subjects, the experiment did indicate support for a tendency toward more positive development among experimental subjects. All three behavior descriptor factors of the Classroom Participation Scale II indicated favorable developments in the experimental groups. It is likely that the classroom interaction, fostered by the teacher in working with the instruments, was at least partially responsible for some of the following teacher observations. Teachers regarded the FIE subjects as engaging in less aggressive interactions; indulging in less disruptive behavior; developing more self-sufficiency and initiative by starting, persisting with, and completing work independently; and adapting to their work demands by helping others and sharing materials.

Slight support in favor of the view that the residential setting is superior to the day center for the successful cognitive and behavioral development of adolescents, irrespective of the program of enrichment administered, may be substantiated by the posttest results. Residential centers appeared to facilitate significantly better development on some factors of general intelligence, as suggested by the superior PMA total scores obtained by subjects studying at the residential centers. A closer inspection of the data shows that scores on the numbers subtest, in particular, contributed to this finding, but analysis of the total research population also reveals that the pictures subtest yielded differences well beyond the accepted level of significance. The superiority of the residential facility was not strongly supported by results on the additional measures of general intelligence, and only the Porteus Mazes showed an effect in favor of this setting. In contrast, the D-48 test indicated superiority of the day center facilities. These findings indicated that setting, as such, may be an important variable, but that the residential facility, in particular, is beneficial for progress on numerical problems and some aspects of verbal capacity as measured by the PMA.

The residential facility did not prove to be superior on the measures of cognitive style (EFT, HFD test), the rapidity-precision complex, and the Postures. In the area of achievement in school subjects, the results suggested that the subjects in the residential setting were superior to those in the day centers. The matched pairs analyses credited the residential center with positive effects in a variety of achievement areas, including Bible, geography, and all basic arithmetic skills with the exception of subtraction, as measured on the Project Achievement Battery. The more conclusive analysis of the total research population attributed superiority to the residential setting in all of these areas plus subtraction, general knowledge, nature, and antonyms. These data are consistent enough to warrant the conclusion that the day centers, at least in the short run, are outperformed by the residential centers with regard to their efficacy in generating cognitive changes in populations of low functioning adolescents.

As on the cognitive measures, differences associated with setting were generally not as sharp as those related to treatment on the non-intellective measures. Of these measures, only factor B of the trait checklist (CPS I) indicated any difference among the settings, suggesting that subjects in the residential centers were more likely to be regarded by their teachers as becoming or remaining depressed, tense, or withdrawn, or evidencing similar behaviors. This finding is not very surprising and is commonly observed in educational settings in which youth are removed from the parental home.

Posttest measures of both Instrumental Enrichment groups and, less dramatically, both residential center groups, proved to be superior to those of their treatment and setting controls, thus demonstrating the independent values of the two experimental conditions on a number of criterion variables. However, the interaction effects did not materialize to any meaningful extent. It would appear that adolescents, similar to those in the present study, can benefit from Instrumental Enrichment, irrespective of the setting, and that they can benefit from residential care, irrespective of the program. None of the combinations of treatment and setting seems more productive than any other in advancing growth in virtually any of the aptitudes and achievements measured.

THE FOLLOW-UP STUDY: PRELIMINARY FINDINGS AND DATA ANALYSIS

The fourth hypothesis, and perhaps the most important, concerns what we have referred to as the divergent effects of Instrumental Enrichment. This hypothesis goes beyond the normal requirement that any gains achieved by an intervention program should be sustained over time. The FIE program is designed to enhance cognitive modifiability and hence the expected changes after exposure to FIE should be *cumulative,* not just sustained, over time. If Instrumental Enrichment is able to provide the individual with the necessary cognitive tools that permit and encourage a continuous process of development in response to exposure to novel experiences, then a divergent pattern of growth should be obtained. As expressed in hypothesis 4, there is a progressive increment over time in the differences of the performance of subjects exposed to Instrumental Enrichment compared to that of subjects receiving General Enrichment and also with respect to their own performance. Although the follow-up study is currently in progress, some preliminary data are available that lend support to the hypothesis of divergent effects. Not all the data are available because the younger subjects were only inducted into the army at a later stage.

Two years after completing the FIE and GE programs, the older subjects were drafted into the army. The follow-up study was designed to investigate their performance on various tests administered by the army to all draftees. The results available at this stage are confined to two measures: the Dapar Intelligence Test and the Hebrew Language Development Test. The Dapar is an intelligence measure derived from an Otis-type verbal test and a nonverbal test based on Raven's Progressive Matrices. A composite score is derived for the two components and is expressed in stanines ranking from 1 (low) to 9 (high) with a mean of 5 and a standard deviation of 2. The Hebrew Language Development Test serves as one of the important classification criteria in the army and is correlated with the rank a soldier achieves in the service. The test consists of about 50% reading, writing, and comprehension, and 50% vocabulary. The mean for the general population is around 7. One of the advantages of using army data is that the performance of other groups on the same measures may be used for comparative purposes.

Before turning to a consideration of the divergent effects hypothesis, comparative data for our research groups and other groups with whom we have worked are presented below, and the long term effects of the intervention programs (FIE versus GE) and settings (RC versus DC) are examined.

The number of subjects and the means and standard deviations for the Dapar and language tests, for each of the original experimental groups and a number of comparison groups, are given in Table 10. From the original 218 subjects comprising the total research population, results are available for 164 subjects on the Dapar and 175 subjects on the language test. (The difference in number of subjects for the Dapar and the language test is a result of the procedure of allowing a period of time to elapse between the administration of the tests.) In addition, Table 10 provides the results for those subjects that received only one year of either FIE or GE. The comparison groups consisted of the following subjects for whom we had army records. The general Youth Aliyah group comprised a subsample of Youth Aliyah graduates and represents a fairly normal segment of the Youth Aliyah population educated in kibbutzim and youth villages and institutions. The subjects rejected by the army consisted of adolescents who did not qualify for army service; they were school dropouts, usually at an early stage of formal schooling, and, consequently, were totally or functionally illiterate and socially, occupationally, and emotionally maladapted. The subjects participating in our experiment were drawn from populations similar to that of the rejected group with respect to demographic variables and levels of cognitive functioning prior to intervention.

For comparative purposes, another set of data is provided, for other groups of similar populations: The percentage frequency of scores obtained on the Dapar Intelligence Test is presented in Figure 1 for a general Youth Aliyah group (a random selection from the general population within Youth

DAPAR 1

	Median score	N
Youth Aliyah random sample	49.0	356
Subjects rejected by the army	22.5	209
RC/GE	42.2	139
DC/GE	39.7	139
FIE: DC&RC	48.3	272

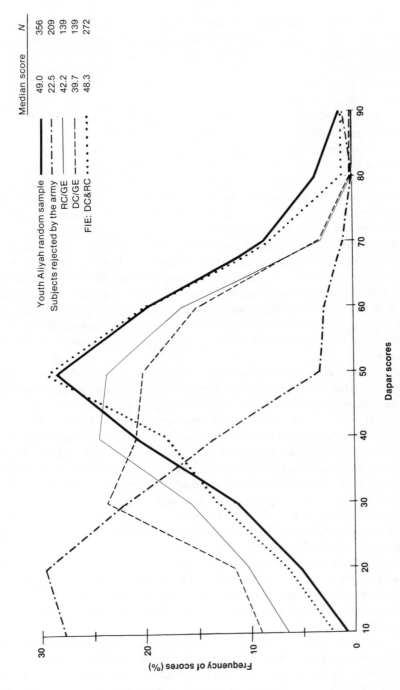

Figure 1.   Frequency of scores obtained on the Dapar Intelligence Test for various groups.

Aliyah), subjects rejected by the army, subjects who received FIE in residential and in day centers, and comparable groups in residential and day centers who received no FIE training. The graph illustrates a clear progression in which the subjects rejected by the army received the lowest scores, followed in turn by the populations from the day centers and the residential centers, neither of whom performed as well as the general Youth Aliyah group. In contrast, the FIE group is virtually indistinguishable from the general Youth Aliyah group with respect to performance on the Dapar test.

When the reader bears in mind that the FIE subjects and their controls in both day and residential centers were selected from a population similar to that of the subjects rejected by the army, these findings demonstrate in a dramatic fashion a number of important points. Not only is it evident that intervention is beneficial, but it also appears that different kinds of intervention may have differential and cumulative effects. Attendance at a day center seems less beneficial than placement in a residential center, but neither kind of setting is sufficient to produce performance levels similar to the general Youth Aliyah group. However, in combination with FIE, the total impact of the intervention is considerably increased. Groups that previously would have been rejected by the army because of their low performance on intelligence tests are not only eligible for army service but are indistinguishable from the general population of Youth Aliyah graduates entering the army.

From Table 10, it is clear that the performance of the Youth Aliyah group (Dapar $\overline{X} = 51.2$; language $\overline{X} = 7.8$) was similar to that of the general Israeli population. The Instrumental Enrichment subjects scored higher on the Dapar ($\overline{X} = 53.8$) but not on the language test ($\overline{X} = 6.35$) than the Youth Aliyah subjects. In contrast, the General Enrichment subjects scored lower on the Dapar ($\overline{X} = 46.4$) and the language test ($\overline{X} = 7.1$) than the Youth Aliyah subjects. The subjects rejected by the army provide an interesting comparison because they represent an approximation of the performance that could have been expected from the experimental subjects had they not been provided with any kind of intervention program (FIE or GE) or placed in either a residential or day center program. For both the Dapar and the language tests, both the FIE and the GE subjects performed far above the very low scores obtained by the group rejected by the army (Dapar $\overline{X} = 24.2$; language $\overline{X} = 4.8$). It is a significant fact that, to our best knowledge, none of the experimental subjects has been placed by the army in the army's special remediation program, established to help integrate youngsters previously rejected.

Another revealing comparison concerns the performance of subjects who received only 1 year of intervention and those that completed the 2-year program. On the Dapar tests, subjects who received FIE for only 1 year scored significantly lower than the experimental subjects who received the

Table 10.   Dapar Intelligence Test and Hebrew Development Language Test: Means and standard deviations for research and comparison groups; figures for subjects who received an intervention program for only 1 year are in parentheses

Groups		Dapar		Language	
RC/FIE	$\overline{X}$	50.4	(43.4)	6.1	(6.4)
	SD	15.0	(13.5)	1.6	(1.4)
	N	31	(54)	38	(58)
RC/GE	$\overline{X}$	48.9	(46.7)	7.0	(7.3)
	SD	10.3	(12.6)	1.2	(0.8)
	N	29	(35)	30	(36)
DC/FIE	$\overline{X}$	56.0	(47.6)	6.4	(6.9)
	SD	13.1	(16.5)	1.2	(1.3)
	N	54	(94)	56	(100)
DC/GE	$\overline{X}$	45.0	(40.8)	7.1	(6.6)
	SD	17.7	(16.6)	1.0	(1.3)
	N	50	(78)	5%	(82)
FIE–Total	$\overline{X}$	53.8	(46.2)	6.3	(6.7)
	SD	14.0	(15.5)	1.4	(1.3)
	N	85	(148)	94	(158)
GE–Total	$\overline{X}$	46.4	(42.6)	7.1	(6.8)
	SD	15.5	(15.6)	1.1	(1.2)
	N	79	(113)	81	(118)
RC–Total	$\overline{X}$	49.7	(44.8)	6.4	(6.7)
	SD	12.9	(13.2)	1.6	(1.4)
	N	60	(89)	68	(94)
DC–Total	$\overline{X}$	50.7	(44.5)	6.8	(6.8)
	SD	16.4	(16.8)	1.2	(1.3)
	N	104	(172)	107	(183)
General Youth	$\overline{X}$	51.2		7.8	
Aliyah	SD	25.5		1.2	
	N	83		76	
Army	$\overline{X}$	24.2		4.8	
rejections	SD	13.1		1.6	
	N	243		265	

2-year program ($\overline{X} = 46.2$ versus $\overline{X} = 53.8$, $t = 3.83$, $p < 0.001$). However the subjects who received only 1 year of FIE did not differ in any meaningful way on the Dapar from the subjects who received 2 years of General Enrichment ($\overline{X} = 46.2$ versus $\overline{X} = 46.5$, $t = 0.12$, NS) and performed at a significantly higher level than the subjects who received only 1 year of General Enrichment ($\overline{X} = 46.2$ versus $\overline{X} = 42.6$, $t = 1.84$, $p < 0.05$). It seems reasonable to conclude that the noteworthy scores of the experimental subjects on the Dapar Intelligence Test may be attributed to the long term effects of Instrumental Enrichment.

The long term effects of FIE may also be demonstrated by comparing the initial performance of the experimental subjects on the PMA test before their participation in the intervention programs with their subsequent performance on the Dapar test. Figure 2 shows the percentage of FIE and GE subjects who scored high (> 130 for the PMA and > 52 for the Dapar). At present, data are available for 153 subjects, 77 from the FIE group and 76 from the GE group. Of the GE subjects who scored high on the PMA pretest, 45% scored low on the Dapar. In contrast, of the FIE subjects who scored high on the PMA pretest, only 15% scored low; 85% continued to score high on the Dapar. The results for the low scoring subjects on the PMA pretest are even more interesting and demonstrate the long term effects of Instrumental Enrichment. For the GE group, 91% of the low scoring subjects on the PMA pretest continued to score low and only 9% scored high on the Dapar test. However, for the FIE group, half (49%) of the low scoring subjects on the PMA pretest scored high on the Dapar.

Not only do these results suggest significant and enduring changes by the FIE subjects, but they tend to confirm the notion of a progressive decline by the GE subjects as well. Of the initially high scoring GE subjects, nearly half (45%) emerged some 4 to 5 years later as low scorers on the Dapar test. What these results suggest is that for low scoring subjects, GE does not produce any meaningful change and that, furthermore, for high scoring subjects not only are no changes produced but the effects actually may be detrimental as evidenced by the deterioration of performance on intelligence tests.

The results for the residential and day center subjects indicate no superiority for one of these settings over the other ($\overline{X} = 49.7$ versus $\overline{X} = 50.7$). This suggests that any advantage that may have been attributable to the setting immediately after the completion of the intervention programs is not sustained over time. However, the combined scores for the FIE and GE groups in each setting tend to mask an important finding. The highest score on the Dapar test was obtained by the DC/FIE group ($\overline{X} = 56.0$), while the lowest score was obtained by the DC/GE group ($\overline{X} = 45.0$), the difference between them being significant ($t = 3.56$, $p < 0.001$). Clearly, the apparent equal performance of the combined residential and day center groups is attributable to the averaging of the high and low scores of the DC/FIE and DC/GE groups. Thus, not only is the hypothesis that residential centers are more beneficial than day centers called into question, but the very opposite may be the case under certain circumstances.

The available data suggest that, in the long term, Instrumental Enrichment may have a greater impact on adolescents in day centers rather than residential settings. This is supported by the fact that a significant difference on the Dapar test was obtained between the RC/FIE and DC/FIE groups in favor of the latter ($\overline{X} = 50.4$ versus $\overline{X} = 56.0$, $t = 1.73$, $p < 0.05$). Support of a negative kind may also be derived from the comparison between the RC/GE

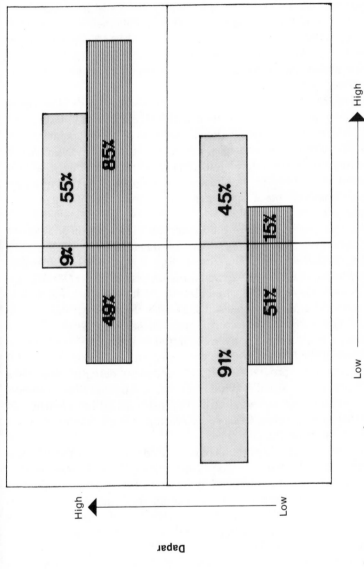

Figure 2. Percentage of FIE and GE students who scored high on the Dapar and PMA tests.

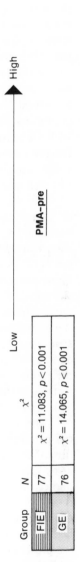

Group	N	χ^2
FIE	77	$\chi^2 = 11.083, p < 0.001$
GE	76	$\chi^2 = 14.065, p < 0.001$

377

and DC/GE groups for which no significant difference was obtained. Although the results suggest that in the long term no significant differences are apparent between the RC/FIE and RC/GE groups with respect to the Dapar test, it is important to bear in mind that initially there was a substantial difference between these two groups on the total PMA prescore. Thus, the difference of 1.48 in favor of the RC/FIE groups over the RC/GE group, although not statistically significant, does represent a substantial improvement over time.

Although the above results call for a reconsideration of our second hypothesis, they also suggest that the negative findings for the interaction hypothesis, obtained immediately after completion of the intervention programs, may require reinterpretation. Although not immediately apparent, with the passage of time an interaction effect does appear to emerge, at least for the Dapar test. However, the interaction is opposite to that hypothesized: it is the combination of Instrumental Enrichment and day center setting that produces the best results.

The superior performance of the Instrumental Enrichment subjects on the Dapar test is even more striking when viewed in the context of the results obtained for the language test. The General Enrichment subjects performed significantly better than the Instrumental Enrichment subjects ($\overline{X} = 7.1$ versus $\overline{X} = 6.3$, $t = 3.85$, $p < 0.001$), thus placing the latter subjects at a clear disadvantage with respect to verbal skills. The fact that the Instrumental Enrichment subjects were not able to surpass or even match the General Enrichment subjects is not surprising, given the initial superiority of the latter on the verbal part of the PMA test at the pre- and even posttest stages. The Instrumental Enrichment program is neither intended nor designed to facilitate an improvement in verbal skills. What is surprising, however, is that, despite their lower performance on verbal skills, the Instrumental Enrichment subjects nevertheless were found to score significantly higher than the General Enrichment subjects on the Dapar test.

The divergent effects hypothesis requires a comparison of the differential performance of the research groups immediately following the completion of the intervention programs and at the time of their induction into the army 2 or 3 years later. Table 11 provides a summary of the subjects' performance on the posttest of the PMA and the Dapar, and Table 12 gives the results of analyses of covariance to test for differences between the research groups (RC versus DC; FIE versus GE). For both the PMA posttest and the Dapar, the PMA pretest scores were used as the covariant. In addition, data are presented in Tables 11 and 12 for the Dapar using both the PMA pretest scores and the language test scores as covariants. Table 12 reveals that for the PMA posttest significant differences were obtained between the FIE and the GE groups and between the RC and the DC groups, in favor of the FIE and

Table 11. PMA posttest and Dapar test: Mean scores for the research groups and mean differences between the treatments and settings

Groups	PMA (Post)[a]	Dapar[b]	Dapar[c]
FIE	167.8	55.8	56.2
GE	162.4	45.2	45.0
FIE − GE	5.4	10.6	11.2
RC	167.6	50.7	50.7
DC	163.6	50.5	50.5
RC − DC	4.0	0.2	0.2

[a]Covariant, PMA pretest scores.
[b]Covariant, PMA pretest scores.
[c]Covariant, PMA pretest scores and language test.

Table 12. PMA posttest and Dapar test: F ratios and significance (p) from analyses of covariance

Source of variance	PMA (Post)		Dapar		Dapar	
	F	p	F	p	F	p
Main effects						
FIE versus GE	7.49	0.007	25.08	0.001	27.48	0.001
RC versus DC	4.06	0.043	0.01	0.999	0.01	0.999
Interaction	0.41	0.999	3.01	0.081	3.32	0.067
Covariant						
PMA (pre)	275.07	0.001	42.75	0.001	32.72	0.001
Language					1.00	0.999

RC groups, respectively. No interaction effect was noted. For the Dapar, the picture is somewhat different. The difference in favor of the FIE group over the GE group is maintained, whereas the difference between the residential and day centers not only ceases to reach significance but is of negligible proportion. Furthermore, even though the interaction is not significant at the 0.05 level, there is a trend toward significant interaction effects ($p = < 0.08$), which increases when the language test is included with the pretest PMA as a covariant for the Dapar ($p < 0.06$). This trend would appear to be attributable to the marked superiority of the Instrumental Enrichment subjects from the day center on the Dapar test.

Evidence for the divergent effects hypothesis lies in the extent of the difference between the FIE and GE subjects on the Dapar, compared to their initial difference on the PMA. Taking into account the fact that maximum scores on the PMA and Dapar are 220 and 90, respectively, and that the standard deviations of both tests are 20, the differences obtained between the

FIE and GE subjects on the PMA posttest and the Dapar are instructive. On the former test, the difference is 5.4 points and on the latter 10.6 points. Thus, it is evident that an increase of nearly double occurs in the magnitude of the difference between the FIE and GE subjects when their Dapar performance is compared with their results on the PMA posttest.

Although the data presented for the follow-up study are incomplete, preliminary analysis has yielded a number of important findings. The overriding conclusion is that cognitive modifiability may be achieved, sustained, and further enhanced after appropriate intervention measures. This is amply borne out by the results of the follow-up study in which the experimental subjects reached the cut-off point used by the army as a selection criterion for officers. Recalling the extremely low performance level of those rejected by the army, a group comparable in many respects with the experimental group at the start of the experiment, the performance levels attained by all the research subjects are testimony to the positive influence of intervention upon the capacity for cognitive modifiability. The superior performance of the Instrumental Enrichment subjects over the General Enrichment subjects 2 or 3 years after the completion of the program, and the fact that the gap between the groups increased, suggests not only that Instrumental Enrichment is effective in producing cognitive modifiability but also that its effects are both sustained and cumulative over time. It still remains to be demonstrated that the divergent effects hypothesis is true not only in the relative sense of comparing the performance of two groups but also in an absolute sense in which the individual's own performance is successively assessed over time. However, even with the data currently available, it is evident that the divergent effects obtained between the experimental and the comparison groups were not the result of the deterioration of the latter. On the contrary, both FIE and GE subjects improved beyond expectation, but more so in the case of those subjects exposed to Instrumental Enrichment.

One of the most interesting findings to emerge from the follow-up study was the unexpected superiority on the Dapar test of the Instrumental Enrichment subjects from the day center compared to the FIE students from the residential center. This finding runs counter to the hypothesis predicting superior performance of the residential center subjects and more specifically to the interaction hypothesis in which superior performance was predicted for the RC/FIE combination. The expectation that the residential setting would produce more positive results than the day center setting was based on a consistent and well established finding. Children in day centers initially perform at higher levels than do adolescents in residential centers, but, on graduating from their prospective programs, the residential subjects invariably surpass the performance levels of the day center subjects (see Feuerstein, 1971; Feuerstein et al., 1976).

What is of particular interest, then, is that the mutually beneficial effects of Instrumental Enrichment and day center setting only emerged after a considerable period of time. Although unanticipated, this finding has both theoretical and practical implications. It may be necessary to reconsider our previous view concerning the residential setting as a preferred environment for redevelopment, at least with respect to cognitive modifiability. Furthermore, the fact that Instrumental Enrichment appears particularly effective in the framework of the less controlled day center setting removes any limitation in the provision of Instrumental Enrichment within a specific kind of setting. Consequently, it would appear from our results that no restriction need be placed on the provision of Instrumental Enrichment to adolescents in a variety of settings and environments.

11
INSTRUMENTAL ENRICHMENT: CURRENT STATUS AND FUTURE DIRECTIONS

In this book we have not attempted to provide the reader with a set of manuals or a list of instructions for the implementation of Instrumental Enrichment. Instead, our aim has been to introduce the concept of cognitive modifiability and to provide a theoretical basis for the redevelopment of retarded performance. At the heart of our theoretical conception is the notion of mediated learning experience, which we believe is the foundation upon which higher mental processes are constructed.

In describing the goals of FIE and the structure and nature of the various instruments comprising the program, we have attempted to show how Instrumental Enrichment is designed to correct the deficient functions produced by a lack of, or insufficient, mediated learning experience. In this respect, the cognitive map is used as both an analytic and didactic guide in the preparation and teaching of the instruments. Because Instrumental Enrichment is not a self-administered, programmed training kit, considerable attention has been given to the topic of teacher training in all its aspects, including the vital support system and in-service training necessary for the successful implementation of the program.

This final chapter provides an overview of the theory underlying Instrumental Enrichment and examines the current status of the FIE program. Then, the results obtained from our research and implementation of the program are summarized, and some conclusions and suggestions for future research and development are offered.

THEORETICAL OVERVIEW

Definition of Cultural Deprivation

The syndrome of cultural deprivation is defined as a reduced level of modifiability in response to direct exposure to sources of stimulation. Low modifiability is considered the major cause of retarded performance and is revealed in an individual's limited use of stimuli impinging on him throughout his life space. The ability to use life experiences for learning is linked to a total lack or more or less severe deficit of mediated learning experience during infancy and childhood, either because the significant figures in the child's environment are unable to mediate the world of stimuli to him or because of the child's incapacity at certain points of his development to benefit from the attempts at mediation undertaken by persons in his environment. The lack of mediated learning experiences affects the individual's functional ability, his cognitive style and attitude toward life, rather than his organic substrata. The concept of modifiability of the culturally deprived adolescent stems directly from this understanding of his condition and its etiology.

Cognitive Structure of the Culturally Deprived Individual

The cognitive functioning of the culturally deprived individual is marked by deficiencies in one or more of the functions that serve as prerequisites to proper cognitive behavior. We have categorized the deficient functions within the three stages of the mental act — input, elaboration, and output — because these phases are found to affect differentially the individual's cognitive processes. They differ as well in both their severity and their resistance to attempts at correction through specific strategies for redevelopment. The peripheral stages of the mental act, input and output, prove much more resistant to change than do elaborational processes, which are established with relative ease and have a higher level of stability following correction. Fluid thinking in elaborational processes is, in the culturally deprived, far more easily acquired by the retarded performer than is the capacity to gather data systematically and communicate end products in appropriate and errorless ways. The latter are examples of functions within the input and output phases, respectively, that need relatively greater investments of time and training to become efficient and stable.

The differential rates of resistance to change exhibited by deficient functions within the three stages of the mental act impose a temporal dimension upon the process of planned redevelopment efforts. The differential rate is also partly responsible for the phenomenon of divergent effects observed among subjects in the Instrumental Enrichment program (see discussion of hypothesis 4 in Chapter 10). The later crystallization of functions at the input and output levels is reflected in increasing measured effects of intervention programs aiming at the induction of modifiability as the impact of the program is assessed at successive intervals, including posttesting undertaken well after the termination of the actual intervention.

Goals of Instrumental Enrichment

The goal of the Instrumental Enrichment program is to sensitize the individual so that he will be able to register, elaborate, and become modified by direct exposure to life events and experiences in such a way that learning and the efficient handling and use of incoming stimuli are increasingly facilitated. Thus, the goal is the development of modifiability as a stable characteristic of the individual. As such, it is contrasted with direct methods of intervention, such as those employed by behavior modification approaches. For practical purposes, Instrumental Enrichment can be equated with the reinstitution of mediated learning experience as the condition necessary for the establishment of appropriate patterns of interaction between the individual and his environment. An intervention program that aims at the redevelopment of the retarded performer as a means to this end must function as a phase-specific, age-adapted substitute for mediated learning experience.

Concept and Meaning of Modifiability

Modifiability is defined within this broader theoretical framework as a meaningful departure from an individual's expected course of development as otherwise determined by his genetic / physiological and / or emotional / experiential background. This conceptualization does not set time limits to the modifiability of the cognitive functioning of the retarded performer, and the redevelopment effort may produce dramatic changes and bring culturally deprived adolescents up to levels of performance characteristic of their nondeprived peers.

The broader significance of modifiability and the ultimate goal of redevelopment is an increase in freedom and alternatives offered to, and perceived by, the individual for his self-realization and the materialization of his culturally and personally determined needs and aspirations. Cognitive factors can be considered key elements to the individual's successful adaptation, particularly in a technological and rapidly changing society. Proper cognitive functioning represents a dimension of autoplasticity of the individual confronted with constant disruption of established states of equilibrium by unexpected changes and cultural discontinuities. Viewed from this perspective, the significance of cognitive modifiability transcends by far the limited goals relating to the individual's academic achievement and vocational-occupational status. Its broader meaning and role are to increase the adaptability of the individual by rendering him more autonomous and flexible and thereby more able to cope with and adapt to new and unpredicted situations, which are increasingly prevalent in our era.

Preferential Modes of Modifiability

The preferred mode for fostering modifiability is first to equip the low functioning individual with those prerequisites of learning found deficient or missing and, second, to strengthen and render their functioning efficient. The Instrumental Enrichment program is committed to dealing with these deficits and their remediation by means of a content-free approach, which is necessary to ensure that the specific prerequisites of cognitive functioning become the temporary target of attack and determine the nature of the learning activity. Dealing with the form rather than with the content, with the process rather than the product of cognitive behavior, Instrumental Enrichment should be contrasted with attempts at modification using strategies involving the supplying of additional information and / or the enrichment of the repertoire of specific skills and behaviors available to the retarded performer. The choice of a content-free focus in Instrumental Enrichment neglects neither the value of information nor the importance of a rich behavior repertoire. However, with modifiability itself the goal of redevelopment, it is ultimately necessary to directly address those functions that, when developed, will ensure the ongoing autonomy of the individual in enriching his storage of information and the behaviors at his disposal by direct exposure to his environment. The program, therefore, does not aim at teaching what to think or how to think but focuses on acquisition of the prerequisites of the thought processes in the firm belief that this will lead to the establishment of both content and form. Changing the cognitive structure seems to be more important and of greater pervasiveness in the adaptability of the individual than the sole transmission of information or premature training in specific tasks. Task-bound activities, unsupported by cognitive development, may limit the individual's capacity to cope with situations that require flexibility and shifts in thinking.

Instrumental Enrichment questions on theoretical grounds, and de-emphasizes in practice, the "concrete" modality of teaching. Our approach is at variance with many of the currently used programs in special education, which emphasize motor enactment and concretization as a way to learn principles and rules. The greater emphasis of FIE on interiorized and representational modalities of learning is a direct outcome of our observations of the inefficiency of the "concrete" modality to serve as a stage necessarily leading to abstract thinking. Our theoretical framework questions not only the necessity of such a preparatory stage at the age of adolescence but also its utility and efficiency, even if allowance is made for it. Our experience with thousands of children who have been confronted with the complex tasks of Instrumental Enrichment has provided ample evidence of the capacity of the low functioning culturally deprived child to cope with abstract, representational, and nonmanipulative modes of problem-solving behavior. In contradistinction, concrete and nonrepresentational types of programs often run the risk of perpetuating the retarded performer's low level of functioning, preserving this as the only way by which he can approach reality.

CURRENT STATUS

Instrumental Enrichment in Israel

Systematic application of Instrumental Enrichment in Israel started 13 years ago with pilot classes in which the material was field tested and didactics and techniques were forged. It continued with a research-oriented program, for which a number of teachers exceeding the strict need of research were prepared. Through the years the program has grown so that there is now a considerable involvement of teachers, master teachers, consultants, curriculum experts, and policy makers. The increase in the number of classes has been artificially constrained by the necessity of providing experienced consultants and master teachers who have had considerable FIE experience. There are, however, 1,300 FIE classes in Israel in 1979, indicating the recognition gained by the program in the field, with teachers and students as Instrumental Enrichment's most ardent proponents.

Corresponding to the growth in the scope of the program has been its increase in range. In addition to the socially disadvantaged, culturally deprived adolescents with whom the material was initially used, the majority of the population in the current program are slow learners and integrated classes in regular junior and senior high schools, and educable mentally retarded (EMR) children in special classes or special schools. The Ministries of Labor and Welfare have joined the Ministry of Education and Youth Aliyah as sponsors of FIE, with classes for trainees in work-study programs and for school dropouts in residential settings or kibbutzim. Sites with pilot programs now include neighborhood houses where parents and their children study FIE together, and hospitals where emotionally disturbed or neurophysiologically impaired children and adult accident victims are exposed to Instrumental Enrichment. There has been the beginning of a downward and upward extension in the ages of populations receiving FIE: from children in fifth and sixth grade to young adults in preacademic studies at the university or in teacher training seminaries (teachers' colleges). Several municipalities, on the advice of either their psychological or counseling services, have instituted FIE in all of their schools for which the program seems appropriate. At this time, it is still premature to evaluate the differential efficiency of FIE with some of the above-mentioned populations.

In addition to the group settings, hundreds of children, ranging in age from early adolescence to young adulthood, and suffering from various distal etiological conditions affecting their cognitive functioning, are being treated through FIE under the direct auspices and supervision of the Hadassah-Wizo-Canada Research Institute. The large number of teachers trained by the Institute for classroom teaching forms a body of manpower available for individual tutoring with FIE and for the more specific problems of diagnostic and prescriptive teaching of the individual retarded performer.

For each of the above-mentioned populations, objectives and didactics are rendered specific. Before implementing FIE with a particular category or age group, a pilot program is carried out with a sample of the population. Thus, before the current use of FIE in 18 teachers' colleges, the program was tried in only two classes of student teachers. In the teachers'-college setting, there were three goals that could have been emphasized individually or in combination. The first was to change the attitude of the teacher toward the retarded performer by teaching the theory underlying FIE. The second was to train the student teachers in didactics and methodology suitable for the teaching of a variety of subjects to all kinds of students. The third was to teach the FIE material, itself, either with a view to the modification of the cognitive behavior of the student teachers, themselves, or to prepare them as teachers of FIE. In the pilot program, it was necessary to find the correct balance between these three objectives and the most efficient and appropriate methods for attaining them. As a result of the 2 pilot years, it is now possible to include student teachers of kindergarten and elementary classes, for whom the FIE program is not yet available, in the teachers' colleges FIE courses. At the present time, methodology is being developed for the use of FIE with classes of deaf children, with parents of exceptional children, with central nervous system disorders, and with children younger than preadolescence.

RESEARCH STUDIES IN ISRAEL

Since the research project described in Chapter 10, a number of more limited and focused studies have been instituted. Some of these have been initiated by educational agencies who introduced FIE into their systems and were oriented to the evaluation of the program's efficiency over a short time period and on specific areas of the individual's functioning. The positive results obtained on these independent evaluations led to the continuation and expansion of the program to other populations similar to those studied. One such study on the effects of Instrumental Enrichment on integrated classes (Solomon, 1976) showed FIE to be highly beneficial in closing the initial gap between the two groups combined into a single class.

Other research projects were initiated by university students fulfilling graduate academic requirements, who became involved in the program either by serving as teachers of FIE or by using teachers and students of FIE as subjects for study. The results of the various studies were generally positive but also pointed to the differential effects of the program as a direct function of the intensity and length of exposure to the material. These studies usually centered on the program's effect on students. Criterion measures for FIE's differential efficiency included, among others, measures of IQ, conceptual tempo, and, in fewer cases, achievement.

A study of particular interest, the subject of ongoing follow-up, is that of 20 students who were exposed to a 2-year FIE program in a Special School for the educable mentally retarded (EMR). The results obtained by these children of "verified" retardation, ranging from moderate to borderline, on the psychometric measures routinely administered to all public school students at the end of the eighth grade, qualified 16 of them for entrance into an academically oriented comprehensive high school. This result can be contrasted with historical controls of previous years in which only one or two, if any, alumni of Special Schools qualified for such admission. Support for the reliability of the finding can be derived from the fact that, in the following year, 15 of 19 children qualified for admission to a comprehensive regular high school. Although the achievement measures of the students were not high enough for high school placement and they lacked much of the content curriculum, these were not considered insurmountable obstacles. Eleven of the Special School graduates entered the comprehensive regular high school and are currently being followed.

One of the group, older than the rest, is currently serving in the army, having successfully passed the army's psychotechnic (intelligence) and language examinations. The single girl in the group applied to, and was accepted into, a high school offering fashion design on the basis of her successful completion of her first 2 years in high school. Of the remaining nine, five were on the equivalent of a Dean's List for outstanding students at the end of the last school year. The school psychologist and counselor report that on the basis of internal examinations and teachers' reports these students show a more positive attitude toward school and teacher, a higher aspiration level, and greater motivation than do their "normal" peers.

A recently completed study (Sar-Shalom, 1978) on the effects of FIE on measures of intelligence, impulsivity, field dependence, and teaching style of student teachers indicated significant differences in favor of the experimental group over their controls in the results obtained on the MEM Test of Verbal Intelligence (Glantz, 1969), in both increased time and decreased errors on the Matching Familiar Figures test of impulsivity (Kagan et al., 1964), and in a test on didactics (Sar-Shalom, 1978). This study draws its meaning from the fact that the changes occurring in the training of teachers for Instrumental Enrichment and their personal use of the material have a spillover effect into areas not directly related to FIE, such as content-oriented and curriculum learning. Although FIE teachers have regularly reported on changes occurring in their own cognitive behavior and approaches to teaching as a result of working with FIE, the Sar-Shalom study is the first stage of further research into the effect of FIE on the cognitive style and instructional methods employed by teachers trained for FIE.

Current plans for FIE research include the study of the optimal intensity and duration of FIE training, the study of teacher variables and training variables, long term and divergent effects of FIE, a microanalysis of the contributions of the various instruments, and the systematic development of bridging from FIE into various content areas. The differential effects of FIE on children whose retarded functioning has differing distal etiologies will be continued and expanded to include a number of distinct populations with whom FIE is not being implemented at present. Victims of internal and external accidents will also be treated through FIE during their rehabilitation, and its effects studied. The use of FIE with senior citizens is being studied as a way of conserving in them operational flexibility.

INSTRUMENTAL ENRICHMENT IN NORTH AMERICA

With the translation of the FIE material into English, work in Instrumental Enrichment started in North America under the coordination of Professor H. Carl Haywood, Director of the John F. Kennedy Center for Research on Education and Human Development. After the appropriate training of teachers and consultants, plus pilot studies, North American research is being carried out with a number of groups including EMR, behaviorally disordered, learning disabled, culturally disadvantaged, neurophysiologically impaired, and delinquent populations, as well as learners of varying exceptionalities. Research is also being carried out on various ethnic subgroups in different locations in the United States and Canada. Research centers include the Kennedy Center, George Peabody College for Teachers of Vanderbilt University in Nashville, with research in Nashville and Louisville directed by Professor H. Carl Haywood and Dr. Ruth Smith; the Ontario Institute for Studies in Education, with studies in Toronto directed by Professors Harvey Narrol and Harry Silverman and Dr. Mary Waksman; and Yeshiva University, with studies in New York City and the Bronx carried out under the direction of Professors Martin B. Miller and Bluma Weiner. Nonresearch implementation has begun in Atlanta and Detroit with other cities soon to follow.

Master's theses and doctoral dissertations have focused on the effects of FIE on cognitive, adaptational, and achievement areas and the cross-cultural efficiency of Instrumental Enrichment with varying populations (Hartley, 1976; Muskat, 1975; Terrell, 1976). In addition to research-oriented implementation, FIE is being taught as practicum by university graduate students fulfilling course requirements, or as a service program in a number of sites in the United States and Canada. Teachers' College, Columbia University, under the leadership of Professors A. Harry Passow and A. J. Tannenbaum, plays an important role in laying the foundation in service-oriented training.

Full scale dissemination of Instrumental Enrichment has been delayed until the completion of the research-oriented implementation and the establishment of a framework for teacher training and consultation. FIE material is currently being translated and field tested in Arabic, and translation into Spanish is planned.

RESULTS SUMMARIZED:
DIFFERENTIAL EFFECTS UPON MODIFIABILITY

Extent of Modifiability

The generally expected development of subjects like those in our target population, whose IQs at the age of adolescence range from 60 to 90, sets very narrow expectations for their capacity to use higher mental processes and so to accede to normal levels of vocational, academic, and social activities. Yet, the results obtained by our research population indicate that both Instrumental Enrichment and General Enrichment groups performed in a way that departed from their expected course of development, in support of the conclusion that various types of intervention can meaningfully affect the course of life of these retarded performers. Our findings are at variance with the general disbelief in meaningful modifiability beyond critical periods, particularly at the age of adolescence, a period in which additional hindrances to producing significant change arise because of emotional and personality determinants. The extent of modifiability produced by the various intervention programs, especially Instrumental Enrichment, shows a dramatic closure of the gap between the performance of subjects in the target population and the norms of their nondeprived peers, particularly on psychometric measures. Such an achievement paves the way for further cognitive development, social mobility, vocational adaptation, and socioeconomic status, previously regarded as inaccessible to these subjects on the grounds of their low level of functioning. The clearest indication currently available is the above-average score obtained by the Instrumental Enrichment groups on the army intelligence test, the score which qualifies these subjects for admission to courses and to training leading to officer rank. This training, in turn, ensures a high status in the army and is also of consequence for opportunities for further development in civilian life. The achievement of the FIE groups should be viewed against the results obtained by the group of individuals rejected by the army reported in the follow-up study (see Chapter 10). These individuals provide an interesting comparative base in that they were similar to our research population with respect to socioeconomic background and initial performance levels but did not receive any kind of intervention before being drafted into the army.

Differential Effects of Programs

It is clear from the outcomes of the controlled experiment, reported in Chapter 10, that the extent of modifiability is a direct function of the nature and duration of intervention. The differential effects of the two programs (FIE versus GE) were found throughout the intellective and non-intellective criterion measures to favor Instrumental Enrichment over General Enrichment. These differences are even more meaningful against the background of the general modifiability evidenced by the retarded performing adolescents across programs and settings. Moreover, although hardly any evidence was obtained for General Enrichment superiority in any measured area, Instrumental Enrichment also proved efficient in areas in which investment in school programs, i.e., instruction in basic school skills and general information, was considerably less for experimental (FIE) subjects than for control (GE) students. Experimental subjects performed as well as comparison subjects, and in some cases even better, in achievement-oriented areas, even though the comparison groups were initially much higher on all achievement measures and benefited from comparatively more training in these areas. Several hundred hours were taken from normal school work in the experimental settings and devoted to work with the content-free exercises of Instrumental Enrichment. This approach, with its particular classroom implementation, was also associated with beneficial developments in such behavioral areas as the adolescent's classroom adjustment, work habits, and interpersonal relations.

The significant effects obtained immediately after termination of the 2-year intervention were consistent in pointing to the superior efficiency of Instrumental Enrichment. However, the results on the army test of intelligence (Dapar) 2 years later indicate that, while Instrumental and General Enrichment both have maintained their effects (as witnessed also by the unusually high rate of army draft), the difference between the two groups in favor of the experimental group has been greatly augmented. This finding, moreover, must be seen in relation to the significantly higher score obtained by control subjects on the army Hebrew language test, indicating that the experimentals achieved their score on the Dapar test in spite of being disadvantaged on the verbal factor. This disadvantage is related to the experimental subjects' initial lower verbal level and the fact that Instrumental Enrichment did not directly attempt to change verbal behavior. Even so, the increment in differences between subjects exposed to the two programs suggests that Instrumental Enrichment produces in the learner a higher level of stable and enduring modifiability. As such, it represents a very important finding because it is counter to the usually observed phenomenon of progressive reductions in the advantages gained through intervention programs. The observed progressive increment of differences suggests that the reported divergent effects are the outcome of changes produced in *cognitive structure* through Instrumental Enrichment's effect on qualitative aspects of the mental capacities rather than on just the *level of functioning* by quantitative addition to the information available to the individual.

Differential Effects of Settings

Our theoretical framework generated the hypothesis that FIE would be more successful in residential centers. The residential setting, by involving the retarded performing adolescent in a total- and group-care program, was considered to provide conditions more powerful for change than the fragmented, partial, and much less controlled program for adolescents at day center facilities. This hypothesis stemmed from previous studies that showed that the day center population initially performed at a relatively higher level than residential students on psychometric measures and usually had advantages in their educational history and demographic characteristics, but benefited less from the program provided by the day center. The settings hypothesis was also confirmed by the data obtained for the first stage of our research covering the 2-year period of intervention. Immediately following this period, subjects of the residential centers were significantly better on some of the central psychometric measures and tests of achievement than their counterparts.

Yet it appears from the preliminary data of the follow-up study that this advantage of the residential facility is not preserved to any meaningful extent over the 2-year period following the termination of intervention. This outcome appears to be related to an emerging interaction effect. Although such an effect was hypothesized between Instrumental Enrichment and the residential center, no meaningful support was obtained for this combination of treatment and setting by the end of the period of intervention. The results of the follow-up study, however, indicate that Instrumental Enrichment and the day center may combine to produce the best performance results, as indicated by scores on the army Dapar intelligence test, for which day center General Enrichment subjects had the poorest scores. It seems, therefore, that the residential center does have a beneficial effect in the short run, but that this advantage is diminished over time by the administration of Instrumental Enrichment in the day center setting; it is in the day center setting that the experimental program eventually proves most effective.

If this finding is substantiated in other areas to be analyzed by the follow-up study now in progress, it is likely that the augmented efficiency of the day center may be ascribed to the introduction of Instrumental Enrichment to the program. This may have an effect on placement policy and funding if it can be shown conclusively that the Instrumental Enrichment–day center combination achieves more than any of the costlier residential center combinations. By the same token, this finding may indicate the potency of Instrumental Enrichment for cognitive redevelopment in an otherwise weaker environment than the residential setting. Studies carried out in regular day schools and in teachers' colleges tend to support this finding. It remains to be established whether these results are attributable to the direct influence of FIE on the students or on the environment itself, by modifying educational policy and goals, the teacher's philosophy, and the readiness to invest in achieving these goals.

Differential Effects of Length of Exposure

The analysis of the preliminary follow-up data indicates a differential effect of length of exposure to Instrumental Enrichment. Although the analysis of the effects of the program was carried out on a pure population of subjects who received the program as a whole, data were also collected for those adolescents who were not included in the population because they dropped out of school or graduated after the first year of the planned 2-year intervention. The results indicate that subjects receiving Instrumental Enrichment for the full 2-year period performed significantly better on the Dapar intelligence test than did subjects receiving only 1 year of the program. The latter, in turn, performed significantly better than subjects receiving the General Enrichment program for just 1 year, and they were not significantly lower than subjects who received only General Enrichment for a 2-year period.

A much more detailed study is necessary in order to conclude definitively from these findings that there are differential effects of exposure, but it is likely that not only *quality* but also *quantity* of investment plays a significant role, since certain instruments are offered only during the second year of the Instrumental Enrichment program.

Areas of Modifiability

That the extent of the phenomenon of divergent effects is a function of both quantity and quality of investment can also be illustrated from the point of view of the areas focused upon within intervention programs. The areas of modifiability proposed in the FIE program encompass a variety of functions, including temporal and spatial orientation, categorization, and syllogistic thinking. These functions are considered necessary both for reinforcing the conceptualized, representational dimensions of mental activity and for serving as carriers for the establishment of relational thinking. The program has not yet attempted to change the linguistic behavior of the culturally deprived adolescent, however. This aspect has not been addressed until now because of the difficulties involved in producing change in the linguistic behavior of this population within the framework of a content-free program. Yet, the specificity with which lack of progress in verbal behavior correlates with the absence of emphasis on verbal ability in FIE makes us reconsider the need to design instruments through which a direct attack on the deficiencies of verbal functioning can be added.

The present lack of emphasis on linguistic functions is reflected in the data obtained from the experimental groups throughout the 4-year period for which data are presently available. The experimental program did not produce a significant FIE over GE difference on the PMA verbal factor, and experimental subjects were significantly lower than the controls on the army test of language development. This is contrasted with the superior performance of the experimentals in virtually all of the intellect-related areas emphasized in the Instrumental Enrichment program and presumably tapped by such tests as the PMA, Embedded Figures Test, Human Figure Drawing, Postures, Lahy, Terman, D-48, and the Porteus Maze test. This differential efficiency of the program indicates that modifiability in Instrumental Enrichment, even though it is generalized over a variety of cognitive functions, is confronted with a specific resistance in the area of verbal functioning that may need to be treated as a *content* of cognitive behavior and therefore given specialized and focused training in order to be modified.

Differential Effects and Areas of Resistance

While our theoretical framework makes provision for areas of greater or lesser efficiency of the Instrumental Enrichment program, other areas of differential efficiency within the program have to be considered in relation to the various stages of the mental functioning. As outlined in the cognitive map, the central phase of the mental act, elaboration, is by far the most accessible to meaningful change. This is strongly supported by our findings in the functions tapped by the EFT and the D-48, both of which indicated significant differences in favor of Instrumental Enrichment. These tests were the only ones to be administered individually, and we adapted a procedure to ensure that the input and output levels of the mental act were adequately dealt with by the subjects. The results obtained on these tests permit us to infer that when input and output are controlled for by individual testing the elaborational capacity of the FIE subjects is reflected in the extent of their superior performance.

The impact of Instrumental Enrichment on the peripheral phases of the mental act is revealed only over a longer time span. The follow-up study, based on data gathered 2 years after completion of the program, provides evidence of the divergent effects of the program, in confirmation of our hypothesis of differential areas of resistance requiring different time dimensions for the efficiency of the program to become fully apparent.

FUTURE DIRECTIONS

Implementation

One of the problems in applied research, especially with innovative programs, is the unfortunate but hardly avoidable need to implement with limited and, at times, insufficient preparation. The time and the means allocated for preparation of materials and staff, for gaining the initial experiences, and for clarifying didactic and even logistic problems are typically very short. There is no doubt that such problems were present during the implementation of our research-oriented program, and the results obtained should be considered against the background of both pragmatic and technical difficulties. The novelty of the program called for caution in its application and for overcoming considerable skepticism on the part of teachers, in general, and policy makers, in particular, regarding its relevance.

For pragmatic reasons, the experimental program had to be tried in settings whose members were convinced relatively easily to take the program and were relatively amenable to controls for research purposes, including controls that allowed for systematic progress toward a well established methodology and didactics. Many didactic approaches to particular problems and many solutions to problems of classroom management were tried during the researched intervention period after only a relatively brief exposure within the framework of the independent pilot studies of the program. Didactic decisions were therefore sometimes made on a theoretical basis rather than on the grounds of more substantial experience. The novelty of the program also generated difficulties in logistics, such as the scarcity of trained personnel when the need arose to find substitutes for teachers with illnesses or pregnancies.

As a consequence of unavoidable problems, the investments in implementation were comparatively larger than are the investments deemed necessary today for the successful implementation of the program. Participant observers, continuous reports, feedback processes, and extensive supervision were all employed in an effort to find the optimal implementation of the program and institute any necessary changes in the program as identified by observation of classes in progress.

Many recommendations may be offered to facilitate the introduction and implementation of FIE. These recommendations derive their strength from our experience not only in the research, but with the thousands of school classes in which Instrumental Enrichment has been administered in the 10 years since the termination of the study reported extensively in Chapter 10. We have learned that when the program is introduced in a new setting it is advisable to call for volunteers rather than to draft teachers. This procedure helps to ensure a higher level of commitment and of motivation to learn and apply the didactics of FIE, which may deviate considerably from what a teacher normally expects in his work. Feedback to teachers should be provided so that they can measure and appreciate the progress of their classes from week to week. We have also developed mastery sheets so that the teacher can monitor and record short term improvement. We have found that FIE teachers make the best progress and enjoy the program most with group seminars and consultation, and that changes from product to process orientation are most easily accomplished through the influence of group dynamics. Furthermore, and perhaps the most difficult recommendation to implement, it is advisable to keep an FIE class intact from the first year to the second, despite the difficulties this may engender in scheduling. Student mobility may result in reduced motivation as a result of the review and repetition necessary to accommodate new students into a veteran class or because of the uneven progress in the program across the original classes.

The years following the completion of the research program have seen the establishment of methodology and didactics and the increasing acceptability of the program on the part of teachers. Teachers who initially rationalize their resistances on the basis of the irrelevancy of the program to the three Rs become converted to the practice of FIE once they learn that they can teach the program and that the children can learn the complex tasks presented in it. Indeed, by the end of the first year of the research program both teachers and students insisted that Instrumental Enrichment be offered, and this attitude is now fairly common. Today, when more than 4,000 teachers are trained to administer the program and when its reputation generates more requests than we can handle, it is clear that Instrumental Enrichment is applicable in educational frameworks varying in both the levels of the children's functioning and in the institutions educating them.

For the implementation of the program, it is now clear that a teacher's increased exposure makes program success less dependent upon extensive supervision and support systems. The cost of the program should therefore be reduced with time. The three major components of program implementation — materials, teacher training, and supervision — will necessarily remain. However, the most expensive of these, supervision, may be reduced to a minimum as a function of the growing experience of the teacher. We are currently translating and expanding the teachers' manuals to meet the realities of the increased dissemination of Instrumental Enrichment in Israel and abroad. Although manuals may reduce the need for supervision, they cannot altogether replace the in-service training provided by supervisors on site. Even then, the manuals should not be regarded as a substitute for initial training. As we have emphasized throughout this book, Instrumental Enrichment requires from the teacher a readiness to respond to the needs of each class and each individual in a unique and innovative manner. Without a thorough training in the theory of cognitive modifiability, including the deficient functions and the cognitive map, the FIE instruments, and the didactics underlying the program, teachers will be unable to function effectively and will be tempted to treat the manuals as instruction booklets rather than as an *aide de memoire.*

The Follow-Up Study

Chapter 10 reported the general impact of Instrumental Enrichment and General Enrichment programs over a 2-year period in two different kinds of educational settings. The need first to establish the differential efficiency of the experimental program assigned a secondary role to some research questions, which, in principle, may be answered by an analysis of the data already available. A follow-up study, now in progress, deals with these questions through a re-analysis of data covering the initial 2-year intervention period and through analysis of additional data obtained in the postintervention period. These additional data, already collected for the most part, cover the areas of achievement, attitudes, aspirations, self-image, vocational-occupational roles, adaptation within the army, and a series of psychometric measures including the army Dapar Intelligence Test.

The re-analysis of data in the follow-up study, as well as the analyses of postintervention criterion measures, introduces three independent variables in addition to the main effects of treatment and setting: 1) initial level of functioning (low, middle, high); 2) sex; and 3) length of exposure to Instrumental Enrichment (1 year, 2 years). The introduction of these additional variables aims at providing answers to important questions of the differential efficiency of Instrumental Enrichment as the first step in what must eventually become a larger research effort to determine the specific impact of exposure to the program on groups of adolescents differing in their level of functioning, as well as in other variables of possible relevance.

The analysis of the additional independent variables should also provide valuable information on the phenomenon of divergent effects, which was generally observed in the preliminary analysis using the army intelligence test as a criterion variable. As already suggested by our preliminary findings, the extent of the divergent effects may presumably be shown to be a function of length of exposure to the program and/or to the impact of the specific instruments offered within the first and the second year. Likewise, the follow-up study will assess the question of divergent effects using the initial level of functioning as an independent variable. Moreover, the data from the follow-up study will enable us to assess the meaning of the achieved change and of the divergent effects in various areas of functioning. This assessment will eventually broaden our understanding of the larger impact of Instrumental Enrichment on the lives of low functioning adolescents. The data of the study will enable us to attribute differential importance to certain postintervention life experiences, such as further schooling or work, in sustaining and reinforcing the impact of Instrumental Enrichment.

Suggestions for Further Research

The theoretical framework of Instrumental Enrichment, as well as the experience obtained from its application in the research program, other studies, and in many additional schools and settings in the last few years, suggests a host of questions for further research. Some of these questions were raised by the results and by-products of research, and others have been suggested informally by our experience in administering the program on a large scale and the great number of professionals involved with the problem of redevelopment of low functioning individuals. Briefly presented, here are some of the research topics that not only are of interest to the authors but also will be of importance for the wider audience of people involved in the planning and use of Instrumental Enrichment.

All the questions for further research have in common the search for a greater understanding of the ways in which Instrumental Enrichment may change the cognitive structure and functioning of different populations or for the improvement of our understanding of the differential efficiency, the economical use, and the precise indications for application of the program.

Extending the Program Toward Additional Areas of Cognitive Functioning   Instrumental Enrichment is now limited to areas of functioning that can be deliberately kept free of content because of the program's emphasis on the prerequisites of cognitive functioning. As such, language has been dealt with only to the extent needed for the communication of instructions to the child and the development of insight. This limitation has imposed strictures on the type of instruments we have been able to develop, and the results of our research point to language as one area that needs a direct and intensive attack in order to become modified. The question in need of research is the extent to which language behavior is as modifiable by the specific methodology and technique of Instrumental Enrichment as are the other areas of cognitive functioning already included in the program. At this point we are exploring this question on a pilot level and are in the process of constructing instruments specifically designed for the area of verbal functioning. New instruments are also being developed involving the cognitive functions underlying the grasp and understanding of analogical thinking, divergent cognitive processes, absurdities and humor, and the differentiation in the perceptual processes between the perceived and the sensed. With these instruments we hope to produce a greater articulation in the mental processes of the retarded performer and also to attack some personality attributes of the culturally deprived adolescent, as well as certain emotional dimensions of his behavior.

Systematic Bridging from Instrumental Enrichment to Content-Oriented Areas   In an effort to assess the possibilities of making Instrumental Enrichment extensions, we are also scrutinizing the problem of bridging between Instrumental Enrichment and areas of content learning. The present research has indicated that Instrumental Enrichment does have an impact on content learning, which eventually may be shown to progressively increase, in line with the divergent effects hypothesis. It may also be possible to anticipate this growth by a direct focus on the carryover from the content-free emphasis on prerequisites of thinking to areas of specific content for learning, such as history, geography, mathematics, and natural sciences. This bridging, which is done today unsystematically by the Instrumental Enrichment teacher, may prove to benefit from a systematization through the presentation of structured materials for this end.

Downward Extension of Instrumental Enrichment   It has already been noted that Instrumental Enrichment has been used successfully in school settings differing from those used in the original research program. The positive response to Instrumental Enrichment in these settings has brought to the forefront the request of teachers and other professionals to consider the possibility of implementing the program with a wider range of populations. Extending the application of Instrumental Enrichment downward in age, below the sixth and certainly lower than the fifth grade, requires the adaptation of both theoretical and structural dimensions of Instrumental Enrichment and, consequently, a very different technique and approach to the didactics of the materials and the teacher-training process. The changes required for application, even within school settings, cannot be limited to just a reduction in the level of complexity or a change in the nature of relationships offered to the child for learning and practice, but will require a very careful assessment of phase-specific characteristics of each stage of child development in considering development of an Instrumental Enrichment model to benefit children of any particular age level.

Upward Extension of Instrument Enrichment   Feeling that the prerequisites of thinking are often a neglected entity in normal education, teachers have often suggested what may be termed an upward extension of Instrumental Enrichment, that is, an application of the program to normally functioning adolescents and young adults. This suggestion has been forthcoming in part because of the instances in which Instrumental Enrichment appears to have benefited individuals whose difficulties were in the peripheral phases of input and output of cognitive functioning while the elaborational phase was well developed. Such an extension will of necessity require adaptation in a variety of areas, including the modalities of presentation, the role of teachers, the rhythm of presentation, and the techniques for the assessment of the efficiency of the program.

Effects of Instrumental Enrichment on Retarded Performers with Differential Distal Etiologies   The study of the differential effects of Instrumental Enrichment on categories of children other than those included in the current program is an attempt to test the basic hypothesis concerning the etiology, nature, and prognosis of modifiability of retarded performance. In the present theoretical framework, a distinction is made between distal and proximal etiologies (refer to Chapter 2, Figure 1) as determining the final product of low functioning retarded performance. Whereas the distal etiology can show considerable variations, including classes of handicap, such as socioeconomic disadvantage, cultural difference, organic damage, emotional disturbance, and educational neglect, wherever it results in retarded performance there is a common, more direct and immediate determinant, which is the hypothesized lack of mediated learning experience (MLE) during and after the early stages of development. Thus, both socioeconomic and organic states can lead to retarded performance because of a lack of mediated learning experience. In the case of the former, the absence of MLE may be caused by the failure of the disadvantaged parents to serve as mediators to their child, and, in the latter, by the impenetrability of the organic child to normal attempts at mediation. Emotional disturbance can also result in retarded functioning whenever it has produced an incapacity of either the parent to provide or the child to accept mediated learning experience.

If this hypothesis is confirmed, the cognitive underdevelopment of children with impaired functioning may be considered to some extent as having in common a proximal etiology and, therefore, may also be accessible to a common strategy of remediation. This hypothesis also implies that difficulties shown by many children on the peripheral phase are more resistant to change than those difficulties experienced in the central processing phase. That is, their central failure is more often attributable to impaired functions at the input and the output phase rather than to impairments at the elaborational phase of the mental act. Obviously, this is also the basic theoretical assumption underlying the prognosis of modifiability and redevelopment of the retarded performer, even at such late stages of development as adolescence. If the hypothesis is confirmed, then Instrumental Enrichment can be considered as a way to bypass and overcome the behavior established by the distal etiology that renders the individual impenetrable to mediated learning experience under normal conditions.

Clinical experience with limited numbers of severely and some moderately retarded children suffering from organic damage, such as cerebral palsy and/or postencephalytic conditions, brings preliminary support for the hypothesis that the causation of retarded performance by these distal etiologies can be prevented and can be overcome. Research in this area would be important also for improved understanding of the continuum between reproductive risk and the caregiving environment, which, in the final analysis, is reflected in the capacity of the individual and the environment to produce the kind of interactive processes necessary for cognitive growth and development given the specific conditions of the organism. Recognizing this continuum may be crucial to the construction of programs that will enable the prevention of retarded performance, even at early stages of the child's development, and in spite of the conditions otherwise liable to produce it.

Implementation of Instrumental Enrichment in Different Settings
Until this point Instrumental Enrichment has been mainly oriented toward classroom programs. Yet, the possibility exists to consider the extension of the program not just to different populations but also to different settings, such as clubs, extracurricular facilities, homes for the elderly, homebound programs, and hospital wards.

The inclusion of such widely different settings naturally raises a multitude of questions, each of which is in need of research. For example, the question of intrinsic versus extrinsic motivation would be doubly in need of clarification before implementation of the program in settings other than the classroom. Instrumental Enrichment has sought to ensure motivation through the structure of the instruments themselves, making them appealing to the learner's need to reach mastery in tasks both complex and novel to him. Therefore, the extent to which the efficiency of Instrumental Enrichment might be increased by adding task-extrinsic criteria such as grades, for success would need to be explored. The general question of the role of feedback also must be posed within the larger context of the possibilities for a self-administered versus a teacher-administered version of Instrumental Enrichment.

Specifically, research has to answer questions relating to the possibilities of introducing horizontal diffusion into the concept of the "teacher," and to what extent the role of teacher might be fulfilled by parents, volunteers, and initiated peers in the redevelopment of retarded performers. The central topics in this area concern finding the most efficient ways to train teachers and the specific weight one should assign to the teacher's understanding of Instrumental Enrichment theory, the area of cognitive functioning, and other aspects related to didactic factors. From another angle, the same question may be asked in terms of the extent and intensity of the supervisory work with the teacher, from the point of view of the quality of the teacher's performance. A whole area of research would be the training of low functioning parents in Instrumental Enrichment in order to provide them with the understanding of cognitive development and the technique for facilitating it in their own children. Such training would be done with two purposes: 1) to gain additional understanding of the MLE processes, and 2) to directly teach the technique to the parents who have been found able to use it profitably with their own retarded adolescent. By the same token, the use of Instrumental Enrichment may also be an important instrument in the hands of volunteers working with the development of retarded performers. As is well known, many of the programs in this area relying upon volunteers are burdened with great difficulties, because the volunteer does not have at his disposal any structured set of instruments for his work with the retarded performer. The extent to which training in, and application of, Instrumental Enrichment might help the volunteer in his work with the retarded performing child in need of redevelopment is therefore also worthy of consideration.

Many of the above-mentioned suggestions are currently being implemented and are under scrutiny. Systematic research in all of these areas not only is relevant and important but is also now possible.

COMMITMENT TO THE CHILD

In describing the materials and methods of Instrumental Enrichment in this book, there has inevitably been an overemphasis on this specific program as an outgrowth of the underlying theory of cognitive redevelopment. However, the necessity of dwelling on the specific techniques and instruments that comprise the program in order to make explicit their nature and function should not be interpreted as restricting the theory of cognitive modifiability to this particular application. Although FIE has demonstrated its efficiency, the theory of cognitive modifiability, the hypothesis of mediated learning experience, and the analysis of the mental act can serve as a basis for constructing other innovative approaches to achieving meaningful change. As we have repeatedly emphasized, we do not consider our work as final or complete; we are constantly seeking elaborations and refinements of its theoretical and applied aspects.

Above all, our commitment is to the child in need of redevelopment. Our task must be to convey to the educator an awareness of the concept of cognitive modifiability and a belief in the child's potential for change. However, belief systems cannot be generated or become operative on the basis of theory alone. They must be supported by real experience. In our work we have found that changes in the ideology of the teacher, which are a *sine qua non* for the successful redevelopment of cognitive processes in the child, can only occur as a result of experiencing the child's mastery of tasks as complex and difficult as those presented in FIE. The teacher's recognition of the child's success with the material, coupled with the child's sense of accomplishment, transforms what is often a frustrating relationship into a productive partnership.

It is only through such a partnership, one in which the teacher acts as a mediator of the world to the child, that the cognitive structure of the child will become modified in the direction of an increased capacity to benefit from stimuli and experience, thereby turning him into one who is both learning and learned.

Rabbi Yehuda, the Prince, described the excellence of one of the sages by likening his train of thought to the movement of "a heap of stones" once disturbed: "When a person removes one from the pile they all go tumbling over each other."[1] Like the heap of stones, whose whole structure is transformed with a change in any of its parts, so we envision the potential for change in the cognitive structure of the culturally deprived child. We would wish to make this cognitive structure open to modifiability to such an extent that each event or experience would not induce an episodic, or isolated, change but would affect the total system in the direction of higher efficiency and greater adaptability to life.

---

[1]From *Avodat Rabbi Nathan,* Chapter 18.

APPENDIX: CHARACTERISTICS OF THE FEUERSTEIN INSTRUMENTAL ENRICHMENT PROGRAM

Program Characteristics	Instrumental Enrichment Program
General goal:	To render the culturally deprived retarded performer more modifiable in his direct exposure to sources of stimuli and in his encounters with academic and life experiences.
Specific subgoals:	Correction of deficient cognitive functions. Acquisition of vocabulary, labels, concepts, operations, and relationships relevant to program. Formation of habits. Production of intrinsic motivation. Creation of insight and reflective thinking. Shift from role of passive recipient and reproducer of information to role of active generator of new information.
Target population: Age:	Ages 11–12 to adulthood for culturally deprived. Ages 9 to adulthood for normal with specific problems.
Level of functioning:	40 IQ to 90 IQ for culturally deprived. Certain learning disabilities } for normal Certain cognitive deficiencies } or gifted.
Minimal abilities:	Accessible to verbal or other kinds of information. Minimal visual-motor functioning. Accessible to training in elementary graphic activity to be used in paper-and-pencil exercises.

Scholastic achievement:	Irrelevant for application. Many instruments accessible to illiterates.
Types of motivation:	Task-intrinsic. Socially reinforced through peer and teacher interaction. Accessible for many scholastically unmotivated children. Appropriate for inhibited young adults who are not willing to accept regression to low level required for acquisition of basic school skills.
Etiology and pathological entity:	Culturally and socially disadvantaged retarded performers. The culturally different. Educable mentally retarded. Retarded functioning with organic or genetic substrata. Unorganized, unmotivated normal individuals who require the acquisition of work habits, strategies, and insight. Perceptual deficits and learning disabilities. Traumatic, organic syndromes.
Settings:	Classroom; resource room. Individual tutorial setting. Prescriptive remedial setting. Extracurricular setting. Under certain conditions, self-administration.
Teachers:	Especially trained for Instrumental Enrichment. No other formal academic prerequisites essential.
Optimal time framework:	Three to five hours weekly, at spaced intervals.
Scholastic framework:	Complementary to regular curriculum. Complementary to content learning or instruction in basic school subjects and mastery of skills in reading and mathe-

matics for those with learning disabilities.
Extracurricular material for settings outside of schools.

Nature of materials: Paper-and-pencil exercises.
Divided into instruments, each of which focuses on a particular cognitive function but addresses others as well.

Rhythm of work: Contingent upon setting.
In classroom, pace regulated by mastery, with individualized attention, as necessary.
In tutorial settings, individualized and flexible.

Nature of peer interaction: Cooperative definition of problem.
Participation in divergent proposals for solutions.
Group discussions for insightful interpretation of FIE activities, generally, and specific tasks.
Peer-assisted interactions.

Interaction with teacher: Presentation of task; explanation of terms; preparation for independent work; exploration of processes and strategies; orienting; producing insightful, reflective thinking; teaching specific content-related elements necessary for FIE; addressing specific deficient cognitive functions and anticipated difficulties in the tasks (see the list of deficient cognitive functions (Chapter 4), the cognitive map (Chapter 5), and the subgoals of the program (Chapter 6)); producing motivation by means of reinforcement; initiating peer interaction; and producing bridging to content areas and life at large.

Nature of exercises: Content-free in that content is not goal *per se* but a carrier for differential focus on cognitive functions to be corrected, developed, and enhanced.

Nature of activity:	Discovery, learning, and repetitive application in varied situations of relationships, rules, principles, operations, strategies, and other prerequisites of adequate cognitive functioning.
Nature of sequence:	Each instrument graded in difficulty, with tasks becoming progressively more complex in their presentation. Repetition of principles and operations with orientation to rules and strategies in various situations that require investment for solution.
Type of feedback:	Self-corrective devices in some instruments. Teacher assists in exploration of nature of process and in interpretation of micro-changes. Mutual feedback through peer interaction. Self-criticism, with the development of criteria and autonomy.
Reinforcement:	Strong task-intrinsic motivation developed with activity. Teacher's reinforcement directed to creating student understanding of his accomplishments.
Evaluation: Teacher:	Student's efficiency in handling tasks himself. Student's mastery and facilitation of transfer to other, similar tasks, including summary pages. Student's spontaneous use of learned rules and strategies in other subject matter or Instrumental Enrichment materials.
Child:	Self-evaluation on objective measurable criteria, such as speed, accuracy, positive responses, decrease in impulsivity as evidenced by decrease in erasures, etc. Self-evaluation on subjective reports,

	feedback from teachers and peers, and evaluations of other teachers.
Program:	Cognitive changes; effects on school achievement; effects on adaptation; effect on school attendance; effect on behavior in other classes and in public, communal areas.
Services given to teacher:	Training in theory and practice of FIE; in-service field training and consultation during classroom visits; orientation; workshops after initial training in didactics and implementation. Lectures on the culturally deprived retarded performer, non-intellective factors in the program, etc.
Spill-over effects of program:	
Teacher:	Training and experience with FIE effect changes in teacher's perception of the child; in his evaluation and expectations of the child's modifiability; in his attitude regarding the capacity of the retarded performer; in lessened use of the concrete in favor of more abstract; in process rather than product orientation. Knowledge of cognitive structure may make teacher more sensitive to aspects of teaching necessary for changes in both cognitive and personality structures or dimensions.
Child:	Increased willingness to cope with school material. Increased motivation and school attendance. Heightened self-image.
Parents:	Exposed to success of the child, parents may modify their levels of expectation and image of the child.
Administrative decisions on program:	Through regular decision-making channels for classroom implementation.

Teacher, educational counselor, psychologist, or educational supervisor for individual, remedial work or prescriptive teaching.

Budget:

From education funds.
Covers the cost of material, training, and in-service supervision and consultation.

Production and distribution of materials used in program:

FIE materials are disseminated only to teachers who have received training.
Material is not bound, but distributed to child page by page.
Material is protected by international copyright.

REFERENCES

Alpert, A. A special therapeutic technique for certain developmental disorders in prelatency children. American Journal of Orthopsychiatry, 1957, 27(2):256–270.

Alpert, A., and Crown, S. Treatment of a child with severe ego restriction in a therapeutic nursery. In The Psychoanalytic Study of the Child. Vol. 8. New York: International Universities Press, 1953.

Alphabetisation, 1969–1971. Paris: United Nations Economic and Social Council, 1972.

Arieli, M. Self-concept and values of scholastic achievements of disadvantaged adolescents in residential and day centers. Unpublished master's thesis, University of Tel Aviv, 1974.

Arthur, G. A. A Point Scale of Performance Tests: Clinical Manual, Vol. I. New York: Commonwealth Fund, 1930.

Ausubel, D. P. The Psychology of Meaningful Verbal Learning. New York: Grune & Stratton, 1963.

Begab, M. J. Barriers to the application of language. In P. Mittler (ed.), Research to Practice in Mental Retardation. Vol. I: Care and Intervention. Baltimore: University Park Press, 1977, A-1-A-5.

Berger, A. New Towns in Israel. Jerusalem: University Press, 1970.

Bergson, H. Matière et mémoire: Essai sur la relation du corps à l'esprit (1919). Paris: Presses Universitaires de France, 54th ed., 1956.

Bernstein, B. Elaborated and restricted codes: Their social origins and some consequences. American Anthropologist, 1964, 66:1–34.

Birk, R., and Eflal, A. Youth centers. In M. Wolins and M. Gottesman (eds.), Group Care: An Israeli Approach. London: Gordon & Breach, 1971, 219–231.

Bloom, B. S. Stability and Change in Human Characteristics. New York: John Wiley & Sons, 1964.

Bruner, J., Olver, R., and Greenfield, P. M. Studies in Cognitive Growth. New York: John Wiley & Sons, 1966.

Bryant, P. Perception and Understanding in Young Children. London: Methuen, 1974.

Clarke, A. M., and Clarke, A. D. B. Early Experience: Myth and Evidence. London: Open Books Publishing Ltd.; New York: Free Press, 1976.

Cohen, E. Development towns: The social dynamics of "planted" urban communities in Israel. In S. Eisenstadt, R. Bar-Yosef, and C. Adler (eds.), Integration and Development in Israel. Jerusalem: Israel University Press, 1970, 587–617.

Condon, W. S., and Sander, L. W. Synchrony demonstrated between movements of the neonate and adult speech. Child Development, 1974, 45:456–462.

Dewey, J. How We Think. Boston: Heath & Co., 1933.

Eisenstadt, S. N. The Absorption of Immigrants. London: Routledge & Kegan Paul, 1964.

Fantz, R. L. Visual perception and experience in early infancy: A look at the hidden side of behavior development. In H. W. Stevenson, E. H. Hen, and H. G. Rheingold (eds.), Early Behavior: Comparative and Developmental Approaches. New York: John Wiley & Sons, 1967, 181–224.

Festinger, L. A Theory of Cognitive Dissonance. Stanford: Stanford University Press, 1957.

Feuerstein, R. The learning potential assessment device. In B. W. Richards (ed.), Proceedings of the First Congress of the International Association for the Scientific Study of Mental Deficiency. England: M. Jackson, 1968, 562–565.

Feuerstein, R. The Instrumental Enrichment Method: An Outline of Theory and Technique. Jerusalem: Hadassah-Wizo-Canada Research Institute, 1969.

Feuerstein, R. Les différences de fonctionnement cognitif dans des groupes socio-ethniques differents: Leur nature, leur etiologie et les prognostics de modifiabilite. Paris: Sorbonne, 1970a.

Feuerstein, R. A dynamic approach to the causation, prevention, and alleviation of retarded performance. In H. C. Haywood (ed.), Socio-cultural Aspects of Mental Retardation. New York: Appleton-Century-Crofts, 1970b, 341–377.

Feuerstein, R. Low functioning children in residential and day settings for the deprived. In M. Wolins and M. Gottesman (eds.), Group Care, An Israeli Approach. New York and London: Gordon & Breach, 1971a, 224–231.

Feuerstein, R. The redevelopment of the socio-culturally disadvantaged adolescent in group care. In M. Wolins and M. Gottesman (eds.), Group Care, An Israeli Approach. New York and London: Gordon & Breach, 1971b, 232–245.

Feuerstein, R. Alleviation of retarded performance. In H. P. David (ed.), Child Mental Health in International Perspective. New York: Harper & Row, 1972a, 185–201.

Feuerstein, R. Cognitive assessment of the socioculturally deprived child and adolescent. In L. J. Cronbach and P. Drenth (eds.), Mental Tests and Cultural Adaptation. The Hague: Mouton, 1972b, 265–275.

Feuerstein, R. The learning potential assessment device: Theory, instruments and techniques. Studies in Cognitive Modifiability. Report No. 1. Jerusalem: Hadassah-Wizo-Canada Research Institute, 1972c.

Feuerstein, R. Mediated learning experience: A theoretical basis for cognitive human modifiability during adolescence. In P. Mittler (ed.), Research to practice in mental retardation. Vol. II. Baltimore: University Park Press, 1977, 105–115.

Feuerstein, R. The ontogeny of learning. In M. Brazier (ed.), Brain Mechanisms in Memory and Learning. New York: Raven Press, 1978.

Feuerstein, R., The Dynamic Assessment of Retarded Performers: The Learning Potential Assessment Device, Theory, Instruments, and Techniques. Baltimore: University Park Press, 1979.

Feuerstein, R., Hoffman, M., Krasilowsky, D., Rand, Y., and Tannenbaum, A. J. The effect of group care on the psychosocial habilitation of immigrant adolescents in Israel, with special reference to high risk children. International Review of Applied Psychology, 1976, 25(3):189–201.

Feuerstein, R., Hoffman, M., Tannenbaum, A. J., and Krasilowsky, D. Selected statistical data on the follow-up study of Youth Aliyah graduates of North-African origin. Report No. 1. Jerusalem: Hadassah-Wizo-Canada Research Institute, 1970.

Feuerstein, R., Jeannet, M., and Richelle, M. Quelques aspects de développement intellectuel chez les jeunes juifs nord-africains. Unpublished manuscript, October, 1953.

Feuerstein, R., and Krasilowsky, D. The treatment group technique. The Israel Annals of Psychiatric and Related Disciplines, 1967, 5(1):69–90.

Feuerstein, R., Krasilowsky, D., and Rand, Y. Innovative educational strategies for the integration of high-risk adolescents in Israel. Phi Delta Kappa, April, 1974, LV(8):1–6.

Feuerstein, R., Krasilowsky, D., and Rand, Y. Modifiability during adolescence. In J. Anthony (ed.), Yearbook of International Association for Child Psychiatry and Allied Professions. The Child and His Family: Children and Their Parents in a Changing World. New York: John Wiley & Sons, 1978, 197–217.

Feuerstein, R., and Rand, Y. Mediated learning experiences: An outline of the proximal etiology for differential development of cognitive functions. International Understanding, L. Gold Fein (ed.), 1974, 9/10:7–37.

Feuerstein, R., and Rand, Y. Studies in cognitive modifiability. Instrumental Enrichment: Redevelopment of cognitive functions of retarded early adolescents. Jerusalem: Hadassah-Wizo-Canada Research Institute, 1977.

Feuerstein, R., Rand, Y., Hoffman, M., Hoffman, Mendel, and Miller, R. Cognitive modifiability in retarded adolescents: Effects of Instrumental Enrichment. American Journal of Mental Deficiency, 1979, 83(6):539–550.

Feuerstein, R., and Richelle, M. Enfants juifs nord-africains. Tel Aviv: Jewish Agency Publication, 1957.

Feuerstein, R., and Richelle, M. Children of the Mellah. Jerusalem: The Henrietta Szold Institute for Child and Youth Welfare, 1963. (In Hebrew.)

Feuerstein, R., Richelle, M., and Jeannet, M. Quelques aspects des structures affectives chez les enfants nord-africains, d'après le test de Rorschach. Unpublished manuscript, July, 1954.

Feuerstein, R., and Shalom, H. Methods of assessing the educational level of socially and culturally disadvantaged children. Megamot, August, 1967, 2–3:177–187.

Finch, F. Kuhlmann-Finch Intelligence Test Manual. Philadelphia: Educational Testing Bureau, 1953.

Finch, F. Kuhlmann-Finch Tests, Junior High School Test. Minneapolis: American Guidance Service, 1957.

Frankenstein, C. The Roots of the Ego. A Phenomenology of Dynamics and of Structure. Baltimore: The Williams & Wilkin Co., 1966.

Freud, S. The loss of reality in neurosis and psychosis (1924). In J. Strachey, A. Freud, A. Strachey, and A. Tyson (eds.), Standard edition of the Complete Psychological Works of Sigmund Freud. Vol XIX. London: Hogarth Press, 1961, 183–190.

Fuller, G. B., and Laird, J. The Minnesota perceptuo-diagnostic test. Journal of Clinical Psychology. Monogr. Suppl. 16, 1963.

Furth, H. G. Thinking Without Language: Psychological Implications of Deafness. New York: Free Press, 1966.

Furth, H. G. Piaget for Teachers. Englewood Cliffs, N.J.: Prentice-Hall, 1970.

Gibson, J. J. Outline of a theory of direct visual perception. Paper presented at conference on the psychology of knowing. Center for Advanced Study in Theoretical Psychology, University of Alberta, 1969.

Glantz, Y. The MEM Test. Ramat Gan, Israel: Bar Ilan University, 1969. (In Hebrew.)

Gough, H. C., and Domino, C. The D-48 test as a measure of general ability among grade school children. Journal of Consulting Psychology, 1963, 27(4):344–349.

Guilford, J. P. The Nature of Human Intelligence. New York: McGraw-Hill Book Co., 1967.

Guilford, J. P. The Analysis of Intelligence. New York: McGraw-Hill Book Co., 1971.

Hamburger, M. Realism and consistency in early adolescent aspirations and expectations. Unpublished doctoral dissertation, Columbia University, New York, 1958.

Hanegbi, R., Krasilowsky, D., and Feuerstein, R. The corrective object relations theory and the treatment group technique. Psychological Processes, 1970, 1, 2.

Hartley, L. B. Effects of a cognitive remediation programme on the reading performance of culturally deprived children. Unpublished master's thesis, University of Toronto, 1976.

Hartmann, H. Essays on Ego Psychology: Selected Problems in Psychoanalytic Theory. New York: International Universities Press, 1964.

Haywood, H. C. Motivational orientation of overachieving and underachieving elementary school children. American Journal of Mental Deficiency, 1968, 72: 828–838.

Haywood, H. C. Summary: Some perspectives on social-cultural aspects of mental retardation. In H. C. Haywood (ed.), Social-cultural Aspects of Mental Retardation. New York: Appleton-Century-Crofts, 1970.

Haywood, H. C., and Burke, W. P. Development of individual differences in intrinsic motivation. In I. C. Uzgiris and F. Weizmann (eds.), The Structuring of Experience. New York: Plenum, 1977, 235-263.

Haywood, H. C., and Dobbs, V. Motivation and anxiety in high school boys. Journal of Personality, 1964, 32:371-379.

Haywood, H. C., Filler, J., Shifman, M. A., and Chatelnat, G. Behavioral assessment in mental retardation. In P. McReynolds (ed.), Advances in Psychological Assessment. Vol. 3. San Francisco: Jossey-Bass, 1975, 96-136.

Haywood, H. C., and Switzky, H. N. Children's verbal abstracting: Effects of enriched input, age, and IQ. American Journal of Mental Deficiency, 1974, 78: 556-565.

Haywood, H. C., and Weaver, S. J. Differential effects of motivational orientation and incentive conditions on motor performance in institutionalized retardates. American Journal of Mental Deficiency, 1967, 72:459-467.

Hebb, D. O. The Organization of Behavior. New York: John Wiley & Sons, 1949.

Howell, R. R., and Stevenson, R. E. The offspring of phenylketonuria women. Social Biology Supplement, 1971, 18:S19-S29.

Hunt, J. McV. Intelligence and Experience. New York: Ronald Press, 1961.

Jensen, A. R. How much can we boost IQ and scholastic achievement? Harvard Educational Review, 1969, 39:1-123.

Jensen, A. R. Educability and Group Differences. London: Methuen, 1973.

Jensen, A. R. Cumulative deficit in IQ of blacks in the rural school. Developmental Psychology, 1977, 13(3):184-191.

Kagan, J. The generality and dynamics of conceptual tempo. Journal of Abnormal Psychology, 1966, 71:17-24.

Kagan, J., Pearson, L., and Welch, L. Conceptual impulsivity and inductive reasoning. Child Development, 1966, 37:583-594.

Kagan, J., Rosman, B., Day, B., Albert, J., and Phillips, W. Information processing in the child: Significance of analytic and reflective attitudes. Psychological Monograph, 1964, 78(1).

Kashti, Y. Socially disadvantaged youth in residential education in Israel. Unpublished doctoral dissertation, University of Sussex, England, 1974.

Kashti, Y., and Arieli, M. (eds.). Residential Settings: Socialization in Powerful Environments. Tel Aviv: Daga Books, 1976. (In Hebrew.)

Konrad, K., and Melzack, R. Novelty enhancement effects associated with early sensory-social isolation. In A. H. Riesen (ed.), The Developmental Neuropsychology of Sensory Deprivation. New York: Academic Press, 1975, 253-274.

Korner, A. Early stimulation and maternal care as related to infant capabilities and individual differences. Early Child Development and Care, 1973, 2(3):307-328.

Levine, S., and Katz, D. Levidal Self-Concept Scale. Jerusalem: Hadassah-Wizo-Canada Research Institute, 1971.

McCall, R. B., Hogarty, P. M., and Hurlburt, N. Transitions in infant sensorimotor development and the prediction of childhood IQ. American Psychologist, 1972, 27:728-748.

Maslow, A. H. Motivation and Personality. New York: Harper & Row, 1954.

Mathieu, J. Notes sur l'enfance juive du Mellah de Casablanca. Bulletin de l'Institut d'Hygiène du Maroc 1947, Nouvelle Serie, VII.

Meeker, M. N. The Structure of Intellect: Its Interpretation and Uses. Columbus, Ohio: Charles Merrill, 1969.

Meltzoff, A. N., and Moore, M. K. Imitation of facial and manual gestures by human neonates. Science, October, 1977, 198:75-78.

Moltz, H. Some implications of the critical period hypothesis. Paper delivered at meeting of American Psychological Association, September, 1972.

Muskat, J. Intelligence, IQ, and the feasibility of cognitive modifiability. Unpublished master's thesis, University of Toronto, 1976.

Neifeind, U., and Koch, J. Problemlosën bei Retardierten Schulern. Darmstadt: Institute fur Psychologie, 1976.

Odier, C. Anxiety and Magical Thinking. New York: International Universities Press, 1956.

Ortar, G. R. Investigation of differences in intelligence level of immigrant and native Israelis of Islam origin. Unpublished doctoral dissertation, Hebrew University, 1951. (In Hebrew.)

Ortar, G. R. Standardization of Wechsler test for Israeli children. Megamot, 1952, 4(1). (In Hebrew.)

Ortar, G. R. Improving test validity by coaching. Educational Research, 1960, 2:137–142.

Ortar, G. R. MILTA Intelligence Test. Jerusalem: Hebrew University School of Education, 1966.

Piaget, J. The Origins of Intelligence in Children. New York: International Universities Press, 1952.

Piaget, J. The Language and Thought of the Child. 3rd. London: Routledge & Kegan Paul, 1959.

Piaget, J. Play, Dreams and Imitation in Childhood. New York: W. W. Norton, 1962.

Piaget, J. La Psychologie de l'Enfant. Paris: PUF, 1966.

Piaget, J. Six Psychological Studies. London: University of London Press, 1968.

Piaget, J., and Inhelder, B. Child's Conception of Space. London: Routledge & Kegan Paul, 1956.

Porteus, S. D. Manuel du test des labyrinthes. Paris: Centre de Psychologie Appliquée, 1956.

Porteus, S. D. Porteus Maze Test: Fifty Years of Application. Palo Alto: Pacific Books, 1965.

Prime Minister's Committee on Children and Youth in Distress. Report submitted to the Prime Minister of Israel. Jerusalem, 1973. (In Hebrew.)

Raven, J. C. Progressive Matrices, Set I and II. Dumfries: The Chrichton Royal, 1947.

Raven, J. C. Progressive Matrices. London: H. K. Lewis, 1960.

Rey, A. Test de copie d'une figure complexe. Manual. Paris: Centre de Psychologie Appliquée, 1959.

Rey, A., and Dupont, J. B. Organisation des groupes des points en figures géométriques simples. Monographies de Psychologie Appliquée, 1953, No. 3.

Rotter, R., and Shamai, N. Patterns of Poverty in Israel. Jerusalem: National Insurance Institute, 1970.

Sameroff, A. J., and Chandler, M. J. Reproductive risk and the continuum of caretaking casualty. In F. D. Horowitz (ed.), Review of Child Development Research. Chicago: University of Chicago Press, 1975, 187–244.

Sar-Shalom, Y. Unpublished research report. Ramat Gan: Bar Ilan University, 1978.

Sexton, P. C. Education and Income Inequalities of Opportunity in our Public Schools. New York: Viking Press, 1961.

Smilansky, S., Shephatia, L., and Frankel, E. Mental development of infants from two ethnic groups. Jerusalem: The Henrietta Szold Institute, 1976, #556.

Solomon, R. Unpublished data, Bar Ilan University, Ramat Gan, Israel, 1976.

Statistical Abstract of Israel. 1971. Jerusalem: Central Bureau of Statistics, Government Press, 1971, No. 22.

Statistical Abstract 1971/2. National Insurance Institute, Jerusalem, 1972.

Stein, J. (ed.). The Random House Dictionary of the English Language. New York: Random House, 1966.

Stodolsky, S., and Lesser, G. Learning patterns in the disadvantaged. Harvard Educational Review, 1967, 37:546–593.

Tannenbaum, A. J., and Levine, S. Classroom participation scale. Jerusalem: Hadassah-Wizo-Canada Research Institute, 1968.

Terman, E. L. Non language multi-mental test. New York: Bureau of Publications, Teachers' College, Columbia University, 1942.

Terrell, B. Teaching thinking: A study involving the application and assessment of Feuerstein's Instrumental Enrichment programme. Unpublished master's thesis, University of Toronto, 1976.

Thurstone, L. L. Primary Mental Abilities. Psychometric Monographs, 1938, No. 1.

Thurstone, T. G. SRA Primary Mental Abilities test. Chicago: Science Research Associates, Inc., 1962.

Thurstone, T. G. Primary Mental Abilities, Rev. 1962. Technical report. Chicago: Science Research Associates, Inc., 1965.

Uzgiris, I. C., and Hunt, J. McV. Assessment in Infancy: Ordinal Scales of Psychological Development. Urbana: University of Illinois Press, 1975.

Vernon, P. E. The Structure of Human Abilities. New York: John Wiley & Sons, 1950.

Vygotsky, L. S. Thought and Language. Cambridge: MIT Press; New York: John Wiley & Sons, 1962.

Whorf, B. L. Language, Thought, and Reality: Selected Writings of Benjamin Lee Whorf. (J. B. Carroll, ed.). New York: John Wiley & Sons, 1956.

Witkin, H. A. Individual differences in ease of perception of embedded figures. Journal of Personality, 1950, 19:1–15.

Witkin, H. A., Dyk, R. B., Faterson, H. F., Goodenough, D. R., and Karp, S. A. Psychological Differentiation: Studies of Development. New York: John Wiley & Sons, 1962.

Yando, R., and Zigler, E. Outerdirectedness in the problem-solving of the institutionalized and non-institutionalized normal and retarded children. Developmental Psychology, 1971, 4(2):277–288.

Zazzo, R. Conduites de Conscience. Neuchâtel: Delachaux et Niestlé, 1962.

Zazzo, R. Le Test de Deux Barrages. Neuchâtel: Delachaux et Niestlé, 1964.

INDEX

Abstraction, 109, 112, 113
Activation-inhibition balance, 78
Active-modification approach, 295, 340
  characteristics of, 1–2
  organism as open system, view of,
    2, 70
Adaptation, 1, 22
  to changing versus constant environ-
    ment, 3
  cognition as focal point of success-
    ful, 4
  of culturally different groups, 5, 24
  as function of capacity to discrimi-
    nate, 76–77
  mechanisms of, 3
  role of familiarity in, 24–25
  role of nonverbal mediation in facili-
    tating, 23
Affective-motivational factors, as a
    basis for distinguishing deficient
    functions, 73, 74–75
Alloplastic adaptation, 70
  defined, 3
Analytic Perception, 174, 183–193, 239,
    247, 270
  anticipated difficulties in, 191
  articulation of internal field in, 184
  behaviors gained in, 192–193
  breakdown of wholes into parts in,
    184–187
  cognitive map used to analyze,
    190–191
  construction of wholes in, 188–189
  elicitation of schemata in, 275–276
  identifying relevant parts of whole in,
    187–188
  insight gained in, 192
  learning to use multiple sources of
    information in, 262
  motivation in, 193
  use of labels and operations gained
    in, 191–192
Anticipation, 279
  in *Illustrations,* 236
  as internal construction of reality,
    30–31

  in *Organization of Dots,* 135, 138,
    141
  in *Representational Stencil Design,*
    263
  in *Temporal Relations,* 205, 206, 207
  of transformations, 246
Arithmomania, child, 94
Arthur's Stencil Design Test, 239
Assessment, 59
  of development, potential for versus
    actual, 2, 61
  of impediments to versus deficiencies
    in development, 2, 61
  need for dynamic measure in, 61
Assimilation-accommodation process,
    23
Autism
  attempt at reversal of, 52
  as a determinant of lack of MLE,
    51–52
Autoplastic adaptation, 24, 70
  defined, 3

Behavior
  aggressive, 5, 64
  automatized, concept of, 111
  cognition as determinant of, 4–6
  comparative, 34–35, 58, 102, 145,
    155, 194, 273
    in *Analytic Perception,* 186, 188,
      189, 190, 191
    in *Categorization,* 175, 183
    in *Comparisons,* 163–166, 167,
      168–169, 173–174
  and concomitant cognitive func-
    tions, 165–166
  in *Illustrations,* 231, 233, 234–235
  importance of using two or more
    sources of information in, 88
  in *Instructions,* 221, 222
  lack of spontaneous, 73, 92–93,
    164
  in *Numerical Progression,* 218, 219
  in *Orientation in Space,* 145, 155